Inventory Accuracy

People, Processes, & Technology

David J. Piasecki

OPS
PUBLISHING
Kenosha, Wisconsin

ISBN   0-9727631-0-4

Library of Congress Control Number: 2002116820

Ops Publishing
P.O. Box 580150
Pleasant Prairie, WI 53158

www.opspublishing.com

Table of Contents

1. Understanding Errors 1
Man versus machine 4
Environmental factors 9
Task relationship to errors 19
Individual's relationship to errors 20

2. Making Accuracy Easy 25
Process evaluation 26
Human-machine interface. 29
    Documents, forms, labels, and reports 30
    Computer programs 40
Procedures and employee training. 46
    Documenting procedures 46
    Procedure format/training materials 49
    Training 52
    Testing 57
    Putting formal checks in place 59
    Other ways to make accuracy easy 61

3. Making Accuracy Expected 63
Management's responsibility 65
Everybody's responsibility 69
Control methods 75

4. Cycle Counting 81

Purpose of cycle counting 82
The standard cycle count program 84
    Running the standard cycle count program 89
    So what's wrong with the standard cycle count program? 92
Cycle count options 95
    Event-triggered counting methods 96
    Other methods 98
    Combining count logic 100
Setting up and running your cycle count program 102

5. Periodic Physical Inventories 133

Conducting a physical inventory 135
    The preparation phase 137
    Physical inventory methodology 140
    Execution 148

6. Accuracy Measurement 151

General accuracy measurement 152
Benchmarking accuracy 163
Specific-process accuracy measurement 165
Measuring the impact of inaccuracy 169
What should my accuracy be? 172

7. Audits, Exception Reporting, and Data Analysis 179

Audits 180
    Accuracy audit 180
    Location audit 185
Exception reporting 187
Data analysis 190
Knowledge of information systems revisited 192

8. Tools, Equipment, & Technology 195

Calculators 197
Scales 198
    Counting scales 199
    Weight verification 204
Machine counters 206
Bar codes 207
    Bar code printing 209
    Bar code scanners 212

Application of a programmable keyboard wedge system 216
Portable computers 218
    Batch versus RF 218
    Hand-held devices 218
    Vehicle-mounted devices 222
    Wearable systems 223
Voice systems 225
Radio frequency identification (RFID) 228
Light-directed systems 231
Full automation 233
Integration 234
Software technologies 238
    Locator systems 238
    Warehouse management systems 243
    Manufacturing execution systems 245
General technology comments 245

9. Specific Processes, Tips, & Misc. 247
How to count? 248
Receiving process tips 252
Putaway process tips 256
Order picking / shipping process tips 258
Returns processing 262
Negative inventory. 265
Non-stock inventory 268
Units-of-measure. 271
Unit packs, multi packs, inner packs, kits, and sets. 274
Lot and serial number tracking. 276
Multi-plant processing. 277
Substitutions 279
Outsourcing 280
Theft. 283
Manufacturing processes general observations 288
24/7 289
Point-of-use inventory and floor stock.. 292
Outside operations 293
Scrap reporting. 297
Work-in-process tracking 299
Backflushing and other issuing techniques 302
Transitions. 308

Glossary 311

Index 335

Understanding Errors

"What does it take to write down the correct location?"

"The customer wanted three! How hard can it be to count to three?"

"How can we be missing $10,000 worth of inventory?"

"How could he forget to load half the shipment?"

"Our employees are idiots!"

"They just don't care."

"They don't try."

"They don't think."

"They won't listen."

OK, most of us have gone through the frustration of inaccuracy. But how many have actually taken the time to try to understand how these situations occur? One of the most common mistakes made when addressing accuracy problems is applying solutions before the problem is fully understood. Often times, companies assume installing a bar code data collection system or implementing a cycle count program will automatically resolve accuracy problems. While both of these are very good tools, they do not guarantee accuracy, and in some cases may have little effect or even negatively impact accuracy. Understanding the nature of errors is critical to applying the appropriate solutions for the specific types of errors being encountered.

There are primarily two major types of errors — those caused by a lack of knowledge and those caused by a lack of focus.

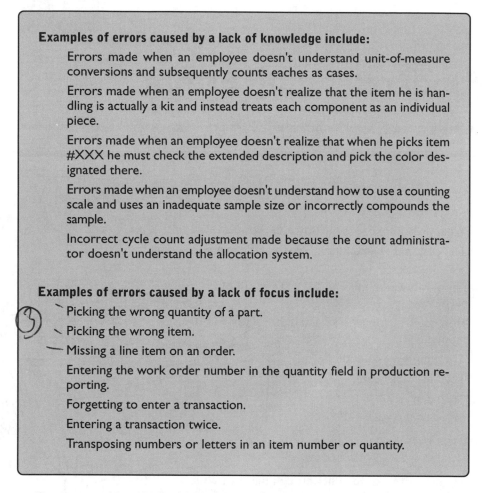

Examples of errors caused by a lack of knowledge include:

Errors made when an employee doesn't understand unit-of-measure conversions and subsequently counts eaches as cases.

Errors made when an employee doesn't realize that the item he is handling is actually a kit and instead treats each component as an individual piece.

Errors made when an employee doesn't realize that when he picks item #XXX he must check the extended description and pick the color designated there.

Errors made when an employee doesn't understand how to use a counting scale and uses an inadequate sample size or incorrectly compounds the sample.

Incorrect cycle count adjustment made because the count administrator doesn't understand the allocation system.

Examples of errors caused by a lack of focus include:

Picking the wrong quantity of a part.

Picking the wrong item.

Missing a line item on an order.

Entering the work order number in the quantity field in production reporting.

Forgetting to enter a transaction.

Entering a transaction twice.

Transposing numbers or letters in an item number or quantity.

Errors caused by a lack of knowledge, although often more complex, are actually easier to prevent than those caused by a lack of focus. Employee training and process changes, such as changing the way a product is labeled, can often resolve knowledge-related errors.

Focus-related errors, however, are much more difficult to control. These errors are commonly referred to as "stupid errors" or "dumb mistakes," in that there seems to be no rational explanation for them. The worker understood what was supposed to be done, but simply was unable to execute correctly. Though it's unlikely you will ever completely eliminate these types of errors, you can significantly reduce them through process changes, training and application of technologies such as bar codes. But first you must understand them.

People have an impressive ability to make errors even under the best-designed processes and controls. I first recognized this ability (or force as I like to think of it) many years ago when implementing a locator system that allowed us to slot products randomly rather than in item number sequence as was previously necessary. Under the previous system, picking the wrong item was the largest source of errors. Since the items had to be stored in item number sequence, which also kept similar items together because the item numbers were assigned based upon commodity classification, you could end up with item XYZ321654, XYZ321645, and XZZ321645, all similar products, stored on the same shelf. It's easy to see how order pickers could mistakenly pick the wrong item.

With our new ability to slot an item anywhere, we were able to separate these very similar items and store them in various areas of the warehouse. So now a picker would be sent to a specific location and would be unlikely to find the previous level of item number and item commodity similarities within that location. Certainly this should eliminate our errors related to picking the wrong item, right? Wrong! While it did reduce this type of error, we eventually started to see errors where the pickers would pick wrong items that were either only slightly similar or not similar at all to the item they were supposed to pick.

So what happened? Well, in the previous system the employees needed to focus on the item number just to find the part. They also expected to find similar items stored in the same area, so consequently would focus more on the item number when picking the part. Under the new system, employees were sent to a specific location and expected to find dissimilar items stored there. They soon adjusted their picking habits to focus less on the item number and were either picking by description, location alone, or just looking for an item number that had some resemblance to the one they were supposed to pick (maybe just looking at the first few characters of the item number). In the end, even though we did make some gains in accuracy, we didn't see the level of overall accuracy improvement we had expected.

Over the years I guess I've become somewhat fascinated with this "force." To better understand it, you need to understand the way people process information, or data, to be more specific. Now, I have to make it clear that I have no formal education in cognitive science and no official credentials for discussing the complex workings of the human mind — but I'm not going to let that stop me. I have spent a lot of time analyzing errors and have developed some definite opinions as to how they occur.

Man versus machine

Consider how a computer processes information. Data is stored in a highly structured hierarchical format that consists of databases containing one or more files or tables that subsequently contain one or more records that contain one or more fields that ultimately contain the smaller pieces of raw data. To access a specific piece of data, a computer program must know the database and table the data is stored in. It will then use selection criteria based upon the data stored in a field or several fields (known as a key) to determine the specific record or records required. Once it has the record(s) it can grab the specific data required based upon the field names. Given the same input, the computer will give you the same output every time it is requested. Even when there are mistakes or bugs in computer programs, they will still provide predictable, consistent output (incorrect output in the case of a computer bug, but still consistent). If you specify that you want the shipped quantity from line #2 on order #12345 in the Sales Order Detail File, you can expect that given the same circumstances the computer will give you the same result every time and not return the shipped quantity one time and the line number the next time or the shipped quantity from line #3 or the date or location etc.

Unlike the computer, the human mind is organic in nature and does not use similar highly structured methods for interpreting, storing, and retrieving data. There is also less consistency in output given the same input. Do you ever wonder why (this is much more entertaining if you use Andy Rooney's voice in your head as you read it) one day you know something such as a date, an address, a company name, a phone number, a password, and another day you cannot seem to remember the information? Yet, days later, you suddenly know it again. Or how you can incorrectly remember information such as confusing a PIN number with an old password or giving out an old phone number rather than your current phone number? Or do you wonder how three people witness a crime and give three very different accounts of what they saw? Or how you can be thinking of a specific word or phrase, yet when you speak it comes out differently? While writing this book I have had several episodes of "what is that word I'm thinking of?" While I'm absolutely certain that there is a word and I know what it is, I just can't seem to access it at the moment. Eventually it will come to me. So what is that all about? I either know something or I don't, right?

The fact is, we really don't know exactly how we interpret, store, and retrieve data. Although I'm sure there is some structure to it, it obviously doesn't follow the same logic as a computer and is not a very highly accurate means of processing detailed data.

We also seem to process information at different levels of consciousness. For example, while driving home from work, you can be thinking about a problem you had at work or what you're going to do when you get home. You're really not paying much attention to where you are, what you have to do at the next intersection, or even whether your foot is on the gas or brake, yet somehow you seem to get home. This "running on automatic" mode primarily occurs when your attention is divided while performing a repetitive task; and while you do somehow manage to complete the task, you are more prone to err because the task is not getting your complete focus.

For example, one day you may need to run an errand on your way home from work. Yet, because you were running in automatic mode, you take your normal highway exit (the one before your intended exit). You were well aware that you were not going directly home, but you "spaced" for a moment and got off at your normal exit. Or, for a more dangerous example, on my route home from work, on a county road that I traveled daily for years, a four-way stop sign was added at an intersection that previously only required the cross traffic to stop. I knew the stop sign was installed, and, when focused on it, I had no problems. However, when I was thinking of something else (divided attention) and driving in automatic mode, I ran the stop sign once and had several abrupt stops before the stop sign finally became part of my automatic mode. I know my eyes saw the stop sign, but the visual image didn't convert into a thought to stop, because, while running in automatic, I wasn't using my complete focus. The information I was using to make driving decisions was based on a mix of what I expected to see — based on repetitive memory — and what I actually saw. Had this been the first time I had ever driven this road, I am certain that I would have stopped at the intersection. In fact, if the stop signs were now removed, I would probably occasionally stop at the intersection since stopping there has now become automatic.

I like to use driving as an example because it is a repetitive and time-consuming task that most people can relate to. The more repetitive and time consuming a task is, the more likely you are to fall into the running on automatic mode. Repetitive and time consuming? Hey, that sounds a lot like work, doesn't it?

When a person processes data there are several points where an error can occur. First, you have the data input, generally in the form of visual or audible information that must be interpreted into a thought. The thought goes into memory and is then later retrieved from memory to perform an action. The action could be writing down a location or quantity, entering data into a computer, picking a specific item or quantity, etc. It's important to understand that an error can occur at any point in this process. People often don't realize that when an order picker reads a pick slip and then reaches to pick the item, he is using his memory to process this information. Though it may have been a split second between the time he read the information to the time he picked the item, it still requires the use of memory, and therefore can have memory-related problems.

Let me try to explain memory-related errors in repetitive environments another way. Say I told you to pick a card from a deck of playing cards and asked you to remember the card for 24 hours. I could probably ask you which card it was after a minute, an hour, or a day, and you would likely be able to accurately remember it. Now, say I told you to pick a new card every hour, and that you only had to remember that card until you picked the next one. You would probably be very accurate for the first several hours. However, eventually your memory would start to get cluttered with previous cards you picked. You would then run the risk of mistakenly remembering the card you picked several hours or days prior as the most recent card picked. Now imagine you are picking orders at a rate of one line every few minutes or seconds. It is very easy to read a pick but remember it incorrectly even a split second later.

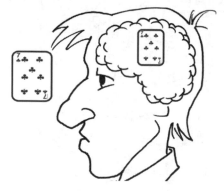

Doing a task once and getting it right is easy.

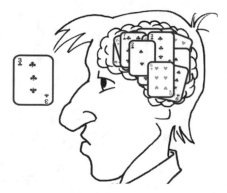

Doing a task thousands of times and getting it right every time is more difficult.

For those of you starting to feel inferior to a computer, you should know that there is a strong desire to get computers to be able to think more like humans. Even though humans have problems consistently processing data at high levels of accuracy, they have an advantage over computers; they can make decisions based upon varying levels of input and can use any stored data (memory, experience) in the decision-making process. A computer requires a specific relationship to be predefined in order to use various pieces of data. That's how people can encounter a situation that they have never encountered before and never anticipated encountering, yet still make a decision for a specific action based upon the given circumstances. A computer, given incomplete or unexpected data, will either crash or do nothing.

By understanding the strengths and weaknesses of people and technologies you have the opportunity to design processes that best utilize the strengths of each to offset inherent weaknesses.

This ability to "fill in the blanks" and take an action even when only minimal data is available, has the negative side effect of sometimes filling in the blanks with incorrect information. This helps to explain the situation encountered when several people witness a crime, yet give different accounts of what happened. Each account of the crime is a combination of what the witness actually saw and what their brain assumed was also happening. The phrase "my eyes are playing tricks on me" should be replaced with the phrase "my mind is playing tricks on me" since it's your brain that is misinterpreting what you saw. The more focused you were on observing the crime, the more accurate your account will be.

This capacity to interpret is what currently separates man from machine. So what does this have to do with inventory accuracy? By understanding the strengths and weaknesses of people and technologies you have the opportunity to design processes that best utilize the strengths of each to offset inherent weaknesses.

Now let's go to some real world inventory-related examples of focus-related errors and possible explanations for the errors.

Paperwork instructs to pick two pieces and the worker picks one piece instead.

✔ There may have been another number on the paperwork with a one in it such as line #1, item number ending with a one or a location ending with a one.

✔ The previous or next pick on the paperwork may be for one piece.

✔ The last time the worker picked this part he picked one piece.

✔ The most common pick quantity for this item is one piece.

Paperwork instructs to pick one piece of a pump; item number XYZ12345 from location BX0240301 and the picker picks the wrong part.

✔ Picker may have transposed a number in the location, saw a similar item number there and picked it.

✔ Picker may have transposed a number in the location, saw a pump there and picked it.

✔ Picker may have gone to the correct location, and saw a similar part number or another pump and picked it.

✔ Picker may have looked at the location and description, and thought of another pump in that area that is picked frequently and picked it instead, disregarding any information on the paperwork.

✔ Picker may have looked at the item number and description, thought of another pump with a similar item number that is picked frequently and picked it instead even though the location is not even close.

✔ Picker may have gone to the correct location, identified the correct item, and then got distracted and physically grabbed the item next to or above the correct one. This is an error type that really surprises people after they implement a bar code validation system and find out that a picker scanned the correct location/item and then picked a different one.

Material handler picks the wrong quantity of a large quantity pick.

✔ Loses track during counting (…54,56,58,70,72,74…)

✔ Counts some of the pieces multiple times.

✔ Assumes wrong case or pallet quantity such as counting as cases of 36 even though marked as 24 because a similar product is stored in cases of 36.

✔ Math error in multiplying cases times quantity per case or layers times quantity per layer etc. (uses memory rather than a calculator such as thinking 12 x 12 = 244 rather than 144).

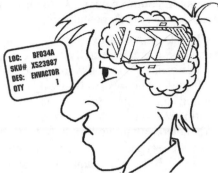

In this example, the "-3" in the SKU# is mistakenly retrieved from the worker's memory as the quantity.

Here the worker looks at the information and assumes it to be an item he regularly picks. His brain will now lead him to the item and location he remembers rather than that which is on the picking document. This is one of the most common types of picking errors.

The objective here is to build a level of understanding as to what drives the thought process in making these stupid errors. Rather than scratching your head, totally perplexed by these errors, you can begin to use your knowledge to explore possible solutions. It's also a good idea to educate workers to help them better understand how they make errors. Only in understanding errors can you truly hope to control them.

Environmental factors

While we've discussed the two major types of errors and the thought process that affects them, there are many additional factors that affect accuracy. I've often said that virtually every decision you make when designing storage and material handling facilities and processes will have some effect on accuracy. While accuracy considerations may not be great enough to change some of these decisions, the knowledge of how these decisions affect accuracy will allow you to develop processes and procedures that take into account the error potential associated with the decision.

Lighting.
Lighting in the warehouse and on the shop floor affects accuracy in several ways. Inadequate lighting can make it difficult to read documents, computer screens, product labels, and portable terminal displays, increasing the opportunity to make

errors. In addition, poorly lit facilities can also affect employee morale resulting in an "I don't care" mentality.

Don't assume more lighting is always better. In some cases lighting can cause excessive glare, especially when using hand held terminals or when lift truck operators have to look towards the light when placing pallets in tall pallet racking. Lighting technology is constantly changing and there is a lot more science being applied to lighting decisions than in the past. It's advisable to use a commercial lighting consultant when evaluating lighting in storage and production areas. Make sure the consultant understands the activities taking place in each specific area as well as the types of documents, equipment, computers, and portable devices being used. If the consultant doesn't show an interest in this level of detail, I would suggest finding another consultant.

Ways of compensating for poor lighting can include using larger, bold fonts on paperwork and labels, glare filters on computer screens, larger fonts and back-lighting on portable displays and adding task lighting and spotlights on lift trucks and material handling equipment.

Noise.

Noise is unavoidable in most manufacturing operations as well as distribution operations that use a lot of automated conveyor systems or internal combustion lift trucks. While noise is primarily a safety issue, it should also be considered as impacting accuracy. For those that may doubt noise can affect work performance, I suggest you move your desk onto the shop floor next to a machine for a day and see for yourself. Anything that distracts a worker or affects their ability to concentrate will potentially impact accuracy.

Temperature.

Like noise, temperature is another environmental factor that can have an effect on accuracy as well as productivity. Workers in cold storage areas will have a difficult time writing information on transaction forms or entering data into portable terminals. Extra measures should be taken to minimize or eliminate the need to do this. Excessive heat tends to be more of a productivity issue than an accuracy issue; however, it can have an impact on accuracy by reducing an employee's ability to concentrate or when paperwork is lost or mixed up through the use of fans. Temperature can also influence the effectiveness of equipment related to accuracy. Portable terminal displays may have problems in extreme environments such as cold storage areas, and scales used to weigh and count materials are designed to work within specific temperature ranges.

Weather.

Inventory losses can occur whenever inventory is stored exposed to the elements, such as water damage, heat/cold related damage, UV exposure damage, and theft. Outside of these obvious problems, there are some other process related special considerations. Product identification such as labels must be able to withstand the elements; this not only includes special label stock and adhesives, but also

printing techniques that won't fade or run. Bright sunlight can also prevent laser scanners from reading bar codes. Certainly, whenever the ability to identify the inventory is compromised, you have increased your risk of errors.

Housekeeping.

Housekeeping can have a significant impact on accuracy as well as productivity and safety. Allowing damaged cartons, gaylords, or other types of containers, or allowing unstable loads to be placed in racking or stacked in floor locations, will eventually result in damaged product or loose product falling on the floor in between loads or racking. Allowing trash to pile up may provide an opportunity for mistaking product for trash. Allowing cluttered aisles and storage areas will result in damage to products by lift trucks and other equipment. Damaged product is a high risk factor for inventory problems because it is often disposed of without the appropriate transaction being entered. Cluttered areas also become "black holes" for lost inventory. Poor housekeeping often allows product to span or share multiple adjacent storage locations, adding confusion to cycle counting and order picking operations. Allowing product to be staged anywhere, such as in aisles, under conveyors, and behind machines, makes it difficult to determine what is supposed to be there and what was mistakenly placed there (lost). Allowing work stations to be cluttered and allowing trash to be left on the floor makes it easier to lose documents that are needed to make inventory related transactions.

In addition to the direct effect on accuracy, you also have the indirect effect that poor housekeeping has on employee morale that eventually affects accuracy. Allowing storage areas and work areas to be dirty and cluttered conveys a message of "we don't care" to the employees. And if you don't care, you can be certain that ultimately they won't care. I'm not saying that every facility can be perfectly organized and spotless all the time. The nature of the activities in a facility, as well as the type of materials being handled, will change the definition of good housekeeping from one facility to another. For example, if you use loose fill in your shipping or receiving areas it is near impossible to prevent some of it from falling on the floor. While you could require employees to pick it up every time a piece hits the floor, you will more likely find a policy of having the floor swept every four hours, every shift, or at least once per day adequate.

Inventory characteristics.
Bulk dry goods and liquids stored in large tanks would obviously have different accuracy characteristics than discrete products such as automobiles or manufacturing equipment. Rolls of steel would have different accuracy characteristics than pre-cut steel sheets. While you're unlikely to change the materials being handled because of accuracy characteristics, you certainly should be taking these characteristics into consideration when developing processes and procedures.

Item packaging/containers.
In addition to the characteristics of the materials being handled, the packaging or containers used to protect and contain the materials for storage and transport can have a significant impact on accuracy. In an ideal environment, you would have all of your materials broken down into a few product groups. Each product group would be stored in standardized containers with standardized quantities per layer within the container. You would have standardized quantities per container and standardized quantities of containers per pallet. All materials would also be received, consumed, produced, and shipped in these same standardized full pallet or full container quantities. Yes, these environments do exist. Unfortunately many operations will find this level of standardization impractical.

Containers can be bags, cartons, totes, gaylords, crates, hoppers, pallets, barrels, tanks, etc. There are various levels of standardization that can be applied:

Same item/container/quantity combination each time a specific item is purchased or produced.

Same container/quantity combination for groups of products.

Use of inner packs (also known as unit packs) such as bags, smaller boxes, dividers, and layers. The use of layers within cartons, totes, gaylords, crates, etc. (usually just a piece of flat cardboard) can often be a very simple means of increasing accuracy; the idea is each layer contains the same quantity of materials arranged in a pattern that greatly reduces or eliminates the possibility of a miscount. Inner packs are also very useful in preventing product damage.

Forcing order quantities, sales quantities, move quantities, and manufacturing production and usage quantities to be exact multiples of container quantities.

The just-in-time movement of the last few decades presents conflicting messages towards standardized containers. On one hand, JIT promotes standardized containers through its efforts to eliminate waste (counting is waste, repacking and returning materials is waste, damaged materials is waste, etc.). At the same time, the JIT move towards ordering just what is immediately needed for components and raw materials and smaller lot sizes, ultimately driving towards one-piece-flow for manufacturing, does not easily coexist within the rigidity of a standardized container/quantity system.

The message to be learned here is that a well thought out strategy that incorporates standardized containers and quantities wherever practical, can provide increases in both accuracy and productivity without negatively impacting overall business strategies. You may find that you can only incorporate this level of standardization with certain product groups or suppliers.

Item identification.
Product identification consists of both the part numbering scheme and the actual physical identification of the product.

The first dilemma encountered when setting up a new inventory system is whether you want to build meaning into your part numbering scheme, and, if so, how much? Meaningful part numbers have historically been the method of choice, however, recent trends are leaning more towards random, meaningless part numbering schemes.

Logic that has been put into part numbers has included:

Product group identification such as sales categories or purchasing commodity classifications.

Vendor identification and/or vendor item number.

Customer identification and/or customer item number.

Product specs such as dimensions, weights, or composition, version identification, color, flavor, facility identification, etc.

The problems associated with building meaning into part numbers include ending up with very long, difficult to use part numbers as well as numbering schemes that are difficult to maintain as new product and product lines are added. With the extensive databases available in most modern inventory management software there is little value to placing this level of information in the item number. If the use of this information is primarily for grouping items for reporting and analysis purposes or for people working at a computer terminal, the information is much better placed in separate fields in the database.

I must admit, however, that I do prefer a little meaning in the part number. For people working in the warehouse, shipping, receiving, or on the shop floor, there is some value in being able to quickly identify the major product group the product belongs to by the part number alone. For example, if I worked for a distributor of computer products I would like to know whether an item was a hard drive, a video card, a memory chip, or a software product by the item number. I would probably not want to try to integrate the vendor identification, model identification or specs into this system. If I worked at a manufacturer that made products that were unique by customer and had only a few customers, I might like the item number to identify the customer. I would probably keep this meaningful portion of the item number to fewer than four characters and have the remaining portion of the item number meaningless.

Another decision related to part numbering schemes is whether the part numbers should be numeric, alpha, or a combination. Purely numeric part numbers provide the quickest data entry but are more prone to transposition errors. A random mix of alpha and numeric characters in item numbers (example: 8FP37W95Q) can make the part numbers difficult to read and enter. Combinations of grouped alpha and numeric characters (such as all items start with three alpha characters and end with four numeric characters, example: BRK4583) tend to be easier to read and reduce problems associated with transposing characters. The primary down side to using alpha characters is their effect on data entry. Entering purely numeric data on the 10-key numeric keypad located on the right of most keyboards is significantly faster than entering alpha or alpha/numeric combinations. Also, if you plan on using portable hand held-terminals, you will find entering alpha characters on them is extremely difficult. A solution to alpha data entry productivity problems is to use bar codes as much as possible for high transaction tasks.

It's generally not a good idea to include special characters such as hyphens, periods, commas, spaces, etc. in part numbers. To make part numbers more readable on documents, packaging, and labels, you can program the computer system to insert a space or hyphen in a specific position to help break up the part number. Your credit card number is an example of this; your card and associated documents may insert a space or dash every four characters to make the number easier to read, however these spaces or dashes are not actually part of your credit card number. Other similar examples are Social Security numbers and phone numbers. While the parentheses, spaces and hyphens make a phone number easier to read, you certainly wouldn't want to have to enter them when making a call.

So how long should your part numbers be? You need to take into account potential future growth (what is the maximum quantity of part numbers you will ever need?), accuracy, and productivity. Long part numbers are more difficult to read, more difficult to enter, and more highly prone to data entry errors. However it is less likely that transposing characters in a longer item number will result in entering another valid part number (in other words, the computer system will

Item Numbering Schemes:

SKU# 473810923847928   *(too long)*

SKU# 7342   *(too short)*

SKU# 3L80BQ98R7   *(too confusing)*

SKU# BPX7349   *(good compromise)*

probably notify you of your error). Short item numbers make it easier to mistake one item for another, or, if you make a data entry error, you are more likely to accidentally enter another valid part number (therefore, no system generated error message).

As a general recommendation, most businesses should find that item numbers between six and eight characters in length, containing a combination of grouped alpha and numeric characters, with some general meaning built into two or three characters, should provide a good balance for a part numbering scheme.

The methods used for the physical identification of materials should also be considered very carefully. Physical identification can include everything from an SKU label on a small parts bin or large container for bulk materials, to individual product packaging or labels, to compliance case labels, to pallet license plates. Poor product identification practices will certainly contribute to inventory accuracy problems. More information on physical identification of inventory is covered in subsequent chapters.

Storage methods.

Different storage methods can have very different accuracy characteristics. While it is unlikely that accuracy will play a key role in storage method decisions (productivity and space utilization will ultimately drive these decisions), processes and technologies can be put in place to reduce or eliminate accuracy issues related to a particular storage method.

Random versus fixed locations. In a fixed locations system, each SKU is assigned a specific location or locations and will always be stored in these predetermined locations. Random location systems allow materials to be stored in any available location. Fixed location systems are inherently more accurate than random location systems, however the need to allocate fixed storage space regardless of the current quantity on hand often results in unacceptably low space utilization.

There is no question that random location systems tend to have a much higher rate of lost inventory than that of fixed location systems. To understand this you need to think about the characteristics of a fixed location system that help in preventing or identifying errors that are not characteristics of a random system. If you are putting an item away in a fixed location system it is very likely that there will already be some of the same item in that location. If you get to the location and your item does not match that already in the location, you are probably at the wrong location. If you put the item away correctly but make a location error when entering the transaction, you may immediately get an error from the system identifying that the location is not a valid location for that item. Or, if this functionality is not available, you can usually set up some exception reporting that can easily identify these errors after the transaction is completed. Often times product that was originally located correctly, ends up in the wrong location as a result of product shifting, falling, or being temporarily moved to count or to get access to other product and is never returned to the original location. In a fixed location system this misplaced product is much more likely to be noticed than in a random storage system.

Application of automated data capture (ADC) technologies such as portable terminals with bar code scanners combined with strict procedures and regular location audits are highly recommended in random storage areas.

Slotting. In fixed location systems, the activity of determining the location for a specific item is called slotting. Historically, items were slotted by simple logical methods such as by SKU number, by product family, or by product description. The driving reason for these types of slotting was to assist the warehouse workers in finding the product. This forced similar items to be stored together, which greatly increases the likelihood of mixing items or picking wrong items. It also tends to result in poor space utilization and poor productivity.

With the advent of computerized inventory systems that allowed physical locations to be easily associated with each SKU there became a means to slot product in a manner that optimizes accuracy, productivity, and space utilization. The advantages of using a locator system and optimizing the product slotting are so great that you'll have a difficult time finding operations that would not benefit in using this methodology. Unfortunately, there are still inventory management software packages being sold (mostly software for smaller businesses) that do not support location functionality. In addition there are a lot of operations that have software that supports locations but have chosen not to use it, or are using the location functionality but have not slotted their product to take advantage of it.

As I mentioned earlier in this chapter, separating similar products does not guarantee the elimination of mixed product or of picking the wrong item. Whenever you add a component to a process (a location in this case) you reduce the focus on the remaining components (item number, description). You also create the need to manage the new component (locator system). All that being said, I still strongly recommend companies consider utilizing locator systems and optimizing their product slotting. Locator systems are discussed in more detail in chapter eight.

High-density storage. High-density storage is characterized by full pallets, crates, bales, rolls, or other large unit loads stored more than one unit deep and/or high. Stacked bulk floor storage, drive-in/drive-thru racking, push-back rack, flow rack, and to a lesser extent, double deep rack, are examples of high-density storage methods. As a general rule, you should avoid allowing mixed SKUs within the same row, bay, or position in a high-density storage system. This is for productivity reasons as well as accuracy reasons.

Although high-density storage is also often random storage, the fact that you do not mix product within a location gives it some of the accuracy characteristics of fixed location storage. In fact, high-density storage generally has a high accuracy rate for both putaway and picking transactions. Unfortunately, if product is somehow mixed or if there is a partial unit load mixed in a high-density storage system it is extremely difficult to identify or rectify. Cycle counting and location audit procedures often must allow the counter to "assume" that all unit loads within a location are the same SKU and the same quantity, as a true visual verification would generally require extensive labor to remove all product from the location.

Standard pallet rack storage. This is the standard single-deep, back-to-back racking configuration that most people are familiar with. Full pallet or other unit-load storage in standard pallet rack will almost always be random location storage. Case and broken-case storage in standard pallet rack may be either fixed or random storage, or, in many facilities, is a combination of fixed locations for picking locations and random locations for replenishment inventory storage.

Case, broken-case, and other manually handled inventory storage in pallet rack presents some additional accuracy issues. Since multiple SKUs are often stored in the same location in this type of storage you are more likely to have product mixed, miscounted, or misidentified. Strict procedures must be in place to ensure clear separations between SKUs. In addition, decking, dividers, and netting should be considered to prevent product from falling or shifting into other locations.

Static shelving. Standard steel shelving is the mainstay of piece-pick type operations and parts rooms. Storage in static shelving usually follows the fixed location model. Parts bins or dividers should be considered to reduce the likelihood of mixing multiple SKUs stored on the same shelf. Solid backs and sides on shelving units will also help to prevent product from falling or shifting into other locations.

Transaction profiles.

Receipts per day, lines per purchase order, quantity per receipt, pallets per receipt, mixed receipts, picks per SKU, picks per day, picks per order, pieces per pick, weight and volume per pick, weight and volume per order, transactions by time of day, transactions by day of week, seasonality, etc. are all characteristics of your transaction profile. While you will probably have very little control over it, your transaction profile will have a significant impact on accuracy. Higher quantities per pick make you more susceptible to quantity errors, higher lines per order make mixed orders and missed items more likely as does multiple pallets per shipment and higher transactions per hour. Transaction profiles will play a key role when defining processes, applying technologies, and setting accuracy standards.

Storage and staging area identification.

Making sure that storage and staging areas are clearly designated and identified should help in improving accuracy. This includes location labels on shelves, hanging signs or painting floors to identify floor storage locations and paint or tape designating staging areas, storage areas, and traffic aisles. This all has to do with organization and identification. Clear storage and staging designations will prevent confusion as to whether something is in storage or is awaiting some type of processing (such as receipt, shipping, manufacturing). Clear location identification will help to avoid picking and putaway errors related to incorrect locations.

Paperwork/documents.

The detailed design of the paperwork and documents used to receive, stock, move, pick, ship, count, adjust, plan, and produce inventory is an often-neglected part of operations. Yet the effects on accuracy and productivity can be significant. This topic is discussed in greater detail in subsequent chapters.

Software.

Inventory accuracy is essentially the comparison of what you have to what you think you have. Since what you think you have is generally tracked on a computer, you'll find that your software's functionality is a key factor in your ability to maintain high levels of accuracy. While only a very small percentage of inventory problems are actually caused by computer error, it is important to note that computer bugs or setup problems can cause inventory accuracy problems. More important are the potential limitations on process improvement forced by the lack of functionality of a particular software system or the lack of knowledge by users of a software system.

Process.

Certainly process design impacts overall accuracy. The most common problem made when designing processes is the tendency to take the narrow view and only focus on a portion of the output requirements. Whether designing a new process or evaluating an existing process it's critical that you take into consideration the effects on customer service, quality, cost, productivity, capacity, safety, and of course, accuracy. Failing to take into account any of these sets in motion the perpetual process-correction cycle, where each process correction creates a new problem, which is then corrected, creating another problem, and on and on. An example would be a process that was designed focusing on quality, cost, and productivity. Once the process is in place, it's found that the process results in excessive lead times that are unacceptable to the customer. Now changes are made focusing on shorter lead times to meet customer service needs and soon the changes result in capacity problems. Quickly the process is adjusted and suddenly you have quality and accuracy problems. The quality people now jump in with changes that end up crippling productivity. Well, you get the idea.

Keep this in mind as you embark on your accuracy initiative. If you start evaluating processes with the sole objective of increasing accuracy, and, in doing so, sacrifice productivity, cost, and your ability to meet your customer's expectations, you are certainly headed for failure.

Technologies used.
There are a variety of technologies available that can be very useful in increasing accuracy. You must realize, though, that access to technology solutions is neither a prerequisite for being accurate, nor is it a guarantee of accuracy. A well-designed process can often negate the need for supplemental technology solutions. Technology applied to a bad process will just result in a high-tech bad process. As with process design, it's important to consider the big picture when evaluating technology solutions to avoid negatively impacting other areas. Specific technologies are discussed in detail in chapter eight.

Task relationship to errors

To further understand errors you must consider the relationship errors have to the task being performed, as well as the environment in which the task is being performed. Certain tasks are more highly prone to errors than others, but more importantly, different tasks tend to have different error type profiles. For example, the most frequent error type for order picking in a distribution/fulfillment operation will usually be wrong items picked, closely followed by wrong quantity and to a lesser extent, missing items. However, the most frequent error type for component order picking in a manufacturing operation will usually be wrong quantity followed by transaction-related errors such as transactions not being recorded or data entry errors. The reason it's important to understand these differences is that when you implement solutions you want to make sure you are implementing solutions that target the types of errors that most frequently occur within the specific task. If you implement a solution targeting wrong item picks in the production order picking process you will have little impact on overall accuracy.

Specific tasks tend to have specific error profiles. Below are examples of the most common types of errors for certain tasks.

Order Picking (Distribution Environment)

>   Wrong item

>   Wrong quantity

>   Missing items

Order Picking (Manufacturing Environment).

>   Wrong quantity

>   Transaction-related errors

Receiving

>   Transaction-related errors

Putaway

>   Wrong location

>   Transaction-related errors

>   No transaction

Production reporting

>   Transaction-related errors

>   Quantity

>   Scrap

Keep in mind that these are generalizations and your specific operation may have very different task error type profiles.

Individual's relationship to errors

Since most errors ultimately come down to human error, it would be negligent to ignore the effects individual workers can have on accuracy. Although the initial focus of an accuracy initiative should never be to start singling out employees, eventually you likely will need to deal with the impact of individual employees on accuracy. Most errors can be eliminated through process definition, employee training, and technology. However, once you've addressed these issues you may still have to deal with the fact that some employees continue to make excessive errors despite your best efforts.

Ultimately this will come down to an employee's unwillingness or inability to follow procedures or to maintain focus. Are some employees naturally more accurate than others? Definitely. Is there a way to determine this type of person during the hiring process? Maybe, but not necessarily. Over the years I've been fortunate to have had some exceptionally accurate employees working for me. I've also hired and fired my share of accuracy nightmares. I've certainly tried to look for characteristics that could help to differentiate the former from the latter during the hiring process. What I found is far from conclusive and fairly generic in nature.

Ability to learn.
Don't confuse this with level of education, although some correlations can be made. People that learn quickly are also able to learn to be accurate more quickly. When it has been identified that they have made an error, they are more likely to make adjustments to avoid making similar errors in the future.

Pride.
People that take a lot of pride in their work are more focused than those that are just there to get a paycheck. While some people naturally take more pride than others, pride is a characteristic that is also greatly affected by the work environment. I should also mention that sometimes employees that take a great deal of pride in their work are not the easiest people to work with. I'm generally willing to accept the trade-off.

Long-term employment objectives.
This is very much related to pride since people with long-term employment objectives within your organization are much more likely to take pride in their work. Individual accuracy also improves with experience; my most accurate employees achieved their greatest levels of accuracy only after several years in their position. Even if an employee has the other accuracy characteristics, they will never achieve these levels if they move on after a year or two. A long-term employment objective is another characteristic that is also affected by the work environment. If your employees do not see any benefit to planning their career within your organization, they will soon become "temporary" employees just passing time and collecting pay.

Gender?
That's right, I've found gender seems to make a difference. Working in warehousing and manufacturing, I've usually had more male employees than female employees, yet the females were predominantly the most accurate. This isn't to say there are not highly accurate men or highly inaccurate women. Nor will I attempt to speculate as to why this is the case. Since there are laws against sexual discrimination, you may even question the applicable value of this statement. I'm not suggesting that you should hire women instead of men, but rather that you should

not exclude them from consideration. It doesn't take a lot of upper body strength to drive a modern forklift, and the average weight of a unit manually handled continues to decrease.

Since most of these characteristics are pretty much ones you should be looking for anyway, the primary purpose here is to help reinforce the value of those characteristics as well as identify the characteristics that can be affected by environmental factors. How you go about identifying these characteristics during the interview process would be a whole other book (and there are many books on interviewing available).

I would, however, like to comment on pre-employment testing. There are two primary categories of pre-employment testing: psychological testing and skills-based testing. I don't hold a very high opinion of psychological testing. Having personally taken several, and also having been given the opportunity to review the detailed results of one in particular, I found the value and accuracy of these tests to be questionable. I do find much greater value in skills-based testing, provided you are careful to ensure the skills being tested match the skill requirements of the position and that the execution of the test takes steps to avoid biases related to language and education. Since many of the production and warehouse positions that have an impact on inventory accuracy are not highly compensated positions, and therefore may not be able to require high school or post-high school education levels, it becomes more important to determine the employee's ability to learn as opposed to determining his current level of knowledge. My preference is to provide the prospective employee information prior to the test that gives examples of the test materials and even instructions as to how to solve the specific problems. This way, your pool of employees that passed the test are not limited to only those that already knew how to solve the problems (biased by education and age), but also includes those that were able to quickly learn (or relearn) how to solve the problems. To avoid language-related biases, you may want to provide the test or portions of the test in additional languages. For example, you could have the English skills portion in English (assuming communication in English is a requirement) and problem solving, mathematical, and other skill portions in the prospective employee's primary language.

OK, there is that other test, the pre-employment drug screen. In my opinion, the inherent flaw in pre-employment drug testing (that it is a onetime test that only detects recent use of drugs) may actually be its greatest asset. Employers are not really looking to eliminate anyone that has ever used, or occasionally uses, drugs, from their work force. Pre-employment drug screening ensures that you do not hire applicants who either lack the self-control to stop using drugs for a short period of time or are just so stupid as to use drugs when they know they are looking for work and will likely be required to be screened for drugs. If you think, as I do, that stupidity and a lack of self-discipline are characteristics that don't mix well with accuracy, then you probably don't want these people working with your inventory and data.

Summary

Understanding errors is the often neglected but critical first step in effectively reducing or eliminating them. Determining whether errors are caused by lack of knowledge or lack of focus, as well as understanding the human and environmental factors that contribute to errors can greatly increase your chances for success in identifying and implementing accuracy solutions. Failing to take this critical first step can result in wasted time, money, and effort on solutions that may not address the specific needs of your operation. Probably the single most important point you should take from this chapter is that making errors is easy. Decision makers that may have never personally experienced working in a highly repetitive transaction environment often have a difficult time accepting just how easy it is to make an error. Their denial leads them to put processes in place that are built upon the assumption that the employees will not make mistakes. Ultimately these processes fail, as the employees cannot achieve these unrealistic expectations.

2

Making Accuracy Easy

The largest obstacle to the success of an accuracy initiative will usually be resistance from workers, supervisors, and managers to accept the changes that may be necessary to improve processes. While there is generally a certain level of resistance expected with any change, accuracy initiatives often fall victim to increased resistance created when the initiative places significant demands on workers too early in the process or the solutions are not well thought out and fail or create additional problems. Since accuracy is highly dependent on cooperation from employees throughout the organization, it is critical that the first phases of your accuracy initiative are not only successful in increasing accuracy, but also successful in reducing the resistance to future changes that will be required. The best way to do this is to start by implementing solutions that make it easy to be accurate. That is, to implement solutions that either make it easier to perform a task or have no impact on the level of effort required for performing a task.

- ✔ Don't start with the "big stick" method by demanding that employees "be more accurate, or else!"

- ✔ Don't start with process changes that negatively impact productivity.

- ✔ Don't start with process changes that negatively impact cycle time or customer service.

- ✔ Don't hastily implement solutions that have not been adequately evaluated.

- ✔ Do start with process changes that increase both accuracy and productivity.

- ✔ Do start with process changes that have a high likelihood for success.

- ✔ Do start with process changes that quickly show improvement.

- ✔ Do get employee involvement.

These do's and don'ts are not hard rules, but rather a set of general recommendations that apply to most operations. There may be times when — due to specific operational needs — it makes sense to start with a process change that negatively impacts productivity or cycle time. This is most likely to occur when a company is having severe accuracy problems and these changes offer the quickest and most significant improvements. If you are putting in place process changes that negatively impact productivity or cycle time, make sure you have a plan to compensate for these changes. Also, as you are evaluating processes, take advantage of making unrelated productivity improvements to offset negative impacts of process changes related to accuracy that may be necessary.

Process evaluation

Making accuracy easy starts with evaluation of the processes in which errors are likely to occur. I'll once again mention the importance of taking the big picture approach to process evaluation. Even though you must evaluate these processes at a very detailed level, you shouldn't lose sight of the overall objectives of your organization. Rather than thinking, "what is the most accurate way to do this?" you should be thinking, " what is the best way to do this, that takes into account the customer service, productivity, quality, accuracy, capacity, safety, and financial objectives of our organization?" Yes, I know it sounds like a catch phrase from one of those management seminars you may have been forced to attend, but it is very important to evaluate processes this way.

Total quality management (TQM) and other quality strategies developed over the past 30 years do a good job of providing tools and methodologies for process evaluation, root cause analysis, and continuous improvement. Since there has been extensive coverage of these concepts in numerous books, courses, workshops, and seminars, I don't intend to spend a lot of time on this topic. I will, however, cover some key points that should be used whenever evaluating processes.

Why do we do this?
This is the first question to ask. Without knowing why you are doing something, you obviously can't expect to effectively improve the process in a manner consistent with improving overall operational excellence. Determining the requirements of the outputs of the process sets the clear objectives of the process. Parts of the process that don't contribute to these objectives should be eliminated. In some cases — though admittedly not very frequently — entire processes can be eliminated by determining that they don't actually contribute to business objectives or by making a minor change to another process that more effectively achieves the objectives.

What are the alternatives?

One process improvement mistake I see regularly is the tendency to focus on making changes to the existing methods without ever considering alternative methods that may more effectively achieve the objective. Usually the result of a lack of imagination combined with a lack of knowledge, this mistake is more common when those responsible for evaluating the process have not had adequate exposure to alternative methods, technologies, and equipment. Educational courses; involvement with professional organizations such as APICS, WERC, MHMS, ASQ, IIE; seminars; books; trade magazines; facility tours; trade shows; equipment and technology suppliers; consultants; and the Internet are all sources of information that will prove to be valuable in evaluating processes. Knowledge isn't gained overnight, so an ongoing commitment to continuing education will prove to be more valuable than last-minute attempts to educate personnel on specific topics.

Process improvement team members should be encouraged to think creatively and to communicate all possible solutions to others working on the team. This is usually done in the form of formal brainstorming sessions, but it should also be encouraged at any point in the process. People are often apprehensive about communicating ideas, especially if the ideas are significantly different than the current or "standard" methods. Most ideas will eventually be dismissed, the people involved need to understand this to avoid feelings of rejection when their suggestion doesn't make the cut, but more importantly they need to understand the importance of their "bad ideas" to the process. If it takes 50 bad ideas to find the best solution, then the effort was well worth it. Often times the best solution will be the result of an evolution of ideas that were initially inspired by "bad ideas" submitted earlier in the process. Also, don't be constrained by standard methodologies. Probably the biggest downside to a formal education is the resulting tendency to use textbooks to run a business. The most successful people are the ones that can determine when standardized solutions are effective and when other means need to be explored.

> *The only people that don't have bad ideas are those that have no ideas.*

What are the costs, benefits, and implications of the solution?

Be careful not to oversimplify this part of the analysis. Costs should include implementation costs, integration costs, training costs, transition costs, and cost of money (interest) if applicable. Benefits should be realistic; it's highly unlikely that a solution will eliminate all errors, so plan accordingly. Costs of errors include both tangible and intangible costs. Tangible costs would include costs such as transportation costs incurred by expediting materials or by correcting shipping errors, cost of production delays and interruptions related to inventory errors, labor costs associated with searching for lost product, clerical costs of correcting errors, and even costs associated with a cycle count program (a reduction of errors should result in a reduction of cycle count frequency). Intangible costs include cost of customer dissatisfaction and costs associated with employee frustration. I generally recommend using only tangible costs in cost/benefit analysis and listing intangible benefits as a footnote. If the tangible costs are not sufficient to justify the solution, managers need to consider the intangible benefits when making the decision. Determining the implications associated with a solution requires comprehensive analysis of the process and all related processes. Make sure you have a clear understanding of the effects of your process change.

What training is required?

Almost every process change will require some level of training. Some solutions may even require a skill level beyond the capabilities of current staff (obviously a key consideration in the solution evaluation process). Failure to consider training requirements is a sure way to sabotage your accuracy initiative. More on training later in this chapter.

How will you implement?

Determining the implementation requirements of the solutions is an important part of the evaluation process. Not only is this necessary to determine costs and develop an implementation plan, but also — if the solution cannot be implemented in the required timeframe — to consider other solutions or temporary fixes.

How will you monitor?

Having a plan to monitor the process change is necessary to ensure the new process is being followed as well as providing a means to quickly identify unforeseen problems associated with the change. Monitoring should start during the implementation and gradually diminish over time as process consistency increases and related problems decrease.

When to reevaluate?

The key to continuous improvement is the elimination of complacency. Just because a process change is working and considered successful, doesn't mean you can put a little check mark by it and call it complete. Setting up a specific time to reevaluate a process — even if there are no perceived problems — will help to ensure that you are on the path to prevention instead of reaction.

As previously mentioned, there is a lot of very good information available to assist continuous improvement processes. It's important to note that although TQM and other similar strategies provide some excellent tools and methodologies to improve business processes, sometimes overly aggressive use of these strategies can actually get in the way of improvement. I've witnessed teams argue for hours (at least it felt like hours) as to how to categorize an identified process input (to fit it into a specific process improvement tool's format) when the categories were primarily listed just to help initiate the thought-process of identifying the inputs, and had no real impact on the analysis. There are also stories of teams that have quickly determined the best solution (usually because it was very obvious) yet still were required to go through an extensive formalized process that not only delayed the implementation of the improvement, but also wasted time that could have been used to improve other processes. Don't let the formal process of continuous improvement overshadow the execution of continuous improvement.

Human-machine interface.

One of the easiest ways to make accuracy easy is to improve the often-neglected human-machine interface. Since inventory accuracy is basically the consistency to which the data in your inventory system is in agreement with the actual inventory in your supply chain, and since most discrepancies are ultimately caused by human error, it would make sense that an accuracy improvement effort should focus on the human-machine interface. Unfortunately most of the human-machine interfaces used in general industry have been designed with functionality being the key objective and usability coming in at a much lower priority. This has actually gotten worse as companies migrate from custom legacy systems to more generic ERP systems. This isn't to say that ERP systems are bad, only that the nature of a software program that is designed with the extensive functionality required to meet the needs of diverse businesses, results in a higher degree of complexity than a program designed with a more specific purpose. This higher degree of complexity is usually characterized by user interfaces that contain substantially more information than the user requires. There are also a lot of computer programmers and system integrators that settle for designing "something that works" instead of "something that works well." Granted, making something that works can often be very challenging and is a respectable goal (especially in the bug-infested world of software programming), however more emphasis needs to be placed on the usability of the program, especially if it is used frequently.

My first personal computer (PC) was a DOS-based system that required you to type commands to execute programs and manage files. I had a spreadsheet program and word processing program that were keyboard and menu driven, and a mouse that didn't do a hell of a lot. You could only run one program at a time and you had to set up your hardware separately for each program. Now on the plus side, it did boot up in a matter of seconds and I don't recall that it ever crashed or froze up on me. While I was pleased with my ability to create and maintain spreadsheets and documents (my initial purpose for the PC was to document procedures and track productivity and accuracy), I was rather disappointed with the user interface. This was the late '80s and I was far from being a pioneer PC user. There were some early incarnations of Windows available but they didn't work that well and there was not very much Windows-based software available.

Eventually Windows 3.0 and the first version of Microsoft Office were released. Now this was more like it! With the exception of it slowing my system down to a crawl (I could have a pizza delivered in the time it took Excel to load), this was the type of interface that would eventually make me a "power user." While I'm not willing to give Bill Gates total credit for my success, the user interface of Windows-based software, including spreadsheet, word processing, database, CAD, flowcharting, presentation, and, more recently, page layout and website design software, provided me with access to tools that I may not have used otherwise. This isn't to say that the graphical user interface (GUI) is always the best interface; I still prefer a good "green-screen" mainframe interface for transaction intensive programs such as most inventory related programs. The point here is that the user interface can have a substantial effect on both productivity and accuracy and efforts to make the user interface more user-friendly are well worth the effort.

Human-machine interfaces are not limited to just the representation of information on a computer screen, but also include documents, reports, forms, labels, keyboards, keypads, buttons, touch screens, bar code scanners, RFID readers, voice systems, scales, optical systems, etc. Basically any method used to pass information from the computer to the user or from the user to the computer is a human-machine interface.

Documents, forms, labels, and reports

The utopian view of paperless business is currently a long way from reality. While it looks good on paper (oops!), in the real world paper is still a key part of business communications. Replacing paper with technology should be a consideration in process evaluation, however you should not automatically assume that paperless is the better solution. There's no doubt that a lot of the paper used in business is a result of the "this is how we've always done it" or "I like to have it in my file" mentality. For archival purposes, paper documents and reports are nearing the end of their useful lives. For the most part, paper documents should have an electronic version stored in your computer system. As long as these electronic documents are preserved and are made readily accessible, you should have no reason to archive a paper-based version. Unfortunately a lot of the software in use today does not do a good job of maintaining or providing access to these snapshot-in-time representations of data. You also sometimes have IS personnel that are unwilling to allocate disk storage to maintaining this data. While you should be encouraged to look for ways to eliminate your physical filing cabinets, you should first verify that the required information is still available and will remain available for a specified period of time. This is especially true with inventory accuracy when you are trying to trace discrepancies. Access to information showing exactly what was on sales orders, pick slips, invoices, work orders, purchase orders, move documents, and receipts at a specific point in time is essential.

Although the end is nearing for the need to archive these paper-based representations of information, it doesn't mean the end is nearing for use of these paper-based documents during the day-to-day execution of operations. In the warehouse and on the shop floor, a well-designed paper document can often be more portable, easier to handle, and easier to read than its electronic counterpart. The key point here being: "a well-designed" paper document. The documents and reports (there's actually very little if any difference between a document and a report) that come with your software are usually very generic and are not optimized for your specific needs. While I don't suggest you modify all of your documents and reports, I do suggest that you look at the ones that are used most frequently. Minor modifications to documents and reports can be very inexpensive and can provide significant improvements in productivity and accuracy.

Document analysis

✔ **Have a clear understanding of the purpose of the document.** Some documents may have multiple uses.

✔ **Determine the printing capabilities of your system.** What choices do you have in fonts, font size, bold, italics, line spacing, grayscale shading, reverse printing (white on black), bar code printing, graphics, etc.? If your current choices are extremely limited, what does it take to obtain more functionality?

✔ **Identify key data elements required to perform the task.** This would be the most important information on the document such as document number, item numbers, and quantities.

✔ **Identify secondary data elements that are necessary but not as important as the key elements**. This is additional information that may be needed but is not looked at every time the document is used.

✔ **Identify data elements that are not needed.** This includes data elements that don't apply to your task or are used so infrequently that removal from the document would not create a substantial problem.

✔ **Identify data elements that are needed but are not currently on the document**.

Making the changes

✔ **Change line spacing.** You'd be amazed at the difference changing the line spacing can have on a cluttered document or report. The costs associated with this type of change should be negligible, although it may mean that you will be using more paper.

✔ **Eliminate unnecessary data elements.** This is also a very simple change. If you don't need the information, have it removed.

✔ **Highlight key data elements.** This is as simple as bolding the key data elements or increasing the font size.

✔ **Subordinate secondary data elements.** If the secondary data elements are already in a small unobtrusive font, you don't need to do anything here. If, however, some secondary data elements are in a larger or bold font you may want to consider using a smaller standard font.

✔ **Subordinate data element identifiers.** This is the text that tells you what the data element is. The importance of these identifiers is diminished based upon the frequency of use of the data element, or the obviousness as to the identification of the data element. For example, if the work order number is the key piece of information that is used every time a worker inquires or reports against the work order, and the work order number is highlighted in a large font in the upper right corner of the document, there is very little value in having "WORK ORDER" printed in a large font designating this fact. While you still may want a tag that identifies the number as the work order number, you would be better off using a very small font that does not detract attention from the key information the user is looking for. For another example, if your part numbering scheme or location numbering scheme is so unique, that the users of the document would always know what it is they are looking at, there is no value in printing the identifiers on the document. The point here is not that we are trying to save ink or toner by not printing this info or using smaller fonts, but rather making these changes will make it easier to focus on the key data elements.

✔ **Group key data elements.** Up to this point, all the changes have been minor and should have taken very little of a programmer's time (depending upon the software, the users may even be able to make these changes themselves). Grouping or rearranging the data elements on the document, while still a simple modification, may begin to add more significant costs. The goal here is to place the key data elements on the document in a manner that is consistent with the task that will be performed. If the document is used for multiple tasks you may want to separate the key data elements into groups based upon the task in which they are used. This way, if a document is used for picking and shipping an order, the picker would be able to focus on one part of the document for his information, while the person responsible for shipping would have all of their information in another area of the document. You also want to try to avoid placing similar key data elements next to each other such as a placing another number field in the same area as the pick quantity on a picking document.

✔ **Adding data elements.** The complexity of this type of modification can vary significantly. If you need to add a data element that already exists on a file that the report or document is based on, or if you need a simple calculation performed based upon data already on the document, this can be very easy. If, however, you need to add a data element that exists on another file, or if you require a calculation based upon data from another file, the complexity of the change can range from a little more difficult to a significant programming effort.

✔ **Changing selection criteria.** This is more common on reports than documents, and is probably not a significant modification. If you are taking a large report and then manually paging through it looking for specific records, you should look into changing the selection criteria to only print the records that have the characteristics that you are manually identifying. Depending upon the software you are using this is also something the end user may be able to do.

✔ **Changing sequencing.** This is also more common on reports but can apply to documents such as pick lists. Sequencing is the sort order of the records on a report. For example: item number sort, vendor number sort, location sort, or required date within vendor number sort. This is also usually an easy change and may be a user option.

It's also important to note that some of these changes may impact the speed at which the program can generate the document or the speed at which the printer can produce the document. If these are on-demand type documents that may result in a worker having to wait for the document to be produced this could be a problem. While some of the changes can get complicated, the majority of them are very minor and inexpensive modifications. Again, I do not suggest that you attempt to modify every document or report that you use. Rather, look at those that get a significant amount of daily usage, such as order picking documents, production paperwork, or planning reports.

More tips on improving documents.

Use alternate line shading to make it easier to focus on individual lines.

Use preprinted color forms to highlight key data elements.

Use color printing to highlight key data elements.

Use alternate text orientations (vertical text) to differentiate groups of data elements.

Use reversed text (white on black) to highlight a specific data element.

Use boxes and lines to focus attention on certain areas of the document.

Add data formats (adding spaces, hyphens, or other characters) to make data elements such as item numbers, locations, and lot numbers easier to read.

Use conditional formatting (format changes based upon data) to highlight special occurrences within a data element.

Order Number / Customer ID / PO #	Line Number / OrdDate / ReqDate	Ordered / Allocated / Backorde	Shipped / Location / OKship	UM	SKU / Description / ExtendedDesc	Xrefvend	Xrefcust	Lot / SerialNo	Weight / Cube / SpecHandling
56174 / 123456 / 987654	1 / 2/1/2003 / 2/1/2003	5 / 5 / 0	5 / BA0901 / YES	EA	SDF123 / 7.253 VALVE FITTING WELKDIN / 7.253 1.25763 O-F-S-W-W-F	HF9378563	IO-SDF123		5.32 / 0.93
56174 / 123456 / 987654	2 / 2/1/2003 / 2/1/2003	1 / 0 / 1	0 / FK0411 / NO	EA	SDP932 / PLATE MOUNTING LEFT YIPDO / 8.250 3.7500 O-F-R-W-G-F	35489657123-1	IO-SDP932		0.56 / 0.28
56174 / 123456 / 987654	4 / 2/1/2003 / 2/1/2003	25 / 25 / 0	25 / JD0813 / YES	EA	SLE765 / HALPIX FELTPOT LEFT UDLO / 3.750 1.5000 O-F-X-W-C-F	89WE-45357	IO-SLE765		0.03 / 0.13
56174 / 123456 / 987654	3 / 2/1/2003 / 2/1/2003	2 / 2 / 0	2 / JK1903 / YES	EA	LZX80321 / 1.750 DUALFLOW SPHINCTERVALVE WELKDIN / 1.750 3.2750 P-F-S-W-W-F	HS4537891	IO-LZX80-321		1.76 / 0.53
56174 / 123456 / 987654	5 / 2/1/2003 / 2/1/2003	1 / 1 / 0	1 / LC2401 / YES	BX	UND2038 / .25 MOUNTING BRKTS / 0.250 0.200 S-F-R-W-S-G	098809214	IO-UND2038		4.75 / 0.89

Figure 2A. Above is an example of the detail area of a generic picking document from an ERP-type software package. Because these programs are designed to be used by a variety of different businesses, the documents tend to have much more data on them than any single business will use. This creates a cluttered document that makes it more difficult for the workers to focus on the data they need to perform their tasks. There are a total of four quantity elements (ordered, allocated, backordered, and shipped), three item numbers (internal SKU #, vender cross-reference, and customer cross-reference, and two lines of description (the second seems to be used for engineering specs or category codes) on this document. You can also see that line number 2 does not have a shippable quantity on it.

Order Number / Customer ID / PO #	Line Number / OrdDate / ReqDate	Ordered / Allocated / Backorde	Shipped / Location / OKship	UM	SKU / Description / ExtendedDesc	Xrefvend	Xrefcust	Lot / SerialNo	Weight / Cube / SpecHandling
56174 123456 987654	1 2/1/2003 2/1/2003	5 5 0	**5** **BA0901** YES	EA	**SDF123** 7.253 VALVE FITTING WELKDIN 7.253 1.25763 O-F-S-W-W-F	HF9378563	IO-SDF123		5.32 0.93
56174 123456 987654	4 2/1/2003 2/1/2003	25 25 0	**25** **JD0813** YES	EA	**SLE765** HALPIX FELTPOT LEFT UDLO 3.750 1.5000 O-F-X-W-C-F	89WE-45357	IO-SLE765		0.03 0.13
56174 123456 987654	3 2/1/2003 2/1/2003	2 2 0	**2** **JK1903** YES	EA	**LZX80321** 1.750 DUALFLOW SPHINCTERVALVE WELKDIN 1.750 3.2750 P-F-S-W-W-F	HS4537891	IO-LZX80-321		1.76 0.53
56174 123456 987654	5 2/1/2003 2/1/2003	1 1 0	**1** **LC2401** YES	BX	**UND2038** 25 MOUNTING BRKTS 0.250 0.200 S-F-R-W-S-G	098809214	IO-UND2038		4.75 0.89

Figure 2B. In this example, I took the document from figure 2A and made some minor changes.

Changed selection to exclude lines without shippable quantities.

Added extra spacing between line items.

Bolded the font on the key data elements (order number, shipped quantity, unit of measure, location, and SKU)

These are very minor changes yet you can start to see that it is becoming easier to focus on the needed data.

Order Number	Line Number ReqDate	Shipped Location	UM	SKU Description	Weight Cube SpecHandling
56174	1 2/1/2003	5 BA0901	EA	SDF123 7.253 VALVE FITTING WELKDIN	5.32 0.93
56174	4 2/1/2003	25 JD0813	EA	SLE765 HALPIX FELTPOT LEFT UDLO	0.03 0.13
56174	3 2/1/2003	2 JK1903	EA	LZX80321 1.750 DUALFLOW SPHINCTERVALVE WELKDIN	1.76 0.53
56174	5 2/1/2003	1 LC2401	BX	UND2038 .25 MOUNTING BRKTS	4.75 0.89

Figure 2C. Here you can see that I've removed all unnecessary data. If you don't actually want to remove the data elements from the program, (in case you may need them in the future) you may be able to change the font color to "white" which will just stop them from printing. This is still the same document as in the previous examples; no data elements have been moved. This is still a very minor modification and the cost should be negligible.

Order Number Line Number ReqDate	Location	Shipped		SKU Description	Weight Cube SpecHandling
56174 1 2/1/2003	**BA0901**	**5**		**SDF123** 7.253 VALVE FITTING WELKDIN	5.32 0.93
56174 4 2/1/2003	**JD0813**	**25**		**SLE765** HALPIX FELTPOT LEFT UDLO	0.03 0.13
56174 3 2/1/2003	**JK1903**	**2**		**LZX80321** 1.750 DUALFLOW SPHINCTERVALVE WELKDIN	1.76 0.53
56174 5 2/1/2003	**LC2401**	**1**	**BX**	**UND2038** .25 MOUNTING BRKTS	4.75 0.89

Figure 2D. Here I've taken it a step further by moving some data elements and increasing the font size of key data elements. Now you have a document that makes it very easy to focus on the key data elements. I purposely moved the line number to the first column to prevent the worker from confusing it with the pick quantity. Normally you would want to place the data elements in the order they would be used. In the case of this picking document, that would be location, SKU number, and then quantity. I chose to keep the quantity between the location and SKU number because the size of the SKU field would have otherwise forced me to place the quantity too far to the right. I also used conditional formatting to make the unit of measure only print if it is not "EA". This helps to focus on nonstandard units of measure.

New Order
56174

B	A 09 01		
	SDF 123		**5**
	7.253 VALVE FITTING WELKDIN		

Order# 56174	Line # 001	Weight 5.32	Cube 0.93
Customer Item # IO-SDF123		P.O. # 987654	
Ordered 5	Shipped 5	Backord 0	OrdDate 2/1/2003	ReqDate 2/1/2003

J	D 08 13		
	SLE 765		**25**
	HALPIX FELTPOT LEFT UDLO		

Order# 56174	Line # 004	Weight 0.03	Cube 0.13
Customer Item # IO-SLE765		P.O. # 987654	
Ordered 25	Shipped 25	Backord 0	OrdDate 2/1/2003	ReqDate 2/1/2003

J	K 9 03		
	LZX 80321		**2**
	1.750 DUALFLOW SPHINCTERVALVE WELKDIN		

Order# 56174	Line # 003	Weight 1.76	Cube 0.53
Customer Item # IO-LZX80-321		P.O. # 987654	
Ordered 2	Shipped 2	Backord 0	OrdDate 2/1/2003	ReqDate 2/1/2003

L	C 24 01	BX	
	UND 2038		**1**
	.25 MOUNTING BRKTS		

Order# 56174	Line # 005	Weight 4.75	Cube 0.89
Customer Item # IO-UND2038		P.O. # 987654	
Ordered 1	Shipped 1	Backord 0	OrdDate 2/1/2003	ReqDate 2/1/2003

Figure 2E. To go even further, I've taken the same data and reformatted it to print on individual pick tags. In this example, the pick tags are labels (actual labels would be larger than those shown).

Since these labels will be attached to the product, I've included information the customer can use to check in the receipt. All customer information is grouped in the shaded area on the bottom half of the pick tags to keep it separate from the data elements used internally.

I've also introduced some different formatting for the key data elements. I've taken the first character in the location (zone) and formatted it as a separate data element. Since this is for a zone picking operation, once the worker has the tags for his zone he no longer needs to look at the zone part of the location. Separating it makes it easier to focus on the remainder of the location. I've also formatted spaces between the different parts of the location. I've done the same with the SKU number.

Since the key data elements are obvious to the workers, I've eliminated their data identifiers ("Location", "SKU", "Shipped"). For the secondary data and the customer data I have retained the data identifiers.

The pick quantity is singled out in a manner that makes it near impossible to confuse it with any other numbers on the tag.

I've also added a bar code containing the order# and line# that could be used during the picking or checking process.

Labels

The same thought process should apply to labels used in your operations. These would include item labels, case and unit load labels, location labels, and license plates used to track product as it moves throughout the facility. Consistency should be maintained between documents and labels used within the same process. For example, use the same font and, if possible, the same font size for the item number on all labels, pick documents, move documents, and putaway documents. Also, if you are adding formats (spaces, hyphens, etc.) to data elements you need to make sure you include these formats in all programs that print or display these data elements. While this may, at first, seem like taking things a little too far, you need to realize that when comparing a picking document to the label of the item being picked, it will be easier (remember, make accuracy easy) if they both look the same. In addition, it probably won't cost any more (assuming you are modifying these documents anyway) to maintain this consistency. Label placement should also be part of the design process and related labeling procedures. Attention to label placement will ensure that labels are clearly visible when inventory is stocked, moved, or picked.

Forms

I would define a paper form as anything that requires a person to write on it. In some cases, a document is also a form, as in a pick slip where the employee marks off items as they pick them and signs off on the order. Forms need to have procedures detailing the correct way to fill them out, how and when they should be used, and where they are to be kept. These instructions should even go so far as to require specific color pens, specific sequence of filling out the form, specific clipboards to be used to fill them out, and specific times of the day to complete the processing of the form. For those of you that are starting to think that this doesn't sound like "making accuracy easy," I would argue that clear and detailed procedures do make it easy because the employee now knows exactly how to perform the task. In addition, if the form is later used by someone else, the consistency achieved through these strict procedures will make their job easier.

With the exception of shipping forms such as bills of lading, there are very few standardized forms used in the warehouse and on the shop floor. Since internal processes vary significantly from one operation to another, standardized forms would be less than effective. Creating custom forms in word processing or spreadsheet programs can be accomplished in a matter of minutes. Using a custom form will help to ensure accuracy and consistency in your documentation. The areas on a form that the employee will be filling out should be large enough to allow legible writing of the information; filling out a form in a warehouse or a shop floor environment is different than in an office environment, so plan accordingly. If the form is later used for data entry, design the form so the data appears in the same sequence as the data entry program. Now I have to admit I do get a little anal when it comes to people using 50th generation copies of forms (a copy of a copy of a copy…) where the form eventually transforms into some type of morphed black and white artwork. Requiring employees to fill out forms that they can't even read will not do much for accuracy and certainly doesn't send the right message as to overall quality. There is absolutely no extra cost in producing clear forms.

This choice shouldn't be a difficult one.

Computer programs

The most obvious human-machine interface would be a program used on a stationary terminal or computer to perform inquiries or enter data. While many of the same considerations applied to documents also apply to the computer programs used, there are some significant differences. Modifying a computer program that adds or modifies data is inherently more complicated than modifying a document or report, therefore a more conservative approach to modifications applies here. This isn't to say that modifications are not justified; if a critical program does not function as needed or does not display the information required to perform the task, a modification should be considered. Also, if screens cluttered with unnecessary data elements make it difficult to focus on key data elements, or make data entry cumbersome by requiring extensive tabbing past this unneeded information, you should consider removing the unnecessary information or eliminating the tab stops.

There may also be some setup options built into the software (therefore not a modification) that allow changes to the way the program works. I strongly recommend that users become more involved with system setup. This is especially true of users of some of the larger ERP systems. These systems often have extensive user definable parameters that can have a significant impact on the functionality and usability of the program. Most business software will come with some online help as well as paper-based or electronic manuals. You may need to talk with your IS department to get access to this information (often there are separate manuals that have the system setup information). Read, read, read! Knowledge is power, but it doesn't come without a price; you need to make a concerted effort to learn. While a technical manual on setting up an ERP system may seem over-whelming, you should realize that you don't need to understand how to set up the entire system. What you need to do, is read the materials that focus on the functionality related to inventory transaction programs and determine if there are better ways to use the software. Initially, system setup is usually done by IS personnel, outside consultants, or the software vendor. While this may have been adequate to get the system up and running, you should not assume that the initial setup is the most effective utilization of the system. IS personnel, software consultants and vendors rarely have adequate operational experience or necessary operational focus to effectively optimize the human-machine interface. As an operations professional, your success is highly dependent upon the effectiveness of information systems; don't leave it all to someone else.

There are also ways to enhance the human-machine interface of computer programs that do not require changes to the host system. The use of macros or bar code scanners with programmable capabilities can greatly improve productivity and accuracy in data entry applications. A macro is a simple computer program that scripts a series of actions. Macros are very useful in highly repetitive tasks by automating the repetitive actions and only requiring the user to enter non-repetitive data and actions. For example, say the normal operation of a receipt program in a specific operation is to type in the purchase order number, tab once, type in the facility you are receiving to, tab twice, type in your user ID, press [enter], press [F5], tab 3 times, enter a 1, then enter the received quantities on the specific lines displayed. By creating a macro, you could enter the purchase order number and then initiate the macro, which will automatically do everything except entering the quantities on the specific lines. The speed of the macro should significantly increase productivity, but also increase accuracy by allowing the user to focus more on the key data elements of the purchase order and the receipt quantities. Most systems will have some type of macro capabilities. Mainframe systems sometimes have play/record keys on the keyboard that allow the actions to be recorded and played back. In other systems this functionality may be built into the software, available in a terminal emulation program, or a separate macro program. There are several very inexpensive macro programs available that will work in most Windows programs.

To take this a step further, you can use a programmable bar code scanner that can perform similarly to a macro with the added functionality to fill in fields with data from the bar code. As with the macro, this can all be done without any changes to the existing software (with the exception of the added requirement to produce a bar code). The specific methods for creating these little scripts vary but the basic logic is the same. You first must map out all of the actions required, keystroke-by-keystroke. Then it's a matter of either recording the actual actions as you perform them on the keyboard, selecting the actions from a series of menus or icons, typing a script of the commands based upon a simple scripting language, or scanning a series of bar codes that represents the actions you want to be performed. Both the use of macros and the use of programmable bar code scanners are very inexpensive ways to make accuracy easy. There is, however, a downside. A macro is not a "smart" computer program; it's basically a script of actions that will occur whenever the macro is initiated regardless of any other factors. If you initiate the macro and you are in the wrong program or the cursor is in the wrong position, the actions will continue anyway. Usually because of data validation inside the host program you will just end up getting an error notification, however under the right (or should I say wrong) conditions you could seriously screw up some data. You should do some "what if" scenarios to determine the likelihood of this happening. If you find a potential problem you may be able to change the script to force an error rather than accept the transaction under these circumstances. It's also important that people using macros understand what they are and the potential dangers.

Comparing manual entry of a miscellaneous inventory adjustment to entry using a macro or programmable bar code scanner.

Manual	With Macro	With Scanner
facility code	initiate macro	scan item bar code
tab	item number	quantity
tab	quantity	enter
tab	enter	
transaction type		
tab		
tab		
item number		
quantity		
enter		

Automated data capture technologies and other automation equipment

In addition to the basic wired bar code scanner discussed previously, there are many other technologies that can be incorporated to improve — and in some cases eliminate the need for — the human-machine interface. These include counting equipment, weighing equipment, portable wireless terminals, flow meters, RFID readers, voice recognition and voice directed systems, automated material handling systems, and light directed systems. The capabilities of these technologies to automatically pass data through a machine-machine interface, or assist the human-machine interface, can have a significant positive impact on making accuracy easy.

Have you ever heard the phrase "don't have a human do anything that a computer (or machine) can do"? If so, it likely came from a technology supplier or systems integrator that has a substantial financial interest in promoting this philosophy. And I agree that it's a good philosophy provided you are taking into account additional factors such as cost, flexibility, and maybe a little reality. Current technology is capable of automating almost every activity that goes on in manufacturing and distribution facilities. Computer technology is capable of generating forecasts, planning materials, creating and sending purchase orders, scheduling manufacturing, receiving materials and paying vendors, shipping products and billing customers, while equipment is capable of loading and unloading trailers, counting materials, putting away materials, picking materials, and processing through various manufacturing operations, all without the need for human intervention. This isn't science fiction; it's science fact. It's totally achievable; it's just not practical in most operations. In reality, human labor is often still more cost effective than the equipment and technology it would take to replace it. Manual systems are also more flexible, allowing businesses to more quickly adapt to changing business needs. While it's easy to agree that this "ultimate" level of automation is currently not very realistic when considering cost and flexibility, it's much more difficult to determine what level of automation is optimal for a specific operation. In addition, applying the wrong technology or automating a bad process can prove to be detrimental to business objectives. A more detailed discussion of these technologies and their applications is discussed in later chapters.

Transaction by exception

Another human-machine-interface-related method of making accuracy easy, is to find ways to reduce or eliminate the number or the detail level of the transactions that humans are doing. This is achieved by using confirmation-type transactions that allow the computer to perform the detailed transactions based upon minimal user input. This automates most of the detailed transaction input, only requiring detailed input on an exception basis. The idea here is that by reducing human input in transactions, you will reduce transaction-related errors. The other advantage is that you will also increase productivity by reducing clerical work.

One technique of transaction-by-exception that is used in manufacturing operations is backflushing. Backflushing is a method for issuing (reducing on-hand quantities) materials to a production order; the materials are issued automatically when production is posted against an operation. The backflushing program will use the quantity completed to calculate through the bill of material the quantities of the components, raw materials, and subassemblies used, and reduce on-hand balances by these quantities. More simply put, rather than having to tell the computer how many of each component you used, you tell the computer how many of the finished product you produced and the computer automatically deducts the quantity of each component based upon how much you "should have used." While I have run into people that seemed to be terrified by the thought of backflushing inventory, I assure you that, under the right conditions, backflushing can be a very effective means of processing these types of transactions. More information on backflushing can be found in chapter nine.

Another transaction-by-exception technique — actually a group of techniques — is the use of confirmation programs to perform transactions. This is possible if your software is capable of creating live documents that direct the details of a transaction. With this functionality, the computer "knows" the details of each specific task; you simply "confirm" that the task was completed, and the computer will complete the associated transactions. Depending upon the specific type of transaction, your computer software may need functionality related to determining on-hand quantities, allocations and availability by specific locations, location capacities, container capacities, material weights and volumes, and special handling characteristics. While this functionality generally falls into the territory of warehouse management systems (WMS), you'll also find that many standard inventory management, manufacturing, and distribution software packages may also have some of this functionality.

Directed picking, putaway, and replenishment. This is the heart of a WMS. Move documents are created instructing the specific quantity and location to pick from, quantity and location to putaway to, and — in the case of replenishment — quantity and location to pick from and location to putaway to. Rather than a physical piece of paper, a move tag is often an instruction on the screen of a portable terminal, an audible instruction coming through a headset, a bar coded label, or a bar coded license plate.

Document-level order picking transactions. This applies to production order pick lists as well as shipping pick lists where multiple items are required. As long as the pick list can designate the specific item, quantity, and location to pick, you should be able to confirm the multiple picks at the document level, as though it was a single transaction. Again, all you are doing is confirming that you did everything that was expected to be done. The only time you would have to deal with the detail of the transactions would be if you did not complete the pick instructions as was intended.

Batch-level transactions. This takes the document level transaction a step further by using a batch program to complete a larger set of transactions. An example of batch-level transactions would be if, at the end of a shift, you confirmed to the computer that all of the pick lists produced were completed as intended. The computer would then complete all of the transactions. This is a little dangerous to say the least, and requires high levels of discipline to ensure all suggested tasks were actually completed.

Advanced Shipment Notifications (ASN). ASNs are used to automate receipt processing. ASNs will include PO numbers, SKU numbers, lot numbers, quantity, pallet or container number, and carton number. ASNs may be paper based, however electronic notification (usually through EDI, however use of XML is growing) is preferred. Since an electronic ASN will transfer detailed shipment data to your inventory system, all the receiving personnel have to do, is confirm the receipt at the ASN level and all transactions are automatically completed. This is usually done by scanning a bar-coded compliance label associated with the entire shipment, or separate labels for each pallet, each crate, or each carton. Since transaction-related errors tend to account for the majority of receiving errors, the use of ASNs can significantly increase accuracy in receiving operations as well as increase productivity. Unfortunately, ASNs require that your vendors are willing and capable of applying compliance labels and sending ASNs. Smaller businesses or businesses that have an extensive supplier base often find it difficult to achieve this level of cooperation from their suppliers. Some supply chains, such as the automotive industry, have achieved some levels of standardization, however there is currently no widely accepted standard for ASNs and compliance labels. As the trend towards collaboration and information sharing grows, especially through the use of the Internet, more businesses will gain access to these technologies.

The keys to transaction-by-exception are information systems that have the logic to direct activities at the detail level, and operations that have the discipline to perform tasks based upon the computer's instructions. You need to maintain highly accurate data, and significantly restrict the ability of the employee to perform the task in a way that conflicts with the computer's instructions. That means not allowing the employee to change the location or quantity recommendations under any circumstances. Since it's difficult to program all potential parameters into a computer, you will occasionally get computer task recommendations that may not be the easiest or most effective means of accomplishing the task. You are better off requiring the tasks to be performed based upon the computer's instructions (even if it's not the best way) and possibly looking into changing the logic for future tasks, than allowing employees to change the tasks and, in doing so, increase the opportunity to make errors. The only time a change is acceptable is if you absolutely cannot perform the task as specified. The most likely cause of this would be incorrect data, such as an inventory shortage. These transactions would have to be handled as exceptions, and there should be a procedure for dealing with these.

Procedures and employee training.

A critical step in making accuracy easy, is ensuring that workers know how to do their jobs. While this may seem obvious, most companies still lack adequate documentation of procedures and employee training. During many years managing warehouses and plant operations, it became very evident that when I invested time into documenting procedures and training employees, there was a significant improvement in overall operations. When I would get involved in other projects and allow training to slip, I would soon see the negative impact.

I also have vivid memories of training from a different perspective than that of a manager. Before I was a manager, I was a young, smart, hardworking guy (I really was) trying to figure out what I was going to be doing for the rest of my life. During this period, I tried quite a variety of entry-level positions, and got a real good feel for what employee training should NOT be. There is nothing more frustrating than to be working hard in a new position, only to find out later that you have been doing the job incorrectly. In one case it was several months before a coworker told me "oh, you're not supposed to do that like that." Now it's not like I was doing the entire job incorrectly, only a small portion. But to me, having always taken a lot of pride in my work, it was a big deal and I was pretty pissed off. While there are certain aspects of a task that can be considered obvious or common sense, you need to think real hard before lumping things into this category. You'd be amazed as to what employees don't know about the products, services, and overall objectives of your organization. It's pretty hard to apply common sense to performing a task when the objective is not clearly understood.

Let me turn on the "way back machine" and tell you a little story about a 16 year old (me) that just got a job as a dishwasher. During a shift overlap, I was doubled up with another dishwasher. I happened to look over my shoulder to see that the other dishwasher had noticed a little residue still on one of the plates that came out of the dish washing machine. Being the conscientious sort, he was not going to send out a dish with a spot on it. So he proceeded to spit on his fingers and then use them to wipe the spot off. When I questioned him on his technique he said "oh yeah, I always do that," not having a clue as to why he should not be spitting on eating utensils. Think about this the next time you assume something is "common sense." Oh, by the way, all those stories you've heard about what can happen to your food in the kitchen of a restaurant — they're all true.

Documenting procedures

Procedures are a combination of rules and instructions for performing a task in accordance with the process defined in the previous process evaluation step. While procedures don't need to have every detail listed, they do need to be comprehensive enough to achieve the required output. Types of information in procedures would include details on how to physically perform the task, equipment used, the correct method for filling out and processing paperwork, the sequence and timing of entering data, any checks that are required to be performed, approval or authorization requirements. Below are some points that should be considered when documenting procedures.

Procedures should be easily understood

Don't turn production reporting into rocket science. Document the procedures in a manner that is consistent with the education levels of the employees. This is important because assuming employees understand terminology that you consider standard may result in some employees not understanding the procedure. I once wrote a procedure using the term "perpendicular" to describe the direction of forklift traffic that required the operator to sound the horn in relationship to specific storage aisles. Later, one of the forklift operators asked me what it meant, qualifying the question with the fact that none of the other operators understood it either. While I was a little surprised at the comment, the fact is, I was wrong in assuming they would understand the term and should have included a better explanation. As this was part of the procedure related to safety issues, it was a serious problem if the employees didn't understand it. Since you probably won't know the exact extent of the employees' vocabulary, you'll need to be mindful during the training to ensure the employees understand the procedures. It's also a good idea to start building a glossary as you develop documentation, especially for nonstandard terminology.

Procedures should be task-specific

Making procedures task-specific not only helps in the training process, it also makes it easier to be comprehensive in documenting the procedures. For example, you don't want to try to document warehouse processing as a single procedure. More likely you will have separate procedures for: receiving materials, stocking materials, picking orders, shipping product. You may even break it down further such as: unloading trailers, receiving raw materials, receiving finished goods, picking replenishment orders, picking customer orders, picking production orders, etc.

Procedures should be position-specific

I know some people won't agree with this, however, I think it makes initial training much more effective. A position-specific procedure only details the procedure based upon the responsibilities of a specific position. For example, if you have a procedure for a machine operator on reporting production, you may have a step that states "if you did not produce the full required quantity, you must report to the group leader before closing the production order." You will need a separate procedure for the group leader stating what is to be done under these circumstances. Why not put it all in one procedure? The main reason is that by including information that the employee doesn't need to know, you are taking focus away from the information the employee does need to know. Putting it all in one procedure can also be confusing as to the responsibilities of the machine operator. This isn't to say that the machine operator shouldn't have access to the additional procedure. Indeed, you should encourage employees to learn about related processes. You just don't want it to conflict with the employee's initial training. I don't consider this as firm a rule as the other points listed here; in fact, I sometimes write procedures that cover more than one similar position and note specific responsibilities within the procedure. It's a bit of a judgment call that needs to take into consideration the extent and complexity of the additional information.

Procedures should not be accuracy-specific
Each procedure should contain all important information related to the task. This means the procedure should include all quality-related, safety-related, accuracy-related, productivity-related, clerical, and physical aspects of the task. A problem often associated with quality initiatives or safety initiatives is that they often end up with separate documents, often kept in separate books than the task procedure. This not only introduces the possibility of them being ignored, but also may result in documents with conflicting instructions. While there are some circumstances where you may have separate procedures, such as having a separate formal forklift-training program, you should still incorporate key parts of the forklift-training program in the task procedures, such as listing hazards that are specific to the task and noting that only certified operators are allowed to operate the lift truck.

Procedures should focus on problem areas
As I previously mentioned, it's unreasonable to expect to put every little detail in the procedure. Too much superfluous information or obvious-type information will clutter the document and take focus away from the more important info. Also, if the procedure gets too big, you're going to struggle to get employees to read it. It's very important, however, to make sure that procedures address, in detail, any areas that have had problems or misunderstandings in the past. Supervisors should consider any issues in which they had previously had to correct employees, and make absolutely sure that the procedure details these issues.

Procedure is not a "wish list"
This is very important. A procedure details the way a task must be performed, not the way you would like it to be performed. If you are not prepared to discipline an employee whenever their actions conflict with the documented procedure, then you need to rethink the procedure. This means documenting a procedure around realistic expectations, not ideal expectations.

Procedures should document any exceptions
While it's preferential to avoid exceptions, in reality there may be a need to have some legitimate exceptions. Document these legitimate exceptions, the alternate procedure, and the specific circumstances under which they apply.

Procedures should be periodically reviewed and updated

Outdated procedure documents can create real problems, as they no longer represent the actual procedure. This pretty much makes all of the documentation questionable and possibly meaningless to the employees. Set a formal timetable for reviewing procedures and publishing and putting into effect revisions (every quarter or six months). Frequent revisions of procedures tend to cause confusion and make it difficult to enforce adherence. Always date procedures and get rid of outdated ones.

Procedure format/training materials

Procedures are generally a combination of lists of rules and step-by-step documentation of instructions. Procedures should follow a logical and consistent format; however, I wouldn't get too hung up on creating a strict format, as some procedures may not fit that well into it. Advances in PC software technology, along with the accessibility to this technology, have significantly changed the format of procedures and training materials from photocopies of typed instructions, to printed documents with photos and diagrams, and computer-based training materials. Not only are these technologies easy to use, they are also affordable to even the smallest businesses (you probably already have the technologies on your desktop computer). By utilizing these technologies to produce more professional training materials you not only make the educational process easier and more effective, you also send a message about the importance placed on procedures and training.

Utilizing technology in training materials:

Scanners, cameras, and graphics programs

The ease of incorporating graphics into training materials is likely the most significant benefit of these technology advancements, and I'm not just talking about clipart. There is some truth in the phrase "a picture is worth a thousand words" and today's technologies make incorporating graphics a snap (actually more like several mouse clicks and some dragging and dropping).

What to include:

✔ **Photos.** Taken with digital cameras, or scanned images of standard photos. Use a graphics program to add text, arrows, or other additional detail.

> Photos of equipment
>
> Photos of specific tasks/actions.
>
> Photos of flows.
>
> Photos of work areas.

✔ **CAD drawings.** It's likely that someone in your organization has access to CAD drawings of your facility. Add arrows, text, and other details to define flows, storage and staging areas, safety issues.

✔ **Scanned images of equipment.** If your equipment came with a manual, it's likely that there are graphic representations of the equipment in the manual. These can be scanned into images and placed in your training materials (get approval from copyright holder before copying).

✔ **Images of computer screens.** If you can access your inventory system from a networked Windows PC (even if it's on a mainframe system), you can take snapshots of the screens to be used in your training materials. Just bring up the screen with the data as you want it to look in your training materials, press the [alt] key and the [Print Screen] key at the same time. This copies the image to the clipboard; you can now go to a graphics program and use the paste command to paste the image. While in the graphics program you can crop the image, resize the image, and add details such as text and arrows, then copy and paste it into your document. There is no doubt that incorporating screen shots into your training materials will greatly enhance your computer training.

✔ **Scanned images of documents and forms.** The best way to show proper use of documents and forms is to scan an image of the correctly filled out document or form. You can then use a graphics program to add text and highlights (arrows, numbers, circles, etc.) to key data elements.

✔ **Flow charts.** Having experienced that people rarely read them, I don't use flow charts as much as I used to. There are, however, some situations where a flow chart is the best way to describe a process, and in these situations you should incorporate them into your materials. Simple flow charts can be produced in most graphics programs, there are also programs designed specifically for flowcharting.

✔ **Tables.** Tables are a good way to represent procedures where the procedure is different based upon other variables such as procedures for use of a counting scale where the sample size and verification is different based upon types of materials and quantities or unloading procedures where there are differences between unloading full truck loads, less than truck loads, rail cars, parcel carriers, etc.

✔ **Drawings.** While most of us don't have the artistic abilities to create complex drawings, there are some simple drawings that can be created using clip art and standard shapes. If you happen to have someone with some artistic talents in your employ, they may be able to provide paper drawings that can be scanned or electronic files of drawings created in a graphics program. There are also many affordable free-lance artists that can be found on the Internet.

Word-processing and page layout programs

Probably the most common types of programs used to document procedures, these would include programs like Microsoft Word, Microsoft Publisher, Corel WordPerfect, Adobe PageMaker, or QuarkXPress. The output from these programs would usually be paper-based training materials that would be printed on your own laser or inkjet printer, or sent to a commercial printer or copy shop for printing. Some of these programs can also convert the document(s) into portable document format (PDF) for electronic distribution, or you can purchase Adobe Acrobat software to convert any document to PDF. Converting a document to PDF will ensure fonts, formats, and page layouts will be consistent regardless of the machine on which the document is being viewed or printed. PDF files can be viewed and printed using Adobe Acrobat Reader software that is available as a free download. Most computers that access the Internet will already have this software loaded. The PDF conversion also compresses the files data, making the PDF file smaller than the original document file. This is especially useful when the original document contains graphics.

Presentation programs

OK, we're most likely talking Microsoft PowerPoint here. Presentation programs are the easiest method for creating computer-based training materials. Mostly known for creating presentations that are intended to be viewed on a big screen with a projector, PowerPoint presentations can also be saved onto a network, giving access to all users, uploaded to the Internet, or saved onto CDs that can be distributed and used on any Windows PC. Limitations of using a presentation program include:

- Slides are limited in size and shape, requiring multiple slides for continued information rather than the ability to scroll down on a page.

- Printing a slide show to be used for paper-based training is not very attractive and takes a lot of paper.

- Slide shows are limited to viewing in a fixed path (forward or backward) that is not very interactive.

Nonetheless, presentation programs can be very useful in creating training materials and are probably best utilized as a supplement to paper based training materials.

Website design programs

This is currently my favorite method for creating computer-based training materials. Although more difficult to use than a presentation program, website design programs provide more functionality and a more interactive interface for training materials. First, I'd like to note that I am not suggesting you should create a conventional web site, to be uploaded onto the Internet to be used as training materials. While this is an excellent idea, the fact that most people are still accessing the Internet through standard modems with slow data transfer rates will force you to be very stingy with graphics or risk extremely long page download times (which will likely result in ineffective or unusable training materials). What I am suggesting, is using the architecture and functionality of a website and running it from a network hard drive or a CD-Rom rather than the Internet. This allows you to access and navigate the training materials from your web browser as you would a web site, however, data transfer rates would only be limited by the speed or your hard drive, network connection, or CD-Rom drive, all of which are much faster than an Internet connection.

The benefits of this are numerous. First, most people by now are familiar with web browsers, web sites, and hyperlinks. This means they will already know how to navigate the training materials. In addition, the initial purpose of web pages and the Internet was to provide an architecture and format conducive to education and the exchange of information, this is exactly what you are trying to do with your training materials. Although you can design a fixed path for employees to go through the training materials, you can also include numerous alternate paths through the use of hyperlinks that provide much more information and make the materials truly interactive. You can also provide hyperlinks to web sites that may have additional related information, or to any files located on your network or the CD-Rom. An example of how you could use this would be to include a link in the training materials related to printing bar code labels to a PDF version of the printer user manual, or the manufacturers website. As many more manufacturers are providing user manuals in a PDF format (it's a very inexpensive way of providing user manuals) you can not only have your internal procedures at your fingertips, but also access to enormous amounts of additional information logically linked directly from your training materials. This starts to turn your procedures and training materials into an extensive company-wide knowledge management system. Although you can print the information from your web-based training materials, web pages do not always translate well into printed documents. If you intend to print the web pages for use as training materials, you need to experiment with the layout during the web design process to ensure the printed versions are acceptable.

Examples of web design software include Microsoft FrontPage, Macromedia Dreamweaver, and Adobe GoLIve. There are also numerous other web design programs available, although not all of them provide a WYSIWYG (what you see is what you get) interface. While some word-processing and page layout programs will allow you to convert a document to HTML, the results are inferior to a good web design program.

Training

Obviously, all of the work on procedure documentation ultimately leads us to employee training. Or does it? There are businesses that have gone through the trouble of documenting procedures, only to put them in a nice binder on a shelf,

never to be seen again. It's true, I've seen it. So how could this happen? Well, not knowing for certain, I have come up with a couple of theories. I'm assuming that at some point, the boss assigned the department managers or supervisors with the task of documenting processes and procedures. Those responsible completed the task and probably had their boss sign off on it. Then one of two things probably happened: either the documentation went directly to the shelf for future reference, or the documentation was handed out once to the current employees and then retired to the shelf. As ridiculous as this sounds, it's more common than you may think. While the boss may have assumed that training would result from the documentation process, he probably didn't specify it and also probably never followed up on it. In other words, he didn't "train" the supervisors and department managers on the task.

Now if you did better by documenting the procedures and actually getting them in the hands of the employees, good for you. Unfortunately, handing out written procedures does not constitute employee training.

When I hear the phrases "conventional wisdom, or "standard practice" I start to get a little nervous because I know I'll probably disagree with whatever comes next. However, when it comes to training and education, conventional wisdom and standard practices apply. People learn differently, therefore training programs that use a combination of methods including classroom training, hands-on or on-the-job training, and individual self-paced or assisted training, tend to be the most successful.

Classroom training

Classroom training is often the core of your training program. This is where you introduce the procedures, elaborate on the purpose and reasoning, and provide a forum for discussion. It's important to try to create a relaxed environment that allows employees to focus on the training. One of the biggest distractions to effective classroom training is anxiety caused by the "hurry up I need to get out of here" syndrome. This occurs when employees are worrying about their work piling up while they are in a training session, or when training is scheduled during off-hours that are inconvenient to employees. While this isn't easily resolved, there should be some strong consideration to these issues. Options include:

❏ Separating employees into small groups for training and train during regular shift while others in the department cover.

❏ Training an entire department during the regular shift while workers from other departments cover.

❏ Providing various off-hours training sessions and allowing employees to choose which sessions they attend.

❏ Trying to agree on a time for off-hours training that is acceptable to all and train the entire department as large group.

Smaller groups and multiple sessions tend to be more operations-friendly and user-friendly, however you risk some groups missing out on important discussions that may have been brought up by an employee in another session. I never said that I had all the answers; you need look at your operation and workgroup and decide what works best for you.

During the training it's important to emphasize that the procedure is the **ONLY WAY** to perform the task. Allowing undocumented exceptions or allowing employees to do it "their own way" will diminish and possibly negate the effectiveness of the procedures. Unless you run into a significant critical flaw in the procedure, I strongly suggest that you do not make changes to the procedure during the training process. If an employee has a "better way" of performing the task, it should be considered for the next procedure revision. At which time, you train all employees on the new procedure and it becomes the **ONLY WAY** of performing the task. Make sure you allow ample time for questions and discussion. Employees should be encouraged to bring up any issues or areas of concern, but the training session should not turn into a debate session. If you involved employees in the process evaluation phase and kept communications open during the procedure documentation phase you should not run into any major surprises during the training.

Repetition is a critical part of training, spreading out classroom training over several sessions allows you to repeat key procedures increasing retention. Also, don't exclude something from the classroom training just because it is included in the on-the-job training. Remember, people learn differently; repeating the training in different ways will increase the success of the training.

On-the-job training
The methods and extensiveness of on-the-job training will vary based upon the specific tasks. Handing a new employee off to Bob saying, "Bob, show the new guy the ropes" doesn't cut it. You should have a formal document describing the requirements of the hands-on training. This should include a check sheet that lists the specific details of the hands-on training. Both the trainer and the trainee should check off each entry ensuring that it was covered and understood.

Individual self-paced or assisted training
Individual self-paced training is as simple as giving employees access to the training materials. As I previously mentioned, people learn differently so it's important to offer alternatives. This does not mean that they can choose to take the documentation home and read it instead of attending the classroom sessions, but rather, that in addition to classroom and on-the-job training they can also study the materials individually. If you've developed computer-based training materials, you should get employees access to the materials, but I also recommend having paper-based materials to hand out. Whereas the paper-based materials may not include all of the graphics, they should include comprehensive text-based procedures.

Assisted training just means providing assistance to anyone needing it. Some employees may require more time, more explanation, and more repetition than others. Rather than risking these employees not understanding the procedures, or slowing the group classroom sessions down to a crawl, you should provide some one-on-one assistance to these employees. You also need to find a means of identifying these employees, as they are unlikely to speak up and say, "hey, I'm really dumb, can you give me some more help?" If you've been working with the group for a while you may already know the ones that may need more assistance. Testing (discussed later) can also prove useful. People are sometimes surprised to find out — after working with an employee for years — that the employee can't read or has other significant learning issues. Assisted training will ensure that all employees receive adequate training.

Language issues
Non-English speaking employees or those to whom English is a second language present additional challenges when it comes to training. Frequently non-English speaking employees are simply left out of the training process (even when they are present during the training). This does not have to be. Though you can have another bilingual employee verbally translate the procedures, you risk errors in the translation and are not providing the employee with alternative learning meth-

ods. There are businesses that will translate your training materials into almost any language. They usually charge by the word, and you can often send them an electronic version of the training materials and receive back a translated version in the same format. Also realize that employees that speak English as a second language, although they seem to speak and understand English well, may learn more effectively if the text-based training materials are in their native language.

New employee training
Much of the classroom training suggestions above assume that you have a large group of workers to train at the same time. They would apply when procedures are first introduced or revised, and during refresher training. However, formal classroom training is usually difficult with new employees that are hired one at a time. Usually new employee training will be limited to on-the-job and individual or assisted training. This doesn't mean that new employees have to miss out on the group interaction of classroom training. Since training should be treated as an ongoing process, classroom sessions should be provided periodically as refresher training, and as training to support new processes and process changes. This not only continues to instill the value placed on training and education, but also provides opportunities to refocus on problem areas and promote discussion that may provide new ideas and insights on process improvement.

Cross-training
While most managers agree that there are benefits to cross training, few take the time to implement an effective and ongoing cross-training program. Often cross-training is pursued as a periodic fad with a big push towards cross-training and then a couple of years ignoring the issue, then another big push, then … Other situations arise when cross-training becomes important only when a specific area is experiencing significant staffing issues. Trying to cross-train when you are short staffed is not likely to enhance operations; in fact it is likely to shortcut the training process resulting in problems related to accuracy, quality, safety, etc. Though most would measure the value of cross-training in the staffing flexibility it provides, cross-training also contributes to making accuracy easy by increasing the employee's knowledge of related processes. This not only helps the employee to better understand their normal responsibilities, but also may inspire creative thinking in identifying and resolving problems, bottlenecks, and unnecessary steps. To get the most benefit out of cross-training I recommend the following:

✔ **Don't start cross-training an employee until they are thoroughly trained and experienced in their current position.** Cross-training too soon will take focus off of their primary responsibilities and possibly confuse them.

✔ **Don't cross-train everyone on everything.** This will generally result in confused employees that know a little about everything but not enough to be effective. It's much more effective to plan cross-training so that there are enough employees throughout the organization to provide coverage for each area, yet each employee is only cross-trained in one or two positions in addition to their own position.

✔ **Cross-train in directly related positions.** Employees will not only learn quicker, be better at their normal position, but will also be able to provide more input on process improvement if they are cross-trained in a directly related position. This usually means cross-training in either a feeding operation or an operation that they normally feed. For example, a machine operator could cross-train at another machine or in a material handling position, while a material handler may cross-train as a machine operator or a receiving clerk. Cross-training a receiving clerk as a machine operator, while still valuable, may not be as effective if their responsibilities don't normally interact.

✔ **Provide incentives for cross-training.** Increased knowledge generally translates into increased responsibilities; make sure that you are compensating employees for the value they are generating through their efforts.

✔ **Provide cross-trained employees with working time in cross-trained positions.** We start forgetting things as soon as we learn them if we are not periodically using the knowledge. Design a schedule that ensures that cross-trained workers periodically get some real working time in the positions in which they've been cross-trained.

✔ **Don't force cross-training on employees.** In some cases this may not be an option, however there are usually enough motivated employees interested in cross-training to meet your objectives. Sometimes you have workers that are very good at what they do and have no interest in cross-training. As long as you are getting enough volunteers to meet your cross-training objectives, I would keep it optional.

Testing

"Make my employees take a test, are you nuts? They'll refuse, they'll all fail, they'll quit!" OK, I'm not going to kid you; a test is going to scare the hell out of some of your employees. And while fear is not the primary objective, it's not totally without merit either. Testing employees on procedures does several things: it emphasizes key points from the procedures, it validates that the employees understand the procedures, it points out areas that were not clearly understood in the training process, it identifies employees requiring more assistance in training, and the mere mention of a test will encourage employees to pay attention during the training.

The design of the test is key to its success. Make the test easy. That's right, make it easy! You are not trying to measure their intellectual capacity, just confirming that they know how to do their job. Think about the types of questions you've always hated on tests and make sure you are not repeating these very same methods of torture. No confusing trick questions, no essay answer requirements, and no complex problems (unless solving complex problems is a day-to-day responsibility of the position). You are designing a test that most employees should be able to score 100 percent on. I recommend a combination of multiple-choice with some true/false questions. The test should focus on critical parts of the procedures; make efforts to include questions on procedural issues that have been problems in the past. An example would be to have a multiple-choice question where one answer is the correct method and another answer is an incorrect method some employees prefer. In this case the question itself is a training tool used to emphasize the correct method as well as point out that the other method is not correct. Trust me, it works. Also, make sure you include questions related to different aspects of the job responsibilities such as safety, quality, accuracy, and housekeeping.

Maximum weight capacity for the reach trucks at full mast extention assuming a 48" deep evenly loaded pallet is:
  - a. 2,400lb
  - b. 3,200lb
  - c. 4,000lb
  - d. 5,500lb

Correct sequence of events for putting away a pallet is:
  - a. Scan bar code on pallet, pick up pallet, drive to location, place pallet, scan location bar code.
  - b. Pick up pallet, drive to location, scan bar code on pallet, place pallet, scan location bar code.
  - c. Pick up pallet, drive to location, place pallet, scan bar code on pallet, scan location bar code.
  - d. Pick up pallet, drive to location, place pallet, scan location bar code, scan bar code on pallet.

Pallets should be positioned in racking to allow clear view of license plate from aisle.
          TRUE   FALSE

Moving double-stacked pallets with the forklift is acceptable if the loads look stable.
          TRUE   FALSE

Moving pallets that do not have license plates is acceptable provided you write the information on a piece of paper and leave it on Bob's desk.
          TRUE   FALSE

In the sample test questions shown above, I am focussing on various aspects of the putaway process. You can see that I am not only using the test to test knowledge, but also to emphasize specific details of the procedure. In this example, the correct answers are: b, a, True, False, False.

So what do you do with the results of the test? The test is part of the training program; you use the results to continue the education process. Any questions that were answered incorrectly by a significant portion of the employees should be addressed in a group setting; obviously something was not clear in the procedures and the training. Changes should be incorporated into the next revision of the procedures and next training sessions to correct any confusion. Other questions answered incorrectly should be discussed with the individual employees, ensuring that they now understand the correct answer. I suggest having the employee initial each incorrectly answered question after they agree that they understand the correct response. Employees doing very poorly on the test will need some additional training. In these cases I would not suggest just going through the incorrectly answered questions, as there is likely a lot more they do not understand about the procedures. You may also find that either language or reading skills are the problem and not the employee's knowledge of the procedures. If this is the case, you may want to give the test again orally or with a translator, even to the extent of elaborating on the question if the employee doesn't seem to understand it. You may also want to allow employees to take the test individually rather than in a classroom type setting. Some employees may panic under the group atmosphere, especially if some employees are finishing the test while they are still on the third question. Do not set a time limit on the test; you are not testing their "test taking" skills.

It's important to let employees know that the test is part of the learning process. There should be no penalty for incorrect answers. Ultimately, everybody passes.

Putting formal checks in place

Certainly it's preferable to have processes in place that achieve 100 percent accuracy without the need for any checks. Do-it-right-the-first-time fanatics will argue that checks are a form of waste (the term non-value-added comes up frequently) and therefore should be eliminated, and that error-free processes are the only acceptable means of achieving quality (or accuracy in this case). They may also argue that allowing checks sends a message that process errors are acceptable, thus undermining the key principles of most quality strategies. While I agree with most of this in principle, I've also spent enough time in the real world to know that while the pursuit of perfection is admirable, the expectation of perfection is unrealistic. I view checks as just another tool that can be used to achieve your business objectives. My general recommendation is to build your processes to be as accurate as is feasible, and — if this level of accuracy does not meet your business objectives — use checks or any other methods available to make up the difference. If it makes you feel better, you can say that you are only putting checks in place as a temporary measure until your process improvement efforts achieve acceptable levels of accuracy.

Checks can take on many forms. Determining the process to check, type of check, and extensiveness of checking, requires evaluating output requirements and process capabilities.

Some examples of types of checks are listed below:

- ❐ Carton count verification of inbound or outbound shipment.
- ❐ Pallet count verification of inbound or outbound shipment.
- ❐ Weight verification of inbound or outbound shipment.
- ❐ 100 percent checking of all inbound or outbound shipments.
- ❐ 100 percent check of randomly selected inbound or outbound shipments.
- ❐ 100 percent check of specific (by customer, vendor, item, order size, destination, etc) inbound or outbound shipments.
- ❐ Verify correct number of line items for inbound or outbound shipments.
- ❐ Quick visual inspection of inbound or outbound shipments looking for obvious errors (usually based upon experience of order checker).
- ❐ Location verification of all receipts stocked prior day or shift.
- ❐ 100 percent checking of all work performed by new employees.
- ❐ Material handler verifying item number and quantity of product prior to moving.
- ❐ Machine operator verifying item number and quantity of materials prior to starting production.
- ❐ Empty location verification.
- ❐ Location audits.
- ❐ Periodic counts of critical raw materials.
- ❐ Cycle counting program. That's right, a cycle counting program is a form of checking.

I assume that checking will continue to be a topic of debate in books, articles, discussion groups, and on the seminar circuit. There are even arguments as to what a check is. Some claim a check that occurs within the process is not a check while one that occurs outside the process is. There is some rationale to this, especially in manufacturing processes, since a problem found during a check that occurs within the process can trigger an immediate machine adjustment, thus reducing the chances of producing an entire batch of defective product. However, once you start down the road of debating semantics, there's no going back. You will now have to argue what a process is, if I extend my definition of a process, I can now argue that my checks actually occur within the process. For instance, if I define the process as order processing instead of order picking, a check that occurs between order picking and shipping is still within the order processing process and therefore is not really a check. None of this really matters, and I only mention it because you are very likely to, at some point, run into a do-it-right-the-first-time fanatic, or, worse yet, a do-it-right-the-first-time fanatic wannabe that will try to convince you that checking is equivalent to doing the "devil's work." Again, I will emphasize that checking is just another tool or method that can be utilized to achieve your business objectives. Checking makes accuracy easy by making accuracy objectives achievable when the base processes are not capable of meeting those objectives. Another advantage of formal checks is in their use as a performance measurement tool. This will be discussed further in the next chapter.

Other ways to make accuracy easy

Make sure employees have easy access to all equipment, information, documents, and forms needed to perform their jobs.

This includes everything from pocket calculators, tape dispensers, and markers, to lift trucks, terminals, printers, and copy machines. Certainly it's easy to see why access to a pocket calculator can contribute to making accuracy easy, but what about the other equipment? Let me give you some examples. If an employee doesn't have easy access to a tape dispenser, they may not adequately reseal a carton that has been opened, possibly resulting in materials falling out of the carton or confusion as to the quantity in the carton. If an employee doesn't have easy access to a label printer, they may choose to manually create or change a label rather than running a new one using the computer's database. This can result in incorrect or unreadable information on the label. If an employee doesn't have easy access to a rolling ladder, they may choose to climb the racking to pick a product. Not only is this a safety issue, but also an accuracy issue as they are now more focused on climbing the rack and not getting caught, than on picking the correct part and quantity. They are also likely to knock some other products over as they do this, opening up the possibility for missing product later. Yes, these are all little things, but removing the contributing factors to errors, no matter how insignificant they may seem, will ultimately add up to significant improvement.

Consider implementing a locator system.

If you are not already using a locator system, you may want to consider implementing one. A locator system can increase the accuracy and productivity of many warehouse tasks, including order picking and cycle counting. There are still some operations that can get by without a locator system and even some that are better off without one. However most distribution and manufacturing facilities will benefit from incorporating locations into their inventory tracking system. Locator systems will be explained in more detail in chapter eight.

Manage capacity and cycle times.

So what does capacity and cycle time have to do with inventory accuracy? When operations approach or exceed capacity, you will usually end up with several things occurring: frequent changes to production schedules, frequent expediting of materials, staging areas full of in-process materials, storage areas overflowing into aisles and staging areas. All of this increases the chances of making errors because there is a lot of confusion, a lot of short cuts taken, and a lot more inventory floating around than can be properly managed. Though capacity is generally considered a manufacturing issue, it's also important to consider the capacity of your warehouse, and your shipping and receiving operations. Cycle time is also related to capacity but is not exclusive to it. Cycle time is the time it takes for inventory to move through an operation or a series of operations, including any time spent "just sitting there." This includes manufacturing operations, receiving operations, putaway operations, picking and shipping operations. Longer cycle times result in more staged and in-process inventory that must be managed over a longer period of time. The more in-process materials you have and the longer they remain in process, the greater the opportunity for error. Though advantages of cycle-time reduction related to increased customer service and inventory reduction are well known, there are also significant internal operational benefits as well. Most significantly, there is less to manage. If inventory is received and stocked the same day it hits the docks, and orders are picked and shipped the same day they are placed, there is that much less inventory and orders that need to be managed. Significant cycle-time reduction can be accomplished by streamlining processes, however, if you don't manage capacity you will struggle to maintain consistently low cycle times. Though not yet generally accepted, many businesses are finding the costs associated with operating with excess capacity are less than the costs associated with operating at capacity.

Change environmental factors to make accuracy easy.
I discussed several environmental factors in the previous chapter that affect accuracy. These include lighting, noise, housekeeping, storage and staging identification, product identification, and use of standardized containers. All of these should be evaluated as part of your make accuracy easy efforts.

Summary

Making accuracy easy is not meant to be a cute little slogan, but rather a mindset that focuses attention on accuracy and productivity improvements likely to be both successful and acceptable throughout the organization. Making accuracy easy focuses on process improvements and employee training. Using the " what is the best way to do this, that takes into account the customer service, productivity, quality, accuracy, capacity, safety, and financial objectives of our organization" method of process improvement will ensure that you are improving the overall process and not just a characteristic of the process. Improving the human-machine interface by improving documents and programs, and by utilizing automated data capture, automation, and transaction-by-exception techniques can be a significant part of making accuracy easy. It's also important to avoid underestimating the value of well-documented procedures and well-trained employees. In the end, operational excellence comes down to the execution of sound processes.

3

Making Accuracy Expected

Before we jump into making accuracy expected, I would like to once more emphasize the importance of the making accuracy easy phase. In addition to the obvious accuracy benefits of the process improvements, Making accuracy easy is critical in gaining the support of both the general workforce and management. Some of the more hard-line approaches that we'll be discussing in this chapter will be much more palatable if implemented after the workforce has experienced the overall improvements resulting from making accuracy easy. The message that the workforce should be taking away from this entire process is that rather than just demanding accuracy, you are creating an atmosphere that is conducive to accuracy.

In this chapter we'll be discussing ways to make accuracy expected. In addition we'll cover ways to make accuracy happen. Many of the concepts detailed here can equally apply to any aspect of quality. Since accuracy is actually a subset of quality, it may make more sense to approach this as "making quality expected." This helps to avoid redundancy and confusion by treating customer service initiatives, accuracy initiatives, and quality initiatives, as parts of a larger overall long-term quality initiative rather than a series of disconnected programs that are often viewed as fads.

Maintaining accurate inventory records and related data is a critical step in achieving overall quality. The fact that you are taking the time to read this book makes it obvious that you've already determined that accuracy was important to your operational success. While I won't spend a lot of time on it, I would like to make some comments on accuracy and it's importance.

❏ Planning systems are only as effective as the accuracy of the data inputs. Accuracy problems will force material planners to increase safety stock levels to help compensate for a lack of confidence in the data. Production planners may fall into the wasteful habit of needing to see the inventory prior to releasing production orders. Frequent adjustments to on-hand quantities related to inventory discrepancies will create havoc with planning systems. Costs associated with increased inventory levels, as well as the time needed to constantly change production schedules, and the time required to expedite and de-expedite incoming materials, can be substantial in operations with accuracy problems.

❏ Manufacturing execution is highly dependant upon the availability of raw materials, components and subassemblies. Shortages may shut down a production run, not only delaying the production of the required products, but also creating additional machine setups and requiring additional handling of other raw materials.

❏ Product quality can be affected when incorrectly picked or identified materials are used in production, when component shortages force last minute substitutions that may not be to spec, or when some old lost component is suddenly found and used in production even though the specs have since changed.

❏ Customer satisfaction is jeopardized when wrong items and quantities are shipped, shipments are missed due to "missing product," shipments are delayed due to production delays related to inventory accuracy, or product is defective because of quality issues related to inaccurate inventory.

All of this stresses the need to emphasize the importance of inventory accuracy in achieving your overall business objectives. In fact, since inaccurate inventory and data can compromise your ability to meet business objectives you must ultimately arrive at the realization that inventory accuracy must be the number one objective of your organization. NOT!!! Actually, inventory accuracy is only one of many factors that are critical to the success of an organization, and while you should be emphasizing the importance of inventory accuracy you should not lose sight of all of the other things a business needs to do right to succeed.

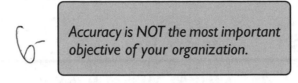

Accuracy is NOT the most important objective of your organization.

The statement "accuracy is NOT the most important objective of your organization" is not meant to be critical of your organization, but rather to help you to base your improvement efforts in reality and not in some fantasy world where everyone will drop everything to help in the effort. Planners' and schedulers' priorities are planning and scheduling, quality personnel focus on product quality, manufacturing personnel focus on meeting the production schedule, warehouse and material handling personnel focus on receiving, stocking, picking, and shipping. While accuracy affects their ability to perform their jobs, and the way they perform their jobs affects accuracy, it is unlikely that accuracy will be their primary focus, nor should it be. What needs to be emphasized is that accuracy is part of everyone's responsibilities, and while it may not be everyone's number one priority it should at least make their top ten list. Making accuracy expected actually comes down to emphasizing responsibility and accountability when it comes to accuracy, and making it clear that this applies to everyone. Yes, I know, the repeated reference to "everyone" is becoming redundant, however it is important to emphasize it as many within your organization may not feel their actions could have any significant impact on accuracy.

Management's responsibility

Accuracy must be an integral part of the attitude of the organization. Sounds pretty good doesn't it? I have no doubt that you could go to any manager or executive in your company and — when presented with this statement — they would wholeheartedly agree and commit to supporting it. The saying "actions speak louder than words" really applies here, as getting people to support this in spirit and getting them to support it in actions are two very different things. This isn't to say managers and executives are lying or just paying lip service; more likely they honestly believe in the statement, but are just unclear as to how to make the statement a reality. They are also likely unclear as to the cause-and-effect relationship between their actions as managers, and actual accuracy in the warehouse and on the shop floor. This is based upon the misguided assumption that accuracy is exclusively controlled at the detailed execution level, that it's solely the responsibility of the workers and supervisors in the warehouse and on the shop floor, and that inaccuracy is simply a performance issue.

So let's take a look at some of the ways managers contribute to inaccuracy.

Not taking responsibility or holding their subordinates responsible for accuracy.

This is probably the biggest issue. Need some examples? How about:

☐ The plant manager that doesn't seem to care how accurate the production reporting is as long as he is meeting the production schedule.

☐ The warehouse manager that's more concerned with keeping the floor cleared and getting the orders out than making sure the transactions are processed correctly (or at all).

☐ The quality manager that makes sure that defective materials are separated from good inventory, however shows little interest in making sure the system is in sync with the physical separation.

☐ The customer service manager that allows the "whatever it takes" attitude to go too far allowing customer service reps to "steal" from other orders.

☐ The materials manager that allows planners to note a component substitution for production without adjusting the corresponding production order's materials list.

I could go on and on.

Usually a single person within an organization is given primary responsibility for inventory accuracy and it ends up being their job to fight these battles with the other managers. While you'd like to think that managers would be able to come to a reasonable solution on their own, this is often not the case. Ultimately, this will come down to whether or not their bosses hold them, as managers, responsible for accuracy. In most cases, the answer is a simple "no." So when you look at taking responsibility for accuracy, you need to start at the top. Is there a clear commitment from the highest levels of the organization to making accuracy part of everyone's responsibility and will managers be held accountable for their actions (or inactions)? If not, your success will be limited to what you can do within the areas under your control and the willingness of others to cooperate. It's important to know where you stand, as it can affect process decisions. You may make changes to processes under your control to compensate for weaknesses in areas not under your control. While this may not be the best solution, it still can be effective.

Breaking the rules

An example of a good control policy to have in place is: "materials cannot be stored, moved, shipped, consumed, or produced, without proper documents." Now who do you think is most likely to break this rule? The owner? President? A VP? Plant manager? Sales manager? All the above? And why did they feel the need to break the rule? Well, customer service, of course. "I'm not going to let a procedure stand in the way of satisfying a customer," they will utter with the greatest conviction.

Hell, you can't argue with that. That is, unless you have a process in place to satisfy the customer without breaking the rules. And, in many cases, you probably already did have that process in place; they just chose to not follow it. Should you call them on it? Probably, but I would give a little warning here. Bringing it to their attention is the right thing to do; however don't be certain that "doing the right thing" won't get you fired. Most owners, executives, and managers are very reasonable folks that truly have the best interests of the organization at heart. However, there are some tyrants out there that don't take criticism well, and are easily infuriated by a subordinate questioning their actions. You know the type: Godlike beings that like to look at their name on the company org chart and take pleasure in the thought of all those insignificant little people below them. Dictators that view their job as a position of power rather than a position of responsibility and have no hesitance in exerting their power periodically just to make that point. I'm quite certain that I am not offending these people by putting this in this book since I know that they would never read this book, because, of course, they already "know it all." Relax; I'm just having a little fun here. I can assure you that this is not the ranting of a disgruntled former employee. I have, however, run into a few of these characters before and have found it somewhat fascinating to watch these relics operate. Well, it's only fun until someone gets hurt, which brings my back to my original point. Life isn't always fair and while I would encourage you to pursue accuracy at all levels, be aware that doing the right thing sometimes has consequences.

OK, back to breaking the rules. Rules are critical to maintaining control, and control is critical in maintaining accuracy. Rules (processes, policies, and procedures) should be designed to meet the overall business objectives of the organization. Since customer satisfaction is likely a key business objective of the organization, rules should not be in conflict with this objective. If rules are not in conflict with this objective, there should be no reason to break the rules. The important point here is to be proactive and anticipate the circumstances under which someone would be inclined to break the rules and make sure you have a process in place that allows the objective to be achieved without breaking the rules. An example would be that if management or sales personnel sometimes bring prospective customers into the facility, and if a prospective customer may want to take some samples of your product with him when he leaves, you should make sure that you have a process in place to allow this to happen without screwing up your inventory.

To ensure that people will follow the procedure, you need to educate them on the procedure and use the making accuracy easy approach in designing the procedure. Don't expect a sales manager to fill out extensive multipart forms, get written approval, and then spend an hour tracking down a stock clerk to retrieve the product. They are just not going to do it. Give them a simple and convenient method of getting the product, and you are much more likely to get their cooperation.

Managers and execs also need to take some responsibility when asking employees to do something out of the norm. If the president of the company goes down to the warehouse and tells an employee to "take those pallets and load them on that truck," I'm pretty certain that it's going to get done. If the president assumes that the employee is "smart enough" to know that he then needs to enter an appropriate transaction, he may be mistaken. The same holds true if a plant manager sees a crate of defective materials and says to a material handler "I know those are bad, throw them away." They'll get thrown out, but will a transaction be entered? The employees are much more likely to think that the president or plant manager "know what they are doing" and had the transactions taken care of or they would have told them specifically to do the transaction. Don't worry, I'm not going to bring up that whole "when you assume" thing.

Not considering the effects business decisions or process changes have on accuracy.

This isn't to imply that accuracy must be a key part of the decision-making process as to whether you will or will not undertake a specific strategic business practice. More likely it would just involve considering the accuracy-related implications of the business decision and ensuring that you are prepared to manage them. Basically it means figuring HOW you will do it, or IF you are capable of doing it, before you DO it. I think information systems personnel will easily relate to this as they are often given the "Hey, we've committed to doing this by next month, we're going to need systems in place by then" task. A more inventory-specific example would be "we've just decided to start outsourcing some of our production, we need to start shipping some raw materials today and redirect some vendor shipments to our new manufacturer." It's not too much to ask to maintain some open communication during the development of these plans with those that will be responsible for the execution. Certainly there are times when unplanned events occur and you have to wing it, but those occurrences tend to be the exception. It's always better to have planning occur before execution, as opposed to during, after, or never.

Not providing the resources necessary to achieve accuracy expectations. These could be financial resources to invest in equipment and technology or labor resources to analyze processes, develop plans, train workers, and perform cycle counts or audits. Write a blank check? I think not. Many accuracy improvements can be made with little or no additional resources, and I strongly recommend starting with the low and no cost improvements. Larger investments should go through some type of cost justification process, however, you must realize that there are intangible savings associated with increases in accuracy that don't fit well into a standard ROI calculation.

Everybody's responsibility

Now that I've finished beating up on management (at least for now), it's time to address the responsibilities of the general workforce. I'll once again mention that accuracy must be an integral part of the attitude of the organization. Every employee needs to understand that they share responsibility for accuracy and that they will be held accountable for accuracy.

Employees must be held accountable for following policies and procedures.
You can't expect employees to never make an error. You can, however, expect them to always follow procedures. You've invested the time to develop processes and procedures designed to prevent errors, you've put in place a training and testing program that ensures the employees understand the policies and procedures.

You now need to be prepared to hold employees accountable for following procedures. If someone is not following the procedures they must be dealt with by means of an appropriate disciplinary action. It's that simple. You may be amazed as to how much just one individual not following procedures can screw up your inventory. If you don't hold the employees accountable, you may as well throw out everything you have done to this point. An error resulting from an employee not following procedures is not a mistake, but rather a deliberate action by the employee to not do what he or she was instructed to do.

I cannot emphasize enough just how important this is. Once procedures are put in place and employees are trained, you must immediately begin to monitor the processes for compliance to procedures. Any deviations from the procedures must be addressed without delay. Let me outline a scenario of a training program that does not follow up with accountability. Initially after the training, most workers will comply, with a few taking a discretionary (when they feel like it) approach to following procedures. If nothing is done to address those not following procedures, you will see a gradual increase in the group of workers taking the discretionary approach. Meanwhile your shrinking group of workers that have been following the procedures, start feeling peer pressure to join the discretionary group or start to wonder "why should I do it if nobody else is?" Eventually, most employees will not be following the procedures, with just a very small group of holdouts. These are generally the employees that take a lot of pride in their work and will try their best to do a good job regardless of what others do, you know — your best employees. While this small group of very conscientious workers is still following the procedures they are starting to think: "What's the point? Does anyone care about what is going on? Why am I working here?"

For most managers and supervisors, disciplining employees is a rather unpleasant part of their responsibilities and many of them will shy away from it by taking the "see no evil" approach. Though no one wants to be disciplined, an environment that fairly applies discipline to ensure company policies and procedures are followed will ultimately have a happier, more productive, and more accurate workforce.

Employees must be held accountable for errors.

Holding employees accountable for errors includes communication when employees make errors, measurements to track accuracy, and standards that communicate expectations. There are several wrong ways to hold people accountable for errors. The most common mistake is disciplining an employee only when an error they made results in an irate customer or an otherwise serious production or inventory problem. This is a very unfair and unproductive means of holding employees accountable, as it is not reflective of the employee's overall accuracy but rather the perceived impact of one specific error. It may turn out that this employee is actually your most accurate employee, and the error in question is the only one he has made in months, while other employees have made significantly more errors. A simple rule of thumb to apply here is to never discipline an employee for a specific error; instead, discipline should be applied based upon a history of repeated errors.

The second most common mistake in holding employees accountable for errors is using a fixed number of errors as a mechanism for discipline. For example, having a policy that states order pickers will be disciplined for making more than X number of errors per month. This type of policy unfairly punishes your more productive employees. For example, one employee picks 10,000 line items and has seven errors, and another employee picks 6,000 line items and has five errors. Which employee is more accurate? If you had a policy of disciplining based upon six or more errors you would be disciplining your more accurate and more productive employee. Accuracy performance should be measured as a percentage of transactions. To use the previous numbers as an example you would come up with accuracy rates of 99.93 percent and 99.92 percent respectively. Manufacturers that are accustomed to using parts per million (PPM) as a means of measuring defects may choose to use the same measurement for accuracy at which point you would come up with 700 PPM and 833 PPM respectively. My preference is to stick with percentages, as PPM tends to be more confusing to workers when their transactions are only in the hundreds or thousands. Also, measuring an accuracy rate as opposed to an error rate puts a slightly more positive spin on communicating accuracy.

Employees will not know what accuracy is, or how many errors are "too many" unless you tell them. When asked "how many errors are acceptable?" supervisors and managers will often answer, "No errors are acceptable." While this may have sounded good when you heard it during a quality seminar, it does not answer the employee's question. If you are going to fire employees whenever they make an error, this answer would be correct. If not, then obviously there is some level of inaccuracy that is acceptable. Communicating accuracy expectations requires that you develop standards. A standard is a statement that quantifies expectations. The first thing you need to consider in developing the standard is, what exactly will it be used to communicate. A standard can describe expectation of average output, a point at which incentives are awarded, or a point at which discipline is initiated. While it may be taking a negative approach, I have found the standard that describes the point at which discipline is initiated (the minimum standard) to be the most important initial standard to have in place. In accuracy this is the answer to "how many errors are too many?" A minimum standard states the level of performance the employee must achieve to keep their job. This is an important statement because it is communicating a clear performance level and a clear action that will be taken if the performance level is not met. It takes subjectivity and unfairness out of the equation and simply states if "A" happens then "B" will happen. Employees now understand the requirement and supervisors or managers now understand their responsibility to act.

You cannot put standards in place unless you have a means of measuring to the standard. In accuracy, this requires measuring the number of transactions and number of errors for a specific employee performing a specific task. While measuring the number of transactions can be pretty straightforward, measuring errors requires that you have a mechanism in place to identify errors and attribute a source to the error. This brings me back to the use of formal checks as discussed in the previous chapter. Your most reliable source for error measurement will be the output of a formal checking process such as order checking, checking of put-away transactions, or a cycle counting or location audit program. If using output from a cycle counting or location audit program you need to be sure the program is aggressive enough to catch the errors within a reasonable timeframe. Attributing an error to a specific employee six months after it occurred is both difficult and ineffective. Programs that incorporate random checks are very useful for determining compliance to procedures and identifying problem areas, but are less effective at measuring individual accuracy. The effectiveness of using customer complaints as a tool to measure order-picking accuracy will depend upon the types of products and the customer base. In some industries only a very small percentage of errors are ever reported. This is especially true of quantity errors, since over-shipments are rarely reported and many customers do not perform 100 percent piece counts at receipt. This is very evident when a company starts an internal checking process and finds that they are catching internally five times as many errors per month as were previously reported by their customers.

Putting a standard in place is not easy and should not be done arbitrarily. Accuracy is relative and an acceptable accuracy level for one facility may be very different from another, as will acceptable levels from one task to another. The environmental factors discussed in chapter one will have a significant impact on the level of accuracy that can be reasonably expected for a specific task within a specific facility. I strongly recommend putting in place the measurement first and analyzing the measurement over a period of time prior to setting a firm standard. You will generally start to see accuracy improvement once the measurement is in place and the employees are aware that their individual accuracy is being measured. You will also likely see a significant spread between the accuracy of employees. Do not take the accuracy level of the most accurate employee and assume that all others should be able to achieve this level, also do not assume that just because several employees are below a specific level, that the level is too high to set as a standard. At some point, setting the standard does get to be a little subjective as you need to ask yourself "how good is the group of employees I am measuring." In a normal mix of employees you may be setting the standard at a level that 70 to 80 percent of the employees are consistently achieving over an extended period of time. Does this mean that you will be firing 20 to 30 percent of your staff? Probably not, as you will generally see a large portion of this group improve once they realize their job is on the line. However, you do need to be prepared for the possibility that they won't improve. Also, this is based on a "normal mix" of employees, a term which can't really be quantified. If you feel your group consists of above average performers, you may set the minimum at a point that all have been consistently achieving, while if you feel you have a large number of poor performers, you may be setting the minimum at a point that few have been consistently achieving. While a minimum standard set too low will lessen the effectiveness of the standard, setting a standard too high will put you in a very awkward position, forcing you to question enforcement if too many employees are not meeting the standard. There is no middle ground; you either enforce the standard or you remove it. Inconsistent enforcement of a standard is unfair and may ultimately end up in court. When in doubt, set it a little low.

Generally, a standards policy will state the standard as a required output over a specific period of time. I generally recommend one-month periods as part of the policy; using periods shorter than a month will make it more difficult to consistently meet the standard (possibly forcing you to lower it), while periods longer than a month will extend the time it takes to get rid of a poor performer. Normal disciplinary actions would include one or two written warnings, a suspension, and ultimately termination. You can see that with monthly time periods, it would take three to four months of substandard performance to terminate an employee. While that may seem like a long time, you need to remember that improvement is the objective here, not termination.

I've been primarily discussing minimum standards but there are also other metrics used to communicate expectations, such as average expected output and incentive level output. I prefer to call these guidelines, targets, or goals. As I've stressed the importance of giving the employees the answer to "how many errors is too many?" it's also important to communicate the answer to "what is an average accuracy expectation?" and "what is above average accuracy?" The purpose of these metrics is to gauge the performance level of the employee and provide incentives for further improvement. Formalized incentive programs have proven to be very useful in increasing both accuracy and productivity, and I strongly recommend them wherever they can be implemented fairly. The combination of minimum standards, guidelines, and goals, will clearly communicate accuracy expectations and requirements, resulting in a workforce that understands the importance of accuracy and their responsibility towards achieving it. Standards should be reevaluated periodically; if improvements have been implemented that make it easier to be accurate you should consider raising the standards accordingly.

It's unrealistic to expect that you will be able to have accuracy performance measures and standards for every position. The more people you have performing a specific task, the frequency of errors occurring within that task, and the efforts required to measure, are factors that should be considered when incorporating performance measures. Order picking processes are the most likely candidates for performance measures, as they often have several employees performing the same task, are critical to customer satisfaction, and may already have a checking process in place. Putaway processes are also prime candidates, especially if "lost" product has been an issue.

Communicating errors.

While I've certainly focused on discipline up to this point, communication of errors is actually more of a training and information sharing activity than a disciplinary activity. As I mentioned before, you should never discipline an employee for a specific error. The communication of errors should be treated as part of the learning and continuous improvement process. Discipline is appropriate for not following policies and procedures or accuracy performance that is below the minimum standard. It's very important to make sure employees understand this. This starts by acknowledging that everyone occasionally makes errors and that the overall objective is to use the errors to further improvement efforts. I know this may be difficult for the " no error is acceptable" folks, but unrealistic expectations do not help the situation.

Communication consists of both performance measures over time as well as detailed communication of specific errors. Employees should be notified and given the details of an error they are responsible for as quickly as possible. In many cases, the employee may remember the circumstances under which the error occurred. This allows them to do some self-diagnosis to determine what they did to cause the error or what they failed to do to prevent it. An example would be that an employee remembers that he had spent a good part of the morning stocking inventory from a specific product group that came in cases of 50, and then stocked one item that was actually in cases of 40 and miscounted it as cases of 50. Another example would be that an employee was supposed to pick one piece of item number HFX789-2 and picked two instead. By seeing the detailed information, the employee may realize that the "-2" at the end of the item number was the contributing factor. This detailed sharing of information allows the employee to better understand how they made the error, allowing them to make personal adjustments to reduce the chances of it happening again. Yes, you could have (and should have) introduced examples like these during the training process, in an effort to prevent it from happening in the first place, however you will find that the "this is how you made this error" approach tends to be more effective than the "this is how you may make an error" approach. Once again this comes back to human nature, as we all think that we are very accurate and that it's the other guy that makes these stupid mistakes. The realization that indeed YOU are the "other guy" making the stupid mistakes can be a turning point in improvements related to personal accuracy.

Keep in mind that this detailed communication of errors is not limited to a training period, but is an ongoing part of continuous improvement. Employees should see every error they make forever. Even though the employee has come to the realization that he makes errors and has greatly increased accuracy based upon this, you do not want to give complacency an opportunity to step in. While being accurate gets easier with experience, the battle to maintain focus is an ongoing one.

I'll once again mention that this communication should not be perceived as negative or threatening. The communication should be treated as information sharing, no different than communicating to an employee which trucks to load, the day's production schedule, or special handling of a new product. This matter-of-fact method of communication makes the situation much more comfortable for both the employee responsible for the error, as well as the person communicating the error, and ultimately provides an atmosphere more conducive to teamwork and improvement. I should also mention that the communication of error details does not necessarily need to come from the employee's supervisor. I will usually leave it to whoever is responsible for identifying and tracing the source of the error; this may be an order checker or a cycle count administrator. These people are already familiar with the error details and can provide input that can help the employee better understand the error. When people other than the employee's supervisor are communicating the error details to the employee, it becomes even more important to stress it as a positive, information sharing activity. Though I had previously mentioned possible contributing factors to errors, I am not suggesting that you should expect an explanation from the employee on the error, or that contributing factors are excuses for errors. Rather, I mean that you should provide the employee with detailed information and any insight that can help the employee determine how they made the error.

Control methods

Control methods include policies and procedures and monitoring of processes for compliance to policies and procedures. While we've already discussed some of these — and will continue to bring them up in subsequent chapters — I wanted to quickly cover these controls as a group.

The ultimate control policy: Materials cannot be stored, moved, shipped, consumed, or produced without proper documents.
This single policy can have a significant impact on accuracy as well as overall control of operations. This requires that nothing comes in without a purchase order, nothing ships without a shipping order, nothing is manufactured without a production order, nothing is scrapped without a scrap order, etc. The intent here is not to cripple operations by creating red tape, but rather to put in place a control system that optimizes operations by avoiding the chaotic conditions that are symptomatic of operations that lack discipline and controls. Achieving this requires you first have processes in place to ensure that all necessary activities can be accomplished within the structure of this policy. This policy works best where "live" documents are utilized. A live document is a document on your computer system that describes a specific transaction or set of transactions and is at an "open" status. Completion of the transaction will update the document to a "closed"

status. As mentioned, this control policy does far more than help in accuracy; it also creates an environment in which you can ensure that everything was shipped on time, production is on schedule, manufacturing is not overproducing or producing early, incoming materials are not bypassing purchasing controls such as approval processes, and outgoing shipments are not bypassing controls such as credit approval.

> *Materials cannot be stored, moved, shipped, consumed, or produced, without proper documents.*

Task authorization.
Controlling who does what. This is another control policy that ensures that the people performing tasks are fully trained, experienced, and authorized to do so. Examples would be: only allowing authorized material handlers to remove or return materials to storage areas, only allowing specific authorized employees to scrap materials, and only allowing specific authorized employees to make inventory adjustments such as cycle count adjustments or other adjustments related to perceived discrepancies.

Monitoring processes.
Monitoring processes is a control designed to ensure that policies and procedures are being followed. Just monitoring the output (as in checks) does not sufficiently ensure that procedures are being followed. It may identify that there is some type of problem, but it is not always adequate to identify the specific problem. Certainly, employees may not appreciate someone looking over their shoulder. However, if you communicate in advance, in a positive manner, and apply it fairly, monitoring processes will be accepted as part of the continuous improvement process. The following is an example of how I monitored a process to ensure that a key procedure was being followed. We were having problems with transactions not being done in a full-pallet-load environment. The systems were very manual and required employees to write down item number, quantity, from location, and to location, to later be entered into the inventory system. For a putaway transaction, the lift truck operator would pick up the load, find an acceptable location, put the pallet in the location, and then write down the details of the transaction. Moving raw materials to production followed a similar flow. The problem seemed to be that operators would occasionally forget to write down a transaction. I changed the procedure to require that part of the transaction be written down as the load is picked up and then the remaining information is written down as the load is stocked or delivered. This resulted in there being two points where the employee would touch the form, greatly reducing the possibility of forgetting to write down the transaction. If the employee forgot to write down the first part, he would catch it at the second point; if he forgets to write down the second point, he should catch it when he picks up his next load. This is a very simple, but also very effective solution, provided the employees follow the procedure. To ensure the procedure was followed I made it clear that I would periodically stop lift truck operators as they are driving with a load, and check their sheet to make sure the

transaction was listed. This was not meant to be a threat, but rather a communication as to how I would perform my responsibilities in ensuring procedures were being followed. I'm not trying to convince you that employees are going to like the idea that they are being checked up on, only that they will accept it as part of the process. I can, however, put a positive spin on this as employees tend to feel pretty good when the boss catches them "doing their job right."

Use formal checks as needed.

Checks are used to identify and correct errors, identify issues related to compliance to procedures, identify process changes, and provide the basis for accuracy measurement. The use of checks was discussed in Making Accuracy Easy, and will continue to come up in later chapters.

Take advantage of built-in checks.

Taking advantage of built-in checks means finding situations where errors can be identified during the normal execution of a task. One of the best examples of a built-in check occurs in many integrated software systems where payment of a vendor invoice requires matching the invoice to a specific purchase order receipt. This is usually called a three-way match since you are matching an invoice to a purchase order and a receipt. Variances observed during this process are generally the result of either the quantity received not matching the quantity invoiced or the unit cost invoiced not matching the unit cost on the purchase order. Depending upon costing methods, industry, and specific materials, minor costing variances can be fairly common. This results in companies allowing specific tolerances such as a fixed dollar amount or fixed percentage. While this may be appropriate for cost variances, they should not be used for quantity variances since a quantity variance may actually be a receiving error and thus an inventory problem. Putting a process in place to ensure that quantity variances observed in accounts payable are communicated to someone in the warehouse responsible for resolving them can prove to be a very simple means of identifying transaction-related receiving errors. The success or failure of this usually falls on the shoulders of the warehouse and their cooperation in verifying the quantity and responding to accounts payable in a timely manner.

Other built-in checks include exception reports or programs that identify — or in some cases have the functionality to prevent the processing of — abnormal transactions such as early receipts, receipts greater than the quantity ordered, receipts less than the quantity ordered, posting production of quantities greater than quantity ordered, shipping quantity greater than quantity ordered, shipping quantity greater than quantity available, transactions to invalid locations, locations over capacity, etc. You should check your software documentation to see if it has functionality that can be set up to identify these situations as they occur (usually in the form of an error message). Also you should promote interdepartmental communication on these types of issues. As an example, a material planner may have a report that highlights early receipts. A very early receipt may actually indicate a receipt error where either the wrong purchase order was received against or the wrong item on the purchase order was received. Communicating this to someone capable of investigating it can quickly correct a potentially significant variance.

Check checks.

As in check (verb) checks (noun). This is actually just another part of monitoring processes (the checking process in this case). The output of a checking process tells you how many errors were caught, but does not tell you how many errors were missed. The problem with checking processes — especially in a fairly accurate environment — is that checking can start to get monotonous and the checkers can get complacent as they start to get used to not finding anything wrong. Then checking starts to shift from "actually checking product" to "putting check marks on a piece of paper as you look at product." As we discussed in "Understanding errors" this is the result of a lack of focus and is a very normal part of human nature in repetitive tasks.

So how should you check checks? There are two approaches. One is to re-check what has already been checked and the other is to intentionally create errors to see if they are caught. Whereas either is useful, my personal preference is the latter. While this may seem sneaky, you should note that it's only sneaky if you don't tell them that you are going to do it. Once again, it's important to be honest with employees and communicate the purpose of monitoring checking processes. I've done this in everything from outbound order checking processes to cycle counting processes, and I can assure you that, if handled properly, this will not insult your employees. I should also note that if you intentionally create an error in an outbound shipment, you damn well better have a means of catching and correcting the error before it ships, should the checker not catch it.

Eliminate unapproved checks.

An unapproved check is an activity where an employee takes it upon himself to physically check on-hand balances or have someone else check on-hand balances solely because they don't trust the inventory system. Examples would be a production planner that regularly has someone physically check raw materials prior to a production run, a machine operator that always goes to the storage area to check raw materials before conducting a machine setup, or a customer service representative that regularly wants a physical check when entering a shipping order. These types of checks are a waste of resources because they are usually conducted in an unorganized manner and have no real logic behind them. They also perpetuate an attitude of inaccuracy since they are based on the assumption that inventory is always wrong. In some cases, unapproved checks can actually cause errors or additional unnecessary disruption of operations. I recall one time when I encountered some frantic planners, rearranging the production schedule because a machine operator told them they were short a critical raw material. I was responsible for inventory accuracy and I simply stopped them and confidently told them that they need to base their schedule on the data in the system and not comments from people out on the floor. I took a quick look at the system and confirmed again that everything looked fine and that they should continue with the initial schedule. I also scolded (yes scolded) the production employee for causing this whole mess. The problem here was that the machine operator decided to go out to the warehouse and verify raw materials for the following day's production schedule. This was not his responsibility, and if he had simply followed the schedule, the material handlers would have brought the materials to him when needed. Instead, by checking for himself (something he was not trained to do), he didn't see some raw materials that were stored in a different location (he didn't bother to check the system for locations) and ultimately concluded that he did not have enough inventory to meet the production schedule. Had I not stepped in, the production schedule would have been changed, the shipping schedule would not have been met, and additional unneeded raw materials would have been ordered. This should serve as an example why unapproved activities should not be allowed.

Granted, you need to achieve an acceptable level of accuracy prior to enforcing this, and it should be explained to people that have been initiating these activities, the reasons for eliminating them. I admit that this can be a hard sell, especially in environments where accuracy has historically been an ongoing problem. Don't assume that just because accuracy has been greatly improved, people will automatically stop these wasteful practices. Old habits are hard to break, and at some point you need to remove the safety net. This isn't to say that an activity such as checking specific raw materials prior to a production run is inherently wrong. If you determine that it is a necessary check, it should be put in place as part of the formal procedure. However, if you have determined that there is not sufficient value in the activity, it should be made clear that the activity is not acceptable.

Control perception of accuracy.
This is usually the culprit behind the unapproved checking activities described previously. Perception of accuracy — or inaccuracy — is an educational issue. Personnel throughout the organization must be aware of operational improvements put in place and the resulting impact of these improvements on overall accuracy. Basically you need to convince people accuracy has improved to the point where they should be able to trust the system, and should conduct themselves in a manner that assumes the data is accurate. The elimination of unapproved checks is a significant step in that direction.

In addition to educating personnel on improvements and overall accuracy levels, you may also need to educate them on the logic of the inventory systems they are using. This is particularly true of allocation logic, which can be rather complicated. When inadequate inventory is available to fill all demand, the allocation system will use specific logic to determine which orders get filled and which orders do not. This may be as simple as first-come-first-served, or more complex when you may prioritize based upon customer, requested date, quantity, ordered date, order type, production demand versus sales demand, shipping method, or order value. It's important that personnel that work with allocations understand them. This is especially true when you have combinations of production demand, sales demand, intercompany demand, future demand, stock orders, emergency orders, etc. When people don't understand allocation systems they will perceive that inventory is wrong when their order did not get processed even though there was inventory on the shelf. This often leads to "going around the system," which will likely create real inventory problems and also compromises the allocation logic that should be based upon company objectives.

Although you may not be able to completely control perception, you can have an impact on it. Sometimes this can be accomplished with basic education, while other times you may need to take a hard-line approach such as preventing people from conducting unapproved checking activities or making personnel — that have been complaining about accuracy — explain the basis for their complaints.

Summary

Making accuracy expected involves communicating accuracy responsibilities and accountability throughout the organization. Managers leading by example, process changes that always consider accuracy, controls and discipline to ensure procedures are being followed, all contribute to accuracy becoming an integral part of the attitude of the organization. Eventually accuracy becomes a habit and your accuracy initiative begins to run on its own momentum.

Understanding errors, making accuracy easy, and making accuracy expected, are the foundation for building an environment that is conducive to accuracy. Though cycle counting and bar code technologies were mentioned in these first chapters, I intentionally underplayed their significance as they are only a couple of tools among many tools used to achieve accuracy. Many operations have cycle counting programs and bar code technologies in place, yet they are unable to achieve high levels of accuracy. This is because rather than taking a holistic approach towards achieving accuracy they have decided to use an overly simplistic approach by throwing the two most highly publicized tools at the problem.

The remaining chapters provide nuts-and-bolts details on tools, techniques, and specific processes. While I certainly expect this information to be valuable, I want to emphasize that you should not lose sight of the concepts discussed in these first three chapters as you get involved in the details of your accuracy improvement efforts.

Accuracy becomes habit.

Cycle Counting

I define cycle counting as any process that verifies the correctness of inventory quantity data by counting portions of the inventory on an ongoing basis. In other words, any process that uses regularly scheduled counts but does not count the entire facility's inventory in a single event. I want to emphasize the broadness of the scope of this definition, as many practitioners take a much narrower view of what cycle counting is, basing their definition on what I call "the standard cycle counting program." Well, I guess you already know how I feel about people's reliance on "standard practices" to run their businesses.

Purpose of cycle counting

Cycle counting is simply a tool — one of many tools — used to help meet the overall business objectives of the organization. The ultimate goal of a cycle counting program is to achieve excellence in customer service and optimize the effectiveness of internal operations. The more specific objectives of a cycle count program are identifying process problems and correcting on-hand balances. Let's discuss these in a little more detail.

Cycle counting ultimate objective.

> Achieve excellence in customer service and optimize the effectiveness of internal operations.

Specific Objectives

> Identify process problems.
>> Used to focus process improvement efforts.
>
> Correct on-hand balances.
>> Used to catch and correct errors before they impact operations.

Identifying process problems.

This is the most publicized objective — often depicted as the sole objective — of a cycle count program. The idea here is to determine root causes for each variance encountered during the cycle counting process, and then use root cause analysis to focus process improvement efforts. This brings up the commonly used phrase that a "cycle counting program should be self-eliminating," in that by improving processes to eliminate the root causes of errors you will ultimately increase accuracy to a point where cycle counting is no longer necessary. Don't feel bad if you don't get to this point as it's near impossible. However, a successful cycle counting program combined with a focus on continuous improvement should result in gradually reducing the frequency of counts.

Basic root cause analysis entails creating root cause categories and assigning variances to the categories over a period of time, then using this measurement to rank the root cause categories by number of occurrences. The resulting ranking is then used to focus process improvement efforts. You will usually start with higher level categories such as shipping error, receiving error, stocking error, production reporting error, or cycle counting error (we'll discuss this later), and then take the highest ranking categories and break them down further such as breaking down stocking errors into putaway error wrong item number, putaway error wrong location, putaway error wrong quantity, replenishment error wrong item number, replenishment error wrong location, replenishment error wrong quantity, location consolidation error, miscellaneous transaction error. Getting down to this level of detail ensures that solutions are designed around real problems not perceived problems. I should also note that although you should focus most efforts on the largest sources of errors, it doesn't mean that you should completely ignore the less frequent errors while you're resolving these higher ranked issues. Or, that you must wait until you have several months of data before you start implementing process improvements. You may find that major problems are clearly identified during the first couple of days of counting or that several lower ranked categories can be resolved with very simple solutions that can be implemented quickly. It serves no purpose to delay making needed improvements just to satisfy the framework of a "formal" evaluation process. You may also find that the most frequent errors are not necessarily the ones causing the biggest problems. An example would be if you have frequent order picking errors that result in rather small variances and less frequent receiving errors that result in much larger variances, ultimately having a more significant negative impact on operations than the picking errors. Again, don't let a formal quality evaluation process become a constraint to process improvement.

Correcting on-hand balances.

While identifying and correcting process problems should be the primary purpose of a cycle counting program, it's negligent to understate the secondary benefits of using a cycle count program to identify errors and correct on-hand balances. There are cycle counting purists that would scoff at this statement and warn anyone making a similar claim that they are dooming their soul to cycle counting hell. Basically they believe that most people are inherently stupid, short-sighted, and lazy, and that acknowledging the benefits of using a cycle count program to correct on-hand balances will result in a complete collapse of root cause analysis and process improvement efforts. Though I don't completely disagree with them, I do feel that it's a disservice to add "ignorant" to this depiction, which is exactly what you do when you choose to not provide valuable information on the basis that decision makers are not smart enough or do not have the self-discipline to effectively use it. So **YES**, there are benefits to using cycle counting to correct errors before they affect operations, and **NO**, it should not be the primary purpose of your cycle count program. That's not so hard is it?

Using a cycle count program to identify errors and correct on-hand balances is similar to the use of any checking process. It helps you to fix errors before they cause a problem, thus providing the benefits of a higher level of accuracy than could be achieved without it. Errors still occur even under very well-designed processes. Unless you have some type of count verification process in place (such as a cycle count program), these errors will eventually result in a short shipment to a customer or a production stoppage. A more specific use of a cycle count program to correct on-hand balances would be to use frequent counts (daily or weekly) of a specific critical raw material to compensate for inaccuracy related to scrap or manufacturing process inconsistencies. Uh oh, here come the do-it-right-the-first-time fanatics arguing, "Fix the problem, not the symptom!" So again I'll mention that in the real world (especially in manufacturing processes) it may be unrealistic to expect 100 percent accuracy in reporting materials usage (bulk materials in particular). Your choices may be to either cripple manufacturing with an impractical materials reporting process, unrealistically expect perfection and always be disappointed, or use frequent counts to achieve overall business objectives. Make your choice.

The standard cycle count program

The following describes what I call "the standard cycle count program"; later in the chapter I will discuss other counting options along with the benefits and shortcomings of each method.

The basic logic of a standard cycle count program is that you randomly count items based upon count frequencies assigned via ABC classification. Counts are usually performed each day during a time window in which transactions are restricted or otherwise controlled. Variances are investigated for root cause and adjustments are made.

Setting count frequencies.
In the standard cycle count program, count frequencies are assigned to SKUs by ABC classifications. ABC classifications are used to rank SKUs based upon a specific driver, such as velocity, units sold/consumed, dollars sold/consumed, or average inventory investment. ABC by velocity (also called ABC by activity, transaction frequency, times sold, or times consumed) ranks SKUs by the frequency of transactions (usually limited to outbound transactions and manufacturing usage transactions), and is generally considered the best driver to use for determining cycle count frequencies. The logic here is the more frequent the transactions, the more likely an error will occur. ABC by units sold/consumed can also be an effective means of setting count frequencies when SKUs have similar units-per-transaction characteristics. However, units sold/consumed does not necessarily follow the same pattern as velocity. ABC classification by dollars sold/consumed or average inventory investment are less effective, especially if you have a diverse SKU base of products with significantly different costs. Though the accountants may appreciate that you are counting your higher cost items more frequently, it does not necessarily provide the best results for improving operations.

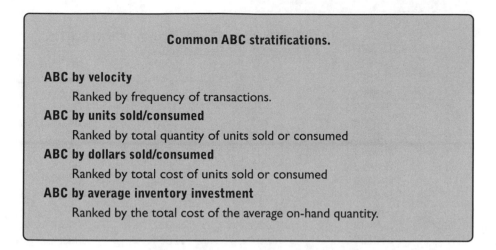

Common ABC stratifications.

ABC by velocity

Ranked by frequency of transactions.

ABC by units sold/consumed

Ranked by total quantity of units sold or consumed

ABC by dollars sold/consumed

Ranked by total cost of units sold or consumed

ABC by average inventory investment

Ranked by the total cost of the average on-hand quantity.

In most operations a small number of SKUs will account for a significant portion of the activity, thus the nature of an ABC stratification is that significantly fewer SKUs are in the "A" bucket than the "B" bucket and fewer SKUs are in the "B" bucket than the "C" bucket.

In the following example, the company has 3,700 SKUs; 200 SKUs account for 50 percent of the transactions with another 500 accounting for 30 percent. If you combine A and B items you now have 700 SKUs (approximately 19 percent of the SKUs) accounting for 80 percent of the activity. This comes pretty close to falling in line with the famed "Pareto Principle" also known as the "80/20 rule," which basically states that a small number of causes are responsible for a great number of effects. In this case the causes are SKUs and the effects are transactions. While it doesn't always come to 80/20, you will find that the Pareto Principle applies to the SKU bases of most businesses. The purpose of applying this principle is to focus efforts where you can expect the most benefits. ABC by velocity stratification is often used to focus efforts related to cycle counting, SKU location slotting for order picking efficiencies, and fill rate requirements for customer service.

Figure 4A. Example of ABC breakdown.

ABC	Transactions	SKUs
A	50%	200
B	30%	500
C	20%	3000

	SKU	Total Annual Transactions	Cumulative Transactions	Percentage of Total
1	546074	537	537	16.3%
2	546373	431	968	29.4%
3	546061	402	1370	41.6%
4	546360	378	1748	53.1%
5	546048	373	2121	64.5%
6	546347	275	2396	72.8%
7	546113	153	2549	77.5%
8	546412	82	2631	80.0%
9	546126	76	2707	82.3%
10	546425	73	2780	84.5%
11	546139	64	2844	86.4%
12	546438	63	2907	88.4%
13	546308	57	2964	90.1%
14	546035	50	3014	91.6%
15	546334	47	3061	93.0%
16	546022	42	3103	94.3%
17	546321	39	3142	95.5%
18	546295	24	3166	96.2%
19	546087	20	3186	96.8%
20	546386	17	3203	97.4%
21	546282	17	3220	97.9%
22	546269	13	3233	98.3%
23	546191	8	3241	98.5%
24	546152	8	3249	98.8%
25	546217	7	3256	99.0%
26	546178	6	3262	99.1%
27	546100	6	3268	99.3%
28	546451	5	3273	99.5%
29	546204	5	3278	99.6%
30	546165	5	3283	99.8%
31	546399	3	3286	99.9%
32	546464	2	3288	99.9%
33	546230	2	3290	100.0%
34	546256	0	3290	100.0%
35	546243	0	3290	100.0%

Figure 4B. Here you can see an example of how ABC is calculated. Total transactions are calculated for each SKU and then the report is sorted by total transactions in descending order. A cumulative transaction column is added. The cumulative number is divided by the total transactions (3290) to calculate a cumulative percentage of total transactions. Now you can assign ABC based upon this cumulative percentage. In this example, eight SKUs represent 80 percent of the total transactions.

The method for actually associating an ABC by velocity stratification to each SKU requires that you determine the total number of transactions for each SKU over a specific period of time (often a year, however, the time frame can vary based upon product life cycles and seasonality). You then sort the SKUs by total number of transactions in descending order, creating a running total of cumulative transactions for each line. In figure 4B, if you choose to associate "A" with the items that accounted for the top 50 percent of transactions, you would end up with the first four items in the "A" category.

While my original example (figure 4A) set the level for "A" to represent SKUs that account for 50 percent of transactions and "B" items to account for 30 percent, there is no standard for setting ABC. You should apply the percentages that best fit your environment. You also do not need to limit yourself to only three rankings (A-B-C), you can choose to expand to ABCDEF or stick with just ABC but create subgroups within each ranking such as AA, AB, AC, BA, BB, BC, CA, CB, CC. When you look back at figure 4B, you can see that having "C" items represent the bottom 20% of your SKUs would result in items with 76 transactions and zero transactions ending up in the same category. You may choose to expand ABC to ABCDEF and have breaks at 50%, 75%, 95%, 98%, 99.9% and 100% respectively to make the categories more specific.

Once you've determined the ABC stratification, you need to determine the count frequency you want to associate with each ranking. In a standard cycle counting program you would count your "A" items more frequently than your "B" items and so on. This again reflects the logic that the more frequent the transactions, the more likely the errors, therefore the more frequent the counts. There are no standards as to the count frequencies. One company may choose to count "A" items ten times per year, "B" items five times per year, and "C" items two times per year, while another company may choose three/two/one or twenty/ten/five. The count frequency should be relative to the frequencies of errors and the impact of the errors on operations. As accuracy improves, cycle count frequency should decrease. When setting the count frequency, there needs to be strong consideration as to the availability of resources to conduct the counts, the time window in which the counts must be completed, as well as the limitations of resources available to investigate the variances.

Now comes the time when you go to your IS department and tell them that you want the cycle count program to "randomly" select items to be counted each day based upon these count frequencies. This is the point where the IS person has an opportunity to laugh at you, pointing out that computer programs function logically not randomly, and that if you can "logically" describe what type of "random" you want, he would be happy to do it for you. Now before you walk away muttering "geek," "spaz," and other well-deserved stereotypes under your breath, you should realize that the IS person is correct; not only do computers not function randomly, you do not really want them to. There are also some other pieces of information necessary, such as the numbers of days per year that you will conduct counts, and any limitations on the number of counts that can be performed on any given day.

Though most cycle counting programs that come with packaged software are based upon this "standard cycle counting" model, you will find that it's usually not as simple as just stating how many times per year you want each classification to be counted. Let me outline some of the ways software handles this.

Generally your inventory system will have a record for each SKU (or SKU/location combination) that contains fields for [Last Count Date], [Cycle Count Period], and [Next Count Date]. Last Count Date is updated whenever the item is on a cycle count that has been completed. Cycle Count Period is often represented as the number of days between counts. To determine the number of days to enter here, you need to know how your software uses these days, such as, is it based on working days (there would have to be a working days calendar to support this) or actual calendar days? If it is working days and your calendar is set for 250 working days per year, you would divide 250 by your cycle count frequency (times per year) to determine the number to enter here. The system will then use this number to calculate the Next Count Date, which is ultimately used to select the items for your cycle count.

Some systems may require you to initially populate Last Count Date and Cycle Count Period manually prior to initiating the cycle count program. To do this you need to calculate dates for each SKU in a manner that spreads your SKUs within each ABC classification, evenly over the dates that fall within the Cycle Count Period for that group. This will result in next count dates being calculated that have fairly consistent numbers of counts on each date. One problem with this methodology is that all of the count frequency data is maintained individually on each SKU; if you decide to change the count frequency or ABC classification, or when SKUs move from one ABC classification to another due to changes in activity levels, the corresponding count data does not change. You would be forced to manage this manually. Another problem occurs when there are disruptions to the cycle count program such as not being able to complete counts one day, or changes to the work schedule such as closing down for a special event. This will usually result in significant variations in the number of counts released on a day-to-day basis. Some programs may allow you to set limits on the number of SKUs that are released for counting on any given day. These systems will use logic that looks at any SKUs with a [Next Count Date] less than or equal to the current date and release SKUs based on the preset count limitation. If using this type of system you need to keep track of your backlog (how many counts behind you are) and determine how the program is prioritizing which SKUs make the release. While you would think that the program would prioritize by Next Count Date, you shouldn't assume this to be true.

Other systems may have batch programs that will populate the Last Count Date and Cycle Count Period based upon user specified criteria. This is much better, as it should allow you to update the cycle count period on all SKUs after

ABC generation programs are run or after changes are made to cycle count frequencies. Always check your systems documentation to make sure you understand the logic it is using prior to running these programs.

More sophisticated systems may be doing all of this behind the scenes based upon initial system setup parameters. You may not even see Last Count Date, Cycle Count Period, or Next Count Date on any screens you use to maintain inventory records, though most cycle counting programs are still using this same base logic.

In my experience, most cycle counting programs are fairly unsophisticated when it comes to managing cycle count frequency and may require some modifications, such as creating batch programs that will populate the cycle counting fields or programming to limit and control the number of counts released each day.

Running the standard cycle count program

Once the initial setup is complete, you're ready to run the cycle count release program. One of the first things you will see in the software documentation (and probably heard about from the software vendor) is that the cycle count program will "freeze" inventory balances. Whoa, that sounds pretty sophisticated doesn't it? You must have bought a good system if it can "freeze" inventory balances for your cycle counting. This means that no one can perform any inventory transactions while you're conducting your counts, right? Well, I hate to burst your bubble, but that's probably not what the system is doing (also you should have realized by now that whenever I say "right?" you can assume the following statement will contradict the prior one). More likely it's just taking a snapshot of current on-hand balances and copying these quantities to the file that is used for cycle counting. The term the software vendor should be using is "copy" not "freeze," because freeze is misleading. This doesn't mean that the software vendor sacrificed functionality by copying instead of really freezing inventory. In fact, you probably do not want to freeze inventory as it brings up a whole lot of additional implications.

> Note: this is the most common method I've seen for handling quantities in a cycle count program. There are some software packages out there that do actually freeze balances, making them off limits for any activities, and there are others that neither copy nor freeze the on-hand balance at the initiation of the cycle count sheet.

OK, so the inventory balances are copied to the cycle count file but there is nothing preventing people from performing transactions against these SKUs. This means that you need to either have a process in place to prevent activities on these items or to track activities on these items. It also means that all transactions associated with any product movement that has already occurred must be completed prior to running the cycle count release program. In an ideal environment you would stop all material movement activities (receiving, putaway, picking, replenishment, manufacturing), make sure all transactions are completed, and then run the cycle count release program. You would then perform all counts, recounts, approvals, and updates prior to letting activities resume. Actually many operations are able to operate in this ideal environment by conducting cycle counts during off hours such as in the evening, first thing in the morning, or on weekends. I address issues related to non-ideal count situations later.

Once you've released the cycle count, you will either print count sheets, print count tags, or make the count data available to portable terminals. For the purposes of the standard cycle count program we'll assume that you will print count sheets. Count tags are rarely used in cycle count programs and will be discussed in the chapter on physical inventories. Using portable terminals will be discussed later. When printing the count sheets you may have some options as to how you want the information to display and sort. If you are using a locator system, you will most likely print the count sheets in location sequence. You may also have the option of printing or excluding the current on-hand balance on the count sheet. Excluding the quantity is known as performing a "blind count." I'll discuss the advantages and disadvantages of blind counting later.

The cycle counters will take the count sheets that display location and SKU, and physically count each SKU/location combination on the sheets, writing the count in the appropriate space.

Next the cycle counters (or a data entry clerk) will enter the counts into the cycle count program. Your cycle count program should display the item/location records in the same sequence as was printed on the count sheet. It's generally just a matter of entering the cycle count number or name (assigned at generation of the cycle count), and then entering each quantity counted.

At this point most systems will allow you to run a variance report to be used for recounts. This report is usually sorted that same way the original count sheets were sorted. Generally each variance is recounted, usually by different cycle counter, and often by a higher-level counter such as a group leader or cycle count administrator. Any variances where a different quantity is counted during the recount process will require editing the quantity in the cycle count program. Some programs (though very few) may even have a separate place to enter the recount into the system.

Next, the cycle count administrator will run another variance report. This report may be sequenced differently than the earlier variance report, such as sorting by item number or dollar variance. You may also have options to only print variances larger than a specific amount or percentage, such as variances greater than $20 or greater than 5 percent of on-hand. The cycle count administrator will use this variance report to investigate discrepancies to determine root cause, and ultimately approve or delete the count sheet. The cycle count administrator may also change counts should he determine that both counts were incorrect or that there was a data entry error on the recount edit.

It's generally a good idea to run a final variance report just prior to approving and completing the cycle count. If the cycle count administrator made a data entry error when editing specific counts, they should catch them on the final variance report. Finally the update is run. This program will usually compare the approved count quantity with the original frozen/copied on-hand balance and generate an inventory adjustment for the difference, while at the same time updating the last count date and possibly the next count date.

Standard Cycle Count Program

Assign count frequency by ABC stratification.

"A" items counted more frequently than "B" and so on.

Initial count is often a "blind count".

Variances are recounted (sometimes tolerances are used to determine which variances are recounted).

Variances are investigated (again, tolerances are sometimes used).

Count sheet is approved (adjustments made).

Well there you go, that is the "standard cycle count program." You may find that your software works very similarly to this, and that this methodology is a good fit for your operation. If you're getting the feeling that I'm about to trash the standard cycle count program, that's not entirely the case. The standard cycle count program works, and many companies have had significant success using this system. What I am going to do is to point out some of the shortcomings of the standard cycle count program, and show that this is not the only way to run a cycle count. I'll detail many different options — some are slight variations while others take a very different direction. It's not that I don't like the standard cycle count program, but rather I don't believe in one-size-fits-all solutions. The standard system may be the best system for you; then again it may not be. I will bring up some much simpler solutions as well as some very complex ones. Some of the ideas that I'm going to discuss are highly unlikely to apply to your operation, some of them I would probably classify as "stupid ideas" (even though they are my ideas). Consider this more or less a brainstorming session that's designed to inspire creative thinking and break away from the barriers of conventional wisdom and textbook standardized practices. There's no doubt that the following sections will, to some extent, add confusion to your cycle count program decision-making process. For any of you who fall into that stupid, shortsighted, and lazy category that want to add ignorant to their repertoire, feel free to skip the following sections. Here we go.

So what's wrong with the standard cycle count program?

Let's start with productivity. Large high-transaction operations will go to great lengths to analyze item profiles and order profiles to determine the optimum storage medium and optimum location slotting to get the highest levels of productivity out of their workforce. This will go as far as finding products that are likely to be picked on the same order and slotting them next to each other to reduce travel times. They then implement a standard cycle counting system that "randomly" picks SKUs and sends cycle counters all over the warehouse to count product. Yes, I know that you print the count sheet in location sequence, but you still have products from every corner of the warehouse counted every day. Just think, if you could get customers to order products in specific groupings such that you could pick all orders out of one small area of the warehouse one day, and the next day's orders would all come from another small area of the warehouse, and so on. Wouldn't that be great for productivity? If only you could get your customers to cooperate. Meanwhile you have a cycle counting program that is completely controlled internally and it never occurs to you to consider productivity in the system design? For some reason, productivity considerations that are critical to all other process improvement efforts are completely ignored when it comes to cycle counting. Operations are constantly struggling with limited resources. Generally the frequency of counts is limited by the availability of resources to perform the counts. Planning a cycle count program that takes into account productivity may allow you to perform more counts with the same resources. Does this sound like it would be a plus for your overall accuracy?

Now let's see if we can to beat up on the logic of using ABC stratifications for count frequency. Using ABC to determine count frequency, assumes that SKUs with the greatest activity would also be the ones most likely to have errors, and therefore should be counted more frequently. Sounds logical, doesn't it? OK, I agree that this may be sound logic, however, I think that it may not always be that simple. ABC doesn't take into account the characteristics of the specific SKUs. As was discussed in the environmental factors section, some SKUs will be more prone to errors based upon their inventory characteristics (bulk materials, small parts), their packaging, and their storage methods. You will also find that certain types of inventory used in manufacturing are more prone to error as a result of the manufacturing process. In addition ABC doesn't consider the impact of the errors on operations. Certain key raw materials may shut down a production line. Shortages on SKUs with long lead times will likely be more serious than SKUs with short lead times.

I'd also like to run through a scenario of a high-volume mail-order fulfillment operation. This operation has 20,000 SKUs and ships thousands of orders each day. The average pick quantity per line is one or two pieces and the most frequent root cause of errors is order-picking errors. The result is that they have a lot of variances, however the variances are generally only a couple of pieces plus or minus. Now let's look at their SKU breakdown, which tends to follow the 80/20 rule pretty close. They have very fast movers that usually have large inventories, frequent receipts, and ample safety stocks (you don't want to run out of an "A" item in the fulfillment business). They then have a lot of very slow movers that they may only stock one or two pieces at a time. In this case, even though they are likely to have more variances on the fast movers, the fact is that even multiple variances on a single SKU will generally net out to only a variance of one or two pieces. With the larger inventories and safety stocks on these items it's unlikely that your inventory will ever get low enough to allow these small variances to affect a customer shipment, and, even if it does, there is almost certainly more already in the pipeline (probably arriving at your dock the same day). Whereas a one or two piece shortage on a very slow moving SKU will almost certainly result in a backorder, and, it's unlikely that there will already be more inventory in the pipeline, meaning the backorder will remain in effect for the entire lead time period.

Also, from a productivity standpoint, "A" items will generally have significantly more inventory, making them more time consuming to count. You may be able to count ten or twenty "C" items in the time it takes to count one "A" item. This brings me to my next point; ABC doesn't take into account the difficulty of counting a specific SKU. Relax! I'm not suggesting that you don't count something just because it's difficult. What I am suggesting is that you may not want to count these difficult items as often. Let's use a desktop computer assembly operation as an example. In addition to floppy drives, hard drives, motherboards, CPUs, video cards, sound cards, memory, and cases, they have two or three different size machine screws used to assemble the computers. These screws are purchased in bulk and are stored in reserve storage as well as at several workstations. You have a counting scale that is used to count them, however the process is still time consuming and the scale count is not 100 percent accurate. They're very low cost, and a smart material planner would probably already have a comfortable safety stock on them. Well, let's put that all together. They're difficult to count and normal variances are unlikely to cause a problem. Do you really need to count these as often as the other components? Remember, since you are probably constrained by limited resources, you'll want to make sure that you are getting the most bang for your buck.

Are you confused yet? Here's a little more. The standard cycle counting program doesn't handle lost inventory well. Basically, a standard cycle count program sends counters to where the inventory is supposed to be. If it's not there you need another process in place to find it. While you may go to a location that has something in it that's not supposed to be there, you won't know that under a standard cycle count program. If lost inventory is a problem in your operation, you will need some type of a location audit system in place in addition to the cycle count program. Also, the design of most cycle counting software forces you to either find the inventory immediately, or deduct it through the count sheet approval process. This can create havoc with planning systems as large quantities of inventory are deducted one day and then appear back in the system a couple of days later when they are found. I'll talk more about this later.

And one more thing; the standard cycle counting process rarely utilized transaction-by-exception techniques. You should expect that when you perform a cycle count, the majority of your items will match the system count. If so, what is the point of writing down the quantity and then entering it into the cycle count program? This only adds an unnecessary opportunity for error. Transaction-by-exception would allow that you only enter variances, and treat "good counts" as a simple confirmation step. This assumes that you are not performing blind counts.

This pretty much closes the "what's wrong with the standard cycle counting program" section. I'd like to emphasize that I'm not saying that the standard cycle counting program is wrong for you. Rather, that it may not be the most effective solution for your environment.

> **What's wrong with the standard cycle count methodology?**
>
> Doesn't take productivity into account.
>
> ABC may not be the most effective means of determining count frequency.
>
> Doesn't handle lost inventory well.
>
> Doesn't take advantage of transaction-by-exception techniques.

Cycle count options

As I said before, this should be treated as a brainstorming session where I will list possible options and give some insights as to their advantages and disadvantages. As you are considering options you should be thinking about the following: Why are you counting? What is the nature of variances? What is the impact of variances? When is the best time to count a specific item? Will productivity gains with a specific method actually make the count program more effective?

Event-triggered counting methods.
- Prior to reorder point.
- Prior to receipt.
- After Receipt.
- Prior to production run.
- After production run.
- Prior to planned shipment.
- After shipment.
- After any transaction.
- When planned order is generated.
- When demand exists.
- When allocated.
- Zero on hand.

Other counting methods.
- Based on lead-time.
- By family, commodity, or other inventory characteristic.
- By physical storage locations.
- Periodic physical inventories.
- Forced counts.
- Opportunity counts and task interleaving.

Combining methods.
- Combining methods to optimize your cycle count process.

Event-triggered counting methods

These initiate cycle counts when certain events occur. You'll find that event-triggered counting methods sometimes inherently follow similar logic to ABC counting, since events may occur more frequently with "A" items. Event-triggered methods also consider the correlation of events to counting productivity and error impact.

Prior to reorder point.

In a reorder point system, you would simply calculate a "pre-reorder point quantity" by using the standard reorder point calculation and adding a predetermined number of days to the lead-time input. The logic here is that inventory is at a reasonably low level (productivity gain) and that a shortage identified at this point may still allow time to get the needed materials in on time, while an overage identified at this point will prevent you from ordering inventory that you do not yet need. You may also find that your ordering patterns naturally result in a count frequency that meets your objectives.

Prior to receipt.

This would follow the same count frequency as the previous, however you would trigger the count by an expected receipt date (usually one or two days prior to expected receipt). This is primarily a productivity-focused method as you would be performing counts while inventory is at its lowest levels. It's extremely unlikely that variances found at this point will give you time to react from a planning standpoint. In fact, any moderate to significant negative variances would likely turn up prior to this point as a shortage to a production or shipping order.

After receipt.

Not very productive since inventory would be at its highest point. The only reason I would suggest this is if you have had significant receipt errors.

Prior to production run.

This would set a specific number of days prior to an expected production run to count inventory related to the production run. For the end item, any variance found here might allow you to adjust the production run to compensate (plus or minus). For the components and raw materials, it may give you time to adjust, but much less likely. It should at least prevent going through a machine setup if there is not adequate inventory. I think this is a better method for the end item than the components.

After production run.

I really like this option in certain manufacturing environments. Generally, in manufacturing environments, the manufacturing process and production reporting tend to be the most significant sources of inventory problems. Counting both finished goods and components/raw materials after the production run will catch production reporting errors and make sure inventory is accurate to facilitate planning the next production run. Components and raw materials should be at fairly low levels, aiding in productivity.

Prior to planned shipment.

This is an unlikely choice, but I thought I would mention it anyway. This will prevent you from waiting until the last minute before you realize you have a shortage; however, it is probably still too late to compensate for a shortage. This may be an option when you are a custom manufacturer and have a tolerance policy where you can produce and ship plus or minus a certain percentage. You may find in the count that you are a little over, allowing you to ship the extra quantity rather than getting stuck with it.

After shipment.

Also an unlikely scenario, however, it may be applicable to specific slow-moving items.

After any transaction.

Similar to after shipment. This could be an option for that very slow-moving inventory you have. After initially counting slow-moving product you may decide to set this parameter to make sure you don't waste your time counting it again if nothing has happened to it.

When a planned order is generated.

Planned orders are generated in MRP and DRP systems. This would be similar to counting at reorder point.

When demand exists.

This would be for components and raw materials or finished goods sold in large quantities where demand would generally result in a production order or purchase order. This allows you to make sure inventory is correct prior to the planning process.

When allocated.

This would be similar to counting components and raw materials prior to a production run or counting finished goods prior to a shipment. This assumes that allocations occur at least one day prior to actual need.

Zero on hand.

This is actually a fairly popular auxiliary count method (used in addition to some other more comprehensive method). This method provides high productivity since there should be nothing to count. Obviously you will not be identifying shortages on a zero-on-hand count. This is also very useful when phasing out a model to find out if you have any more prior to removing from catalog.

Other methods

Based on lead-time.

This focuses on the impact of variances and would generally be used as a factor combined with other factors (such as ABC) to determine count frequency. This is especially valid if you have some inventory that has extremely long lead-times, such as from overseas manufacturers. There's no doubt that a significant shortage on one of these items can have a major impact on the business.

By family, commodity, or other inventory characteristic.

This actually consists of a couple of methods. First would be to prioritize counts and set count frequencies based upon any logical inventory characteristic. You may determine that a specific product group is more prone to error and therefore decide to count that group more frequently. In addition, you may find that certain product groups are more critical to operations, or that the magnitude of the errors on specific product groups are larger than on others. This would also include using inventory characteristics to schedule less frequent counts of difficult to count product groups. The other part of the method is, that in addition to using these characteristics to set count frequencies, you may also want to schedule product groups to be released together on the same count sheet. This would make sense when there are inventory characteristics that require special methods of counting, such as grouping items that require scale counts, grouping items that require special material handling equipment, or grouping items that have unique units of measure such as linear feet, cubic feet, gallons, or pounds.

By physical storage locations.

For those of you that thought this was getting too complicated, here is the ultimate in simplicity. Cycle counting by physical storage area is essentially conducting a wall-to-wall physical inventory a little bit at a time. You simply determine how much you want to count each day and start at one end of the warehouse. Depending upon the operation, you may choose to count one aisle a day, a couple of sections a day, or a couple of shelves a day. The next day's count will start where the previous day's count ended. You achieve high productivity because you virtually eliminate any travel time between counts, and the fact that you are counting everything in a location helps to find lost product, thus eliminating the need for additional location audits. This does not necessarily mean that everything will have the same count frequency. If you logically slot your product for physical storage (such as designated areas for fast-moving product, designated areas for certain product groups, etc.) you can choose to count some physical areas more frequently than others. Despite the very simplistic logic behind this method, I find it very effective in many environments, especially small to mid-sized operations where the product is relatively easy to count. The elimination of travel time allows you to count significantly more inventory with the same resources, which ultimately allows you to be more effective, even though you are not applying a highly scientific approach to count frequencies.

Periodic physical inventories.

This is actually an alternative to a cycle count and is usually only an option in fairly small operations. Examples of this would be coming in once a month on a Saturday and conducting a wall-to-wall physical inventory, or dividing the facility into sections and designating one day each week where an entire section is counted (these sections would be larger than that described in the "cycle counting by physical storage area"). For periodic physical inventories to be effective, you need a small enough operation such that all inventory can be counted, investigated, and adjusted within a short time frame. For these operations, periodic physical inventories can prove to be just as effective as a cycle count program. The primary reason you would choose this over a cycle count program is it does not disrupt daily operations by requiring daily resources and daily transaction controls.

Forced counts.

Forced counts are a supplemental part of most counting programs. The forced count sheet contains items that have been identified through other processes as likely having variances. Examples would be items involved in a shipping error (not caught internally), items identified through a built-in check such as a variance in a receipt/invoice matching process, items that couldn't be adjusted on a previous regular count sheet due to questionable transaction timing, items that are part of a control group count, other items on a production order where a reporting problem is suspected, or similar items to an item that had a variance on a regular count sheet. Forced counts may be part of the daily cycle counting routine or may be handled as individual counts whenever the need is identified.

Opportunity counts and task interleaving.

This is a productivity-focused methodology that is generally only used in environments where workers' activities are controlled via portable radio frequency terminals. You still require some other logic to set count frequencies and then coordinate this with daily tasks to have a warehouse worker perform the count while they are already at the location doing another task. An example would be that you use standard ABC logic to set count frequencies. When an item comes up for count release, rather than releasing a count sheet, the item goes into a queue and waits until an unrelated task (order picking, putaway, replenishment) comes up for that item/location combination. When the warehouse worker is instructed to perform the task, the terminal will also inform them to verify the count. I have mixed feelings about this methodology. I like the productivity opportunity here as it completely eliminates travel time associated with cycle counting. However, I have concerns about the disruption to the primary task and the coordination of dealing with variances. If a worker is picking an order and the computer suddenly instructs them to perform a cycle count it takes focus off of the order picking process, opening up an opportunity for error. It can also slow down the order picking process. Then there's the issue of how to handle variances. Remember, this is occurring during normal operations and there are no special transactional controls in place. Your choices may be to allow the variance to immediately make an adjustment (danger! danger! danger!), require that someone is immediately available to investigate variances (probably negates productivity gains), or use the output to confirm matching counts and then automatically submit variances for a more conventional cycle counting process (this is likely your best bet). While the last option sounds like a duplication of effort, it actually isn't since it only applies to counts that resulted in variances. This means that the more conventional cycle counting process would actually start at the recount step.

Combining count logic

This is where things start to get interesting. The various methods for determining what to count and when, detailed above, are not mutually exclusive. The real art comes in mixing various methods to come up with a truly unique method — or set of methods — that provides the best results for your unique operation. Let me outline a couple of examples:

Company #1.

We're going to start with a standard cycle counting program and add a series of modifications to increase productivity and effectiveness. We're going to maintain the basic logic that "A" items get counted more frequently than "B" items and so on, but we're going to add logic to time the counts of "A" and "B" items to coincide with their lowest inventory levels (one week prior to receipt). We're also going to add a category "D" for the extremely slow movers that will be counted only after another inventory transaction has occurred. In addition we're going to create a series of override codes that allow us to hard code the count frequencies of specific items due to their specific characteristics (some low-cost, difficult-to-count items will only be counted twice per year, and some critical items that are highly prone to error will be counted twelve times per year, regardless of ABC classification). Here's the information we're going to need to do this:

The Data.

    ABC classification by velocity.

    Cycle count period by ABC (in calendar days).

    Override code.

    Cycle count period by override code.

    Last count date (on each item).

    Next count date (calculated).

    Last activity date (based upon receipt, sale, or inventory movement transactions).

    Next scheduled receipt date.

The programs.

I've attempted to describe the programs in a way that follows programming logic, but is not too confusing to nonprogrammers. This is not actual programming syntax, however it should give nonprogrammers insights into how the program will actually work, and how they should communicate their needs to programmers.

Batch program to run each night to update next count date based upon ABC count frequency or Override count frequency. Basic logic would be:

> **IF** the item has an override code,
>
> **THEN** use the [Override Cycle Count Period]
>
> **ELSE** use the [ABC Cycle Count Period]
>
> [Cycle Count Period] plus [Last Count Date] equals [Next Count Date].

The cycle count release program would use the following logic:

> **IF** item has an override code
>
> > **AND** [Next Count Date] is less than or equal to Today
>
> **OR IF** [ABC] is equal to "A" or "B"
>
> > **AND** [Next Count Date] is less than or equal to Today
> >
> > **AND** [Next Scheduled Receipt Date] is greater than or equal to Today.
> >
> > **AND** [Next Scheduled Receipt Date] is less than or equal to Today plus 7
>
> **OR IF** [ABC] is equal to "C"
>
> > **AND** [Next Count Date] is less than or equal to Today
>
> **OR IF** ABC is equal to "D"
>
> > **AND** [Next Count Date] is less than or equal to Today
> >
> > **AND** [Last Activity Date] is greater than or equal to [Last Count Date]
>
> **THEN** release for count,
>
> **ELSE** do not release for count.

Company #2.

We're going to do basically the same thing as company #1, with the exception that any C or D items with quantity on hand less than 25 will not be released to the count sheet, but rather will be released to a queue. The order pickers are operating from RF terminals and every pick request checks the queue for a match. If it finds a match, it requests that the order picker counts the location after the pick. The idea is that you gain productivity through the task interleaving, and since the items are relatively slow-moving and have small quantities, you are not significantly slowing down the picking operation and should be able to easily resolve discrepancies.

Company #3.
Company #3 is a large distribution and manufacturing operation. The facility has several distinct physical storage areas. SKUs are exclusive to a specific storage area. Storage area A is used for finished goods that are produced and shipped in full pallet load quantities only. Storage area B is for finished goods that are stored and shipped in case or broken case quantities. Storage area C is for raw materials that are stored in bulk, including rolls of steel and containers of plastic. Storage area D is for smaller components used in manufacturing and assembly processes. Here we've decided to cycle count storage area A by counting one complete aisle each day. Storage area B uses a conventional ABC cycle count. Storage area C has a physical inventory completed each month. And in storage area D we count the components after each production run.

I'm not suggesting that your cycle count program needs to be this complex. And please, do not set up your program to exactly match any of these scenarios, these are just examples I used to show some of the possibilities. Also, do not expect that the cycle count program that came with your software is going to be able to do any of this without modifications. As with any modification, you need to weigh the benefits of the added functionality against the costs.

Setting up and running your cycle count program

Since I already ran through the standard cycle count process, I'm not going to repeat that information here, however, I will elaborate on some of the issues previously discussed as well as introduce some additional topics. The person responsible for managing the cycle count program and approving the specific cycle counts I will refer to as the "cycle count administrator," though I don't want to infer that a specific hierarchy should be imposed, that all these responsibilities belong to one person, or that every company needs a full-time cycle count administrator. For small companies this will likely just be part of the responsibilities of a related position. I will also refer to the people performing the counts as "cycle counters." Again, I am not suggesting that you must have full-time cycle counters.

Determine count methods and count frequency.
I think I pretty much covered this. I'll again mention that you should consider the characteristics and needs of your unique operation when determining the meth-

ods to use. Small operations will likely want to stick with something fairly simple, while large complex operations may find that a complex cycle count program will be the most effective option for them.

Know your inventory system.

This is critically important for the people designing the cycle count system as well at the person(s) that will be responsible for running it. The cycle count administrator must thoroughly understand every type of transaction that can affect on-hand balances, when and where they occur, and how to identify them. This includes a thorough knowledge of production reporting, sales order processing, returns processing, receipt processing, putaway, replenishment, picking, location consolidation, outsourced services, quality rejections, scrap processing, and any other process that affects inventory. He must also have a thorough understanding of allocation systems. Allocations refer to actual demand created by sales orders or production orders against a specific item. The terminology and the actual processing that controls allocations will vary from one software system to another. Basically, a standard allocation is an aggregate quantity of demand against a specific item in a specific facility. I have heard standard allocations referred to as normal allocations, soft allocations, soft commitments, regular allocations. Standard allocations do not specify that specific units will go to specific orders. A firm allocation is an allocation against specific units within a facility such as an allocation against a specific location, lot, or serial number. Firm allocations are also referred to as specific allocations, frozen allocations, hard allocations, hard commitments, holds, or reserved inventory. Standard allocations simply show that there is actual demand, while firm allocations reserve or hold the inventory for the specific order designated. Confusion over allocations can result in substantial cycle count adjustment mistakes in operations where tight control over transactions is either not enforced or not practical.

The cycle count administrator must also have a thorough understanding of their cycle count program. This is especially important when it comes to how the cycle count program uses cycle count quantities to make inventory adjustments. Systems that copy (freeze) the on-hand quantity at cycle count generation (as described under standard cycle counting program) will usually make an adjustment equal to the difference between the actual count and the on-hand quantity at the time the count was generated. Under this scenario, if the initial on-hand quantity was 10 pieces and the count was 10 pieces the program would make no adjustment even if other transactions occurred prior to updating the cycle count. However if your system does not copy the on-hand quantity, it is probably comparing the count quantity to the current on-hand quantity. In this case if the initial quantity was 10 and the count was 10 but there was a shipment transaction for 2 pieces that occurred after the count was performed but before the cycle count was approved, your system would compare 10 (the count) to 8 (the current on-hand) and make an adjustment for +2. In this case, that is not what you wanted to happen.

Confusion over allocations and transactions, or confusion over how the cycle count program uses quantities, as well as miscounts and data entry errors, can result in a cycle count program doing more harm than good. This is not an unusual occurrence as many cycle count programs (and annual physical inventories) are plagued with "bad adjustments." So much so, that when I go into companies and conduct audits, the first thing I look for when I find a variance, is an equivalent offsetting previous cycle count or physical inventory adjustment.

In addition to this critical knowledge, the cycle count administrator should also be knowledgeable in the tools available to help in determining the sources of errors. More on this later.

Control transactions.

Transaction control is critical in cycle counting programs. For the most part this is a timing issue. Specific requirements must be set as to exactly when transactions must occur. The cycle count administrator must have absolute confidence that these requirements are being met.

In the ideal environment (I'll again mention that many companies are able to perform counts this way) there will be a specific time cutoff when all tasks that may affect inventory are stopped (often this is simply the end of the work day). There then needs to be a process in place to ensure that all transactions associated with these tasks (orders shipped, orders picked but not shipped, inventory that has been processed through receiving, materials consumed or produced in production processes, any product movement, or any miscellaneous adjustment) has been completed prior to generating the cycle count. Some systems may require batch programs to be run to update on-hand quantities; I've frequently seen this with sales order processing systems that update inventory upon generation of an invoice via a batch program run at the end of each day. Tasks that affect inventory are not to resume until the cycle count and all recounts are completed. You may be able to resume normal operations after the counts but before the final approval and update is run, provided your system copied the initial on-hand balance and that the cycle count administrator is aware that transactions are now occurring.

When controlling transactions, there must be clear delineation of inventory based upon status. In a receiving area, this would require a clear physical separation between inventory that has been received (included in on-hand balance) and inventory that has not yet been received (not included in on-hand balance). In manufacturing areas, this would require a physical separation between materials already issued to production (no longer included in on-hand balance, now part of work-in-process) and materials staged or stored and not yet issued to production (still part of on-hand balance) as well as completed items that have been reported (included in on-hand balance) and completed items that have not yet been reported (not included in on-hand balance). On the outbound side this would require a physical separation between inventory reported as shipped (no longer in inventory) and inventory that has been picked and staged but not yet deducted (still included in on-hand balance).

For the most part you want to make every effort to avoid having inventory at questionable statuses. This means if your software requires that orders must be invoiced or reported as shipped in order to relieve inventory balances, you should not pick the orders until they can be shipped. The same is true of inventory for production orders; if it's not going to be issued to production right away, do not pick it. I often see companies pick and stage sales orders or production orders several days — sometimes weeks or months — in advance. Their reasoning is usually something like: "I like to set it aside and hold it to make sure it is available when I need it" or "if I have time to pick it now, why wait until the last minute when I may not have enough time." Part of this attitude is a distrust of the inventory system to reserve inventory and the other part is an effort by a warehouse worker to be proactive and "get ahead." In either case, this creates serious problems for cycle counting, and should be avoided whenever possible. I rarely see situations where there is no other way but to stage these orders. If you don't feel you can avoid this, you should at least try to significantly limit it and put in place a process for tracking these "in limbo" orders. One method for keeping track of this would be to transfer these inventory balances to a staging location such as a machine location or a shipping location. When I say, "transfer" I am talking about an inventory transaction that moves the balances from one location to another in a location tracking system. This way the inventory balances will appear on the cycle count sheets as being in shipping or at a machine as opposed to still showing in the storage area. If this is not possible, you at least need a means for the cycle count administrator to easily identify that items on his count sheet for that day are also sitting in staged orders. Be aware that this will probably be an ongoing problem for your cycle count program and will almost certainly result in inventory errors, especially when staged orders contain small quantities of multiple SKUs.

Start with control group.

This is another one of those rare "standard practice" recommendations that I actually agree with. When you first start your cycle count program, you should select a small number of SKUs to use as a control group. The items should be chosen such that they are representative of the diversity of your inventory and processes. This would include some of each: purchased items, raw materials, components, subassemblies, finished goods, small items, large items, bulk items, fast movers, slow movers, etc. You will want to repeatedly count these over a long enough period of time to turn up most major inventory problems. How often and for how long you count them will depend primarily on the frequency of transactions. For very high transaction environments, you may count the same items every day for three to six weeks. For a lower transaction environment, you may count the items once a week for a period of several months. The objective is to quickly identify your major sources of errors. By repeatedly counting the same items, you will be able to narrow down the error to a specific time period, making it much easier to track the source.

Although identifying major root causes is generally touted as the reason for the repeated counts of a control group, I strongly recommend it for a secondary purpose; it helps to prevent you from screwing up your entire inventory before you realize you do not understand your inventory system and are not cycle counting properly. I've mentioned this before, but it's certainly worth mentioning again. Confusion over allocations and transactions, or confusion over how the cycle count program uses quantities, as well as miscounts and data entry errors can result in a cycle count program doing more harm than good. Bad adjustments are more common than most would think, and it can be a major mistake to assume that you are above making these types of errors. By limiting the cycle counting initially to a small control group, you limit the number of SKUs that you can screw up, and by counting them repeatedly, you will quickly figure out if you are doing something wrong (either that or you will be running around the facility like an idiot, blaming everyone else).

> *Starting with a control group helps to prevent you from screwing up your entire inventory before you realize you do not understand your inventory system.*

You may want to start the control group counts prior to designing your formal cycle count program by simply running a report, writing down quantities, or using screen prints, and then manually entering adjustments. This can help you get a feel for your inventory accuracy, the time involved in counting and reconciling, and the types of errors encountered. You can use this information when designing the formal count program. I still suggest continuing the control group on the formal cycle count program to test the system. I also recommend going back to a control group whenever a new cycle count administrator starts, or if you are encountering errors in the regular cycle count program that you are having a difficult time in determining the source.

Blind counts versus non-blind counts (verification counts).

A blind count usually refers to a cycle count or physical inventory count where the counter is given SKU and location information, but no quantity information. A more extreme version of a blind count occurs when the counters are given no information and must document the SKU number, location, and quantity, as they count. For the purposes of this discussion we'll limit focus to the pros and cons of including or excluding quantity information on cycle counts. The primary reason for conducting blind counts is to prevent counters from "cheating." Cheating occurs when the cycle counter chooses to use the system quantity rather than actually counting the inventory. This is most likely to occur when the cycle counter encounters a particularly difficult item to count. In addition, listing the quantity may occasionally trick honest counters into thinking the count is correct, when it is not. For example, say you have full pallet loads of materials that, depending upon the product group, will either be in quantities of 12, 16, or 18 cases per pallet. If you have a pallet of 16 cases that is incorrectly in the system as 18 cases, the cycle counter may see that the item number matches and that it is a full pallet, and the fact that the quantity 18 is on the count sheet will convince the counter that the full pallet case count is 18. While this may sound the same as cheating, it is not, because "assumptions" about units-per-pallet and units-per-case are generally accepted when counting standardized unit-loads.

The problems with blind counts are that they are more time consuming and have a much lower first-pass accuracy rate. The lower first-pass accuracy requires that you do more recounts, further increasing the resources required per count. If you haven't personally spent much time counting you may be thinking, "What's the difference? Either way you still have to count the product, don't you?" So let me explain a little further. If I am counting via a blind count sheet, I will have to be much more careful with my counts. Yes, I know this sounds like a good thing, but let's keep going. Even being careful, I find that I make a lot of mistakes and may even resort to counting everything twice to avoid getting nailed with counting errors. Now if I am conducting verification counts (where the expected quantity is listed) I will probably conduct a much more streamlined count process. I will first quickly count the item (not nearly as carefully as in the blind count) and if my quick count matches the system count, I will move on to the next item. If my quick count does not match the system count I will conduct a second, more thorough count. In addition, a variance may cause me to look behind the location for inventory that may have fallen or look more closely at the inventory to see if something is misidentified. It's very unlikely that I would do this if I did not know that the quantities didn't match (blind count). If you're concerned about the accuracy rate of a "'quick count" you have to realize that the item would already need to have a variance that exactly matches the mistake you made in the quick count. While this is possible, it is extremely unlikely. The value of a verification count is that not only does the initial count go quicker, but also that it results in less items needing to go through the formal recount step. It also opens the door to using transaction-by-exception techniques for entering the count data by only entering counts for variances. This not

only makes the data entry faster, but also more accurate, as you eliminate the possibility of miskeying a count that was initially correct.

It's probably obvious by now that I prefer verification counts to blind counts. My primary motivation for this is that I can get significantly more counting done with the same resources than if I conducted blind counts. So how do I deal with the cheating factor? This comes right back to the making accuracy expected topic. You have to monitor processes for compliance to procedures, and you have to hold employees accountable for following procedures. It's pretty easy to find out if employees are "cheating" on cycle counts; you simply take some items that would be tempting to cheat on, and make sure that the quantity does not match the system count. If the cycle counters report it as a match, they are cheating and should be disciplined. Remember that failure to follow procedures is not a mistake; it's a willful violation of company policy. To remove the "sneaky" aspect of setting up the employees, make sure that, as part of the training program, the employees are clearly informed that these types of checks will be occurring. You should also educate them that the alternative (blind counts) would make their jobs more difficult. To avoid mistakes related to verification counts, it's important to emphasize the sequence of events in the counting procedures, primarily that you must count the item first, and then match the count to the count sheet, not the other way around. These types of very simple procedural details can prove to be significant in reducing errors.

Conducting blind counts and recounting all variances is ultimately the most accurate means of cycle counting but not necessarily the most effective. The term "effective" is important here as you must weigh the advantages of counting more inventory with the risk of "cheating" or count errors. In maintaining my one-size-doesn't-fit-all position, I'll once again encourage you to look at the characteristics of your operation and make up your own mind.

Blind counts versus verification counts.

Blind counts
- Lower first pass accuracy
- More recounts
- Safest method if you recount all variances.

Non-blind counts (verification counts)
- Higher first pass accuracy
- Greater productivity.
- Risk of cheating.

Training cycle counters.

Sure, I've already covered training, however, I feel that it's important to bring it up again at key points. Cycle counters must be trained on procedures, acceptable counting methods, use of counting equipment and technologies. I've just covered the importance of something as simple as the sequence of events used to count inventory. Cycle counters must also be trained on when cases must be opened and counted versus accepting case quantities, when inventory must be moved to verify obscured inventories, and how to verify questionable items. Something not to be overlooked when training cycle counters, is instructing them on how to count. There will be more on counting methods in chapter nine.

Recounting variances.

The nature of cycle counting — primarily the large quantities often counted — makes it highly prone to errors, and a procedure that includes recounting of variances is highly recommended. Many cycle count programs have adopted tolerances to focus recount efforts. The basic logic is that if the variance is smaller than a predetermined dollar amount or percentage of on-hand, it is not recounted. Cycle count software often has built-in functionality to allow exclusion of counts within tolerance from variance reports. While there are valid reasons for using tolerances, I have to warn you that there are also a lot of problems associated with tolerances. First off, the purpose of a variance recount is to catch counting errors. You have to look at the types of variances you are experiencing and determine what your exposure is to bad counts prior to implementing tolerances. You also need to look at the potential effect of an undetected bad count. Just because a variance is less than $20 does not mean that it will not create a serious problem, such as a production interruption or irate customer. The problem with tolerances is that they are often viewed simply as a financial issue when they should be viewed as an operational issue. Tolerances are also used at various other points in the cycle counting process, such as in root cause investigation and accuracy measurement. While it may make sense to use a tolerance in one place, that does not mean that it makes sense to use it in another. For the most part, I recommend recounting all variances, especially if you are conducting blind counts. A situation where I would consider using a tolerance would include very large quantities of difficult-to-count low-cost materials that are counted by mechanical means, where the tolerance is set to correspond with the realistic accuracy of the mechanical counting method.

Recounts should not be blind counts. It's important that the person conducting the recount knows the expected inventory quantity so they are able to perform some field-level troubleshooting. This may include, opening sealed cases to verify quantities, looking for fallen product, checking for misidentified product, looking in nearby locations, etc. The person conducting the recount should — whenever possible — not be the original cycle counter as it's easy for the same person to make the same mistake on the recount. It's also common that the person conducting the recounts has a higher skill level than the initial cycle counters.

Reconciling variances.

Reconciling variances is important for two reasons. First, it is used to confirm correctness of counting and recounting prior to approving adjustments. In addition, it is used to determine root cause, which is ultimately used for process improvement. Though the reconciling process may ultimately result in an inventory adjustment, the focus should be on investigation, not execution.

There are always time constraints on the reconciling process and it is unlikely that you will always have the time to conduct a comprehensive investigation of each and every variance. This is where, once again, the issue of tolerances comes into play. Having spent a lot of time investigating variances, I have found that categorically ignoring variances based upon a tolerance can be a mistake. A very small variance may be your first exposure to a new problem, or, when further investigated, may turn out not to be a variance at all. My preference is to look at all variances and use my experience to focus investigation efforts. Reconciling variances is as much art as it is science, and its effectiveness is highly dependant upon the skill level and experience of the person conducting the investigation (generally the cycle count administrator). This person needs to develop a "feel" for the operation, which helps him to quickly determine root causes and to also identify "bad counts." This is basically developed as the result of a high level of knowledge of the operation combined with accumulated knowledge of previous errors. What the cycle count administrator is looking for when he looks at variances is to identify combinations of characteristics that point to specific root causes. A highly skilled cycle count administrator can often make a fairly accurate judgment as to root causes on a large percentage of the variances within a matter of minutes or seconds simply by looking at the variance and looking at the item history and characteristics in the computer system. OK, I admit, this judgment is basically an educated guess. However, you have to realize that there is not always hard evidence, and you do have to manage your time effectively. This means making "educated guesses" where you have a fairly high level of confidence in the accuracy of the guess, and focusing investigation efforts on variances that don't easily fit into known patterns. The reality is, that even though you will focus process improvement efforts on root causes detected during your cycle counting, you may not be able to eliminate all of these root causes. When you evaluate variances you want to determine:

Is this a known source of errors?

Is this a new source of errors?

Is this not a variance?

Once your cycle counting program has been well established, you will find that most variances fall into the category of being a known source of errors. You should make the appropriate corrections and measurement based upon the specific type of error. For variances that don't fit the profile of a known error source, you must now determine what the new error source is. This will require a full investigation of the error. The other question that needs to be asked is: Is this not a variance? Just because an item has been counted and recounted doesn't guarantee that the final count is correct. It's important for the cycle count administrator to be able to say, "this doesn't make sense; I do not believe that this is a valid variance." Obviously **something** is wrong. However, an inventory adjustment may not be the solution, it may actually create a problem. The most common situation would be that inventory was miscounted based upon incorrect identification, confusing units-of-measure, confusing storage configuration, mixed inventory, or lost inventory. The inventory may need to be recounted, straightened up, sorted, or located, but not adjusted. This is a critical part of the cycle count reconciliation process as it is the point where you prevent the cycle count from "screwing up" your inventory.

Exactly how you go about evaluating and reconciling your variances will vary from one operation to another based upon the characteristics of the inventory, the types of processing, and the investigation tools available. While the most important tool is the knowledge of the cycle count administrator, the second most important tool will likely be your transaction history file. Yes, your transaction history file is your friend; get access to it, develop a relationship with it, understand it, and protect it. Most current inventory systems maintain a transaction history file where individual transactions that affect on-hand balances are registered. The level of detail maintained and the functionality of the tools available to access it may vary as will the terminology used to describe it. It may be called an item history file, an item register, a usage file, a transaction file, or a ledger file. The most basic file will usually contain the item number, the date, the quantity, and the type (usually a transaction type code) of each transaction. More detailed files will include exact time of transaction, user id, location, related documents such as shipping order number or production order number, and even the identification of the specific program that generated the transaction.

Access to the file may be through reports or online programs. Ideally you want to access the file through a program that allows you to select various filters and possibly sort orders. Filters allow you to look at specific groups of transactions, such as transactions occurring in a specific location or specific date range, or only looking at certain types of transactions such as receipts, sales, manufacturing usage, previous cycle count adjustments, etc. The item history file gives you detail on what has reportedly happened to the item over a period of time. The term "reportedly" is key, because an inventory variance suggests that a transaction was incorrectly reported, not reported, or incorrectly executed, and thus the actual history (what really happened) differs from the reported history. A quick look at an item's history tells you the frequency of transactions, the size of transactions, and the types of transactions (manufacturing, shipping, etc.). This gives you the transaction profile of the item, which is important in focusing root cause analysis (you don't start looking through manufacturing paperwork on an item that's not used in manufacturing, you don't check receiving records on something that hasn't been received in over a year, etc.).

Transaction history programs may also provide a running on-hand balance that can be useful in narrowing down the time frame of an error that resulted in a substantial shortage. The shortage would have to have occurred after that last time the on-hand quantity was less than the variance quantity. Cycle count administrators should have extensive knowledge on the item history file and the programs used to access it. This would include knowledge of all transaction types, the programs that generate them, filtering and sorting capabilities, timing of entries into the history file (live, batch), running total calculations, and transactions that may not be included in the file. Sometimes, transaction history files do not include all transactions, or some transactions may have been deleted or purged after a specific period of time. It's important that the cycle count administrator is knowledgeable of, and included in, decisions related to this file.

Information found in transaction history files:

Item number.

Location.

Lot number.

Transaction quantity.

Transaction date/time.

Transaction type code.

Document numbers.

User ID.

Program ID.

While the transaction history file will likely be one of the first places the cycle count administrator will look when evaluating variances, there are a lot of other pieces of information that may be needed or useful. These include records related to purchase order receipts, manufacturing receipts, manufacturing usage, bills of material, location transfers, shipments, returns, rejections, previous cycle counts and physical inventories. Although there are times when you may need to access paper-based documents, it's best to try to get as much information as possible from the data in your computer system. The cycle count administrator should have access to, and have an understanding of, any programs and reports available that can provide this information. Key programs would include programs that show on-hand balances by location, open purchase orders, open production orders, open sales orders, open transfer orders, open replenishment orders, allocations, inbound quantities, outbound quantities, in-transit quantities, bill of materials, where-used, routings, costs, size, weight, packaging information, unit-of-measure information, vendor information, customer information, and planning information.

Because each operation is different and each error is different, there is not a specific sequence of events that can be used for investigating variances. Below I list some questions that you should consider while evaluating and investigating variances.

What is the size of the variance?

What are the current on-hand quantities?

When was the item last counted?

What was the result of the last count? Previous counts?

How is the item counted (manually, mechanically, case counts, pallet counts)?

What shipping activity has occurred since the last count?

What manufacturing activity has occurred since the last count?

What receiving activity has occurred since the last count?

What location transfer activity has occurred since the last count?

How does the size of the variance compare to previous transactions?

Is the item finished goods, raw material, component, or a combination?

If the item is used in production, is it prone to scrap?

If the item is used in production, what recent activity has there been on the items it is used to make?

What is the frequency of transactions (fast mover versus slow mover)?

What is the physical size of the item?

How is the item stored?

How is the item packaged?

Is it possible that the item may be misidentified?

Is the same item stocked under multiple item numbers?

Is the item part of a vendor managed inventory or consignment program?

Does the item have multiple units-of-measure?

Does the item have an unusual unit-of-measure?

Does the item have multiple storage locations?

What activities have occurred, or can occur in the location of the variance?

Are there any current allocations?

Are there any past due allocations?

Are there any open purchase orders?

Are there any past due purchase orders?

Are there any cancelled or deleted purchase orders?

Were there other items on the same purchase order as recent receipts?

Were there other items received from the same vendor on the same day as recent receipts?

Are there any open shipping orders?

Are there any past due shipping orders?

Are there any cancelled or deleted shipping orders?

Is the item capable of being direct shipped from supplier or another facility to the customer?

Have there been any recent direct shipments of the item?

Are there any open production orders?

Are there any past due production orders?

Are there any cancelled or deleted production orders?

Have there been quantities received that are not consistent with the ordered quantities?

Have there been quantities received that are not consistent with the invoiced quantities?

Have there been any early receipts?

Have there been quantities produced that are not consistent with production order quantities?

Have there been quantities of raw materials or components consumed in production that are not consistent with produced quantity of the finished item?

Is scrap quantity reported against production orders consistent with normal process scrap?

Is this item properly coded (issue code) on bills of materials and materials lists?

Have there been manufacturing quantities reported on dates that are not consistent with the production schedule?

Is any part of the manufacturing process outsourced?

Is there any identification on the product that can cross-reference it to a specific purchase order, production order, etc.?

Are there any unusual transactions such as rejections, scrap, returns, samples, or reversal transactions?

Are there any transactions performed by unauthorized personnel?

Are there items with similar item numbers stored near the item?

Are there items with similar descriptions stored near the item?

Have there been other items with exact offsetting variances?

Is there any quality-related information in the system that suggests a rejection, yet no corresponding inventory transactions?

Are there any unidentified materials stored somewhere in the facility?

Are there any materials that do not have a current disposition staged somewhere in the facility?

Now that's not so hard is it? OK, you don't have to answer all these questions on each item. Usually the answers to a few questions will eliminate the need to ask many of the questions listed here. The trick is in determining which questions to start with on a specific variance. That's where the experience and knowledge of the cycle count administrator comes in. While taking a quick look at the size of the variance, the current on-hand quantities, open allocations, open orders, and transaction history may be the normal starting point, from there the investigation can go just about anywhere. You are looking for combinations of characteristics and events that can narrow down the investigation. Some examples are listed below:

If the variance quantity exactly matches a recent transaction, that's a pretty good place to start.

If the variance quantity is substantially larger than your normal shipping transactions, you may be able to rule out a shipping error.

If the previous cycle count adjustments are consistently similar (always positive or always negative), you may want to focus on bill of material errors, scrap reporting errors, or theft.

If you have an offsetting variance on a similar item stored in the same area, you should look into picking errors or mixed stock.

If a variance is similar to the quantity on a cancelled purchase order, production order, or shipping order, it may be that the order was actually processed and should not have been cancelled.

If the variance is similar to a recent receipt and the inventory was received early (significantly earlier than the requested date), it's likely that this is a receiving transaction error where another item was actually received and the wrong purchase order or purchase order line was received against. Look for a past due similar quantity and you may find the correct item.

If the variance would offset the difference between the received quantity and the invoiced quantity on a purchase order, you probably have a receiving transaction error.

If the entire quantity of a recently stocked item in a random storage area is missing, you probably have a location error.

If the same item is stocked under different item numbers, you should count all of these item numbers.

If a missing quantity was received but never transferred into a valid storage location and the received quantity and invoiced quantity match, you probably either have a putaway transaction that was not entered (lost product) or may have inventory sitting in a staging area without a disposition.

Variances on items with confusing or unusual units-of-measure make receiving errors, picking errors, cycle counting errors, or quantity labeling errors, very likely.

If the item is mechanically counted and the variance is within the accuracy tolerance of the counting equipment, you can just make the adjustment or ignore it.

If the item is mechanically counted and the variance is outside the accuracy tolerances of the counting equipment, you may want to manually recount the item (or a sample quantity) and check the accuracy of the counting equipment and the accuracy of the person using the counting equipment.

If you have a shortage on a component and a corresponding overage on an end item, it likely points to a production reporting error or production that occurred without a production order.

If the quantity produced against a production order is not in sync with the materials issued against the production order you likely have a production reporting error (produced five computers but only issued four cases, or vice versa).

If the ordered quantities (purchase orders, replenishment orders, or production orders) are greater than would be expected based upon current planning information (demand, safety stock, reorder point, on-hand balances), this may point out there was demand that no longer exists (such as a cancelled order). You should see if the cancelled order quantity matches the variance.

If system information reflects recent quality problems, yet there are no rejection-related transactions and you are missing a substantial quantity of inventory, you should check with the quality department to see if a transaction was missed.

If you are missing a quantity that is equivalent to a recent customer return quantity, you may either have a transaction problem related to the return or the return was to correct a previous shipping error that was either not correctly reported or the associated balances were not correctly reconciled.

If the current on-hand balance is negative, you should look at the most recent transactions.

If the quantity variance is similar to the quantity on an open shipping order that is past due, its likely that the order was shipped or at least picked and that the transaction was not completed.

If the variance offsets the previous cycle count adjustment, you need to review your cycle counting procedures.

If the item is stored in a manner by which some inventory may be hidden or obscured (such as falling behind other items), you should check the location and adjoining locations more closely.

If you're aware of areas where inventory tends to accumulate, you should check these areas before making any negative adjustments. Actually, you should put in place procedures to eliminate these areas.

Though I can't possibly list every combination of events and the likely root causes, these examples should give you a pretty good idea of the logic used to narrow down the investigation. The basic process involves starting with the most likely causes and working your way down to the least likely. However, there is also some valid logic in checking the easiest causes first. For example, you look at a variance and determine it is likely the result of one of three root causes. However, the most likely cause requires checking physical documents, and one of the less likely causes can be verified with a couple of clicks on your computer. You don't want to spend twenty minutes going through paperwork just to find the actual cause could have been determined with a couple of mouse clicks. This may sound like the old joke where a person loses his car keys in one area but is searching in another area because "the light is better here." In the case of investigating variances, it does make sense to prioritize your investigation by a combination of the likelihood of the root cause and the ease of verification of the root cause.

Understand the effects of adjustments.

Before you take that final step in the cycle count process that actually makes the inventory adjustments, you need to consider the effects of adjustments. First I want to address the problems with adjustments related to lost inventory. Lost inventory can be a problem in any operation, but is more likely to be a problem where inventory is stored randomly. In these operations, lost inventory will often represent an entire receipt, production run, or an entire unit-load (pallet, container, etc.) of inventory. These are significant adjustments and can create havoc with planning systems. What generally happens is the adjustment is made reducing the on-hand balance of the lost inventory. The following day, the planning system will instruct the planner to immediately order more inventory or expedite an existing order; this may require phone calls to vendors, changes to a production schedule, or expedited transportation services. In a manufacturing environment, it may also initiate planning changes to lower level components and raw materials. Eventually the lost inventory is found, and the on-hand balance is increased to reflect the current physical counts; this may be days, weeks, or months after the initial adjustment. If there are still pending orders for more of the item, the planning system will recommend canceling or de-expediting orders, which will result in more phone calls to vendors and changes to production schedules. It will also likely result in excess inventory of the item or lower level components. If the time period has been months and the item has a short product life cycle or is at the end of its product life cycle, you may be stuck with obsolete inventory.

The best solution is to put in place systems that prevent lost product. Until you achieve this level of accuracy you will need other options. The second solution is to find the inventory prior to approving the cycle count. This usually involves the dreaded "walk-through" where you walk around the storage areas looking for a specific lost item. This is not a very good use of labor resources and is practical only in smaller storage areas where you have a pretty good chance of finding the lost product relatively quickly. The third solution is to have a process in place to find lost inventory in a timely manner (probably not same day). This will usually be accomplished by location audits, which will be discussed later. If you're operating under the third option, the cycle count administrator needs to ask the questions "Am I sure that the inventory is still in the facility?" and "What are the chances that this will be found before it is needed?" The first question should be answered based on the variance investigation; the second question would be answered based upon the current remaining on-hand balances of the item, inbound quantities of the item, expected demand for the item, and the aggressiveness of the location audit program. For example, you may have a location audit program that cycles through the storage area once every four weeks. You should then be able to assume that the item should be found within four weeks of the date it was lost. If you are pretty sure it was lost two weeks ago, you can assume it will be located within the next two weeks. Now you need to look at the planning data in your system to see if you can get by for two weeks without the lost inventory. If so — or even if close — I would suggest that you do not adjust the on-hand balance to reflect the missing inventory.

My preference under this situation is to create a logical variance location (this assumes you are using a locator system) and transfer the lost inventory balances to this location. The reason for this is that even though you are not deducting the inventory, you still want to have visibility to the variance. You also do not want other workers to waste their time going to a location where you already know the inventory does not exist. When the inventory is found, it is simply transferred from the variance location to the actual location. I like to use this logical variance location scenario whenever items are stored in multiple random locations and lost inventory or offsetting balances between locations are an ongoing problem.

In addition to lost inventory, there are other situations where you need to carefully consider the effects of making a cycle count adjustment. In integrated business software systems, your planning, execution, and financial processes are all interconnected. The result is bad data in one area will have an immediate impact on the others. How this relates to cycle counting adjustments is simple — well, maybe not so simple. If the error is related to production reporting, receipt processing, facility transfer processing, and in some cases, sales order processing, you may find adjusting the on-hand balance doesn't really fix the whole problem. Remaining data such as allocations, incoming quantities, and in-transit quantities, may remain out of sync. As an example, if you had a purchase order for 500 units of item XYZ and mistakenly received the quantity as 300, the planning system would still show 200 open on the purchase order. At this point your inventory balance is wrong, but the planning system is actually operating OK. If the extra 200 turn up during the cycle count and you use the cycle count program to make the adjustment, your on-hand balance is now correct, but the planning system still thinks that 200 more are coming in. Also, if you are conducting a three-way match of the invoice, receipt, and purchase order to pay the vendor, you will have a problem. In this case, what you should do is, reduce the cycle count quantity by 200 to prevent the cycle count program from making the adjustment (formally called "faking the count") and then process the 200 units through your normal receiving process.

The issue is even more complex with facility transfer processing (transferring inventory from one facility to another), where you may also have in-transit quantities involved. In both of these situations you should try to make the corrections through the original programs using the original purchase orders and transfer orders. With production reporting errors, you have a little more leeway, especially with small variances. Generally, once the production order is complete, any remaining allocations or incoming quantities related to that specific production order will be removed. The best thing to do with a variance that can be tied directly to a production reporting error is to fix the error through the original program using the original production order number. However, if the variances are small, you can usually get away with just adjusting through the cycle count program. Large variances or variances on orders that will not be completed in the very near future should not be adjusted through the cycle count program. For errors on sales orders you have some similar problems, in that historical data is not correct. Since making corrections through the sales order process may result in some very confusing invoice and statement data (which is no way to impress a customer) it's generally better to just make the cycle count adjustments unless the variance is enormous.

I know this makes cycle count adjustments much more complicated, but your inventory accuracy efforts must consider the importance of accurate planning data as well as on-hand balances. I'll once again mention the importance of the cycle count administrator having a thorough understanding of all related processes. It's also important that the cycle count administrator is very careful when making these types of corrections, since "faking" cycle counts and using receiving, shipping, and manufacturing, programs to correct inventory balances is not near as simple as just approving a cycle count and letting the system take over. You also need to realize that faking the count sheet may compromise some of your accuracy reporting systems. We'll discuss this in more detail in chapter six. Some cycle counting programs will allow you to cancel or skip individual counts on the count sheet. This means that you can cancel the specific count rather than faking it. If your system has this functionality, make sure you understand what exactly is happening when you "cancel" or "skip" the count.

Dedicated accuracy personnel?

Though impractical in many operations, there are some real benefits to having employees that specialize in cycle counting and related processes such as audits and checking/inspection processes. The primary benefit is that dedicated accuracy personnel will have inventory accuracy as their primary focus rather than just part of their responsibilities. Also, since they are spending all or most of their time working on accuracy-related issues, their knowledge of these issues will increase substantially more than if they were just doing it an hour or so a day. This allows you to start to give the cycle counters more of the responsibilities that would normally be performed by the cycle count administrator. On the downside, full-time accuracy personnel often experience difficulties in maintaining a positive attitude, as they essentially spend all of their time dealing with mistakes. It's important to counsel personnel on this issue prior to them starting in the position so they have a good understanding of what they are getting into. It's also important to emphasize the value of their accuracy-related duties to the organization.

Unfortunately, it's often difficult to schedule accuracy-related activities to fit into full-time positions. In these cases you have no choice but to have other workers "sideline" as cycle counters. I used the term "sideline" because that is usually how they will view their cycle counting responsibilities. This can be a tough hurdle to overcome as they may rush through cycle counts to get back to there primary duties, or, even if they are not rushing through the cycle count, they are probably thinking about their other work piling up on them. Making sure the employees realize that their performance is being evaluated on their cycle counting duties as well as their other duties will help in maintaining proper focus on count activities.

Supplements to your cycle count program.

Each cycle counting method will have certain drawbacks. Frequently you will find that supplementing your cycle counting program with location audits and other checks will greatly enhance your overall accuracy program (more on this in chapter seven).

Cycle counting without special programming.

I've dedicated a substantial portion of this chapter to the inner workings of cycle count programs (I'm talking about the actual computer programs here), so it may come as a surprise to find that I frequently choose not to use the programs even when they are already available. If you were paying attention in the "Understanding effects of errors" section, you've realized that I'm recommending that many of the adjustments not be made within the cycle count program. This is done by "faking" the count to prevent the cycle count program from making the adjustment. That's just a lot of extra work as far as I am concerned. There's also the issue of transaction-by-exception, which most cycle counting programs that I've run into are not set up to perform. This means that I have to either modify the software, or continue to waste time and risk errors by having cycle counters enter all of the "good counts" as well as the variances.

So how do you cycle count without cycle counting programs? First of all, you need to have a relatively simple method for selecting items to count, such as counting by ranges of physical storage locations (aisle A, section 13 - 24) or counting by ranges of item numbers (item# BJK452 - BJK502). Next you need to be able to print a report based upon your selections, that has all relevant count information (item number, location, description, quantity on hand) and prints in a sequence that makes sense (usually by location). I will generally create the report as a custom report or as a query output so I can get the information just the way I want it. Yes, I guess this would be considered programming, but it's very minor programming. Now the cycle counters can take the report, count the inventory, and circle the on-hand quantity if the count matches, or write in the count quantity if it doesn't. The recounts can be conducted with the same report. Finally, the count administrator uses the report to investigate variances and manually makes the appropriate adjustments. Pretty simple, eh? See figure 4K at the end of this chapter for example of "no programming" count system.

If you have a locator system, you can incorporate the logical variance location scenario I previously discussed into this by having the cycle counters transfer inventory to or from the variance location to make the on-hand quantity in the location they counted correct. For example, if I'm missing five pieces in the location I counted, I would transfer five pieces from that location to the variance location, or if I'm over five pieces, I would transfer five pieces from the variance location to the location I counted (this would result in a negative quantity on hand in the variance location). Now, the cycle count administrator can run another report showing all items with a quantity on hand (positive or negative quantities) in the variance location. This is essentially the variance report used to investigate discrepancies and make adjustments.

The drawbacks of these basic count systems are that you must stick with a fairly simplistic count frequency method, you must manually maintain any count accuracy measurement (discussed later) and there is no system updating of count information such as last count date.

12/12/2002

Cycle Count # 1082

Counter ID # _123_

LOCATION	SKU	Description	UM	Count
PA0101	RND8739	.50 ROUND TUIT	EA	182
PA0102	WGS4322	.5 FLC TAPE	EA	73
PA0203	JEK8439	.25 SPRING CLAMP	BX	23
PA0205	MIL6548	FOLTIN BINDING SMEKERS	EA	4
PA0208	BLG1598	3.5 ASSON GEAR	EA	2
PA0324	WPL6702	LST GT UPNGO	EA	32
PA0408	XPF4321	CHNG RESISTOR	EA	3
PB0404	KEW2976	LGE GNEP KEY	EA	2
PA0514	LKE4783	NUTHA QUAL STRGY	EA	53
PA0527	RND8978	.25 ROUND TUIT	EA	23
PA0530	FRP7896	HESREP JUNCTION GUNKEL	EA	3
PA0602	LZX8032	1.750 DUALFLOW SPHINCTERVALVE	EA	27
PA1404	KKJ9874	LCKOF EFERTT	EA	6
PA1406	LPS1223	CMPLT WST TYM KIT	EA	1
PB0104	SDP9321	PLATE MOUNTING LEFT YIPDO	EA	73
PB0113	JKL6588	.156 FELL SNUBBER	EA	227
PB0207	FLC2033	PLL CBL 18.4	EA	23
PB0210	REW9284	BUSNS TRANSFORMER	EA	25
PB0214	LSK4872	BSKT CASE	EA	0
PB0323	SDL5683	LARGE DUST COLLECTOR	EA	2
RA1200	KSD2483	ROLL STL .3275	LF	3500

Figure 4C. Blind Count Sheet

This is an example of a simple blind count sheet. Since no quantities are printed on the count sheet, the employee has no idea if his count matches the system quantity. The cycle count number in the upper right portion of the count sheet is the key to entering the count data. Since the employee does know if the counts match, he must enter all counts into the system.

				12/12/2002	
			Cycle Count #	1082	
			Counter ID #	*123*	

LOCATION	SKU	Description	UM	Quantity	Count
PA0101	RND8739	.50 ROUND TUIT	EA	183	*182*
PA0102	WGS4322	.5 FLC TAPE	EA	(73)	
PA0203	JEK8439	.25 SPRING CLAMP	BX	(23)	
PA0205	MIL6548	FOLTIN BINDING SMEKERS	EA	(4)	
PA0208	BLG1598	3.5 ASSON GEAR	EA	(2)	
PA0324	WPL6702	LST GT UPNGO	EA	(32)	
PA0408	XPF4321	CHNG RESISTOR	EA	(3)	
PB0404	KEW2976	LGE GNEP KEY	EA	(2)	
PA0514	LKE4783	NUTHA QUAL STRGY	EA	(53)	
PA0527	RND8978	.25 ROUND TUIT	EA	(23)	
PA0530	FRP7896	HESREP JUNCTION GUNKEL	EA	(3)	
PA0602	LZX8032	1.750 DUALFLOW SPHINCTERVALVE	EA	(27)	
PA1404	KKJ9874	LCKOF EFERTT	EA	5	*6*
PA1406	LPS1223	CMPLT WST TYM KIT	EA	(1)	
PB0104	SDP9321	PLATE MOUNTING LEFT YIPDO	EA	(73)	
PB0113	JKL6588	.156 FELL SNUBBER	EA	213	*227*
PB0207	FLC2033	PLL CBL 18.4	EA	(23)	
PB0210	REW9284	BUSNS TRANSFORMER	EA	(25)	
PB0214	LSK4872	BSKT CASE	EA	1	*0*
PB0323	SDL5683	LARGE DUST COLLECTOR	EA	(2)	
RA1200	KSD2483	ROLL STL .3275	LF	(3,500)	

Figure 4D. Verification Count Sheet

In this example, the quantities are printed on the count sheet. My preference with verification counts is to have the counter circle the quantity if
it matches and only write in quantities if they do not match. This makes
the count sheet cleaner and reduces the chances of the counter writing
the count incorrectly or illegibly. It also makes data entry into a program
designed for transaction by exception (entering only the bad counts)
easier.

					12/12/2002	
					Cycle Count #	**1082**
					Counter ID #	_____

LOCATION	SKU	UM	Quantity	Count		Notes
PA 01 01	**RND 8739** .50 ROUND TUIT 42 PER LAYER		183	_____	1	
PA 01 02	**WGS 4322** .5 FLC TAPE		73	_____	2	
PA 02 03	**JEK 8439** `BX`		23	_____	3	
	.25 SPRING CLAMP					
PA 02 05	**MIL 6548** FOLTIN BINDING SMEKERS		4	_____	4	
PA 02 08	**BLG 1598** 3.5 ASSON GEAR		2	_____	5	
PA 03 24	**WPL 6702** LST GT UPNGO		32	_____	6	
PA 04 08	**XPF 4321** CHNG RESISTOR		3	_____	7	
PB 04 04	**KEW 2976** LGE GNEP KEY		2	_____	8	
PA 05 14	**LKE 4783** NUTHA QUAL STRGY		53	_____	9	

Figure 4E. Modified Count Sheet

Here I've made a series of changes to improve the cycle count sheet. Since cycle counting is often done using clipboards, I've moved everything to the left to prevent having to try to write on the edge of the clipboard (also leaves room for the counter to write notes associated with the count). I've also reformatted the key data elements to make them easier to read and added conditional formatting on the unit of measure to only display when UM is not "EA".

Two new data elements were added. The small number to the right of the count line is the line number. Since we are entering only the counts that do not match, we can use the line number as a "skip to" in the entry program. I've also added a data element that contains special notes for cycle counters. It only displays (gray shaded) if there is a note for that item (line #1 has a note that states the count per layer).

Variance Recounts

12/13/2002
Cycle Count # 1082

LOCATION	SKU	UM	System Qty.	Count Qty Variance	Recount Qty
PA0203	JEK8439 .25 SPRING CLAMP	BX	23	22 -1	
PB0207	FLC2033 PLL CBL 18.4	EA	23	22 -1	
PC0102	KLF4438 VLV DISK RRC	EA	4	0 -4	
SB0101	BLG1598 3.5 ASSON GEAR	EA	16	14 -2	
SB0201	JKL6588 .156 FELL SNUBBER	EA	2,313	2,340 27	
SB0201	JKL8493 KIKNTH HEAD GASKET	EA	233	228 -5	
SC1402	FLC2033 PLL CBL 18.4	EA	53	50 -3	
SC1505	JKL6588 .156 FELL SNUBBER	EA	1,323	1,309 -14	

Figure 4F. Cycle Count Variance Recount Report.

This is an example of a report used to recount variances. The report follows the same location sort as the original count sheet. The difference between this and the original count sheet is it only prints item/locations that had variances and it prints the original count quantity along with a variance calculation.

The original cycle count quantity is shown more prominently here since that is the number the person conducting the recounts is verifying. I recommend following the same logic as in verification counts by simply circling the count quantity if it matches the recount, and only writing in a count if it differs from the original counter's quantity.

Only recounts that differed from the original count will need to be entered into the count program.

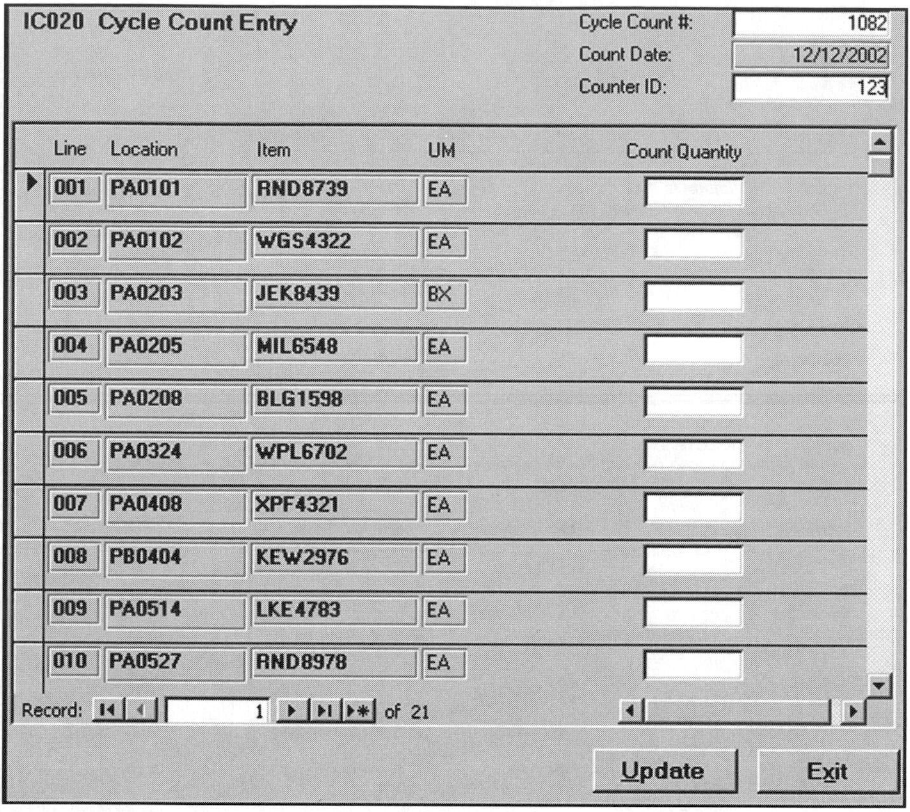

IC020 Cycle Count Entry				Cycle Count #:	1082
				Count Date:	12/12/2002
				Counter ID:	123

Line	Location	Item	UM	Count Quantity
▶ 001	PA0101	RND8739	EA	
002	PA0102	WGS4322	EA	
003	PA0203	JEK8439	BX	
004	PA0205	MIL6548	EA	
005	PA0208	BLG1598	EA	
006	PA0324	WPL6702	EA	
007	PA0408	XPF4321	EA	
008	PB0404	KEW2976	EA	
009	PA0514	LKE4783	EA	
010	PA0527	RND8978	EA	

Record: |◄ ◄ [1] ► ►| ►* of 21

Update   Exit

Figure 4G. Cycle Count Entry (Blind Counts)

This is an example of a simple cycle count entry program used with blind counts. The cycle counter would enter the cycle count number to bring up the detail of the count sheet. The detail area should be in the same sequence as the original count sheet (location sequence in this example). The cycle counter would then enter each count line by line until all counts are entered.

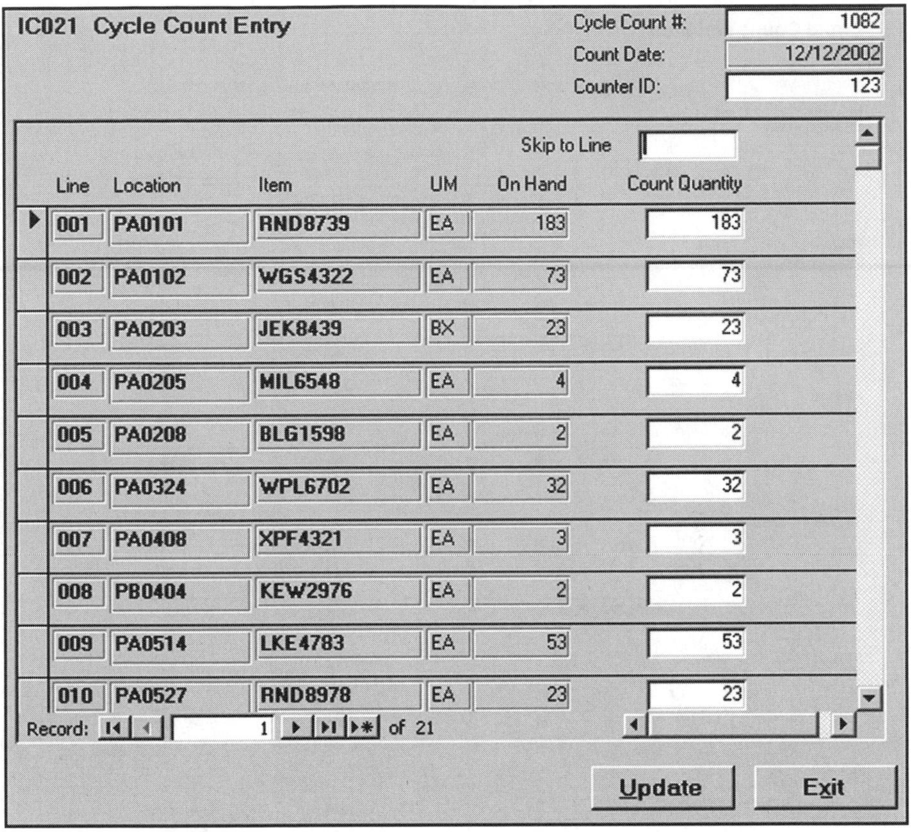

IC021 Cycle Count Entry					Cycle Count #:	1082
					Count Date:	12/12/2002
					Counter ID:	123

					Skip to Line		
	Line	Location	Item	UM	On Hand	Count Quantity	
▶	001	PA0101	RND8739	EA	183	183	
	002	PA0102	WGS4322	EA	73	73	
	003	PA0203	JEK8439	BX	23	23	
	004	PA0205	MIL6548	EA	4	4	
	005	PA0208	BLG1598	EA	2	2	
	006	PA0324	WPL6702	EA	32	32	
	007	PA0408	XPF4321	EA	3	3	
	008	PB0404	KEW2976	EA	2	2	
	009	PA0514	LKE4783	EA	53	53	
	010	PA0527	RND8978	EA	23	23	

Record: |◄ ◄| 1 |► ►| ►*| of 21

Update   **Exit**

Figure 4H. Cycle Count Entry (Verification Counts)

This is an example of a cycle count entry program designed to be used with verification counts. This program has the functionality to use transaction-by-exception techniques for data entry. When the cycle count number is entered the detail will come up with the on-hand quantities preloaded into the count quantity fields. Now the cycle counter only needs to enter the variances. If the count sheet is large, he can use the "skip to" functionality to go directly to a specific line number.

The person conducting recounts would generally use this same program to enter any counts that differed from the original count. Once the original counts are entered, they will come up in the detail area instead of the default on-hand quantity.

```
Cycle Count Variance                                              12/23/2002
                                                              Cycle Count #  1082

                        System   Counted   Variance    VarianceAmount    VariancePercent

BLG1598        $25.43
3.5 ASSON GEAR
              SB0101   EA   16      14        -2          -$50.86          -12.50%
              SF0106   EA   16      18         2           $50.86           12.50%
                            32      32         0           $0.00            0.00%

FLC2033         $1.87
PLL CBL 18.4
              PB0207   EA   23      22        -1           -$1.87          -4.35%
              SF0102   EA  467     473         6           $11.22           1.28%
              SC1402   EA   53      50        -3           -$5.61          -5.66%
                           543     545         2           $3.74           0.37%

JEK8439         $0.07
.25 SPRING CLAMP
              PA0203   BX   23      22        -1           -$0.07          -4.35%
                            23      22        -1           -$0.07          -4.35%

JKL6588         $0.13
.156 FELL SNUBBER
              SB0201   EA 2,313   2,340       27           $3.51           1.17%
              SF0105   EA 6,543   6,525      -18           -$2.34         -0.28%
              SC1505   EA 1,323   1,309      -14           -$1.82         -1.06%
                        10,179  10,174       -5           -$0.65         -0.05%

JKL8493         $6.46
KIKNTH HEAD GASKET
              SB0201   EA  233     228        -5          -$32.30         -2.15%
                           233     228        -5          -$32.30         -2.15%

KLF4438        $16.35
VLV DISK RRC
              PC0102   EA    4       0        -4          -$65.40        -100.00%
                             4       0        -4          -$65.40        -100.00%
```

Figure 4I. Cycle Count Variance Report

This is an example of a variance report that would be used by the cycle count administrator to evaluate variances after the recount is completed. Once again, we are only printing variances on this report.

We are sorting and grouping by item rather than location. This allows us to see all locations for the item that had variances, and also allows us to net out the location variances for each item. In the case of the first item on the report, you can see that the two location variances netted out to zero. Which means even though you have location-level variances for this item, your facility-level inventory is correct.

We also have variance amount and variance percentage calculations shown on this report.

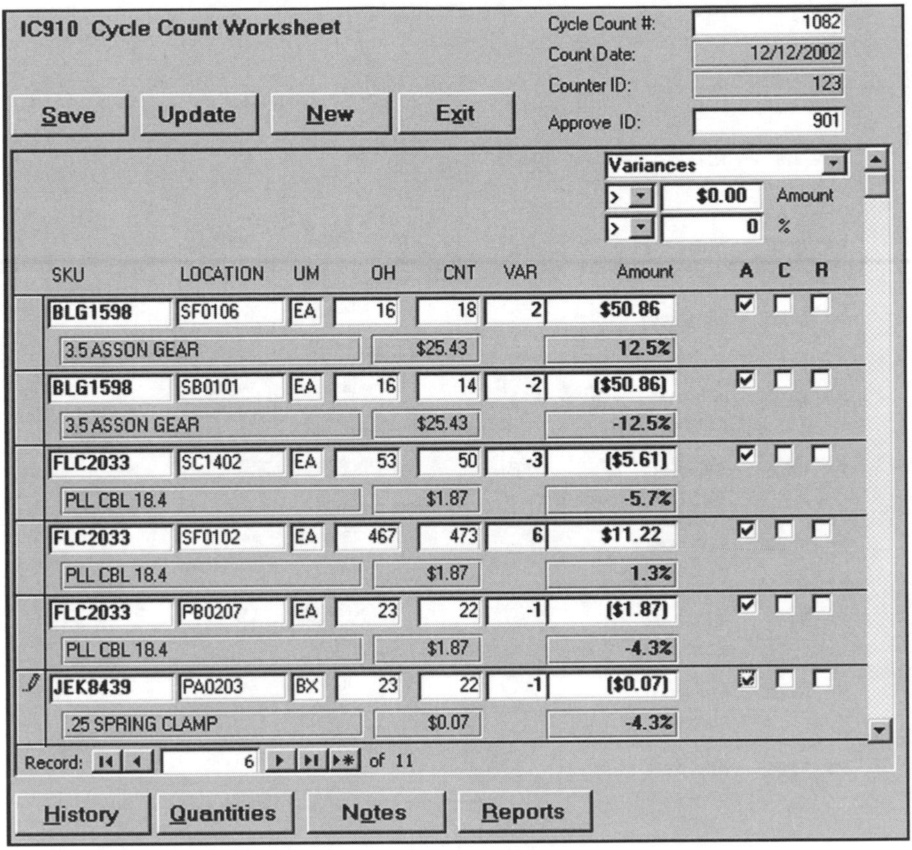

Figure 4J. Cycle Count Variance Online Worksheet

This is an example of an online variance worksheet. Filters incorporated into the program allow you to look at all counts, variances only, or variances greater than a specified amount or percentage.

The program provides direct access to the item history inquiry program and other programs useful in investigating variances.

This program also allows you to cancel specific lines from the count sheet as well as force additional recounts though a set of check boxes (A = approve, C = cancel, R = recount).

It also has the ability to add notes to specific detail lines of the count sheet.

I should note that most cycle counting programs do not have the level of functionality shown here. Most cycle count programs will just have a variance report and a batch program used to approve and update the count.

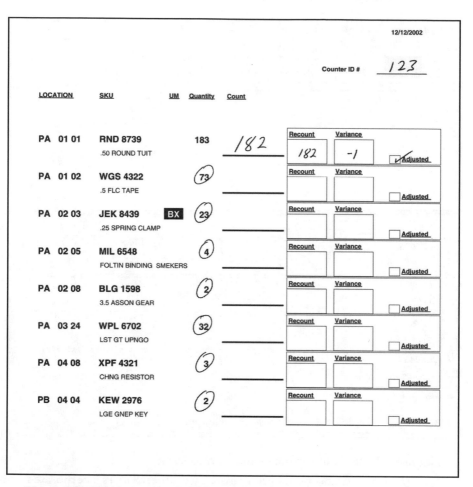

Figure 4K. "No programming" Count Sheet / Worksheet

This is an example of a cycle count sheet used on a system that has no special programming for cycle counting. This is simply a report based on the inventory file. You'll notice that there is no cycle count number on this sheet. Since the recounts and adjustments will have to be done manually I have designed a worksheet area that provides space for recount information, variance calculations, and adjustment information.

The initial cycle counter would conduct the counts and then hand the sheet off to the recount person who would recount only the variances. The cycle count administrator would then use the same sheet to evaluate the variances and make adjustments.

This simplified counting process can be very effective.

12/17/2002

Counter ID # ________

LOCATION	SKU	UM	Quantity	Count	Recount	Variance	Adjusted
PA 01 01	RND 8739 .50 ROUND TUIT		183	______			☐ Adjusted
PA 01 02	WGS 4322 .5 FLC TAPE		73	______			☐ Adjusted
PA 02 03	JEK 8439 .25 SPRING CLAMP	BX	23	______			☐ Adjusted
PA 02 05	MIL 6548 FOLTIN BINDING SMEKERS		4	______			☐ Adjusted
PA 02 08	BLG 1598 3.5 ASSON GEAR		2	______			☐ Adjusted
PA 03 24	WPL 6702 LST GT UPNGO		32	______			☐ Adjusted

Figure 4L. With Bar Codes.

Here I've added two bar codes (SKU and Location) to the "no programming" cycle count sheet. Since there is no programming to automate the inventory transactions in this example, the bar codes can be used by the cycle count administrator when making the adjustments. This will reduce the chances of a data entry error and also provide an increase in productivity.

When using small bar codes like this on reports used at a workstation or desk you would probably be using a pen-type wand scanner rather than a pistol-type scanner to read the codes. The bar codes can also be used to scan the item number into inquiry programs you would be using to investigate the variances. This also makes them a useful addition to separate variance reports. You may choose to combine the two bar codes into a single bar code depending upon your specific use.

Summary

Cycle counting is a tool used to identify root causes of errors that will be used to focus process improvement efforts, and to compensate for process problems by catching and correcting inventory balance discrepancies before they negatively affect operations. In addition to the standard ABC cycle count methodology most are familiar with, there are many other options, including some simple methods as well as some very complex methods and combinations of methods. For those that may be new to cycle counting and are feeling a little overwhelmed by the various options outlined in this chapter, I recommend starting simple with either a standard ABC count program or a simple location based strategy. After you have gotten comfortable with running a cycle count program, you can then go back and consider the benefits of some of the other options.

5

Periodic Physical Inventories

A physical inventory (also known as a wall-to-wall physical) is the activity of counting all inventory within an organization or facility and reconciling the counts with the inventory records. Usually this requires shutting down warehouse and manufacturing operations for the duration of the count and reconciliation process. Physical inventories are taken on a periodic basis (annually, semiannually, quarterly, or monthly) based on company policy, with the much-maligned annual physical inventory being the most common.

The problems associated with taking a physical inventory are well known:

✔ They occur too infrequently to contribute to continuous improvement process.

✔ Interruptions to operations results in capacity and customer service issues.

✔ Physical inventories are rarely accurate.

There's nothing new here, I've seen these problems documented in business textbooks going back to the 1930's. Infrequent physical inventories are not only an ineffective means of maintaining accurate inventory records, they are also frequently a source of inventory accuracy problems. This is one of those rare occasions where virtually all of the experts are in agreement.

So why do so many companies continue to conduct annual physical inventories? As much as I'd like to blame this solely on accountants and their unwillingness to let go of antiquated accounting practices, it's actually a little more complicated than that. Accountants are responsible for providing an accurate accounting of the value of the company's inventory for tax purposes and financial reports provided to owners, shareholders, and financial institutions. Though they are responsible for accurately reporting the inventory value, they rarely have much control (despite the title "controller" some of them carry) over the day-to-day operations that affect the accuracy of inventory records. The result is they need a way to verify the accuracy of the inventory records. Historically, this has been through a physical inventory count. And I'll agree that, for the purpose of aggregate inventory reporting, a physical inventory can be effective. The accountant wants to be confident that if he reports ten million dollars in inventory, that he actually has ten million in inventory and not nine or eleven million. While physical inventories are often inaccurate at the detailed item level, they will generally come "close enough" at the summary level. Good for the accountants, bad for operations.

Basically the accountant is taking the easy way out by requiring a physical inventory. It provides them with documentation to support the numbers they are reporting. Sure, they know that it's not 100 percent accurate at the aggregate level, and probably suspect that it's even less accurate at the detail level, but what are their options? This is where operations managers need to share the blame for the perpetuation of the annual physical inventory. Most businesses operate with inadequate inventory practices resulting in unacceptable accuracy levels. If you were an accountant, would you be willing to sign off on the accuracy of the inventory numbers in these environments?

This puts it back in the hands of the operations managers to put in place systems that ensure consistent accuracy, and then prove this accuracy to the financial folks. If you think this is leading up to a cycle count program, you're only partially correct. There are many companies with cycle counting programs in place that still have unacceptable accuracy levels, and the flaws in cycle count accuracy measurement (discussed later) are not going to help much in proving the accuracy levels. What is needed is consistent accuracy and a means to verify it. While cycle counting can be a tool used to help achieve accuracy, the existence of a cycle counting program does not ensure accuracy. All right, I'm not going to repeat the entire book up to this point, but you get the idea. Build an accurate environment, prove the accuracy, and then talk about getting rid of the annual physical inventory.

Though cycle count results can be used to prove the levels of accuracy, I prefer conducting periodic audits instead. A periodic accuracy audit is similar to a cycle count with the exception that its purpose is solely to determine accuracy levels. Accuracy audits are discussed in detail in chapter seven.

So, am I saying that physical inventories are bad and should be avoided at all cost? Actually not. In the chapter on cycle counting, I reference using frequent periodic inventories (usually monthly) as an alternative to a cycle count program in smaller operations. If you can count all of your inventory and adequately investigate count discrepancies without creating excessive interruptions to operations, frequent periodic physical inventories may be an effective option to cycle counting. I also have no problem with using an annual physical inventory to prove accuracy in an environment that already uses cycle counting, provided the same conditions exist (can count and adequately investigate count discrepancies without creating excessive interruptions to operations). However, if your inventory is too extensive or if you are in a 24/7 environment and do not want to shut down operations, you should look into combining cycle counting with periodic accuracy audits to replace your physical inventory.

I should also note that, contrary to many rumors, an annual physical inventory is not a federal tax law requirement. Companies are required to accurately report the value of their inventory and other assets. While there are specific requirements on how you value your inventory, there are not specific requirements on how you prove the existence of the inventory (as in a physical inventory count). Physical inventory requirements are the result of corporate policies, not federal laws (I cannot completely rule out that there may be some odd state or local laws requiring a physical inventory). Changing the company policy requires convincing the policymakers of the merits of the alternative you are suggesting. Essentially you need to convince the policymakers that the company is better without the physical inventory than it is with it. Explaining the problems associated with a physical inventory along with a well-documented alternative (cycle count program, periodic audits) should do the trick. Your documented alternative will now become a part of company policy. This is usually much easier in small to mid-sized privately held companies than it is in publicly held companies or government agencies.

Conducting a physical inventory

If you are going to conduct a physical inventory there are specific steps that will greatly increase the success factor. First let me go into a little more detail on the problems that plague many physical inventories.

Problems with the execution of physical inventories.

Inexperienced, poorly trained counters.

Inadequate time and resources to investigate discrepancies.

Confusion over open orders and allocations.

Accumulations of unidentified inventory.

Incorrect adjustments.

Safety problems.

Poor morale.

Inexperienced, poorly trained counters.

The extensive resources required to conduct a physical inventory often results in the need to recruit (volunteer, draft, shanghai) workers from throughout the organization regardless of their skill levels. These people may not have much, if any, experience handling the inventory. Counting errors, misidentification of inventory, misunderstanding of units-of-measure, and confusion over storage locations are much more likely when using inexperienced counters.

Inadequate time and resources to investigate discrepancies.

I'm not even going to go into root cause analysis here. Often you do not even have the time or resources to perform recounts or determine the correctness of the adjustment (is this really a variance, or should it be investigated further?), yet alone try to determine root cause.

Confusion over open orders and allocations.

While this is also a problem with cycle counts, it can be a disaster in a physical inventory.

Accumulations of unidentified inventory.

As counters proceed through the inventory they come across items that are not properly identified; since there is rarely adequate time or resources available to identify the materials, they just tend to accumulate. If they are not identified prior to the adjustments being made, you can assume that you just deducted all of this unidentified inventory.

Incorrect adjustments.

Physical inventories are plagued with incorrect adjustments. These are the results of all of the problems mentioned above as well as simple data entry errors that result from the often-massive numbers of transactions.

Safety problems.

I have to mention this as safety practices that are enforced during normal operations are often completely ignored during the physical inventory. For some reason, people seem to think that under special circumstances (such as a physical inventory) the normal rules do not apply. Counters climbing on pallet rack and shelving, squeezing in between pallet loads, climbing over machines, climbing over piles of inventory, balancing on the top rungs of ladders or the rails of rolling ladders, being raised on the forks of a forklift, operating material handling equipment they are not trained and certified to operate, smoking in the warehouse (which is against fire codes), or trying to manually lift very heavy items are practices that are "tolerated" during a physical inventory even though they may be cause for dismissal on any other day. I have no doubt that there are numerous injuries and even some fatalities that are a direct result of the lack of safety practices during physical inventories.

Poor morale.

With the exception of a handful of employees that love the overtime, most of the people that will be part of the physical inventory process do not want to be there. Not only does this affect their performance during the physical inventory, but also the performance of their regular duties in the days prior to and after the count. Prior to the physical inventory they are likely getting depressed at the thought of the physical inventory and after the process is completed they are depressed over the inaccurate and unorganized process they were just a part of.

OK, so it's the end of the year and the warehouse workers and all of the salaried employees are gathered together on a Saturday morning to perform the annual physical inventory. The coffee and donuts help to put color into the faces and cover up the odors enveloping those who had overindulged themselves the night before. People are wandering around not sure what they should be doing, when the boss walks in with stacks of reports, cards, and colored stickers and says "OK here's how this is going to work." By noon it's obvious that less than half of the warehouse has been counted and the pizza lunch has left everyone with an enthusiasm deficit. At two o'clock, one by one, people start approaching the boss with the reasons as to why they have to leave. Suddenly the pressure increases on those remaining to get finished. Five o'clock and the last of the counters are abandoning ship, there's an enormous pile of paperwork marked "discrepancies" and several piles of product marked "unknown," "what's this?" and "needs to be identified." The boss surveys the scene and instructs the people in charge of investigating the overwhelming pile of discrepancies to "just make the adjustments, we need to get out of here."

The preparation phase

So how do we conduct a physical inventory and avoid the many pitfalls? It's all in the preparation. This includes preparing the count plan, preparing the inventory, preparing the equipment, preparing the facility, preparing the workers, preparing the paperwork, and preparing the information. The success of a physical inventory is as much if not more dependent on what occurs before the count than what occurs during the count. For large complex operations, preparation should start months before the physical inventory is scheduled. I should mention that one of the most valuable preparation methods would be to have a cycle count program in place. Having a cycle count program means that you are starting off with at least some experienced counters, a cycle count administrator that is experienced in investigating discrepancies, and probably a higher level of accuracy resulting in less variances during the physical inventory.

The steps listed below are not necessarily intended to be followed sequentially. Some steps, such as conducting test counts and training counters, may be repeated at several different points prior to the count, while others, such as preparing forms, data, and equipment, may have lead times associated with them.

Preparation

Conduct test counts.

Prepare count plan.

Train workers.

Paperwork and forms.

Data and programs.

Prepare inventory.

Prepare facility

Equipment and supplies.

Conduct test counts.

If I were going to conduct a physical inventory in a facility, the first thing I would do is conduct an initial accuracy audit (see chapter seven). This will give me some idea of the number of variances I can expect to run into, the time it takes to resolve the variances (recounts and investigation), the time it takes to conduct the count, the equipment and information needed, and specific problems and any other unknowns that I may run into during the count. This would just be my initial test count. After the count plan has been developed I would conduct additional test counts using the count plan to verify that the count plan works and confirm initial assumptions made during the initial test count. I would also use subsequent test counts as part of the training process. If you already have a cycle count program in place, it can serve as part of the test count step; you should, however, conduct additional test counts using the actual physical inventory count plan. I also suggest you conduct several counts of a control group to test your process (see cycle counting chapter for more control group information).

Prepare count plan.

Preparing the count plan requires determining all resource needs (time, people, equipment, information) and documenting procedures for conducting other preparations, training, controlling transactions, initial counts, data entry, recounts, variance investigations, adjustments, measurement, and any follow-up activities.

Train count personnel.

Yes, here comes that "training thing" again. Training the personnel that will be conducting the counts and related activities is extremely important. This should included training them with the specific forms, reports, portable devices, or other informational tools used, as well as training them on item identification, units-of-measure, location system, count methods, material handling equipment, and safety issues. I'm not going to pretend that companies are willing to put everyone that will be involved in the physical inventory through a six-week training program (though it wouldn't hurt). What is reasonable to expect, would be to put all count personnel — and I do mean everyone — through an approximately one-hour classroom training session that goes through the procedures, forms, and equipment, and then have them all conduct test counts. This gives you more test count information to work with and gives the counters some real experience before the count date. You will also be able to detect employees that either didn't understand the procedures or have other difficulties. Key individuals involved in the physical inventory — such as team leaders or those responsible for investigating variances — should have more extensive training.

Prepare paperwork and forms.

This includes designing and testing reports, tags, labels, bar codes, forms, or any other materials used during the physical inventory process.

Prepare data and information systems.

This includes all data and programs used to generate the count paperwork and forms, programs to enter count data, programs to identify variances, programs to make inventory adjustments, and programs to summarize the results of the physical inventory. It also includes evaluation of procedures for identifying and tracking any in-process inventory such as shipping orders picked but not shipped, production orders started but not yet completed, and incoming inventory that has not yet been processed. Ideally you want to conduct the physical inventory with no in-process inventory. If this is not possible, efforts should be made to reduce in-process inventory to the lowest possible levels. See chapter on cycle counting for more detailed information on controlling transactions.

Prepare inventory.

If you want your physical inventory to go faster, with fewer count errors and no piles of unidentified inventory, you need to prepare your inventory prior to the count. This includes, but goes far beyond, doing a little straightening up. Location audits can be used to identify and correct incorrectly located inventory, this is very valuable since incorrectly located inventory requires manual processing (usually must be hand written onto count sheets or tags and then manually entered) during a physical inventory count. Inventory found that is not properly identified (missing labels or other identification) can be investigated and labeled accordingly. Difficult to count items can be pre-counted and containers can then be sealed and identified with counts. Inventory that has fallen behind or between racking and shelving should be put where it belongs. An aggressive cycle count program or series of test counts can correct a lot of errors prior to the physical inventory. And please, make an effort to get rid of obsolete inventory prior to the physical inventory.

Prepare facility.
Clean it up and make sure all storage and staging locations are properly marked. Also, find all the little nooks and crannies where miscellaneous inventory accumulates and clean them out. This includes areas around production equipment, under conveyors, under and around workstations, on stock carts, and in the dark corners of storage and dock areas. Move all unnecessary equipment out of the way and prepare specific areas for picking up and dropping off reports, forms, and any other materials related to the count process.

Prepare equipment and supplies.
Make sure you have all necessary equipment and supplies readily available for the count process. Counters searching for tape machines, calculators, clipboards, markers, strapping cutters, and carton knives, or waiting for a needed piece of material handling equipment are not doing what you need them to do — count the inventory. Make sure you have plenty of all the low cost supplies and equipment and consider renting additional material handling equipment. Most material handling equipment suppliers will rent lift trucks and other equipment by the day. Having a couple of extra lift trucks and pallet jacks will not cost that much and can prevent a lot of aggravation. Also consider renting man-up order selectors or a scissors lift to help in counting racked inventory. Counting scales can also be rented for short periods of time. Make sure you train and certify the employees that will be using this additional equipment.

Physical inventory methodology

As with cycle counting, there are many decisions that need to be made when designing a physical inventory count process. Unlike cycle counting, you don't need to worry about what to count (count frequency) since you will be counting everything. Decisions on how you count may not be so easy. There is no such thing as a "standard physical inventory." Over the past 100 years, businesses have developed various methodologies — some simple, some extremely complex — for conducting their physical inventory count. Some take advantage of technological changes, while others have just recreated old manual systems on a computer. Before we go into these, let's consider the objectives of the physical inventory process.

The objectives of a physical inventory may or may not be similar to the objectives of a cycle count program. If you are conducting frequent physical inventories (monthly) in a small operation, the objectives may be the same as would be for a cycle count for the same operation. However, if you are conducting an annual physical inventory, the objectives are more related to fulfilling an accounting requirement than any operational requirements. The basic objective is simply to count everything and make sure that the system data is in sync with the actual inventory. It's very unlikely that you will be conducting much, if any, root-cause analysis during an annual physical inventory. You also need to realize that you only get one shot at this; if you run into items where open orders and other activities have resulted in questionable on-hand balances, you do not have the option of skipping these items and counting them again some other day.

Blind counts revisited.

Cycle counting practitioners have been slowly coming around to appreciate the benefits of not conducting blind counts. Unfortunately, this open-mindedness has not made it's way into physical inventory count processes. Some people are simply adamant that annual physical inventories must be conducted as blind counts, with others going even further by requiring duplicate sets of blind counts (everything counted twice by separate counters). I don't really understand this double standard since the advantages and disadvantages of blind counts are no different for a cycle count than for a physical inventory. Time and resources are the biggest constraints during a physical inventory, and conducting verification counts will allow you to conduct the physical inventory in less time, with fewer counters, and with less aggravation, than with blind counts. As long as the counters are trained and understand their responsibilities, you should be able to expect accurate results without resorting to blind counts. Testing the counters by "planting" some variances will assure you of the accuracy of the counting. More detailed information on blind counts was included in the chapter on cycle counting.

Special programming requirements.

You don't necessarily need special programming to conduct a physical inventory. In its simplest form, a physical inventory process only requires a report that lists each item with the quantity on hand and a program that allows manual adjustment of those quantities. At the other end of the spectrum you have counts entered into portable terminals that update a database that compares counts to on-hand quantities and creates variance reports or variance screens, and ultimately automates the adjustment process. Since a physical inventory usually only occurs once per year, you may find it difficult to justify extensive programming to support elaborate counting processes unless you are in a very large complex operation and want to use technology to minimize operational downtime. Many software packages will come with programs designed for conducting physical inventories. For most small to mid-sized operations I would generally suggest that you use the programs that came with your system, or go to a simplified report-and-manual-adjustment system, rather than designing your own physical inventory programs.

Minor programming such as creating custom reports or forms to use as count sheets or count tags are reasonable investments. Be careful to avoid developing unwieldy systems that look good in a flow chart, but are a disaster in the warehouse and on the shop floor.

Count sheets, tag counts, and other options.

Choices, choices, choices. Choosing between using count sheets or conducting tag counts only starts the decision making process as each of these choices have numerous variations within them. When making your decision, it's important to consider the complexity of some of these choices and the benefits they provide.

Count sheets. Count sheets are basically reports designed for use in the counting process. Count sheets will have multiple items per sheet sequenced in a manner to support a logical counting process (see previous chapter for examples of count sheets). A physical inventory may consist of one large continuous count sheet (this isn't to imply that it is on a single page) or a series of separate count sheets logically broken up to simplify the counting. The most desirable method for sequencing and breaking count sheets is by physical storage locations. You may choose to run one continuous count sheet sorted by location, separate sheets for groups of locations (such as for an entire aisle or zone), or a separate sheet for each location (when multiple items share locations). For operations that do not use locations, you will want to try to sequence count sheets in a manner that is consistent with your storage methods. If your inventory is stored by item number sequence, an item number sequenced count sheet is fine; however, if your inventory is stored using some other logic, an item number sequenced count sheet is going to result in a whole lot of hunting and page flipping which will ultimately add to the possibility for errors. Breaking the count sheets by commodity or vendor, and then sorting by item number within these breaks, may make the counting easier.

The recommendations made in "making accuracy easy" related to documents, forms, and reports should be considered in designing count sheets for physical inventories. Make sure that fonts used are easy to read, only include necessary data fields, leave ample room to write in counts or comments, and leave clear space between each count line. The data fields should be positioned in a logical manner. Specific areas should be designated for writing in count quantities, variances, and notes. A count sheet may be a live document as described in the cycle counting chapter, or may simply be a report. With a live count sheet you would then enter the count quantities into the system as with a standard cycle count. With a simple report-based count sheet you would calculate the variances and manually enter adjustments (as with the "no programming" cycle count described previously).

An additional form is usually necessary to document any inventory found that is not on the count sheet. You could just write the information on the count sheet, but I find this sloppy and more prone to error than using a form. Just create a simple form that has areas for all the specific information needed.

It's common in physical inventories to physically mark each item/location combination, as it is counted, to provide a visual verification that everything was indeed counted. This is generally accomplished by using stickers (often colored stickers) or by putting a check mark or other identification with a marker on the item. There is some value in this, though it's not always necessary. If you are going to physically mark the inventory, you should try to keep it as simple as possible. Don't require counters to write their name or initials and the count date on the product. If you want this information, I suggest that you preprint labels with the info for each counter. This can be done on any ink jet or laser printer with standard off-the-shelf label stock in sheet form, or, if you have access to thermal transfer label printers you can run them with that equipment. If you want the visibility of color on the labels, you can choose colored label stock, get a colored ribbon for the thermal transfer printer, or use an ink jet or color laser printer. You generally only mark one container or one unit of an item stored in the location (the one in front on top). This is another one of those situations where a specific sequence of events is necessary. Counters should count an item and then sticker it, count the next item and then sticker it, and so on. Failing to have a specific procedure may result in an employee going to a location and placing stickers on everything there before starting the count. This can result in the employee missing something during the count, yet because they already put a sticker on it, it will not be noticed by a visual inspection.

Count Date:	*12-31-02*
Counted By:	*Bob*
Count Number:	*8763*
Quantity:	*174*

Count Date: **12/31/02**

Counted By: **#123**

#123

1202

The first label shown here is an example of one commonly used during physical inventories. Requiring counters to manually fill out a label for each count is simply a waste of resources.

The second label is an example of a preprinted label that lists the counter ID and the count date. You would assign counter IDs to each counter and print enough of these for each counter prior to the physical. The primary reason for having labels that identify the counter is to emphasize accountability. Though you should be able to track down the counter in other ways, the sticker serves as a reminder to the counter that they are responsible for their counts.

The third example shows a very simple label that is designed to obscure the purpose of the label. Though you will understand internally what the label is used for, your customers will not. The small number in the lower left corner is a date code.

Whenever applying any type of label to inventory you should have a specific procedure for label placement. In this example the requirement is to place the physical inventory labels in the lower left corner of the first carton for each SKU.

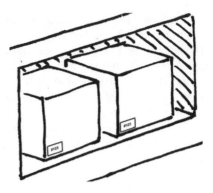

Tag counts. Tag counts involve printing separate inventory tags for every item/location combination and then using these tags rather than count sheets. Tags are usually produced as live documents with individual document numbers for each tag. This is just a sequential number used to assist in data entry and keep track of the tags. Tags are often multipart (usually three ply) forms (requires dot matrix printer) that allow a copy to be left on the item in the location after the count. The usual process — though there are many variations — involves running all the tags prior to the physical inventory and placing them in each specific location. They are either attached (taped, stapled, glued, adhesive sleeves, magnetic sleeves, thumbtacks) to the inventory or to the shelving or racking at the location. The counters will proceed from location to location, counting the inventory, writing the count on the tag and removing one copy to be used for data entry. The tag number is used as the key for data entry (enter tag number and then quantity counted). A variance report is run to be used for recounts (sometimes the variance report is another set of tags). The person conducting the recounts will go to the location, count the inventory, fill out the second count area on the form and take the second copy to be used for data entry. After all counts are entered, a missing tag report will be run showing any tag numbers that do not have counts entered. After accounting for all missing tags, the variances are investigated and approved resulting in inventory adjustments.

Tag counts take the visual verification concept to the next level by leaving a tag on the item that not only identifies it was counted, but also details the item information, the counts, recounts, and often the counter's initials and date. Sometimes companies have attempted to get around the dot matrix printer form requirements by producing multiple labels or multipart labels and then requiring the counters to write the quantity and other information multiple times (eeeeeck!). Business forms companies can usually show you examples of forms designed for tag counts, and will have some neat tricks that allow you to print on a laser or thermal transfer printer and still provide the multipart form capabilities.

This version of a tag count is surprisingly rather common (especially in older companies) and is basically an evolution of methods used decades ago (pre-computer) when an inventory record was a card or piece of paper kept in a book or filing system. The tags (which were cards or carbon forms then) could then be matched against the inventory card for the specific item. While it is a workable solution, it can be very cumbersome and you really need to ask yourself "what is the real benefit to all of this?" For the weeks and months after the physical inventory, you will likely be sweeping up the remaining count tags as they fall off of the items and locations, or are removed when the product is picked (you usually don't want this stuff going to your customers). I'm keeping an open mind that maybe someday I'll run into an operation where this methodology makes sense, but I think it's a long shot.

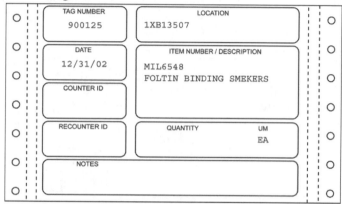

Here is an example of a multipart form used for tag counts. After the counter writes in the count and their ID, they would remove the first ply of the form and turn it in for data entry. The remaining copies of the tag (probably two more copies) would remain with the inventory in the location. If a recount is conducted, the second counter would take the second copy of the tag, leaving the final copy on the inventory.

There are variations on the tag count that can prove to be more effective. Here's how I would do it: First, I'd get rid of the three-part forms and placing the forms on the inventory prior to the count. I would print a simple tag (possibly with a small removable label portion) and hand these out to the counters. I would assign document numbers to each tag and include a bar code of the document number to facilitate very simple data entry later. I would not conduct blind counts, instead I would print the quantity on the count tags and the counters would circle them if correct and write in the quantities if not. The counters can then count each item, write in or circle the quantity, and, if you have a small removable label portion, they can place that on the product. The removable label portion would be used the same way a sticker was used with the count sheet (I would not have the counter write the quantity on it).

After the counts are completed I would manually sort the tags into two piles, one for counts that matched (hopefully the larger pile) and the other for variances. I would create a separate program for entering the "good counts" that only required scanning the bar codes (no entering of quantities). Basically you would just scan scan, scan, scan, scan, scan, scan, scan, scan, and it would sound something like this: beep, beep, beep, beep, beep, beep, beep, beep, beep. Bad counts would be entered through a different version of the program that required you to enter a quantity after scanning the bar code. Rather than a missing tag report, I would just reprint all tags that had not been scanned, and instead of a variance report I would reprint all tags with variances, and include the original count quantity on the tags.

Yeah, that sounds pretty slick. While it may seem as though the differences between the two tag count options are minimal, you will find, in practice, these small changes can make a big difference.

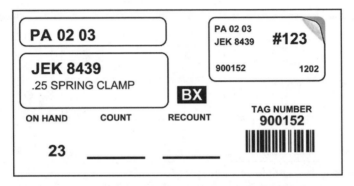

This is an example of a single-part bar-coded count tag as previously described. The tag has a removable label designed into the upper right portion. Assuming you can assign counters as you print the count tags, you can preprint the counter ID on the removable label part of the tag. This label will be used as the count verification sticker that will be placed on the item after it is counted. All the counter needs to do is circle the quantity if the count is correct, write in the quantity if it does not match, and then attach the label portion to the item.

This is the way the count tags would look when they are turned in. The tag on the left shows how a good count would be filled out, the one on the right shows a variance. You can now sort the tags by good counts and variances and then use the bar code to facilitate the data entry.

Counting with portable computers. If you do not have bar codes on your product identifying the item number (and possibly the quantity), I do not recommend attempting to use portable computers to conduct a physical inventory. And, even if your inventory is bar coded, I still may not recommend using portable computers. Generally when we talk about portable computers, we are talking about the small hand-held units. The small and difficult to read screens combined with the small and difficult to use keypads on these devices can prove to be counterproductive and can even increase error opportunities. That being said, there are environments where the use of portable terminals can be beneficial. If you have raw materials where the quantity per unit-load is not consistent from one unit-load to the next, and the item number and quantity are bar coded on the material or containers, portable computers with bar code scanners are the way to go. A more specific example would be rolls of steel, where each roll has a bar code designating the item number and the weight (which is the stocking unit-of-measure) and each roll will vary in weight. To manually count this you would have to manually add up each roll weight. Using bar code scanners and portable computers, you could just scan each roll, and then use a program to make the calculations. Also, if you have palletized loads of finished goods or raw materials that are stored in single depth pallet rack, and each palletized load has a license plate with a bar code that identifies the item number and quantity (must not have broken unit-loads), and each location has a bar code label, you could just scan each pallet load and location to conduct the inventory.

Basically I am suggesting that if you have bar-coded inventory, where scanning the bar code not only validates the item number (and probably location), but also eliminates the need to count the inventory, there are a lot of benefits to using portable computers with bar code scanners. The design of a physical inventory program using portable computers and bar code scanners under the conditions I just described is very different from the design of other counting methods. This would truly be a blind count, where you are simply scanning in all of the information to build a database file that will then be summarized by item/location and compared to the inventory database file to determine variances. Recounts of variances should be conducted manually via a variance report similar to the recount step in a count sheet based physical inventory. This is to prevent an incorrect bar code label from generating an adjustment, and to provide the person conducting the recount with additional information.

In these types of operations, the use of portable computers and bar code scanners will be a tremendous improvement over conventional counting systems. You don't necessarily need elaborate programming and RF communications to conduct this type of count. A simple program on a batch computer to gather the data and a couple of queries on your inventory system is all that's needed. In most other types of operations, you will find that portable computers become cumbersome and slow down the process.

A big mistake when using portable terminals in a physical inventory is to duplicate count sheet or tag count methodology on the terminals. This overcomplicates the process and is not effectively utilizing the technology.

Execution

If you've invested adequate time and resources into the preparation phase, the execution phase of a physical inventory should run smoothly. The biggest issue immediately prior to starting the count will be the verification of transactional control. This will usually involve running an assortment of open order and staging location reports to confirm that everything that was supposed to be processed, was actually processed. It should also consist of a quick walk-through to potentially identify undocumented, in-process materials. This usually consists of a lot of "what's this doing here?" questioning of floor personnel.

It's very important to resolve all transactional control issues prior to initiating the count. Failure to do so may result in some very complicated data adjustments to compensate for incomplete transactions. For example, if a large shipping order was picked and shipped, but the system was not updated, you will have to manually add all shipped quantities into the counted quantities of each item on the order. You are much better off delaying the initiation of the count until you have accounted for all of these open issues rather than trying to reconcile them during or after the count.

Once you have the transactional control issues taken care of you should go ahead and initiate the count. If the preparation and training were adequate, this should start out fairly smooth. It's a good idea to conduct some quick checks shortly after the counting has started. Focus should be placed on checking the counters with the least experience first to ensure they understand and are following procedures. You don't want to wait several hours before you find out someone is having some real problems.

You generally want to start conducting recounts of variances as quickly as possible. If you are not conducting blind counts, you may want to just use the original count documents to conduct the recounts. If you are conducting blind counts, you will need to enter the count data first and then run variance reports. It's a good idea to use a printed floor plan of all storage operations to keep track of progress. It's simply a matter of marking off the areas that have been counted with one color, and then marking them again after recounts have been completed with another color. You may also want to use this to document the person that was counting in each area.

The reconciliation process is by far the most difficult part of most physical inventories. There are usually only a handful of people (or sometimes just one person) that have the skills and knowledge to effectively investigate and approve physical inventory adjustments. If you're in an environment where items will be stored in multiple locations that can be anywhere in the facility, you may not be able to start reconciling until everything has been counted. If items can be stored in multiple locations but will be within specific designated storage areas, you should plan your counting so the counters focus on one area at a time to allow reconciliation to start as soon as each area is completed.

If you did not read the chapter on cycle counting, you should go back and read the sections on reconciling variances and understanding the effects of adjustments. While it's unlikely that you will have the time to conduct thorough root-cause investigations during a physical inventory, you still need to go through some of the same logic just to determine if the adjustment is valid. So why would you need to do this if the inventory was counted and then the variances were recounted? Certainly the count must be valid, right? Not necessarily. You may have inventory that was incorrectly identified, mixed inventory, cases or other containers that have incorrect quantities on the labels, and remember those open orders that I keep referring to? The people in charge of reconciling the counts need to determine if they need the identification of inventory verified, if they need to sort the inventory, if they need an additional recount, if they need containers opened and hand counts conducted, or if they need to research open or recently processed shipping orders, production orders, or receipts. This is where time often becomes your enemy as you struggle to keep up with the variances. The more variances you have, the more likely it is that you will not adequately investigate them, ultimately resulting in more incorrect adjustments. If you had been proactive and aggressively pursued counting inventory and making adjustments (cycle counting) prior to the physical inventory, your efforts will be rewarded at this point.

If you are using a physical inventory program that will automatically make adjustments, you should run and review a final variance report before running the update. If you are using your cycle count program to make the adjustments, be aware that the program will likely update the last count date on all items; this may create serious problems for your cycle count scheduling. If you are making the adjustments manually, you should go back and check the adjustments to make sure they were entered correctly. If you have a transaction history file that contains the date and time of the transactions, you should be able to produce a report sorted by time that can be compared to the paperwork you were using to make the adjustments.

Immediately following the completion of the physical inventory there are still a couple of things that need to be done. You should prepare reports on the results of the physical inventory and make notes on what worked and what didn't work. This should help make the next physical go smoother. After a few days, you should consider cycle counting through the items that had variances during the physical. The approach here is pretty simple, start with the largest adjustments based on either dollar value or quantity, and work your way down the list. It's highly unlikely that all of your physical inventory adjustments were correct and this is the best way to find out.

Summary

There is no debate on the problems associated with periodic physical inventories. The real question is: What do you do about it? You can either make it work, or find an alternative. The option of making a periodic physical inventory work is generally more realistic for smaller operations. Investing the time in planning and preparation can compensate for many of the problems associated with physical inventories. For larger or more complex operations, you may find that "making it work" is just not realistic. In addition, companies that lack the capacity to permit shutting down operations will also find a periodic physical unrealistic. I am amazed at the number of businesses that consider high levels of customer service a key objective in the success of their companies, yet seem to think nothing of shutting down production and shipping operations for two or three days (while customers are waiting for product) to conduct their annual or semiannual physical inventory. Building an accurate environment and putting in place a process for proving the accuracy is what is needed to eliminate a periodic physical inventory in these environments. There is no doubt that cycle counting is part of this solution, however you also need a process for continuous improvement and probably periodic accuracy audits to prove the accuracy.

6

Accuracy Measurement

Have you ever heard the saying "You can't improve what you don't measure?" The "can't" part of the statement is a little bit of an exaggeration. A more accurate statement is "you probably won't improve what you don't measure." Measurement generally provides a method for controlling a process, incentive to make improvements (if your performance is evaluated based upon the measurement), documentation of the results of improvements, and information to assist in the improvement process. Measurement comes in many different forms, from high-level measurement used to review the performance of the business to detailed measurement used to control and improve specific processes. As accuracy is critical to the successful operation of your business, you should probably have a plan to measure it.

General accuracy measurement

Inventory accuracy measurement is generally a summarized measurement of the output of a cycle count program or a periodic physical inventory. It's given as an accuracy percentage based upon snapshot-in-time counts (in cycle counting it would be a series of counts over a period of time). There are several different methods of this type of measurement:

Good count bad count.

This is probably the most common method of measurement associated with cycle count programs. Good count bad count measurement divides the number of good counts into the total number of counts. A count is defined as a specific item/location combination, or, in other words, each line on the count sheet. The definition of a "good count" gets a little muddy as tolerances are introduced into the equation. In its purest form a good count would be a count that exactly matched the system quantity. For example, if I went to location 123 and counted 25 pieces of item XYZ, and the system quantity was listed at 25, I would have one good count. If the system quantity were 26, I would have one bad count. Tolerances are frequently introduced into good count bad count to allow counts that are close but do not exactly match system counts to be considered good counts. For example, in the same scenario where I counted 25 but the system quantity was 26, and I had a 5% tolerance, it would still be considered a good count.

So why would you want to consider a count as a good count if it didn't match exactly? Let me give you another example. If your inventory is made up of small nuts, bolts, and washers with average inventory quantities on each item being in the tens of thousands, you would rarely have counts that matched exactly to the piece. Because of the rigidity of a pure good count bad count system, this would result in almost every count being considered a bad count. Whether you are off by one piece or ten thousand pieces doesn't make a difference, it's still a bad count. Obviously this rigid measurement in this type of environment is not going to produce useful and meaningful results (we do want the measurement to be useful and meaningful don't we?). This is where tolerances come in. I consider tolerances to be a necessary evil when using good count bad count in many environments. I don't particularly like using tolerances, but then again, I don't particularly like good count bad count anyway. Unfortunately, no matter where you set the tolerance, you still end up with the situation where one piece will make the difference between a good count and a bad count.

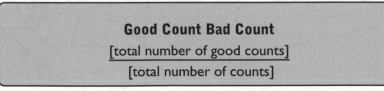

Good Count Bad Count

[total number of good counts]

[total number of counts]

You also have the issue of determining what tolerances are reasonable for the specific items being counted. There are many differing opinions on what a reasonable tolerance is. One view is that tolerances should only be used where materials are machine counted and the tolerance should be set to reflect the machine tolerances. Another view is that tolerances should be set at a point where the variance would potentially become a problem to operations. The machine count tolerance is a given, you cannot possibly expect your inventory to be more accurate than the counting method. The operational impact tolerance, however, is subject to debate. I agree that considering the impact of variances is important. The problem lies in how you quantify the point at which a variance is likely or unlikely to impact operations. Unless you formally allocate a specific quantity of safety stock to inventory variances (highly unlikely), this tolerance becomes very subjective.

Unfortunately, there seems to be a trend in companies taking a simple approach by applying a 5% tolerance across the board. While keeping it simple has some merits, in this case it is not a good idea. Though there may be some items where allowing a 5% tolerance is justifiable, I would say that they are the exception more than the rule. I have a hard time believing that 5% variances on all items are unlikely to affect operations. Another approach commonly used is to apply a fixed dollar tolerance where any variance less than the dollar tolerance amount is considered a good count. The dollar amount chosen is highly dependant on the type of materials you are handling and the volume in your operations. Most common are amounts between $5 and $50, with $50 being more common than I would like. Once again, there are operations where $50 or more tolerances are justifiable, but they are the exception. The benefit of a fixed dollar tolerance over a percentage tolerance is that it will automatically apply only to lower cost items (unit cost must be less than tolerance amount). The problem with a fixed dollar tolerance is that it assumes a connection between the cost of an item and its potential impact on operations. You may have some items where the value of the entire stocked quantity is less than the tolerance. Does this mean that if you lose the entire quantity stocked it is still considered a good count? I would hope not.

So what should you do? You need to look at the characteristics of your inventory and determine if tolerances make sense for your environment. It's unlikely that you should need tolerances for all items, or the same tolerance for all items where a tolerance is justifiable. Let's go back to the computer assembly operation I discussed in chapter five. I would likely have a fairly large tolerance (maybe 5%) on the little machine screws used to assemble the case and components. I would first verify the planning methods and safety stock calculations to determine the potential impact of a 5% tolerance. I may also have smaller tolerances (maybe 2% or 3%) on the internal power connectors and communication cables. I would probably not use tolerances on other components such as cases, power supplies, drives, motherboards, CPUs, memory, graphics cards. If I did chose to use a tolerance on these other items it would be very small (1% or less).

You can also combine tolerances to take the value and the percentage of the variance into account. For example, you can set the tolerance to designate a good count if the percentage variance is no more than 3% and the dollar variance is no more than $10. This is a simple means of assuring that the tolerance percentage is only applied to lower cost items.

Another way to get around the black-and-white rigidity of a good count bad count measurement is to calculate several versions of the measurement with different tolerances applied. For example your measurement may show that with pure good count bad count you are at 75%, with a 2% tolerance you are at 90%, and with a 5% tolerance you are at 98%. By showing multiple calculations, you get a much better picture of your overall accuracy. You may also want to combine some fixed dollar tolerances at each level.

Net piece variance.
Net piece variance compares the sum of the piece variances to the sum of the expected on-hand quantities (system count). For example, if on item XYZ you are expected to have 100 pieces and only have 95, and on item ABC you are expected to have 100 pieces and have 104, your variances are -5 and +4 respectively. This gives you a net sum of -1, which, when divided by 200 (the sum of the expected quantities) you get a net piece variance percentage of -0.5%. This translates to a net piece accuracy percentage of 99.5%.

Net dollar variance.
Net dollar variance is calculated similarly to net piece variance with the exception being that you are comparing dollar amounts (pieces multiplied by unit cost) rather than pieces. If you used the previous example and applied the unit costs of $10 for item XYZ and $5 for item ABC, you would have dollar variances of -$50 and +$20 respectively. This gives you a net sum of -$30, which, when divided by $1,500 (the sum of the value of the expected quantities) gives you a net dollar variance percentage of -2.0%. This translates to a net dollar accuracy percentage of 98%.

Net variance measurements will generally show a deceivingly high accuracy rate since positive and negative variances will offset each other. Because of this, net variance calculations are not a very good measure of detailed accuracy. They do, however, serve a couple of purposes. Net variances will show a bias in variances (either positive or negative). For most operations you will find that you generally have almost as many positive variances as negative variances. This is representative of operations where execution-level human error is the cause of most errors. A consistent positive or negative bias may point to other problems such as bill of material problems, scrap reporting problems, or theft problems. From an accounting standpoint, the net dollar variance is the most important measure of accuracy as it describes the accuracy of the total inventory value. You can also see from the previous example, that there can be a significant difference between net piece and net dollar accuracy measurements (99.5% and 98% respectively). In a net piece variance measurement, a positive variance of one 5-cent screw can offset a negative variance of one $500 component.

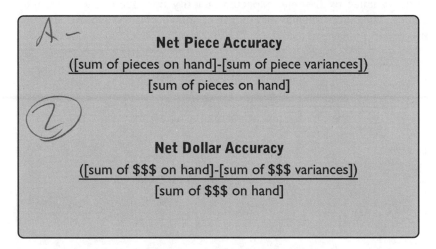

Gross or absolute piece variance.

Gross piece variance, also known as absolute piece variance, compares the sum of the absolute (disregarding positive or negative sign) piece variances to the sum of the expected on-hand quantities (system count). For example, if on item XYZ you are expected to have 100 pieces and only have 95, and on item ABC you are expected to have 100 pieces and have 104, your absolute variances are 5 and 4 respectively. This gives you a sum of 9, which when divided by 200 (the sum of the expected quantities) you get an absolute piece variance percentage of 4.5%. This translates to an absolute accuracy percentage of 95.5%. Absolute accuracy measurements are a much better means of showing operational accuracy than net accuracy measurements.

Gross or absolute dollar variance.

Absolute dollar variance is calculated similarly to absolute piece variance with the exception being that you are comparing dollar amounts (pieces multiplied by unit cost) rather than pieces. If you used the previous example and applied the unit costs of $10 for item XYZ and $5 for item ABC, you would have absolute dollar variances of $50 and $20 respectively. This gives you a sum of $70, which, when divided by $1,500 (the sum of the value of the expected quantities) gives you an absolute dollar variance percentage of 4.7%. This translates to an absolute dollar accuracy percentage of 95.3%.

Average absolute variance.

There is also a supplemental measurement related to absolute accuracy. Average absolute piece or dollar variances are calculated similarly to the previously mentioned absolute measurement, with the exception being that you divide the total absolute variance (pieces or dollars) by the number of variances (do not include good counts). This would display the average absolute variance as a piece quantity or dollar amount. To calculate as a percentage, you would divide the total absolute variance by the total expected quantity or value of the items that had variances. This supplemental measurement shows you the average size of your variances.

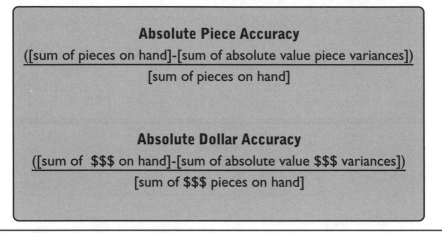

Absolute Piece Accuracy

$$\frac{([\text{sum of pieces on hand}]-[\text{sum of absolute value piece variances}])}{[\text{sum of pieces on hand}]}$$

Absolute Dollar Accuracy

$$\frac{([\text{sum of \$\$\$ on hand}]-[\text{sum of absolute value \$\$\$ variances}])}{[\text{sum of \$\$\$ pieces on hand}]}$$

Comparing the calculations.

On the following page (figure 6A) is an example of the various calculations applied to some sample data. On top is the detail of a small count sheet (only 21 counts). On the bottom of the page are the results of the calculations discussed on the previous pages.

You can see that there is a significant range of accuracy percentages that result from the same data by using different methods of calculating accuracy.

With good count bad count measurement you have 7 bad counts with no tolerance, 5 bad counts using a 2% tolerance, and 3 bad counts using a 5% tolerance. This results in good count bad count accuracy percentages of 66.67%, 76.19%, and 85.71% respectively.

If you look at the net accuracy calculations, you can see that there is a significant difference between the net piece results and the net dollar results (99.76% and 98.20% respectively). This is because there were a couple of small piece shortages on some higher priced items. This resulted in a positive net piece variance of 5 pieces, but a negative net dollar variance of $70.73. In a larger count sheet you would probably see a narrower gap between net piece and net dollar accuracy results.

You can also see that the absolute accuracy results are significantly lower than the net accuracy results. This is almost always going to be the case since some variances will offset others in the net calculations.

Item	Cost	System Quantity	System Value	Counted Quantity	Piece Variance	Absolute Piece Variance	Dollar Variance	Absolute Dollar Variance	%
RND8739	$0.37	183	$67.71	182	-1	1	-$0.37	$0.37	-0.5%
WGS4322	$10.48	73	$765.04	73	0	0	$0.00	$0.00	0.0%
JEK8439	$3.85	23	$88.55	23	0	0	$0.00	$0.00	0.0%
MIL6548	$7.68	4	$30.72	4	0	0	$0.00	$0.00	0.0%
BLG1598	$76.48	2	$152.96	2	0	0	$0.00	$0.00	0.0%
WPL6702	$23.87	32	$763.84	33	1	1	$23.87	$23.87	3.1%
XPF4321	$0.24	3	$0.72	3	0	0	$0.00	$0.00	0.0%
KEW2976	$93.50	2	$187.00	1	-1	1	-$93.50	$93.50	-50.0%
LKE4783	$2.53	53	$134.09	53	0	0	$0.00	$0.00	0.0%
RND8978	$7.94	23	$182.62	20	-3	3	-$23.82	$23.82	-13.0%
FRP7896	$18.43	3	$55.29	3	0	0	$0.00	$0.00	0.0%
LZX8032	$1.57	27	$42.39	27	0	0	$0.00	$0.00	0.0%
KKJ9874	$4.68	5	$23.40	5	0	0	$0.00	$0.00	0.0%
LPS1223	$87.50	1	$87.50	1	0	0	$0.00	$0.00	0.0%
SDP9321	$10.39	73	$758.47	75	2	2	$20.78	$20.78	2.7%
JKL6588	$0.03	213	$6.39	199	-14	14	-$0.42	$0.42	-6.6%
FLC2033	$12.48	23	$287.04	23	0	0	$0.00	$0.00	0.0%
REW9284	$3.94	25	$98.50	25	0	0	$0.00	$0.00	0.0%
LSK4872	$4.25	1	$4.25	1	0	0	$0.00	$0.00	0.0%
SDL5683	$3.78	2	$7.56	2	0	0	$0.00	$0.00	0.0%
KSD2483	$0.13	1347	$175.11	1368	21	21	$2.73	$2.73	1.6%
Summary		2118	$3,919.15	2123	5	43	-$70.73	$165.49	

Tolerances

	0%	2%	5%
Good Counts	14	16	18
Bad Counts	7	5	3
Total Counts	21	21	21

Accuracy Measures

Good Count Bad Count 0% Tolerance	66.67%
Good Count Bad Count 2% Tolerance	76.19%
Good Count Bad Count 5% Tolerance	85.71%
Net Piece Accuracy	99.76%
Net Dollar Accuracy	98.20%
Absolute Piece Accuracy	97.97%
Absolute Dollar Accuracy	95.78%

Figure 6A

Transactional variance calculations.

Unlike the other accuracy measurements, transactional variance measurement compares the variance quantity to the quantity consumed during the count period rather than the on-hand quantity at the time of the count. This type of tracking is far more useful in determining process problems. Unfortunately, it is also much more difficult to implement and maintain this method. To calculate transactional variances you must determine the total quantity consumed (consumed in production or shipped to customers or branches) between the previous count date and the current count date. You then divide the variance quantity by this usage quantity. You would generally summarize this measurement by commodity or some other logical grouping of inventory. In manufacturing, this type of measurement on raw materials can prove to be very valuable in pinpointing problems relating to bills of material such as incorrect required quantities and scrap and yield percentages. While the results of on-hand based measurements may have been inconsistent, you may see a consistent pattern when you recalculate the variance percentage based upon transacted quantities. This type of measurement is also valuable in high volume order picking operations to determine if certain products or groups of products are more highly prone to error. This is a rather specialized form of accuracy measurement and, since it is also rather difficult to calculate, is not used frequently.

Root cause measurement.

Root-cause measurement should also be maintained as an output of the root cause analysis conducted as part of your cycle counting program. Since root cause determination is not always an exact science, the cycle count administrator may want to break down the measurement into groups based upon the evidence to support the root cause determination. If you are fairly certain of the root causes you list them under "fairly certain," others may be listed under "best educated guess." Root cause measurement is usually provided with several levels of detail. You will usually start with higher level categories such as shipping error, receiving error, stocking error, production reporting error, or cycle counting error, and then take the highest ranking categories and break them down further such as breaking down stocking errors into subcategories like, putaway error wrong item number, putaway error wrong location, putaway error wrong quantity, replenishment error wrong item number, replenishment error wrong location, replenishment error wrong quantity, location consolidation error, and miscellaneous transaction error.

What measurement should you use?

Unfortunately, none of these measurements by themselves show a clear picture of your inventory accuracy. Good count bad count shows the number of SKUs affected but does a poor job of showing the magnitude of the actual variances or any bias in the variances. Net variance measurement shows the bias but does not describe the number of SKUs affected or the magnitude of the actual variances.

Absolute variance measurement shows the magnitude but does not describe the number of SKUs or any bias.

In addition, any measurement that compares the variance to the current on-hand quantity is subject to the timing of the count. For example, if I counted item XYZ today with the on-hand quantity being 100 and had a variance of -5, my accuracy measurement would be very different than if I counted the same item tomorrow after a receipt of 500 was put into inventory. I still have the same variance of -5, however it now likely qualifies as a good count (assuming at least a 1 percent tolerance), and the effects on gross and absolute calculations would be significantly different. This means that if you tried to take productivity into account in designing your cycle count program by timing your counts to when inventory was relatively low, you are essentially handicapping the accuracy reporting results. Also, since all of these accuracy measurements are generally calculated based upon the output of a cycle count program, your accuracy is also dependant upon the items chosen for counts (count frequency distribution). So once again, if you are focusing your counts on items that are more prone to error (as you should be) you are further handicapping your accuracy reporting results. Similarly, measurement that comes from forced count sheets (those are cycle count sheets where items are hand selected based upon a suspected variance that turned up in the course of business) is going to reflect extremely low accuracy rates since you already suspect there are variances on the items. On the flip side, if you are manually making corrections based upon supplemental checks such as location audits, are these corrections reflected in the measurement? Should they be? These are good questions because the accuracy measurement is supposed to reflect overall accuracy. If you include variances from forced counts and audits, you are biasing the results to incorrectly understate the overall accuracy. If you don't include them it could be argued that you are now biasing the results to overstate the accuracy. There are other factors such as the number of locations an item is stored in that can also change the results of the accuracy measurement.

A savvy and principled cycle count administrator may find himself in a dilemma as doing the right thing in determining what gets counted and when is in conflict with the standard his performance is being measured against. A savvy and unprincipled cycle count administrator may figure out that by counting items only after they are received (sacrificing productivity), frequently counting items that have a low opportunity for error (sacrificing effectiveness), and using other methods to correct known errors (from audits or forced counts) he can significantly improve the reported accuracy numbers, and, in doing so, get himself a raise or bonus.

More bad news.
You should recall from the chapter on cycle counting that I mentioned there are times when you should be making the inventory corrections in the original program that created the error. This was mentioned related to errors where the failure to use the original program (receipt program, production reporting program, etc.)

to correct the error would leave bad planning data in the system. In doing these types of corrections, the cycle count administrator would usually "fake" the count to prevent the cycle count program from duplicating the adjustment. If you are using the cycle count database files as a source for your accuracy measurement (most common method of measuring accuracy), you will find that you have just compromised the accuracy of the reporting by making these "bad counts" appear as "good counts." Since these types of errors are often very large in comparison to the errors you are allowing the cycle count program to correct, you are definitely changing the measurement.

One way to get around this would be to go ahead and allow the cycle count program to make the adjustment, then make the correction through the original program and enter a miscellaneous adjustment to offset the adjustment made by the cycle count program. This can be a little dangerous, so your cycle count administrator better be on top of his game. If these types of adjustments are fairly infrequent, this methodology is a reasonable solution. For more frequent adjustments, you need to weigh the extra work and risk of error (each additional transaction creates an additional risk of error) against the value of the measurement. You may also choose to take all of your accuracy measurement off-line. This would require a separate means of accumulating the accuracy data, which essentially translates to more work for the cycle count administrator or a clerical person.

Where is all of this leading?
Accuracy measurement is important yet imprecise. As long as you understand the flaws in accuracy measurement, you can still make effective decisions based upon it. That is why you are measuring, isn't it? Though none of the measurement methods by themselves will clearly describe your accuracy, combinations of several methods can prove to be an effective means of evaluating it. Using a scorecard approach by calculating several (or all) methods and separately displaying their results provides a knowledgeable manager with a clear picture of accuracy. You may also choose to weight specific measures and calculate a single composite measurement number that you feel best reflects the accuracy and its impact on operations.

To further enhance your accuracy measurement, you may choose to break down your inventory into groups and measure the accuracy of each group. Examples include breaking down your inventory by various ABC categories, separating production usage inventory from finished goods inventory, or grouping by commodity classification.

I've developed a preference for using the results of periodic accuracy audits as the basis for accuracy measurement rather than the results of cycle counts. Since the primary goal of an accuracy audit is to provide an accurate measurement of accuracy, you will find that many of the cycle counting conflicts do not apply. In most cases the accuracy rate from a periodic audit should be higher than the accuracy rate calculated based upon cycle count data. One reason is that an audit

Month Ending 12/31/2002

	Totals	Accuracy Percentage
Total Items/Locations counted	2200	
Total Pieces Counted	135250	
Total Dollars Counted	$1,754,358	
Piece Accuracy		
Net Piece Variance	-254	99.81%
Absolute Piece Variance	3542	97.38%
Dollar Accuracy		
Net Dollar Variance	-$437	99.98%
Absolute Dollar Variance	$45,375	97.41%
Good Count Bad Count		
Bad Counts No Tolerance	347	84.23%
Bad Counts 1% Tolerance	148	93.27%
Bad Counts 3% Tolerance	76	96.55%
Bad Counts 5% Tolerance	21	99.05%

ScoreCard

Weighting		
50%	Net Dollar Accuracy	99.98%
30%	Absolute Piece Accuracy	97.38%
20%	Good Count Bad Count w/1% tolerance	93.27%
	Weighted Score	**97.86%**

Figure 6B. Above is an example of a month-end summarized accuracy report. I've also added an example of a weighted scorecard at the bottom of the report. In this example, I chose to use net dollar accuracy, absolute piece accuracy, and good count bad count with a 1% tolerance accuracy as the key accuracy metrics for the scorecard. I weighted them at 50%, 30%, and 20% respectively. In this case, the weighted score is being used to communicate accuracy to the executive staff, that is why net dollar variance is weighted more heavily. The weighted score of 97.86% is the result of this composite calculation.

A weighted score is a nice way to communicate accuracy to those that are unlikely to look at the detail. It's also easy to plop into a graph to communicate long-term performance. For my own purposes, I would still want to see the separate accuracy measurements.

will focus more on a representative sampling of your overall inventory and not on items that are likely to have problems. Another reason is that a cycle count always occurs at the end of the cycle count cycle (I hope this makes sense) when the likelihood of a variance is the greatest. With an accuracy audit, you will be counting items that are at various points in their cycle count cycle. In other words, some of the items in the audit may have just recently been counted, making them less likely to have a variance (unless you're doing a really bad job of cycle counting). This provides a much better picture of the true day-to-day accuracy of your on-hand balances. If you do chose to use periodic audits (quarterly or semiannually) for your internal accuracy measurement, you should try to refrain from aggressively "fixing" the inventory just prior to the audit. You want the output of the audit to reflect normal day-to-day conditions. If the audit is being conducted for external purposes, the external auditors will likely assume that you were attempting to "fix" everything prior to the audit, so you may as well go ahead and give it your best shot.

You will find that the same advantages of using the output of an accuracy audit also apply to using the output of a physical inventory for your accuracy measurement. Hold on there, partner! I'm not saying that a physical inventory is a better means of achieving accuracy than a cycle count program, only that it is a better means of measuring accuracy.

When deciding how you are going to measure accuracy, you need to consider the value of the measurement along with the costs and resources required to produce and manage the measurement. Accuracy measurement should be a tool that helps to manage and improve accuracy, not an unwieldy system that sucks up resources and takes focus away from accuracy improvement activities.

As important as accuracy measurement is, I think companies need to ease up a bit on their focus on "the numbers." Being someone that spends significant amounts of time analyzing data, I readily admit that managing by the numbers is a big part of my management strategy, however, there are times when the numbers can get in the way of effective management. I believe I've demonstrated that these types of accuracy measurements are at best imperfect, in some cases misleading, and in other cases completely inaccurate. Some companies complacently sit back boasting high rates of accuracy (often the results of large tolerances and flawed measurements) while their customers and employees scratch their heads thinking, "there's no way!" In other companies, those responsible for accuracy are constantly beat up because the numbers aren't "high enough" even though their accuracy initiatives have greatly improved operations and customer satisfaction.

Put in place measurements that are reasonable, useful, and meaningful. Educate those that use the measurement on the logic behind the measurement and any known flaws in the measurement. Make sure the measurement does not get in the way of improvement.

Benchmarking accuracy

Two of the most frequent questions I am asked are "what should my accuracy be?" or "how can I benchmark my accuracy?" If you were even moderately paying attention during the previous sections you should realize how difficult it is to try to compare accuracy measurements from one company to another (external benchmarking). On top of confusion over the various measurement methods, tolerances, and controlling factors, you also have to consider the characteristics of the operation you are trying to compare yourself to. Are the inventory characteristics similar? Are the storage characteristics similar? Are the order profiles similar? Are the manufacturing processes similar? What types of technologies are being used? Unless you can get detailed answers to all of these questions and have access to their raw data, it is unlikely that you can conduct a fair comparison. And even if you could, what does it tell you? Should you settle for the same accuracy rate as company X or is it realistic to expect the same accuracy as company Y?

OK, I admit it; I look at benchmark data every chance I get. There's no harm in looking. I compare the benchmarks with my own experiences and frequently come the conclusions that "these numbers are crap." Now if I did not already have something to base the comparison on — as is often the case of those looking to use benchmarking data — I may be making business decisions based upon "crap." To be fair, "crap" can mean a number of different things here. In some cases the benchmarks — in my opinion — are too low or high based upon the other information provided, and in other cases there is just not enough information included to even make a general comparison.

There is also a misconception related to benchmarking that assumes companies currently recognized as being successful must be the standard by which all others should be measured. There are a lot of factors that lead to the success of an organization, and it's naive to think that just because a company is successful, all of their practices should be considered "best practices." And, with the rash of accounting scandals that are dominating the headlines as I am writing this book, it's questionable as to whether "successful" companies are really successful.

Many business professionals are coming to the conclusion that rather than trying to emulate another business, they will be more successful if they look to set their own standards. This follows the logic of continuous improvement, that by continuously focusing on improvement, regardless of what other companies are doing, you will be the best that you can be. This answers the question of "what should my accuracy be?" with "better than it currently is."

I am not going to deny that there is value in benchmarking. Sometimes a company truly does set a new standard. These are the situations where you look at the numbers and say, "I didn't think that was possible" and "how did they accomplish that?" The problem is that unless you can first answer the questions "are the numbers real?" "how are they calculating the numbers?" and "what are the characteristics of the operation?" the benchmark is of no value to you. This is the most significant problem with benchmarking inventory accuracy. If you can build relationships with other businesses that have similar operations to your own, where you can ask these questions and get detailed answers you have a better chance of sharing and making use of benchmarks. If you have expectations that you can simply pull accuracy numbers from a benchmark report or from an industry magazine article and apply them to your operation, you should plan on being disappointed.

Unlike external benchmarking, internal benchmarking seeks only to compare an operation to itself over a period of time. Let's face it, internal benchmarking is just a fancy term that describes the measurement we maintain in the normal operation of the business. Internal benchmarking can be very useful provided the method and data used to produce the measurement has not changed. Even a flawed measurement system that is maintained consistently over an extended period of time will prove to be more valuable than constantly changing "optimized" measurement systems. Long-term accuracy measurement will not only display the effects of process improvements, but will also reveal the effects of process deterioration.

Specific-process accuracy measurement

Though general snapshot-in-time accuracy measurements combined with root-cause analyses are useful in monitoring and improving accuracy, the results do not give the levels of detail you can obtain through accuracy measurement of specific processes. For the most part, specific-process accuracy measurements are the results of measuring the output of some type of checking process. As cycle counting, physical inventories, and accuracy audits are checking processes for general accuracy, checks such as outbound order checking are checking processes for specific processes (order picking in this case). As with cycle counting, process checks are designed to not only catch errors and correct them before they affect operations, but also to provide information to be used in the continuous improvement process.

Shipping accuracy as reported by customers.

There is no doubt that measuring customer complaints is important. For distribution and fulfillment operations, shipping accuracy measurement is given as much — if not more — importance than general accuracy measurement. As with general accuracy measurements, shipping accuracy measurement is also imprecise and misunderstood. Shipping accuracy measurement based upon customer complaints is not a measurement of the actual shipping errors, but rather the perceived shipping errors that customers caught and felt were important enough to report.

Let's break this down a little further; "perceived" errors are not always actual errors. If the shipment was correct and the customer made a mistake checking it in, the customer has a perceived error. If you cannot convince the customer that it is not an actual error, you need to track it as a customer complaint of an error. The number of errors that customers "caught" are sometimes far less than actual shipping errors. If your customers are not conducting thorough inspections at receipt, they are likely to only catch very obvious errors. Errors that the customer felt "were important enough to report" may only be a portion of the errors that the customer caught. If you ship to other business, they may not report small quantity variances based upon their own tolerances. Over-shipments are far less likely to be reported than short-shipments. And, if a customer receives a more valuable and desirable item in place of what they should have received, are they going to call and report it?

So let's review. Sometimes customers report errors that are not errors, customers only catch a portion of actual errors, and only report a portion of the portion they caught. The number of over-reported errors due to perceived errors is usually minimal in comparison to the number of unreported errors. Depending upon the industry you are in and your customer base, the difference between reported shipping errors and actual shipping errors can be astonishing.

Unless you are going to go to your customer's location and check the order as it is received (not a bad idea for occasional spot-checks), you really have no other choice than to base shipping accuracy on customer complaints. And, even with its drawbacks, shipping accuracy measurement based on customer complaints is fairly effective at showing improvement or deterioration of actual accuracy because the percentage of reported errors to actual errors tends to remain fairly consistent over time. This means that if your customers are reporting more errors, you are probably making more errors; if they are reporting less, you are improving. Exactly how many errors you are making is unknown. What I'm really trying to say here is that shipping accuracy as reported by customers is a very important measure of customer satisfaction and operational performance. However, you should not be misled into thinking this is an accurate measure of actual errors.

Shipping accuracy is generally reported as either a percentage of line items shipped, a percentage of orders shipped, or, in rare cases, a percentage of units shipped. Reporting shipping accuracy as a percentage of line items shipped tends to be most common. A line item is an individual pick from an order; it represents one trip to one location to pick whatever quantity is required for the order. Some companies may consider picks of the same item from several locations to fill a single requirement on an order, as a single line item, though considering each location pick as a separate line item tends to be more common. To calculate shipping accuracy, you must take the total line item errors, order errors, or unit errors, subtract them from the total line items shipped, total orders shipped, or total units shipped, and then divide the result by the total line items shipped, total orders shipped, or total units shipped. For example, if you shipped 1,000 orders containing a total of 3,000 line items and 6,000 pieces, and had a total of 2 errors (on separate orders) consisting of a shortage of 1 pc and a shortage of 5 pcs; your order accuracy would be 99.80%, your line items shipped accuracy would be 99.93%, and your units shipped accuracy would be 99.90%. Though you may also report accuracy as the specific number of errors, the key measurement should always be reported as a percentage of transactions.

Error-type analysis should also be part of your shipping accuracy measurement. This is basically breaking down the shipping errors into categories such as, incorrect quantity over shipment, incorrect quantity short shipment, incorrect materials shipped, missing line item, and mixed orders.

Picking accuracy measurement based upon internal checks.
The difference between this and shipping accuracy is that it is the output of an internal checking process. If you don't have a formal internal order checking process, you can conduct periodic audits of outbound orders to determine your internal picking accuracy. Based upon the level of checking conducted, this measurement will give you a much more accurate measure of picking accuracy. The purposes of accuracy measurement from an internal checking process include validating the need for the checking process, measuring process accuracy to provide information to be used for process improvement, and providing accuracy mea-

surement of individual workers to be used to evaluate performance and possibly provide incentives.

Picking accuracy measurement based upon internal checks is calculated exactly the same way as shipping accuracy, with accuracy percentage by line items shipped being most common method used. Picking accuracy measurement can be compared to shipping accuracy over an extended period of time to try to estimate the percentage of actual shipping errors reported by customers. If you are just putting in place an internal order checking process you can compare the changes in the number of reported errors to the number of errors caught internally. For example, if you had been averaging 30 errors per month reported by customers prior to starting the internal check, and the number dropped to 10 errors per month after the internal check was in place, you can now compare the difference of 20 errors to the number of errors caught internally. If you averaged 40 errors per month caught internally, you can now make the assumption that customers are only catching and reporting half of the errors actually made. If you go back to the pre-check period where you used only the customer complaint measurement, you probably thought you were making 30 errors per month when more likely you were making 60 errors per month. Now, your order picking process is still producing 60 errors per month, your checking process is catching 40 of these, 20 are getting out to customers with only 10 being actually reported back. Some operations may find that, after implementing a formal checking and measurement process, their actual errors were three, four, or even five times the number of reported errors. These higher error rates will likely help to better explain the general inventory accuracy problems they had been having.

Receiving accuracy measurement.

Receiving accuracy measurement is somewhat unique since the receiving process is, for the most part, a checking process. The difference is, this checking process is not checking an internal process but is rather a check of the shipping accuracy of a supplier. External errors caught during the receipt check-in process should be documented and communicated to the supplier. Since it's likely that your supplier is rating his accuracy based upon customer complaints, your failure to notify the supplier of errors will only perpetuate the problem. This measurement would be calculated similarly to shipping accuracy measurement (since that is what it actually is). The important use of this measurement is in providing information to your suppliers to help them improve and also to help in determining the requirements for your receipt check-in process.

Once you get past the receipt check-in process, there is rarely another formal check in place to verify the receipt process. Measurement of the accuracy of the receiving process is usually based upon output from built-in checks (three-way invoice match or errors caught during putaway, inspection, or repack) or from the output of a cycle count program. It can be valuable to periodically conduct an audit of receipts to verify process accuracy. Receiving accuracy is generally measured as a percentage of receipt transactions (line items received).

Putaway accuracy measurement.

Putaway accuracy is measured as the output of a putaway checking process, location audit process, or cycle count process. Putaway errors are usually the result of placing the materials in the wrong location or processing the transaction incorrectly. Putaway errors tend to be rather easy to identify through any of the previously mentioned checking processes since the variance quantity and location is generally easy to associate with a specific putaway transaction. As with picking accuracy, the purposes of putaway accuracy measurement include validating the need for the checking process, measuring process accuracy to provide information to be used for process improvement, and providing accuracy measurement of individual workers to be used to evaluate performance and possibly provide incentives. Putaway accuracy measurement is less important in operations that use fixed putaway locations rather than random putaway storage. Putaway accuracy is measured as a percentage of total putaway transactions.

Location replenishment accuracy measurement.

In this case I'm referring to measuring the accuracy of the process of replenishing forward picking locations from reserve storage locations. Replenishment is actually a process that consists of two subprocesses — picking the replenishment inventory, and putaway of the replenishment inventory. Replenishment errors are most likely to be quantity errors that occur during the picking step of the replenishment process. This results in offsetting location imbalances. It's unlikely that you will have a formal checking process in place to check replenishment transactions, therefore replenishment accuracy measurement is usually based on errors caught during the putaway step, through a location audit, or through the cycle count process. You can also periodically conduct 100 percent audits of a group of replenishment transactions to determine accuracy. Location replenishment accuracy is measured as a percentage of replenishment transactions

Manufacturing accuracy measurement.

The diversity of the transactional methods used to move, consume, and produce inventory during manufacturing processes makes it difficult to outline a generic means of measuring the accuracy of these processes. However, since accuracy in manufacturing processes tends to be much lower than in warehousing and distribution processes, it's very important to find ways to measure these processes. Manufacturing transactions may include transactions related to the movement of inventory to machines or workstations, issuing inventory to manufacturing, reporting against operational steps, moving from one operation to another, reporting scrap of raw materials, reporting scrap of in-process materials, reporting scrap of finished materials, and reporting production of finished materials.

Sources for manufacturing accuracy measurement would include:

✔ Production reporting paperwork audits.

✔ Production order variance reports (WIP variances).

✔ Variances between manufacturing operations.

✔ Staging location variance audits.

✔ Open production order audits.

✔ Cycle counts.

✔ Periodic 100 percent production transaction audits.

✔ Comparing physical scrap to reported scrap.

There's no doubt that measuring the accuracy of a manufacturing process is more difficult than measuring the accuracy of a warehouse process, such as order picking. It's also unlikely that this measurement will be highly comprehensive. Nonetheless it is still important to maintain some level of manufacturing accuracy measurement. Though process improvement is certainly an objective of manufacturing accuracy measurement, a more important objective will likely be using the measurement to emphasize personal accountability. As I've previously mentioned, accuracy is unlikely to be a top priority of manufacturing personnel. By measuring accuracy and ensuring that this measurement is considered when evaluating each employee's performance, you are communicating that, although it may not be their primary responsibility, they are still responsible for the accurate processing of information related to their duties.

As with most other forms of accuracy measurement, manufacturing accuracy should be measured as a percentage of transactions.

Measuring the impact of inaccuracy

In all probability the most meaningful measure of accuracy is the measure of the impact of inaccuracy. This is the measure of the number of times customer service or general operations is negatively impacted due to inaccurate inventory or inaccurate inventory processes. Measures of the impact of inaccuracy would include:

Shipping errors.
Yes, we already covered this, but due to its direct impact on customer service I thought I would list it again here.

Missed shipments due to inaccuracy.
This is a measure of the number of times that an expected shipped quantity cannot be shipped due to an incorrect on-hand balance. More simply put, this is the number of times when, according to the inventory system, the order should have shipped but did not because the warehouse was missing the required inventory.

Backorders due to adjustments made within lead time.

This is a little different from missed shipments due to inaccuracy in that it measures the number of times demand cannot be met due to an adjustment that resulted from an incorrect on-hand balance. In a standard reorder-point system this would include any adjustments that either brought the inventory balance below reorder point or occurred after reorder point had been reached, and ultimately resulted in backorders up to the quantity of the adjustment.

Production interruptions due to inaccuracy.

Similar to missed shipments, this is the number of times that you should have had enough inventory to complete the production run, but due to an incorrect on-hand balance, you could not. These are shortages on orders that have already been released to the shop floor.

Production schedule changes due to inaccuracy.

These are scheduling changes to orders that have not yet been released to the shop floor, that are the result of an inventory adjustment made to correct on-hand balances.

Expediting or de-expediting due to inaccuracy.

This would include schedule or quantity changes made to existing supplier orders or the creation of new supplier orders as a direct result of an inventory adjustment made to correct on-hand balances.

Excess or obsolete inventory caused by inaccuracy.

This is that lost and found scenario I discussed in the chapter on cycle counting. Basically this is when "found" inventory results in excess or obsolete inventory.

Vendor payment problems due to inaccuracy.

This is the result of problems in the receiving process that prevent the processing of a vendor payment. This can be a problem as you may lose out on discounts or may have further shipments held as a result of being past due.

Labor hours spent searching for lost inventory.

I think you can figure this one out.

Safety stock to compensate for inaccuracy.

I admit that it's unlikely that you will be able to put a number on this one, but I thought I would mention it anyway. If you have specifically calculated safety stock to compensate for inaccuracy, you should use those numbers.

Cost of checking.

The do-it-right-the-first-time fanatics should be pleased that I included this one. The costs of conducting your cycle count process, physical inventory, accuracy audits, location audits, order checking, and any other process checks that are in place to catch inventory errors are all the direct result of inaccurate processes and the financial impact should be reported. While you may never be able to eliminate your cycle count program and other checks, increases in process accuracy

Accuracy Measurement

General accuracy measures.
Good count bad count.
Net piece accuracy.
Net dollar accuracy.
Absolute piece accuracy.
Absolute dollar accuracy.
Transaction-based calculations.
Root cause measurement.

Specific process accuracy measurement.
Shipping accuracy.
Picking accuracy.
Receiving accuracy.
Putaway accuracy.
Replenishment accuracy.
Manufacturing accuracy.

Measuring the impact of inaccuracy.
Shipping errors.
Missed shipments due to inaccuracy.
Backorders due to adjustments made within lead time.
Production interruptions due to inaccuracy.
Production schedule changes due to inaccuracy.
Expediting or de-expediting due to inaccuracy.
Excess or obsolete inventory caused by inaccuracy.
Vendor payment problems due to inaccuracy.
Labor hours spent searching for lost product.
Safety stock to compensate for inaccuracy.
Cost of checking.
Cost of accuracy measurement.

should result in reducing the extent and frequency of these checks, thus reducing the total cost.

Cost of accuracy measurement.
Don't forget that all this measurement is a result of inaccurate processes. These costs should not be ignored.

Though measuring shipping errors or missed shipments due to inaccuracy is pretty straightforward, trying to determine whether or not a backorder is a result of a previous inventory adjustment, or whether an adjustment made today will result in schedule changes can get fairly complicated and may not be a realistic expectation. I like these measures because they reflect the true impact of inaccuracy and can be the best way to document improvement. They also serve as the basis for the cost-justification of improvement expenditures. Since some of these measures are difficult to maintain and may require coordination between multiple departments, you need to be realistic in your expectations of them. As with some of the other measurements discussed, many of these "impact" measurements are more likely to be conducted periodically as audits rather than being conducted as an ongoing daily measurement process.

What should my accuracy be?

Didn't we already cover this under benchmarking? I really struggled with the decision of whether or not I would include any specific accuracy numbers in this book. My initial intent was that I would not. I have no problem confronting the disappointment and possible criticism from those that would expect an "accuracy book" to give "accuracy numbers."

The "right" accuracy for you is different from the "right" accuracy for anyone else, and any numbers that I provide are as likely to be "wrong" for you as "right." I liken the question of, "What should my accuracy be?" to be similar to asking, "What should my profits be?" "What should my overhead be?' or "What should my inventory turns be?" You simply can't answer these questions without conducting a thorough evaluation of the specific operation, and, even with an evaluation, you still may not be able to accurately answer the question.

What changed my mind was the thought that some readers may not have had any experience with accuracy and are simply looking for any information that can give them a place to start. Though the numbers I provide may not be directly applicable to their operation, as long as I explain the variables they may be able to use these numbers as a point-of-reference in "ball parking" an accuracy number that may apply to them. I would again like to warn you that these numbers should only be used as "ball park" measurements and that you need to consider the uniqueness of your operation when trying to determine what is right for you.

Let me start with some numbers that have been passed around the industry for some time. The statement usually goes something like this: "you need at least 95% accuracy for your planning systems to work and you should set a goal of achieving 98% accuracy for your planning systems to work effectively." I've heard this 95% number used as though there were a specific point where your computerized planning systems would start smoking and then explode. I don't know where these numbers originated; my guess is a consultant got tired of repeatedly going through the long explanation of "why I can't tell you what your accuracy should be" and decided to throw in a couple of ballpark numbers. Others likely began to repeat these numbers until what began as a "ballpark number" became "scientific fact."

One of the problems with these numbers is that I don't know what they are based on. Maybe the originator of the numbers elaborated on the calculation; however the context in which I have run into these numbers has not included any explanation of the calculation. My best assumption would be they are based upon a good count bad count calculation with tolerances (probably 5%) in place. I am only assuming this since this has also become the most frequently stated means of measuring accuracy. So this means that if the inventory on 98% of my stocked items is off by 5% or less and 2% is off by more than 5%, I am in good shape. I don't think so, especially if this is a distribution or fulfillment operation. If you are a manufacturer that uses a lot of low-cost components, this may be reasonable. And to go back to that 95% number; I would agree that if you are getting less than 95% accuracy with a 5% tolerance, you are likely having problems planning your inventory; however, there is no specific accuracy point at which a planning system fails to work. A single significant error on a key raw material in one operation may throw production planning into a tailspin, while another operation may have sizable errors on several raw materials and still be operating. The fact is, any error can have an effect on planning systems, and these systems will gradually become less effective as the quantity and size of errors increases. So there is not an actual point where planning systems fail to work. I suggest measuring the impact of errors (as previously discussed) to determine the extent to which accuracy is affecting your planning systems.

If you want to use these numbers as rough guidelines for a manufacturing operation that has a lot of low-cost components or bulk raw materials, I would say go ahead. For distribution or fulfillment operations, or for manufacturers that use a lot of higher value components, I think the 5% tolerance is unacceptable. I would certainly want to know how many of the 98% good counts were "perfect counts" and how many had variances that approached that 5% tolerance. I also need to once again bring up the argument that good count bad count measurement by itself is just not an adequate measure of accuracy.

On the following pages, I am giving examples of accuracy rates that are reasonable to expect within a given environment as opposed to accuracy rates that are required for systems to run effectively. I'm also giving examples of some specific process accuracy rates.

Description of Environment	Net Dollar Accuracy	Absolute Piece Accuracy	Good Count Bad Count
Piece-pick finished goods warehouse, manual paper-based system, moderate cycle counting, additional checks such as order checking and location audits, mix of low-cost and high-value items, mix of fast and slow movers.	99.95% to 100%	96% to 99%	75% to 95% No tolerance 95% to 99% 2% tolerance
Same as above but with bar code data collection on major processes	99.97% to 100%	97% to 99%	80% to 95% No tolerance 96% to 99% 2% tolerance
Case-pick finished goods warehouse (all materials received, moved, and shipped in case quantities) , manual paper-based system, moderate cycle counting, additional checks such as order checking and location audits, mix of low-cost and high-value items, mix of fast and slow movers.	99.96% to 100%	97% to 99%	90% to 98% No tolerance
Same as above but with bar code data collection on major processes	99.98% to 100%	99% to 100%	99% to 100% No tolerance
Full pallet finished goods warehouse (all materials received, moved, and shipped in full pallet quantities) , manual paper-based system, moderate cycle counting, additional checks such as order checking and location audits, mix of low-cost and high-value items, mix of fast and slow movers.	99.97% to 100%	98% to 99%	97% to 99% No tolerance
Same as above but with bar code data collection on major processes	99.99% to100%	99% to 100%	99% to 100% No tolerance

Description of Environment	Net Dollar Accuracy	Absolute Piece Accuracy	Good Count Bad Count
Manufacturing raw materials and components inventory, point-of-use as well as pick-to-order materials, mix of low-cost and high-value items, mix of fast and slow movers.	99% to 100%	95% to 98%	50% to 80% No tolerance 85% to 98% 2% tolerance
Same as above but with bar code data collection on major processes	99% to 100%	96% to 99%	60% to 85% No tolerance 88% to 98% 2% tolerance
Manufacturing raw materials and components inventory, point-of-use as well as pick-to-order materials, primarily fast-moving low-cost materials	99% to 100%	93% to 97%	40% to 80% No tolerance 75% to 95% 2% tolerance
Same as above but with bar code data collection on major processes	99% to 100%	93% to 97%	40% to 80% No tolerance 75% to 95% 2% tolerance
Manufacturing raw materials and components inventory, primarily slow-moving high cost materials, pick-to-order processing	99.95% to 100%	98% to 100%	98% to 100% No tolerance
Same as above but with bar code data collection on major processes	99.95% to 100%	98% to 100%	98% to 100% No tolerance

Description of Environment and Task	Picking Accuracy	Shipping Accuracy with moderate order checking in place.
Piece-pick or case-pick operation with average pieces or cases per pick less than 3	99.80% to 99.90%	99.90% to 99.98%
Same as above with bar code item/location verification	99.90% to 99.95%	99.93% to 99.99%
Piece-pick or case-pick operation with average pieces or cases per pick between 3 and 10	99.70% to 99.85%	99.88% to 99.96%
Same as above with bar code item/location verification	99.80% to 99.90%	99.90% to 99.97%
Piece-pick or case-pick operation with average pieces or cases per pick between 11 and 75	99.00% to 99.50%	99.20% to 99.70%
Same as above with bar code item/location verification	99.10% to 99.60%	99.20% to 99.70%
Piece-pick operation with average pieces per pick greater than 75	accuracy gradually decreases as quantity per pick increases	
Same as above with bar code item/location verification	very little change	

Description of Environment and Task	Picking Accuracy	Shipping Accuracy with moderate order checking in place.
Full-pallet-pick operation from single depth pallet rack	99.70% to 99.85%	99.95% to 99.99%
Same as above with bar code item/location verification	99.95% to 99.99%	99.95% to 99.99%
Full-pallet-pick operation from high density storage	99.80% to 99.90%	99.95% to 99.99%
Same as above with bar code item/location verification	99.95% to 99.99%	99.95% to 99.99%

Description of Environment and Task	Putaway Accuracy with no checking process.
Putaway into fixed picking locations	99.80% to 99.90%
Same as above with bar code item/location verification	99.98% to 99.99%
Putaway into random storage areas, worker chooses location	98% to 99.95%
Same as above with bar code item/location verification	99.98% to 99.99%
Putaway into random storage areas, system chooses location	99% to 99.95%
Same as above with bar code item/location verification	99.98% to 99.99%

WARNING:

The examples on the previous pages are intended to be used as "ballpark" numbers and are not a replacement for a thorough analysis of an operation. I only list them to give you a rough idea of what can be expected in a variety of environments. Pay close attention to the environment and task descriptions and take into account any characteristics of your specific environment that are not listed.

Summary

You should now realize that accuracy measurement can be rather complex and that there is no simple answer to the question, "what should my accuracy be?" Accuracy measurement is important yet imprecise and those that use the measurement must understand how it is calculated and any potential flaws in the measurement system. Though I have outlined many ways to measure accuracy, you should only put in place the measurements that make sense for your operation. Many of these measurements can be conducted periodically on an as-needed basis rather than being a required ongoing day-to-day measurement. It's also important to mention again that you should be careful to avoid having the measurement become your "accuracy program."

For those just starting to measure accuracy, I suggest basing your measurement on quarterly accuracy audits and taking a scorecard approach by listing net dollar accuracy, absolute piece accuracy, and good count bad count at different tolerance levels. This combination should provide a pretty good description of your snapshot-in-time inventory accuracy. I also recommend measuring shipping accuracy and putting in place formal checks or spot checks to determine accuracy of key processes such as order picking or putaway. This should be plenty to get you started, and as you get a better feel for your operation and your measurement needs, you can begin to develop a long-term measurement system.

7

Audits, Exception Reporting, and Data Analysis

A cycle counting program is only one method used to "check" your inventory accuracy and focus improvement efforts. You will find that supplementing your cycle counting program with audits and other checks can greatly enhance your overall accuracy. The checks described in this chapter may be implemented as ongoing processes or simply used periodically to check processes. It is not intended that a company would use all of the checks described here. Checks are used to validate processes and make up for process deficiencies; use them where they provide the most benefit.

Audits

Accuracy audit

I've mentioned conducting accuracy audits at several points in this book. An accuracy audit provides a snapshot-in-time measure of your inventory accuracy based on count results of a sampling of your inventory. Hey, wait a minute, isn't that a cycle count? Not really. The primary purpose of an accuracy audit is to determine your accuracy level. The primary purposes of a cycle count program are to focus process improvement efforts and to correct on-hand balances. These differences in purpose change the "what, how, and when" decisions related to counting. As discussed in the chapter on measurement, the output of a cycle count program may not be the best measure of accuracy. And while a well-executed physical inventory process can provide an accurate measure of accuracy, it may not be worth the effort and disruption to service that is often needed.

To conduct an accuracy audit, we need to develop a sampling strategy that provides an accurate representation of the inventory. This is best done by first breaking down the inventory into logical groups and then taking a random sampling from each group. If you are using the audit as a measure of financial accuracy, you will find an ABC stratification by inventory investment to be a very useful grouping. For a measure of operational accuracy, you will likely prefer using an ABC by transaction frequency. You may also choose to break out separate categories for finished goods and raw materials. Use groupings that best reflect the primary objective (financial versus operational) of the audit. You can still re-stratify the results of the audit later to provide measurement that reflects secondary objectives. For example, you may choose to use a financial stratification during your sample selection if the purpose of the audit is to provide a validation of the financial representation of your inventory (such as replacing an annual physical inventory). This sampling will provide the best results for that objective. However, you can still use the count results to provide measurements that are useful in evaluating operational impact of accuracy by re-stratifying the results. Though the measurement may be less accurate for the secondary purposes, it can still be useful.

When you break down each category, you will need to determine key summary information such as: total inventory dollars, total number of items, total units on hand, total units consumed (within specific time period), and total transactions (within specific time period). You now need to determine the sample size for each group. While you could go with a keep-it-simple approach and just count a fixed percentage of each category, you will find that it will be more effective to base your count percentage on the importance of each group to your primary objective. When using an ABC stratification by inventory investment for financial objectives, you will likely want to count a larger percentage of your "A" items than "B" items, and an even smaller percentage of "C" items. Since the nature of ABC (the 80/20 rule) is such that you will likely have only a small number of items in category "A", you can easily count a significantly larger percentage of "A" items than "B" or "C" items without dramatically increasing the total number of counts that need to be conducted. In some cases, you may even find that you can count all "A" items and then just a percentage of "B" and "C" items.

Inventory Breakdown

Finished Goods (by average inventory investment ABC)

ABC by Inventory Investment	Inventory Value	% of Inventory Value	Number of SKUs	% of SKUs
A	$1,000,000	50%	100	4%
B	$600,000	30%	350	15%
C	$380,000	19%	1100	47%
D	$20,000	1%	800	34%
Total	**$2,000,000**		2350	

Raw Materials (by average inventory investment ABC)

ABC by Inventory Investment	Inventory Value	% of Inventory Value	Number of SKUs	% of SKUs
A	$500,000	50%	75	5%
B	$300,000	30%	280	18%
C	$190,000	19%	750	49%
D	$10,000	1%	435	28%
Total	**$1,000,000**		1540	

Grand Total	**$3,000,000**	3890

Figure 7A. In this example, I've broken down the inventory into finished goods and raw materials. I've then broken it down further by ABC (based on average inventory investment) within each group.

You can see that 80% (based on value) of the finished goods inventory is accounted for by only 19% of the finished goods SKUs (450 actual SKUs). Similarly, 80% of the raw materials inventory is accounted for by only 23% of the raw materials SKUs (355 SKUs).

If the primary objective of the audit is for financial purposes, you can see that by putting most of your efforts in the A and B items, you can account for a significant portion of the total inventory value without having to count a significant number of SKUs

Inventory Breakdown

Finished Goods (by average inventory investment ABC)

ABC by Inventory Investment	Inventory Value	% of Inventory Value	Number of SKUs	% of SKUs
A	$1,000,000	50%	100	4%
B	$600,000	30%	350	15%
C	$380,000	19%	1100	47%
D	$20,000	1%	800	34%
Total	$2,000,000		2350	

Audit Sampling

Audit %	Number of SKUs	Inventory Value
30%	30	$300,000
10%	35	$60,000
3%	33	$11,400
2%	16	$400
	114	$371,800
	4.9%	19%

Raw Materials (by average inventory investment ABC)

ABC by Inventory Investment	Inventory Value	% of Inventory Value	Number of SKUs	% of SKUs
A	$500,000	50%	75	5%
B	$300,000	30%	280	18%
C	$190,000	19%	750	49%
D	$10,000	1%	435	28%
Total	$1,000,000		1540	

Audit %	Number of SKUs	Inventory Value
30%	23	$150,000
10%	28	$30,000
3%	23	$5,700
2%	8.7	$200
	82	$185,900
	5.3%	19%

Grand Total $3,000,000   3890

Figure 7B. As you can see in the example, I have decided to count a significantly larger percentage of "A" items than others, yet this larger percentage did not have a significant impact on the total items counted. The net result is that by counting 114 SKUs (4.9%) out of the finished goods group, we are counting 19% of the inventory value within that group. Though there is likely statistical methodology that could be used to determine percentages to count within each group, I simply applied the "educated guess" method here. To get a rough idea as to the accuracy of the sampling I will generally take the results of half the SKU's from each sample and compare them to the results of the full sample. If the resulting accuracy calculations were close, I will feel pretty comfortable with the sample size chosen, if not, I may need to increase the sample.

In addition to SKU-based sampling, we will also want to conduct some location-based sampling. SKU-based sampling is a "system-to-floor" check where you take quantities from the inventory system and go out to the floor to see if the inventory is actually there. This is achieved through the ABC sampling discussed previously. Location-based sampling is a "floor-to-system" check where you compare what is actually on the floor to the inventory system. Though this sounds very similar to system-to-floor counting, there is one distinct difference. A floor-to-system check will identify inventory that may not be on the books (the system). This may be "lost" inventory, or inventory that was put into storage without following the correct procedure. It may also be inventory that was removed from the books (obsolescence, scrap, etc.) but was not removed from physical storage. This inventory would not turn up in a random "system-to-floor" audit or in a cycle count process that uses similar methodology.

To conduct location-based sampling, you simply select some small physical areas within the facility and conduct physical inventories of these areas. If you have various storage configurations within your operation, you should choose a sampling from each. For example, you may break down your storage areas by finished goods piece-picking locations, finished goods case-picking locations, finished goods reserve storage, bulk raw materials storage, discrete component storage, and point-of-use storage. You should select small areas within each storage configuration and verify that everything stored in these locations is also listed in the inventory system. Examples of selecting small areas may include randomly selecting one section of racking from every aisle or every nth aisle, or verifying every nth storage lane in a bulk floor storage area.

You can conduct your location-based sampling through a formalized process using location reports to validate the locations, or you may just choose to walk through the storage areas and randomly write down items, quantities, and locations to later check against the system. I also like to look for storage areas that did not have any counts conducted through the SKU-based sampling. This is a good way to find the oddball storage areas that are more likely to contain "off-the-books" inventory.

A comprehensive accuracy audit will also include some verification of offsite storage areas, work-in-process, non-stock, and in-transit inventories. These topics are discussed further in chapter nine.

The results from all counts should be combined into the final accuracy audit report. You should calculate the pure results of the counts, but also extrapolate the results against the total inventory to "project" the expected variances that would likely result from a complete physical inventory. For example, if you had a net variance of -$1,000 that resulted from counting $500,000 of "A" items you get a net variance of -0.2 percent. You can now multiply the total value of all "A" items by this percentage to project an expected variance. If the total value of "A" items is $2,000,000 you could project a net dollar variance of -$4,000.

The output of the audit is used to "prove" your accuracy. If you are using the audit to replace a periodic physical inventory, the output will either prove that you have achieved a level of accuracy that is sufficient to eliminate the need for a complete physical, or it will prove that you do indeed need to conduct a physical. The audit process described here is intended to be used internally to check accuracy or by external auditors to verify accuracy. The audit process is not a simple one, but can be very effective in proving accuracy in environments that would otherwise require costly plant shutdowns to conduct a physical.

Audit Results

Finished Goods

ABC	Number of SKUs	SKUs / Locations Counted	System Value	System Quantity	Good Counts	Good Count %	Net Piece Variance	Net Piece Accuracy %	Absolute Piece Variance	Absolute Piece Accuracy %	Net Dollar Variance	Net Dollar Accuracy %	Absolute Dollar Variance	Absolute Dollar Accuracy %
A	30	52	$300,000	5378	48	92.3%	-37	99.31%	127	97.6%	-$1,368	99.54%	$5,376	98.21%
B	35	48	$60,000	3457	45	93.8%	54	98.44%	140	96.0%	$983	98.36%	$2,481	95.87%
C	33	40	$11,400	1163	39	97.5%	-4	99.66%	4	99.7%	$42	99.63%	$42	99.63%
D	16	16	$400	149	16	100.0%	0	100.00%	0	100.0%	$0	100.00%	$0	100.00%
Total	**114**	**156**	**$371,800**	**10147**	**148**	**94.9%**	**13**	**99.87%**	**271**	**97.3%**	**-$343**	**99.91%**	**$7,899**	**97.88%**

Raw Materials

ABC	Number of SKUs	SKUs / Locations Counted	Inventory Value	System Quantity	Good Counts	Good Count %	Net Piece Variance	Net Piece Accuracy %	Absolute Piece Variance	Absolute Piece Accuracy %	Net Dollar Variance	Net Dollar Accuracy %	Absolute Dollar Variance	Absolute Dollar Accuracy %
A	23	49	$150,000	2475	40	81.6%	24	99.03%	354	85.7%	$852	99.43%	$7,632	94.91%
B	28	47	$30,000	1056	38	80.9%	67	93.66%	407	61.5%	-$439	98.54%	$1,238	95.87%
C	23	34	$5,700	10537	32	94.1%	-259	97.54%	1008	90.4%	-$143	97.49%	$568	90.04%
D	9	9	$200	107536	1	11.1%	-864	99.20%	8467	92.1%	-$8	96.00%	$25	87.50%
Total	**82**	**139**	**$185,900**	**121604**	**111**	**79.9%**	**-1032**	**99.15%**	**10236**	**91.6%**	**$262**	**99.86%**	**$9,463**	**94.91%**

| **Grand Total** | **196** | **295** | **$557,700** | **131751** | **259** | **87.8%** | **-1019** | **99.23%** | **10507** | **92.0%** | **-$81** | **99.99%** | **$17,362** | **96.89%** |

Figure 7C. This example shows the summarized output of an accuracy audit. There is still probably a bit too much information here for most people to digest. I would likely create another report similar to the weighted scorecard example in the previous chapter to communicate results to upper management. In the case of a financial audit, the net dollar variances and net dollar accuracy percentage would be the most important data. This report is a good example of how net accuracy increases as you move from detail calculations or subtotals to higher level summarized calculations. In this example the net dollar accuracy was 99.91% for finished goods and 99.86% for raw materials, yet when you look at the combined measurement you get a net dollar accuracy of 99.99% This is higher than either of the other rates because finished goods had a negative net dollar variance and raw materials had a positive net dollar variance. In the end, even though there were a significant number of variances, they netted out to just -$81.

Location audit

The most common supplement to a cycle counting program is a location audit process. As previously discussed, most cycle count programs are not designed to locate lost inventory. If lost inventory is an ongoing problem in your environment, an aggressive location audit process can be very effective in locating it. The difference between a running location audit process and a location-based cycle count process is that you are not doing any counting in the location audit process. This allows you to very quickly move through large storage areas. The basic process includes running a report for a specific storage area listing all items stored and sorted by location. The auditor starts at the first location and compares everything stored there to the report. This is another process where the sequence of events is critical; the auditor should first look at each item in the location and then verify that it is on the report. This is important because the primary goal of a location audit is to find inventory that is not listed in the location, not identify inventory that is listed but not in the location (though you are doing this as well).

If you didn't quite understand the significance of the previous statements, I suggest you read them again and think real hard about the sequence of events, since you will need to communicate this to your auditors. To restate it a little differently, you want the auditor to look at the location and ask "Is this item on the report?" not look at the report and ask, "Is this item in the location?" In doing so, you will also determine which items may be missing, however that is not the primary objective here. If you find something that doesn't belong there, it's much easier to determine from where it is missing, than finding that something is missing and then trying to determine where it is. Remember, no counting is occurring during the audit (you should document quantities of any "found" items), you are simply verifying that the item or items stored in the location are listed in the system as being stored there. Also, you don't need to maintain frozen quantities or transaction control during an audit, which means you can conduct audits during normal operations. All you need to do is to make sure that any material movement that occurred during the audit has been updated in the inventory system before you start to investigate any variances. This way, if something was put in a location between the time you ran the audit report and the time the auditor actually checked the location, you should be able to inquire on the item in the system and see that it is actually not a variance.

Unless you are conducting frequent periodic physical inventories or a location-based cycle counting process, you will likely need to conduct location audits. If lost product is an infrequent problem in your environment, you may choose to just conduct location audits on a periodic basis. If lost product is a significant problem, an aggressive ongoing location audit process can provide significant operational improvement by identifying and correcting errors before they affect operations.

Location Audit Report

LOCATION	SKU	Description	Quantity	UM
SB0101				
	DKJ2135	ACRNM CIRCULATOR	50	EA
	JKL6588	0.156 FELL SNUBBER	2,313	EA
	KYN6093	THERMISTOR 134	78	EA
	WGS4322	.5 FLC TAPE	124	EA
SB0102				
	BLG1598	3.5 ASSON GEAR	16	E
	FLC2033	PLL CBL 18.4	127	
	FLG4651	2.75 BRN ENGAGER	2,000	
	JKL8493	KIKNTH HEAD GASKET	233	
	KKJ9874	LCKOF EFERTT	10	
	LSK4872	BSKT CASE	1	
	MIL6548	FOLTIN BINDING SMEKER	10	
	WPL6702	LST GT UPNGO	43	
SB0103				
	JEK8439	.25 SPRING CLAMP		
	KLF4438	VLV DISK RRC		
	LZX8032	1.750 DUALFLOW SPHINCT		
	REW9284	BUSNS TRANSFORMER		
	SDF1236	7.253 VALVE FITTING WELK		
	SDL5683	LARGE DUST COLLECTO		
	SDP9321	PLATE MOUNTING LEFT Y		
SB0104				
	KEW2976	LGE GNEP KEY		
	RND8978	.25 ROUND TUIT		
	XPF4321	CHNG RESISTOR		

Location Audit Form

Auditor ID: *123*
Date: *1-4-03*

Location	SKU	Quantity
SB0102	*KEW2976*	*36*
Notes: *1 bx date 6-5-02*		
Location	SKU	Quantity
Notes:		
Location	SKU	Quantity
Notes:		
Location	SKU	Quantity
Notes:		
Location	SKU	Quantity
Notes:		
Location	SKU	Quantity
Notes:		
Location	SKU	Quantity
Notes:		

Figure 7D. Above are examples of a location audit report and the location audit form used to document "found" inventory. In this example, there are multiple items per location so the report groups the items by location to make it easier to use. Though the quantity is printed on the report, the auditor should not be counting and verifying the quantity of any items that are correctly located. If something is found that is not on the report, the auditor will fill out the form. It is necessary to count and note the quantity on any found items. It's also useful to write in any notes that can help in investigating the discrepancy.

I'll again mention how important it is to train the auditors to look at what is in the location and then look to see if it is on the report. The primary objective of a location audit is to find inventory that is not located correctly, not identify inventory that is missing from the location.

Exception reporting

Empty location report.

In full-pallet-load storage configurations where each location holds only one pallet, you can run an empty location report and use it to verify there is actually nothing in the location. This can be a very fast means of finding lost product under the right conditions. The basic idea here is that if you have limited empty locations, you can quickly check them, and anything found there is likely "lost" inventory. To create an empty location report, you need a locator system that maintains a "location master." A location master is a file that contains all valid locations. If your locator system does not include a location master file, and you feel an empty location report would be valuable, you can create a separate file to use as a location master.

Multi-item location report.

Another exception report that is very useful in this same environment is a multi-item location report that shows any location containing more than one item. Since you are in a full-pallet-load storage area with one pallet per location, any location showing more than one item must have some type of problem. This same exception report can be used in any area where you limit your storage to only one item per location. Unlike an empty location report, a multi-item location report does not require a location master file. All you need to do is run a query that counts the number of items (with quantity on-hand greater than zero) in each location. Then select on the output by only showing locations that contain more than one item.

New location report.

A new location audit report is a tool to verify the accuracy of new item/location combinations. Any item placed in a location where it had not already existed would come up on the new location report for verification. This can be a tricky report to produce if the item location file does not maintain a "created date" on each record. If your item/location file has a created date on each record, all you need to do is run a report of all records created since the last time you conducted the new location audit. This would generally be a daily audit report.

Open shipping orders.

Monitoring open shipping orders is an important part of any operation. Shipping orders will often have statuses assigned and updated as they are processed from order entry to shipping and invoicing. For the purpose of inventory accuracy you will want to monitor any orders that have been released to the warehouse for shipping, but have not yet shipped. My general recommendation is that you do not release orders to the warehouse unless they are going to ship that day. This way, at the end of the day, the open shipping order report should be blank. If it is not, you either have an order that was supposed to ship and did not, or you have an order that shipped without the system being properly updated. Either of these is a problem. Though there are some operations where this may not be feasible, most operations should be able to operate under this policy. This policy will not only make cycle counting easier, it also makes it easier to manage the shipping process.

If you cannot operate under this "clean every day" policy, you will want to structure the open shipping order report in a manner that makes it easy to identify potential problems. I still suggest running and reconciling this report every day. If you find that you have a lot of open orders on a daily basis and the reconciling process is difficult, it may give you the incentive to reduce the number of reasons that an order is released and not shipped.

Open production orders.
Monitoring open production orders will usually be much more complicated than monitoring open shipping orders. It's extremely rare that an operation can process all production orders, and end the day with a blank open production order report. Instead, you will likely monitor open production orders by comparing them with the production schedule. Past due production orders (or orders that are off schedule in any operation) should be investigated. In operations that pick all materials for a production order and issue them at once you should follow a similar policy as with open shipping orders where you do not release the order for picking unless it will be picked and issued that day.

The tools you use to monitor open production orders will vary from one system to another. Make sure you are very familiar with any statuses that may be used in the production order process. Structuring open production order reports by statuses, operations, and scheduled dates should provide a much more workable audit.

Production order variance report.
This is one the most useful, yet most underutilized, reports in many manufacturing operations. The production order variance report (also called the WIP variance report) identifies completed production orders where the value of the finished materials does not match the value of the materials, labor, and overhead reported against the order. This is a critical part of maintaining accurate work-in-process records. Work-in-process and the production order variance report are discussed in more detail in chapter nine.

Closed production orders with remaining allocations.
There are many variations on how you would approach this, but basically you are looking for manufacturing orders where all or some of the components that were expected to be issued, were not. Depending upon your processes, you may choose to run this when a production order is started, rather than waiting for it to be completed (closed). In most systems, this is actually a fairly simple report to create by comparing required quantities to issued quantities on the production order materials list. To be more exact, you may chose some more complex pro-

gramming and compare the actual quantity of finished goods produced to the actual quantities of materials used.

Past due receipts.
A past due receipt is generally a supplier problem (late delivery), a receiving processing problem (not processed quickly enough), or a receiving transaction problem (an inventory problem). The trick to managing past due receipts lies in a good understanding of internal processes and past vendor performance. This will help in determining "most likely cause." Usually, past due receipt monitoring would be the responsibility of the planner/buyer. They are the ones that would best know if there was a supplier delay. On the other hand, they are not the ones that should be investigating receiving problems. Thus there needs to be some communication between the planner/buyer and the receiving department to ensure the planner/buyer is looking into vendor delays and the receiving department is looking into possible receiving problems.

Early receipts.
Monitoring early receipts can be important in controlling inventory levels, but can also point out receipt errors. If a receipt transaction is entered against an incorrect purchase order or incorrect item, it is very likely to result in an early receipt. Like past due receipts, early receipts will likely be monitored by the planner/buyer who should communicate potential errors to the receiving department.

Staging location reports.
If using staging locations (see locator systems in chapter eight) you will find it important to monitor quantities showing in them. If your database maintains a last transaction date on the item/location record you can create a report that sorts and selects by last transaction date. Since staging locations are usually for short-term storage, you would select based upon the expected length of time inventory would reasonably remain in a staging location in your specific operation. Often this is just a matter of a day or two. Inventory remaining beyond this time is likely some type of a problem. To use the example of a receiving staging location, quantities remaining beyond the normally expected putaway cycle time could be the result of inventory that was put away without a transaction being entered or inventory that was incorrectly received (therefore it could not be put away), while a difference between received quantity and putaway quantity would likely identify a receiving or putaway quantity error. Monitoring shipping, machine, inspection, and other staging locations can identify similar errors.

Open move documents.
Move documents are used in warehouse management systems, and monitoring them is essential in maintaining the WMS as well as your inventory accuracy. The problems identified through open move documents are similar to those uncovered by monitoring staging locations. Generally you will monitor both open move documents and staging locations. You may even create reports that compare open

move documents to quantities in staging locations to look for inconsistencies. Since move documents are almost certain to have a date on them, it is easy to create open move document reports based upon date.

Locations over capacity.

This generally also falls into the domain of operations that have a WMS in place. Obviously a location over capacity is some type of a problem, and, if you are able to set up location capacities, you should consider monitoring locations over capacity. Often a WMS will allow you to set parameters that prevent entering a transaction that goes beyond the capacity of a location, or at least, give the worker an error message. I generally recommend that you work within this policy and do not allow overriding the WMS. For those that feel they need the flexibility to override the WMS, you should periodically monitor locations over capacity to identify potential inventory problems as well as potential problems related to the setup of the WMS.

Negative inventory.

Monitoring negative inventory is probably one of the more obvious types of exception handling tasks. Though not desirable, negative inventory may be a "normal" part of your operation. See chapter nine for more detailed info on negative inventory.

Data analysis

Auditing the accuracy of the data that affects your inventory is a critical part of maintaining an effective inventory planning and execution system. This includes monitoring item masters, bills of material, routings, location masters, vender masters, customer masters, item cross references, multi-plant relationships, and unit-of-measure conversions. There are no simple "canned" exception reports for this type of data analysis since the variety of processes, software systems, and types of problems encountered tend to be unique to each operation.

Data auditing is often initiated by an error root cause identified during a cycle count process. I go by the motto "a specific type of error rarely occurs only once" and use this to help guide the creation of exception reports. With a reasonable knowledge of your inventory system database and a little imagination, you can often create exception reports based upon characteristics consistent with a specific error to identify additional data problems.

The following are some examples of exception reports created when a specific problem is uncovered.

✔ An inventory shortage is traced back to a missing component on a bill of material. You suspect that there may be more BOMs that may be missing this item. If this item is always used in a specific family of end items, you can create a report of all items in that family that do not have the item in their BOM. If the missing item belongs to a family of parts that must always be used to make another family of parts, you can report on all end items within family "A" that do not contain a component in family "B." If the item is always used in combination with another item (such as a nut with a washer) you can create a report of every BOM that contains item "A" but not item "B."

Some other checks that may turn up BOM problems would include summing up the "quantities per" of all components on each BOM by end item product family. In many cases, all items within a product family will contain the same number of components (though they may be different components). By summing the quantities per BOM, you can identify inconsistencies in BOMs within each family. You may even find that by summing the weights of all components on each BOM and then comparing it to the weight of the end item, you may be able to identify BOM problems (a weight version of a cost rollup).

✔ Now let's say you trace another shortage back to an incorrect stocking type on the item master. In this case a stocked item was listed as a direct ship item and therefore was not reducing on-hand balances when shipped. You may now run a quick report of any item with a direct ship stocking type that shows on-hand balances or has a physical storage location. You may also run a report on previous shipping orders that shipped from your facility that had items on them with direct ship stocking types.

✔ Next you encounter an overage that is the result of an incorrect unit-of-measure conversion. The purchasing unit-of-measure is eaches and you stock them as cases (12 per case). The unit-of-measure conversion was set at 24 eaches per case. Therefore every time you received 24 eaches, one case was added to inventory when actually there were two cases. You may now choose to run a report based on product family or vendor showing the unit-of-measure conversions and either specifically selecting on those with a 24-to-1 conversion or you may choose to look at all conversions for inconsistencies.

You can see that each of these examples is based upon a very specific error. Exception reporting is used to identify combinations of factors that are common to specific types of errors. While this isn't an entirely proactive approach (since it is initiated by an error) it is proactive in the sense that it helps in correcting data that would otherwise result in additional inventory errors in the future. Certainly you should also be looking to change the processes involved in creating the data problems to prevent recurrence. Exception reports may be run periodically when errors are recurring and process changes have not adequately eliminated them, or may be run only once to correct errors that are not likely to recur.

Knowledge of information systems revisited

I once again want to emphasize the importance of knowing your inventory system and having the technical skills to extract and make use of the information. This includes some basic knowledge of database structure along with query and reporting tools. Your business software contains extensive amounts of information that can be used to increase accuracy and improve operations in general. If your job is highly dependant upon this data, you should look to gain the skills necessary to take control of the data. Cycle count administrators, inventory analysts, planners, buyers, warehouse managers, and accountants, all fall into this category.

There are custom reporting and query tools available that allow nonprogrammers to access and manipulate their business data. A nonprogrammer using these tools can create the majority of the audit reports discussed in this chapter. There are also user-definable parameters in most software systems that allow you to change the way your system works. Granted, you will need some technical skills beyond that of ordinary system users, but you didn't get to where you are by being stupid, did you? It's clear that we have become increasingly dependant on information systems for the management and execution of operations, and your choice is to either be a master of technology or a slave to it. To sit back and relegate all responsibility for setting up the parameters of your software, as well as responsibilities for extracting data from your systems, to your IS department is no longer an acceptable option.

Inventory accuracy is achieved by keeping physical operations in sync with information systems. To focus solely on physical operations because you have an inadequate understanding of information systems will certainly impede your progress in this endeavor. I frequently encounter processes where extensive labor is dedicated to manually performing a task, when a simple custom report or system parameter change would have greatly simplified the task.

Summary

Audits and related checks can be extremely helpful in achieving higher levels of accuracy. It is important to point out that the need for audits is the result of flawed processes. While I don't expect us to get away from using audits to help in maintaining high levels of accuracy, we should avoid getting into the habit of using audits as a permanent replacement for process improvement. We should also monitor the amount of resources we are dedicating to audit-related tasks. Audits that become a standard part of day-to-day operations should be reviewed periodically to determine if they could be eliminated through process changes. Just because you didn't have an effective solution when you implemented the audit, does not necessarily mean that there is not an effective solution currently available. You should also treat an audit process like any other process, making sure you have designed it in a manner that takes into account productivity. Sometimes a minor change such as a change in data selection criteria, data elements, or data sequencing can greatly improve the usability of an audit report.

8

Tools, Equipment, & Technology

OK, I admit that up to this point, I may have underplayed the value of technology in solving accuracy problems. The technology available today, even to the smallest of businesses, is truly amazing and can certainly play a key role in improving accuracy. The reason I sometimes play down technology related to operations improvement, is people often have the misconception that they can solve all of their problems with technology alone. This just isn't the case. If you go back and compare the key operational issues of industry 75 years ago to those of today, you will find that despite our access to technology we continue to have the same problems. The reason for this is not that technology has failed, but rather our expectations of, and dependence on, technology has resulted in us getting sloppy in managing the fundamentals of operations. We dedicate managers and consultants to software selection processes, but do not invest in resources to work on process improvement. We focus on software implementations and ignore employee training. And we purchase high-tech gadgets but don't enforce accountability.

When you go back and consider what it took to manage inventory prior to access to computers, and then consider the improvements that "should have been" achieved through the implementation of technologies, you will likely come to the conclusion that we must be doing something wrong since we have not achieved these levels of improvement.

[WHERE WE WERE] + [TECHNOLOGY ADVANCES] ≠ [WHERE WE ARE]

Though technology vendors will often describe their products as "solutions," they are actually just tools. You need to think of the process as the solution, and the application of technology as a potential part of the process. You need to match the technology to the process, making sure it is the best technology for the specific process. And, you need to make sure you are taking full advantage of the existing technologies you already own.

You should evaluate the application of technology just as you would any new process or process change. This once again brings up the question, " What is the best way to do this, that takes into account the customer service, productivity, quality, accuracy, capacity, safety, and financial objectives of our organization?" Sometimes the answer to this question does not include technology. Anyone familiar with lean production methods should be aware of the use of kanbans to signal production or procurement and to control quantities of materials. Kanbans are containers or cards that signal the previous operation or supplier to make and deliver more. Once you have emptied a container, the container or card is returned to the source. You limit the inventory by limiting the number of kanban containers or kanban cards. Japanese manufacturers turned to the use of low-tech kanbans because their high-tech planning and execution systems were ineffective at managing these processes, resulting in excess work-in-process and raw materials. They were smart enough to realize that technology is not always the best solution. I should add that they could have changed their planning and execution system to follow the simplified logic of a kanban system, which would have resulted in an effective high-tech solution. In either case, the technology that was initially put in place was the "wrong technology."

I should also note that putting information related to technology into a book is somewhat of an exercise in futility as some of the information will likely be obsolete shortly after if not before the book hits the shelves. I purposely waited until the last possible moment to write this chapter to try to be as current as possible. I'm also timing the writing of this chapter (late September of 2002) to coincide with Frontline Solutions Expo that comes to Chicago every year. Frontline Solutions is the premier data capture trade show and conference, and, if you are looking for the latest and greatest in technologies related to bar codes, scanners, wireless technologies, voice technologies, and RFID, this is the place to go. I also plan to create a companion website (http://www.accuracybook.com) to provide more current information as well as links to other sites that would have information useful to readers of this book.

www.accuracybook.com

Calculators

Sometimes the simplest technologies get overlooked. Think of how exciting it would have been 40 years ago if someone would have come to your plant or warehouse with little electronic calculators that fit in your pocket, didn't require batteries, and cost less than ten bucks. Well, 40 years later, the availability of these devices is taken for granted; yet, their use is not optimized. There are two primary mistakes made related to pocket calculators in warehouse and shop floor environments. They are often not readily available to the workers and they are not the right design for the task.

Buy extras. Make sure calculators are always readily available to those that need them. Pocket calculators are going to get lost, broken, or stolen; and while you may minimize these factors, you will not totally eliminate them. If you have employees that need to count product or make other related calculations, they should always have access to a calculator. If an employee has lost, accidentally taken home, or broken their calculator, the fact that you may have "just given them one last week" has no bearing on the fact that they do not have one today. Refusing to buy more is not punishing the employees as much as it is punishing your processes.

As for using the right design, a warehouse or shop floor is not a college class-room. Your employees are likely doing very simple calculations while they are also conducting physical work. Lighting conditions may not be optimal and they may even be wearing gloves. What you want in this environment, is a simple design, large buttons, and a large display. Just because these devices are inexpensive shouldn't mean that you do not need to invest a little time in research. It's doubtful that you will need scientific functions, multi-line displays, or graphing capabilities, so don't clutter up the design with these features. You also do not want the smallest design available, an employee should not need a stylus or pencil to press the buttons. The ones that tend to work best in this environment will have 20 to 24 button keypads, 8 to 10 character displays, and are designed to fit in a shirt pocket. You should also consider physically attaching calculators to lift trucks, stock carts, or other types of mobile equipment that are used by the workers.

For workers that may need to do a lot of calculations at a fixed workstation or desk (cycle count administrator, transaction auditors), get them a large desktop calculator. As with the pocket calculator, focus on simple design, large buttons, and large displays. Remember that we are applying the right technology to the right task. While a pocket calculator may be the right technology for non-stationary tasks, a larger desktop calculator will prove to be more accurate and productive for a desktop application.

Scales

Scales are an important part of many inventory processes. In addition to their use in freight calculations, they are used to measure bulk materials when weight is the unit-of measure, they are used to count large quantities of discrete items, they are used to verify the accuracy of automated filling systems, and they are used as a check to verify accuracy of outbound shipments. Scales can be stand-alone pieces of equipment or integrated into manufacturing and material handling equipment. Scales integrated into the carriage of a forklift or in-line scales integrated into a conveyor system are examples of mechanically integrated scales. Scales may also be integrated with information systems providing real-time exchange of data.

Scales come in a variety of configurations determined by the required capacity, required accuracy, the specific process, and the characteristics of the load being weighed. These can range from small bench top scales to large scales used to weigh tractor-trailers and rail cars. There are several things that you need to understand about using scales.

Capacity. Capacity is important for more than just preventing you from overloading the scale. The accuracy of a scale is relative to its capacity. If you were weighing a 20-lb. package, you would get a more accurate measure from a 50-lb. capacity scale than a 500-lb. capacity scale. You generally want to get the lowest capacity scale that will meet your weighing needs.

Accuracy. While I already mentioned that capacity affects accuracy, the design of the scale also affects accuracy. The phrase "you get what you pay for" often applies here as less expensive scales tend to be less accurate. The accuracy you need is relative to the task, if you are weighing palletized loads for transportation documentation, an accuracy (also known as sensitivity) rating of +/- 0.5 lb will likely meet your needs. However, if you are check-weighing cases of lightweight products, this same accuracy would be unacceptable.

Maintenance and calibration. Scales need to be properly maintained and periodically calibrated to ensure accuracy. The rated accuracy of the scale assumes that it is properly maintained and calibrated.

Operating conditions. Scales are designed to operate within specific environmental conditions. If you will be using the scale in extremely hot or cold environments or in wet or corrosive environments, you need to make sure your scale is designed to operate in these conditions. Air movement and vibrations can also affect the accuracy of a scale.

Tare. Tare weight is the weight of the container that holds the materials you are weighing. The container may be a bag, a box, a tote, a pallet, a crate, a drum, a trailer, or a rail car. Most scales will have functionality that allows you to automatically reduce the displayed weight of the load by the tare weight. This is done by entering the tare weight manually, accessing the tare weight from a database, or weighing the container separately to set the tare weight.

The applications for scales in inventory-related processes are extensive as is the variety in the levels of integration with equipment and information systems. Though I can't cover everything, I will focus on two common uses for scales that are closely tied to inventory accuracy. This includes the use of counting scales and the use of scales in order weight verification. I'll also give a brief description of an interesting application of weighing technology designed to provide real-time inventory information.

Counting scales

If you work with large quantities of small parts you are likely already familiar with counting scales. The difference between a counting scale and other electronic scales has nothing to do with the scale itself, but rather with the technology used to calculate and display the output. Counting scales have functionality that allows them to convert a counted sample into a unit weight and then use the unit weight to convert the weight of the materials back into a piece count. Let's go though a basic counting scale process:

A container is placed on the scale.

The [TARE] button is pressed, weighing the container and registering the tare weight into memory. The scale will now display 0.

A sample quantity of the material being weighed is counted and placed in the container.

The sample quantity is entered into the scale keypad.

The scale weighs the sample and container, deducts the tare weight and divides the resulting weight by the sample quantity to calculate a piece weight. It then divides the weight of the sample by the piece weight and displays the piece count (which should be the sample count).

The remainder of the material is placed into the container.

The scale weighs the material, deducts the tare weight, and divides the remaining weight by the piece weight to display the total piece count.

A counting scale is simply combining a series of measurements with some simple math to convert weight to pieces. The accuracy of the process is dependant upon the following:

The sensitivity of the scale relative to the piece weight of the items being weighed.

The accuracy of the tare weight.

The accuracy of the sample count.

The consistency in the unit weight of materials being weighed.

The relationship of the sample count to the total count.

The sensitivity of the scale relative to the piece weight of the items being weighed is important when counting very small lightweight items. For example, if you are using a scale to count small paperclips you need to make sure the scale is sensitive enough to register the weight of a single paperclip. Some scales will give an error message if the piece weight is outside of the sensitivity limits of the scale; this does not necessarily mean that just because you did not get an error message your count is correct. In operations that have a diverse range of items that need to be scale counted you may require multiple scales with different capacities and sensitivities to meet your accuracy objectives.

The accuracy of the tare weight can also be an issue when weighing lightweight items since even a slight breeze can affect the tare weight registered. I generally recommend using the smallest container possible and the smallest scale possible for the weighing process. Also, if you are using the counting scale to weigh several containers of an item, you need to make sure the weight of each container is consistent, or you need to weigh each container separately and reset the tare weight.

It's not unusual to count several cases of an item by setting the tare weight of the first carton, conducting a normal scale count process on the first carton, and then using the same tare weight and piece weight to count additional cartons. This will be accurate provided that the difference in weight of each of the containers is less than one-half the weight of a single piece. For heavier items this is usually not a problem, however, for very lightweight items a difference as minor as one carton having a little more packing tape on it or a carton that has gotten wet or soaked with oil may distort your results.

The accuracy of the sample count is critical. Employees need to realize that there is no "magic" in a counting scale that will automatically identify if you miscounted the sample. If you use a sample of 100, but miscounted and only added 99 pieces, the resulting count will register 100 pieces for every 99 actual pieces. That means that if you actually have 10,000 pieces, the scale will register 10,101 pieces. There is also a misconception that if you throw a few pieces onto the scale after the sample has been registered, and the scale registers the added pieces correctly, that the sample count was accurate. In the previous example where 99 pieces were used as a 100 sample, additional pieces would register correctly until you reached 50 additional pieces. Therefore you could have counted out as much as 49 additional pieces and added them to the container and received "correct" results. I always recommend that you verify the original sample count with another counted sample of equal or greater quantity.

The importance of the consistency in the unit weight of materials being weighed should be obvious. You are using weight to determine pieces; therefore if the weight per piece is not consistent, the resulting total piece count may be incorrect. Inconsistency in unit weight is the result of inconsistencies in the manufacturing process or in the materials used in the manufacturing process. While the likelihood of inconsistency is greater when you have the same item supplied by multiple suppliers or your inventory consists of several production runs of the item, you can also find inconsistency within the same run from the same supplier. All materials will have some inconsistency in weight per unit; problems arise when the difference in weight between one unit and another is large in proportion to the average unit weight, and the units used for the sample are not a representative sampling of the total materials being weighed.

So how do you know if the materials being counted are consistent in weight? You can count the materials using several separate samples. If you get several different counts, you have either counted a sample incorrectly or your unit weight is inconsistent. You can also display the unit weight on most scales. Count several small samples and compare the unit weights or just weigh several pieces individually. Large inconsistencies should show up in the sample verification process; however, very small inconsistencies may not register unless you are counting a quantity significantly larger than the sample. This is where the relationship of the sample count to the total count comes into play. The further away the total count is from the sample count, the more likely that any inconsistencies in unit weight or issues related to the sensitivity of the scale will affect the accuracy of the count.

Does this mean that if you expect to count 10,000 pieces you need to hand count a 2,000 sample? Fortunately most counting scales will allow you to easily compound samples. This is achieved by using a sample to count up to a larger quantity that is likely still accurate based upon the original sample quantity, and then reweighing the new quantity as a larger sample. For example, you would start with a 50 sample, then hand count another 100 to verify the initial sample. You can then reweigh the 150 pieces as a 150 sample. You now have a 150 sample (which is pretty good) but you are expecting the total count quantity to be 5,000, which is 33 times the sample size. While the 150 sample would likely be adequate to count up to 500 or 1,000, it may not give the needed accuracy to count to 5,000. What you can do is add materials (not counting them) to the container until the scale count reads 1,000 pieces, and then reweigh as a 1,000 sample. Now you have a sample that is reasonably accurate based upon your initial hand-counted sample, but also large enough to provide reasonable accuracy for a 5,000 count. Though this may sound like a lot of work, it is actually very easy on most current models of counting scales.

Figure 8A shows an example of a scale counting procedure. For those of you that may have been using counting scales with 10 and 20 samples you have probably noticed that I am recommending substantially larger sample sizes with 100 being the smallest (50 sample and then another 50 to verify sample). It takes very little time to count a 50 or 100 sample, and the added level of accuracy is well worth the minimal additional effort required. This procedure is actually a compromise; if I wanted the ultimate in accuracy I would likely use even larger samples and add some additional verification steps (such as repeating the entire process to see if you come up with the same count). As you look to balance accuracy and productivity you will likely find that this count procedure is a reasonable one. As with all process decisions, consider the unique characteristics of your operation and the materials you will be counting. Operations counting smaller quantities of heavier items may find a smaller sample size suitable while those counting very large quantities of very lightweight items may require larger samples.

There are several ways to eliminate the need to count out a sample. These involve recording the piece weight calculated in an initial count, so it may be used during subsequent counts of the same item. Some scales will have an internal database that will allow the storage of specific item piece-weights, others will integrate with an external database, and others will print a bar code of the piece-weight (and possibly tare weight) that can be placed on the storage bin. While all of these are timesavers and may increase accuracy (especially if a very large

Quantity to Count	Procedure
100 or less	Count by hand
101 to 300	Count a sample of 50, weigh sample, count another 50, add to scale and verify that scale reads 100, if not 100 you must recount samples and possibly go to higher sample. if scale reads 100, reweigh at sample 100 and then add remaining product.
301 to 1,000	Count a sample of 50, weigh sample, count another 100, add to scale and verify that scale reads 150. If not 150 you must recount samples and possibly go to higher sample. If scale reads 150, reweigh at sample 150 and then add remaining product.
over 1,000	To weigh very large quantities, use the previous procedure to obtain a verified sample of 150, then add product until scale reads 1,000, reweigh at sample 1,000 and then add remaining product.
Very light items	For some very light items you may need larger sample sizes. It's imperative that you always check your original sample with another sample of at least the same quantity as the original. Moving air and vibrations can also affect the proper weighing of very small items.

Figure 8A. Example of procedure for determining sample size.

sample is used for the initial count) there are some potential problems. If the initial sample count is conducted incorrectly, your count will be wrong every time after that. In addition, you are much more likely to encounter piece-weight variances under these conditions since you will be using a sample from one production run to measure all subsequent production runs. You will also have piece-weight variances and tare-weight variances when weighing porous materials or containers due to changes in humidity or other environmental factors (the same item or container will have a different weight in January than it did in July). If items are packaged, any changes in the packaging will change the item weight.

Don't let these potential issues frighten you away from automating your counting process. In many cases you will find this automation of the process will give you gains in both productivity and accuracy. Just make sure that your initial sample counts are accurate and periodically conduct audits (with new sample counts) to verify the consistency of product weight. Also, make sure the process is quick and simple. For the most part this should be as simple as scanning a bar code to access the data and update the scale. If your process requires manual entry through a series of prompts, you may just as well have counted a sample.

One more method used to eliminate the need to count out a sample is called reverse sampling. Reverse sampling is used primarily in picking operations when you are picking a large quantity that is smaller than a known case quantity. Since the case quantity is known, you can sample at the case quantity and then either remove materials until the count drops to the difference between the case quantity and the pick quantity, or remove all materials and then use the sample to count the new quantity.

The decision to incorporate the use of counting scales into your operation is a fairly simple one. If you are frequently hand counting large quantities of small parts, you should definitely plan on using counting scales. The only real decision comes in when you choose the specific scale you will be using and the sampling methodology. As I mentioned before, you generally get what you pay for with counting scales. Though you can buy a counting scale for under $500, you will find that going to a more expensive scale will be worth the additional expense. Not only will it be more accurate, it will also likely have greater functionality that allows your employees to be more productive. Proper training is critical when employees will be using counting scales. Employees need to understand all of the variables discussed here as well as the operational procedures specific to the piece of equipment they are using.

Weight verification

Check-weighing is most commonly known as a system that verifies the accuracy of manufacturing filling processes. Applications would include using a scale to control the filling process or using an in-line scale after the filling process to verify the weight. An example would be cases of canned foods zipping across an in-line scale built into a conveyor system. In this situation, the tolerances should be very small, as you would expect a high consistency in weight from one case to the next; any case underweight or overweight would be diverted off of the line for inspection.

Similar concepts can be applied to outbound order checking processes. This is usually performed as part of the shipping process in view of the fact that shipments must be weighed anyway to determine shipping charges and produce shipping documents. Since most companies now have some type of computerized shipping system, it's just a matter of providing the expected shipment weight to the system along with some tolerances and a little programming to compare the weights to identify any shipments that are out of the tolerance. While this is far from a comprehensive order checking system, it can prove to be valuable in catching certain types of errors.

Before you can embark on order weight verification, you obviously need a way to determine the expected weight of the order. This requires that you maintain accurate weights for all shippable items in a computer database and have a means of using this data to calculate total weight at the order level. Tolerances are needed to account for shipping containers and packing materials. These tolerances can be tightened if you can also maintain the weights of shipping materials in a database and use these to more accurately estimate the expected shipping weight. Methods of incorporating shipping materials into the expected shipping weight calculation would include having the computer "predict" the materials that will be used, or identifying the materials used and entering them into the system during the shipment-processing step. This may be done by scanning a carton ID bar code, using an in-line measurement device to identify the carton size, or manually entering shipping material information. Tolerances for pallets are difficult since pallet weights can vary significantly, especially if you are shipping on used pallets. The idea here is to use whatever technology may be available to keep the process as simple as possible. We're trying to create a "built-in" check here that doesn't significantly impact the process already in place.

You will then need a process in place for dealing with shipments that are not within the tolerances. Depending upon the materials being shipped and your order profiles, this can either be a quick visual check or a complete unpacking and 100 percent inspection of the contents of the shipments. Process flaws such as incorrect item weights or tolerances that are not reasonable in respect to the types of shipping materials used, will likely result in an unmanageable process where excessive time is wasted checking "good" orders.

Scales used as a real-time inventory system?
This is a rather unique application of weighing technology. Small load cells are incorporated into shelving or parts bins and used as sensors, communicating the bin weight to a computer. The computer than converts the bin weight into a piece count for each item. It's kind of like having a separate counting-scale permanently assigned to each storage bin. This allows the computer system to know the quantity in each bin at any given point of time (hence the name, real-time inventory system). I'm aware that this technology is currently being used as part of a vendor managed inventory (VMI) program. The supplier is the owner of the system, and he uses it to track the quantity of inventory at the customer's location.

The concerns with this type of a system would be cost, accuracy, and the question of how you have it interface with your inventory systems. Do you want count changes from the weighing system to automatically initiate inventory transactions? Probably not. It's always important to consider the implications of adopting alternative systems.

Machine counters

Machine counters have been around for a long time and come in many forms — from mechanical counters that increment each time a machine cycle has been completed; to flow meters that measure and control liquids, gases, and bulk dry materials; to computerized systems that measure combinations of activities. In many cases, machine counters can be used to either initiate or validate inventory transactions. Using the production machine to track the number of units produced or consumed is likely to be far more accurate than having the operator count and keep track of them. Virtually any machine can be retrofitted with devices that can accumulate data related to the machine operations. As with any equipment, training and procedures must be in place to ensure proper use of machine counters.

Bar codes

A bar code consists of a series of bars and spaces that . . . well, if you don't know what a bar code is by now, I doubt my explanation is going to help you anyway. I am also not going to focus on the detailed specifications of bar codes because it's way boring and, unless you are designing the equipment and software that generates, prints, and reads bar codes, you simply don't need to know all the little details. There are a few things you should know about bar codes related to symbologies, check characters, and quiet zones. A symbology is basically a "bar code version" that consists of a set of specifications that determine how the bars and spaces are converted to numbers, letters, and characters. Bar code symbologies are broken into two primary groups: one-dimensional bar codes, and two-dimensional bar codes.

1D symbologies are the ones we are most familiar with, consisting of many different symbologies including UPC, Code 128, Code 39, and Interleaved 2 of 5. There may also be variations within a specific symbology. The symbology you use may be dictated by supply chain partners through a standardized compliance label program, or, if only used internally, can be chosen based upon specific application. Some symbologies can only be used with numeric data while others can contain alpha characters as well as some special characters. Some symbologies are fixed-length, which means they are limited to a specific number of characters, while others are variable length. Let's keep things simple here. If you are in a supply chain that uses compliance labels, you will simply use whatever your supply chain is using. If you are looking for a flexible symbology to use internally on documents, labels, containers, locations, license plates, etc. you will find that Code 128 is a good choice.

Example of a 1D symbology.

This is an example of a Code128 bar code.

2D symbologies are capable of storing significantly more data then their 1D counterparts. Rather than using bars and spaces, 2D codes will use a pattern of smaller geometrical shapes to store the characters. Examples of 2D symbologies include PDF417, MaxiCode, and Data Matrix. If you've seen a UPS shipping label recently, you should have noticed a postage-stamp-sized pattern of what appears to be a bunch of dots around a three very small concentric circles. That's a MaxiCode code, and the dots are actually little hexagons. 2D symbologies are often called "portable databases" since rather than containing a very minimal amount of data used to access a database, they can actually contain the equivalent of a complete database record. 2D symbologies can only be read by scanners specifically designed for reading 2D codes; most scanners currently in use do not have these capabilities.

Examples of 2D symbologies.

Above is an example of a PDF417 code and to the right is and example of a DataMatrix code. 2D symbologies are capable of holding much more data than their 1D counterparts, but also require special scanners to read them.

Check characters. (also called check digits) are used in many symbologies to ensure an accurate read of the bar code data. A check character is a character, or set of characters, that is the result of a calculation based upon the characters in the bar code. When a bar code is created, the program will calculate the check character(s) and include them in the bar code. When the bar code is scanned, a program will read the characters in the bar code and perform the same calculation, it will then compare the check character(s) in the bar code with the results of the calculation to determine whether or not it was a "good read." In addition to check characters, 2D symbologies may also incorporate redundant data to ensure accurate reads.

Quiet zones are blank areas that must exist around a bar code to enable the scanner to detect the beginning and end of a bar code. The exact size of a required quite zone is relative to the specific symbology, however, all you really need to know is that you shouldn't have a bar code butted right up against another bar code, text, or graphic.

You should consider using bar codes whenever you have a need to take paper-based data and enter it into a computer. Places to use bar codes in inventory-related activities include: labels on individual items, cases, or unit-loads; location identification; production documents; picking documents; shipping documents; receiving documents; putaway documents; replenishment documents; cycle count and physical inventory tags or documents; kanbans; and compliance shipping labels.

When choosing between using 1D or 2D symbologies you need to look at the application and the amount of data you need to incorporate into the bar code. Most inventory-related warehouse and shop floor tasks can easily be accomplished through the use of 1D bar codes. I have had no problems in getting anywhere from 20 to 30 characters in a code 128 bar code that is still reasonable in size and easily readable with a good quality scanner. For the most part, all you need is enough data in the bar code to access the appropriate record(s) in your inventory database. There is also no need to limit a bar code to a single data element. For example, to use weight verification as part of a shipping manifesting process, you can incorporate the destination zip code, the shipping method code, and the expected shipping weight into a single bar code. You can then use software to parse and format the separate data elements as you scan the bar code. This allows you to place a shipment on a connected scale and scan a single bar code to accomplish the shipping manifesting task as well as providing the estimated weight to be used in the weight verification process.

There are also applications where it may make sense to print multiple bar codes. In these cases you will want to make sure each bar code is unique to prevent using the wrong bar code. This can be done by using different bar code symbologies or by adding a data identifier to the bar code. A data identifier is a character added to the bar code to identify the type of data in the bar code. You will then program the scanner to take actions based upon the data identifier. For example, you may add the letter "Q" to the first position of any bar code that represents a quantity, and the letter "P" to the first position of the bar code that represents the part number. This way, if a worker accidentally scans the quantity bar code when he should have been scanning the part number bar code, the system can recognize the error and send an error back to the user or not accept the scan.

I have no doubt that the use of 2D codes will increase in popularity in upcoming years, but unless you absolutely need the extra capacity of a 2D code you will find that you can save some money by using the currently more affordable 1D technology. You may also save time since 1D symbologies can usually be read more quickly and from greater distances than 2D.

Bar code printing

You can print a bar code on just about any printer, including dot matrix, laser, inkjet, thermal transfer, and direct thermal printers. Your choice in printers should consider the volume of labels or documents you will be printing, the use of the bar code, the required print speed, and the material on which you will be printing the bar code. Unless you are printing on multipart forms, there is little reason these days to use a dot matrix printer for bar codes. Inkjet printers are fine for relatively low volume printing of bar codes, provided you take care not to smudge the bar code prior to the ink drying. For higher volume printing of bar codes on documents, a laser printer is the preferred method. You can also use a laser printer to print bar codes on sheet-fed label stock. For high volume bar code labels, or frequent print-on-demand bar code labels, thermal transfer and direct thermal bar code printers are the equipment of choice. Thermal transfer uses a ribbon that prints onto the labels by means of a hot print head. Direct thermal operates similar to thermal transfer (often the same printer can operate as thermal transfer or direct thermal) except that rather than using a separate ribbon, the label stock is heat sensitive and the application of the hot print head to the label stock will produce the bar code. The down side of direct thermal is that the labels have a short life-span; exposure to heat and light will gradually fade and discolor the label. Though direct thermal is adequate for temporary applications such as shipping labels, you will likely find thermal transfer to be your best bet for most other labeling needs. For very high volume printing needs such as on packaging for consumer goods, you may choose to have the printing done by a professional printer.

The difference between a standard printer and a printer designed specifically to print bar codes (a bar code printer) lies in the way the bar code data is communicated to the printer. With a standard printer, the bar code software will create a bar code image and send the image to the printer as a graphic. With a bar code printer, the software can send a set of commands that the printer will use to create the bar code. The difference between the two methods is speed. Passing a graphic image to a printer is substantially slower than passing data. If you don't want your workers wasting time while waiting for the label to print in print-on-demand applications, you should use specialized bar code printers. There are also add-on devices currently available that can convert many standard printers to bar code printers.

Thinking of portable bar code printers? Yes, even the battery operated bar code printers that you hang from a belt or shoulder strap have become very affordable recently. I would caution against using these devices unless you really need to print labels in remote areas. Requiring a worker to carry around a portable printer all day even though they may be only a few steps away from a fixed printer will not do much for productivity. Portable bar code printers will usually be connected to a portable terminal, also carried by the worker. If your workers are working off of a lift truck or even a stock cart I would recommend attaching the portable printer to these pieces of equipment rather than to the worker.

Bar code verifiers are devices used to check the quality of printed bar codes. There are portable or fixed units that are used to selectively verify bar codes and there are also in-line verifiers that will verify bar codes as they are printed. Bar code verifiers are frequently used in high volume bar code printing applications such as checking UPC bar codes on consumer product packaging. For most internal applications, you probably do not need a bar code verifier.

You'll also need software to generate the bar codes. An extensive variety of software products are widely available today to generate bar codes. These products include stand-alone programs specifically designed for bar code printing, bar code fonts that can be used in many Windows applications, and ActiveX controls that can add bar code functionality to many existing programs.

Bar code label software is used to design and print labels with or without bar codes. You'll want to make sure the bar code label software you purchase is compatible with the operating system, database, and printers that you will be using. Most newer bar code label software will provide a graphical user interface that allows you to design the labels in a WYSIWYG format. You can also link objects (bar codes or other data) on the label to your database. If you are using a bar code printer and need the higher print speed, you need to make sure that your software is designed to send the bar code data as print codes (rather than a graphic) to the specific printer.

ActiveX controls are small computer programs that can be plugged into existing ActiveX-compliant applications to provide added functionality (bar code printing in this case). ActiveX controls for bar code printing have become widely available and are fairly inexpensive. Though many applications for ActiveX controls may require a programmer, they can also be used by non-programmers in document design and report generation programs. For example, if you use Microsoft Access to produce documents or reports, you can insert an ActiveX control into the document or report to produce a bar code.

The term "bar code font" can be a little misleading since you cannot necessarily just type data into a program using a bar code font and expect to produce a usable bar code. Though the bar code characters actual exist as a font, an additional program may be needed to convert the data (adding start characters, stop characters, and calculating check characters) prior to applying the bar code font. For desktop publishing applications, simple low-cost bar code font software may be all that's needed for periodically generating bar codes. For more demanding applications, programmers can use bar code fonts to develop more sophisticated applications. There are also utilities available for many popular software products that allow you to incorporate bar code fonts into them.

If you are using a bar code printer or a standard printer with an add-on bar code device a programmer simply needs to add some code that identifies the data to be printed as a bar code, and the printer hardware will then generate the bar code automatically, eliminating the need for any additional software.

There are also other development tools available that simplify the process of adding bar code printing capabilities to applications. Covering these in detail is beyond the scope of this book as well as beyond my own level of technical knowledge. Your software provider should be aware of products that can be used with their applications.

The wide variety of software and printers currently available to generate and print bar codes makes it very easy and affordable to add bar code printing capabilities to your operations. Though you may need a programmer to integrate bar code printing into current applications, the costs associated with this should be minimal. You'll also find that many software developers are adding bar code printing functionality to their manufacturing and warehousing software products, negating the need for further integration.

Bar code scanners

Bar code scanning technology has become more accurate, more functional, faster, and much more affordable in recent years. A vast variety of products are available to scan bar codes that range from pen-style wands, to laser and CCD hand-held scanners, to fixed mount omnidirectional scanners. When choosing a specific device, you need to consider the task the scanner will be used in, the conditions under which the scanner will be used, the frequency of use, the bar code symbology being used, and the distance from which the bar code will be scanned. You also need to understand how you will be interfacing the scanner with your system. Below, I've put together a glossary of key bar code scanning technology terms.

Wand scanners
These are the pen-type devices used to read bar codes. These are contact scanning devices that require you to draw the device across the bar code to read it. Though not very useful in most warehouse applications (scanning locations or items), wand scanners can be used to scan bar codes on documents at workstations. Standard wand scanners are not capable of reading 2D symbologies. I have, however, seen some new imaging devices that have similar designs to wand scanners that are capable of reading 2D symbologies.

Hand-held scanners
These are the pistol-shaped devices (as shown above) most people are familiar with. You basically point it at the bar code, pull the trigger, and it beeps when you've completed a good scan. Options in hand-held scanners include: laser or CCD scanners, decoded or undecoded, 1D or 2D symbology scanning, corded or cordless, various programmable capabilities, keyboard wedge functionality, compatibility with smart stands, ability to scan at various scan distances (depth of field), and even omnidirectional scanning capabilities.

Cordless scanners
Cordless scanners (also known as wireless scanners) should not be confused with portable terminals or portable computers (although the line is becoming blurred as more features are added to cordless scanners). Cordless scanners are basically hand-held scanners that have had the cord replaced with a radio transmitter. Though

they may have some programmable features, they are not "smart" the way a portable computer is. You generally need to be within view of the computer or terminal the cordless scanner is communicating with to ensure the transactions are being completed properly. A cordless scanner consists of two devices; a scanner and a base station. The base station is connected to your system the same way a corded scanner would be. The scanner then communicates directly with the base station. Cordless scanners have relatively short operating ranges (usually within 50 feet of base station). They are useful in situations where it is easier to walk a few feet to the bar code than to bring the bar coded materials to the workstation.

Fixed-position scanners

Fixed-position scanners are devices that are physically mounted to equipment or workstations. The bar code is then passed in front of the scanner to register the scan. Fixed-position scanners may be small scanners similar to a hand-held device mounted to a workstation, or they may be large high-speed omnidirectional scanners used in grocery checkouts or high speed conveyor applications.

Smart stands

These are stands that allow hand-held scanners to be used as fixed-position scanners. When you place the scanner in the stand it becomes a fixed-position scanner and you can just pass a bar code in front of it to register a scan. There is no need to pull the trigger. This can be very useful when a person working at a computer uses a bar code on a document to initiate a transaction. Rather than having to constantly pick up the scanner and point it at the document, they can just place the document under the scanner in the stand.

Omnidirectional scanners

As its name would infer, an omnidirectional scanner has the functionality to scan in several directions negating the need to orientate the scanner with the bar code. The most common application of omnidirectional scanners is the use of in-counter devices in supermarkets and retail establishments. Omnidirectional scanners are available as fixed-position devices and hand-held devices. For high volume applications such as in-line scanning of materials on a conveyor system, you need to make sure that the scan speed of the device is fast enough to keep up with the movement on the conveyor.

Laser versus CCD

Laser scanners use a laser beam that moves back and forth horizontally across the bar code. This back-and-forth movement is what creates the visible red line across the bar code during a scan. Laser scanners have been in use for decades and are capable of longer scan distances (depth of field) than CCD scanners. CCD (charged coupled device) scanners act like a digital camera, taking a picture of the bar code, which is then decoded. CCD scanners are generally less expensive than laser scanners but provide a limited depth of field. Some CCD devices actually require contact to the bar code, while others are capable of scanning only within a few inches. Longer-range CCD devices are becoming available with scan ranges up to 12 inches, however these do not come close to comparing to the capabilities of a laser scanner. Because CCD scanners are actually "imaging" devices, this same technology is used in higher priced devices to scan 2D bar codes and collect images such as signatures. Due to the depth-of-field limitations of CCD scanners, their use in warehouse applications tends to be rather limited. In my personal experience, I have generally preferred laser scanners over CCDs primarily because of the longer scan distances and faster read rates. This may not be a fair comparison since I have only used a few CCD scanners, and they were rather "low-end" models.

2D scanners
As previously mentioned, 2D bar code symbologies require special scanners to read them. There are both laser and CCD scanners designed to read 2D symbologies, though the advantages of a laser scanner with 1D bar codes don't seem to apply here. 2D symbologies are generally scanned from a relatively short distance (less than 12 inches). As of the writing of this book, the vast majority of scanners being sold are not capable of scanning 2D symbologies. I have no doubt that the number of 2D capable scanners will increase over the next few years. 2D scanners are generally capable of also reading 1D bar codes.

Depth of field
Depth of field describes the working distance of a particular scanner from the bar code. This cannot be listed as a single range since the depth of field is also dependant upon the density (size) of the bar code and the reflectivity of the media on which the bar code is printed. For instance, a particular laser scanner may have a working distance of 1-3 inches when scanning a very small bar code, or a working distance of 12-18 inches when scanning a larger bar code. If you tried to scan the small bar code from greater than 3 inches or the large bar code from less than 12 inches, you will not get a good read. If you used a different model of scanner you would likely have different working distances. There are also long-range scanners specifically designed to scan at longer distances. These are the devices most often used with lift truck mounted computers when the driver may be scanning a location bar code from more than several feet away. Generally, you can assume that a long-range scanner will have trouble scanning relatively close bar codes, however, manufacturers have developed some scanners that serve both purposes. Also, the term "long-range" can be deceiving when describing scanners since some CCD scanners described as long-range versions may only have a maximum scanning distance of 12 inches. Some manufacturers use terms like extra long range or extended range to describe their longer-range devices.

Decoded versus undecoded
Decoded scanners have logic built into them to convert the bar code into ASCII characters and then pass the ASCII characters to the connected device. Undecoded scanners require separate hardware/software for decoding the electronic signal and converting it into data. The choice of a decoded scanner over an undecoded

scanner will be dependant upon the method chosen for integration. A decoded scanner can be used alone (without additional hardware or software) in a "keyboard wedge" application (discussed later) to provide a very simple means of getting scanned data into a computer program. An undecoded scanner will need to be connected to a device that can decode the signal. This may be a separate decoder, a portable terminal with built in decoder, or a computer with a decoding program.

Autodiscrimination

Autodiscrimination describes the functionality of a bar code scanning system to recognize the bar code symbology being scanned. This allows a single scanner to read several different symbologies without the user having to "tell" the scanner what symbology is being scanned. Autodiscrimination is actually part of the decoding function, and will therefore be either part of a decoded scanner or a separate decoder used with undecoded scanners. Most decoded scanners and decoders come with this functionality and also allow you to program them to read only certain symbologies (this prevents someone from scanning the wrong bar code when multiple bar codes are present).

Keyboard wedge interface

With a keyboard wedge interface, the scanner is connected between the keyboard and the computer or terminal. Any data scanned will be sent as ASCII characters and immediately appear on the computer screen just as though it were typed on the keyboard. More simply put, the computer doesn't know that a scanner is attached and treats the data sent from the scanner as though it were keystrokes from a user. The advantage of a keyboard wedge interface is that there is no need for special software or programming on the computer. In its simplest application, you just connect the scanner, make sure your cursor is in the correct field, and scan the bar code that contains the data you need. A decoded scanner with the appropriate cable is all that is needed to accomplish this, however, you can also accomplish it with an undecoded scanner connected to a decoder with a keyboard wedge interface.

Decoders

Decoders (often called wedges) are interface devices that allow you to connect one or more scanners or other devices (such as scales and credit card readers) to a computer or terminal. Decoders are often called wedges because they frequently use a keyboard wedge interface to connect and communicate with a computer or terminal. Decoders may also connect via a serial port. If connecting through the serial port, you will require additional software on the computer to "do something" with the data being sent from the decoder. Since I've already mentioned that you can get decoded scanners with a keyboard wedge interface, you may be wondering why you would decide to use a separate decoder and an undecoded scanner. The primary reasons would include the ability to connect multiple devices and the added programmable functions (see programmable) some decoders offer.

Programmable

The term programmable is used to describe the functionality of some decoders and scanners. Unfortunately the term "programmable" is a little vague and can mean anything from some basic hardware configuration to full programming functionality. The programmable functionality most of us "nonprogrammers" are looking for is the ability to program the scanner or decoder to take different actions for different bar codes based upon data identifiers, format the data from the bar code, and script the keyboard wedge input. This would include the ability to parse the data (separate the various data elements when multiple data elements are placed in a single bar code) and add additional keystrokes. And do all of this without actually writing any "code."

The way many of these devices accomplish this "nonprogrammer programming" is by providing a set of bar codes that represent specific actions or characters. By scanning a logical sequence of these bar codes you are programming the device to take the specific actions you require. Some of these devices may provide software that allows you to develop the script on a PC and then download it to the device.

Clonable

Cloning is used to copy programming from one device to another. This functionality can be especially useful when you have several decoders that will be used at separate workstations, but will use the same programming. Rather than having to program each device individually, you can program one device and then use that device to copy the programming to additional devices.

Application of a programmable keyboard wedge system

When people talk about "barcoding" their plant or warehouse, they are generally referring to the use of batch or RF portable computers (discussed next) with bar code scanning capabilities. And while a keyboard wedge application is not a replacement for a full-blown RF system, it is a good way to start into the world of automated data capture. Keyboard wedge systems are very inexpensive and can be implemented in a matter of minutes or hours (provided you already have a bar code available). Most keyboard wedge applications in a warehouse or shop floor environment will be related to automating transactions associated with live documents. These would include: production reporting, pick confirmation, shipping confirmation, shipment manifesting, putaway confirmation, cycle counting, and receipt processing (if advanced shipment notifications are being used).

To implement a programmable keyboard wedge scanning system, you need to look at the program that the transaction is processed through and map out the data elements and keystrokes required to complete the transaction. Let's use a production-reporting program as an example. The program may require an operator to enter the production order number (eight characters), tab past three unused fields, enter the operation number (two characters), tab two more times, enter the machine ID (six characters), tab once, enter the user ID (eight characters), tab 4 times, enter the good quantity produced, tab once, enter the scrap quantity, press enter to accept. What I would do is add a bar code that includes the order number and the operation number to the production order for each operation. I would also provide a bar code label that contains the machine ID and the worker ID. Assuming that the worker usually works at the same machine, he could simply apply the label to his clipboard. I would apply a data identifier to each bar code (maybe MO for the manufacturing order and ID for the machine ID). I would then program the wedge device so if it encounters a bar code starting with the characters "MO," it should ignore the first two characters (MO), return the next eight characters, enter three tabs, return the next two characters, enter two more tabs and end. I would then program the device so if it encounters a bar code starting with the characters "ID," it should ignore the first two characters (ID), return the next six characters, enter one tab, return the next eight characters, enter four tabs and end. Now all the user needs to do is to scan the bar code on the production order paperwork associated with the operation they completed then scan their machine ID/user ID bar code on their clip board, and manually enter the quantities completed. While this is certainly a productivity improvement (especially with the hunt-and-peck one-fingered data entry method many production operators use), it is also an accuracy enhancement since it automates most of the data entry, allowing the worker to focus on the manual entry of the quantity.

I should mention again that this type of programming is simply a script of actions — similar to macros. There is no validation logic that ensures the right data is going into the right field. The user needs to make sure he is in the correct program (screen) and that the cursor is in the correct field prior to scanning the first bar code. Since the actions described in the example didn't include scripting the [enter] key, the results of incorrectly scanning something would probably not cause any serious problems, however, [enter] is often used when scripting simple transactions or ones that go though multiple screens. In these cases, a user mistake could cause a serious problem. If there are other programs used frequently at that workstation, or if there are other bar codes that may accidentally be scanned, you should test these combinations to see what the end effect would be. In many cases you may just initiate an error message, however, under certain conditions you may actually complete an incorrect transaction. Sometimes you can find ways to change the script to force an error under those conditions.

Though I focused on programmable keyboard wedge applications (because of their low cost and ease of implementation), you can also use scanners with "real" programming to accomplish many similar transaction-related tasks or more complex tasks that don't fall into the capabilities of a programmable wedge device.

Portable computers

These devices are known by a variety of names including portable terminals, portable data terminals (PDTs), RF terminals, batch terminals, industrial computers, hand-held computers, vehicle mount computers, and portable digital assistants (PDAs). Although they are sometimes programmed to act like "dumb terminals" these are all actually full-fledged computers. I must admit that I've been somewhat disappointed in the lack of progress made in portable industrial computer design, especially with hand-held units. If you think 386 processors, DOS operating systems, and monochrome displays are ancient history, you better think again as these are the specs of many of the hand-held portable data collection devices available today. To be fair, DOS is very capable of processing the simple screen prompts and communications used in many warehouse and shop floor tasks. But come on, we are in the 21st Century . . . DOS? On the plus side, costs have come down over the years and I'm hopeful that more quickly evolving technologies being developed for devices such as PDAs and other personal wireless communication systems will soon make industrial portable data collection terminals smaller, lighter, and more functional.

Batch versus RF

Batch devices are used to collect data into files on the device and are later connected to a computer to have the files downloaded. RF devices use radio frequency waves to communicate live with the host system or network. While batch devices were heavily used in the past and still have viable applications today, the introduction of wireless standards and the growth in wireless networks has made RF technology much more affordable and easier to maintain and implement. Batch terminals can be useful for processes like cycle counting or physical inventories, but are less desirable for transactions related to receipt, putaway, picking, and production reporting.

Hand-held devices

As previously mentioned, I have been less than impressed with advances in hand-held devices. I should also say that I have a lot of problems with the basic concept of hand-held devices. First of all, "hand-held" implies that you will be using one hand to hold the device. Well, in most warehousing/material handling environments this is a problem since that hand can no longer be used to handle materials or operate controls of material handling equipment. In addition, hand-held terminals generally have very small LCD displays that are difficult to read. They also have very small, confusing keypads that can make data entry extremely difficult. This doesn't mean that these can't be valuable tools in your operation, only that they are not the wonderful devices that you may have imagined them to be. Hand-held devices often come with integrated bar code scanners, however they can also be used with a separate scanner or without a scanner (not recommended).

In my opinion, the standard hand-held device designs that look like large pocket calculators have little use in a material handling operation outside of maybe a cycle count program. While the addition of a pistol-style handle with a trigger to initiate the scan improves the device by making it easier to scan bar codes and easier to holster between scans, I think these devices still have a way to go before they appear on my list of highly recommended technologies.

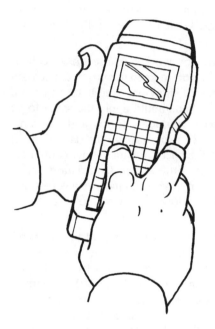

Here is an example of a standard hand-held industrial computer. This is not a very efficient means of completing inventory transactions in a material-handling environment.

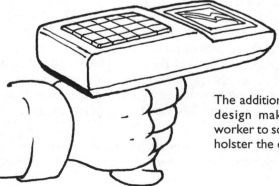

The addition of a pistol grip in this design makes it easier for the worker to scan a bar code and then holster the device.

When designing processes utilizing hand-held devices, your objective should be to make every effort to avoid using the keypad and screen. Basically you want your workers to just point and shoot, only using the screen or keypad if something goes wrong. Now I expect that promoters of "paperless" picking and putaway processing through the use of these devices will disagree, however, I have seen enough operations where workers are standing in an aisle, staring at these little computer screens trying to figure out their next task, when they should be "doing" their next task. I've also seen the interruption to processing that occurs when workers need to take their other hand (their only free hand) to use the keypad. They're not getting a hell of a lot of warehouse work done when they have their eyes and both hands committed to performing a transaction. I guess the use of the word "automated" in the term "automated data capture" really doesn't apply here.

Certainly there are tasks that may require the worker to use the screen or keypad. In these cases you should make every effort to keep the prompts and data entry as simple as possible. The prompts should show only the bare minimum amount of data necessary to perform the task. You should apply the same logic discussed in "Making Accuracy Easy" related to documents, forms, and programs to these devices. For example, you should look to subordinate the data element identifiers. These are the text descriptions of the specific data elements on a report or computer screen. Rather than filling the little screen with data descriptions like "Item Number," "Location," or "Quantity," you can just use a very small "#," "L," or "Q" to identify these elements. This allows the worker to more easily focus on the actual data.

As I said before, the keypads on these devices are very difficult to use, especially with alpha characters. Limit data entry to numeric data as much as possible and also eliminate the need to have to enter tabs or enter keys. I frequently see applications where the device is designed to scan in all the data, yet the programmer decides to require the worker to press the enter key to complete the transaction. While this doesn't sound like much, you once again need to put this in the context of a physical material handling process. Why should you require the worker to take their other hand and reach over to press an [enter] key when the final scan could have automatically completed the transaction. If it is absolutely necessary to have a step that requires the [enter] function, you can create a separate bar code label that initiates the [enter] key. These labels can then be strategically placed where the worker can easily scan them, such as on the cage of their lift truck, on a stationary object by their workstation, or even on the employee. That's right, they can slap a label on their sleeve, pants leg, or even the top of their shoe. This way, they can complete the transaction without needing to use their other hand. Or better yet, make use of voice technology (discussed later) to initiate the enter command.

Options on these devices are numerous. Most still use the standard monochrome displays, however full color displays and even black-and-white (with grayscale) displays are available. I never liked the monochrome so I'm pleased to see these newer options. My personal preference continues to be black text on a white background. If you recall when personal computers started to become popular in the late eighties and early nineties, everyone was using color schemes like white text on blue backgrounds, red text on black backgrounds, just because they could. We all figured "we are no longer limited to paper and ink." Eventually most users started to realize this was just plain hard to look at and started to change their programs to more conventional color schemes. Now, most computer programs load with a default black on white. Coincidentally the exact same scenario developed with web sites almost ten years later. Remember all of those websites with red on black, yellow on black, green on purple, blue on red, ... and the immediate headache that occurred as soon as you started to try to read the text on them. Now, black on white has also become the norm for the web. Should we translate this knowledge to our use of portable devices with their even smaller screens? I certainly hope so. Unfortunately a color display (required to do black-on-white, although the grayscale screens are a good option) consumes significantly more power than does the older monochrome display. While this may not be a big issue in a desktop application, it is an important consideration in battery-operated devices. Touch screens (discussed later) are also becoming available on many of these devices.

Some of these devices will also provide various keypad options to better suit the type of entry your workers will be doing. Take the same advice that was given related to pocket calculators here and select the simplest design with the largest buttons possible. Since I'm hoping that I have convinced you not to do any alpha entry, you should focus on a large numeric keypad.

Options related to integrated scanners include: 1D or 2D, laser or CCD, image capturing capabilities, and scanner orientation. If you decide to use a separate scanner with these devices you should look for a low power usage model. There are also small hand, wrist, or finger-mounted scanners available.

Though DOS remains the most common operating system on portable handheld industrial computers, I expect that to change dramatically in the next few years. Windows CE devices are becoming more common and will likely replace DOS as the most common operating system very soon. There are also devices available with Palm and Linux operating systems.

The growth of personal digital assistants is having a positive impact on portable devices used in industrial applications. The larger market for PDAs provides larger investments in research and development that will ultimately result in technology gains that should trickle down into industrial devices. Though I don't expect to see warehouse workers using a stylus to enter data (at least I hope I don't), advances in touch screens, color displays, smaller more powerful devices, graphical user interfaces, more energy efficient devices, and higher performance batteries, will certainly aid in the evolution of portable industrial devices. One of the terms you may encounter when comparing industrial devices to personal computer devices is "ruggedized." Though there is no standard definition for what ruggedized is, it basically means that the device has been designed for an industrial environment where it is more likely to get dropped or otherwise bounced around. There are also industrial devices specifically designed to work in very dirty environments or in cold storage environments.

Vehicle-mounted devices

Vehicle-mounted devices are larger computers that have more similarities to a notebook computer than a hand-held device. Vehicle-mounted devices have several advantages over hand-held devices including larger screens (even up to full sized screens), larger keypads similar to a standard keyboard on a notebook computer, and you can't drop, loose, or forget to charge them. You're also more likely to find a graphical user interfaces (Windows) with vehicle-mounted devices than with hand-held devices. When using a full-screen vehicle-mounted device, integration can be much simpler as you can use your existing programs designed for desktop computers (although you should still consider simplifying the screens). Obviously you need to be performing tasks using some type of a vehicle (lift truck, tug, cart, etc.) to use these devices. Vehicle-mounted devices will generally use a separate wired or wireless hand-held bar code scanner to input data. These are the same scanners discussed previously that would otherwise be integrated with a desktop computer or terminal. Tips for using vehicle-mounted devices are similar to those for hand-helds (simple prompts, minimal data entry). You should also consult with your vehicle manufacturer for recommendations on where to mount the device to ensure safe operation of the vehicle. As demand for these devices grows, I would expect to see lift truck manufacturers integrating them into the designs of their vehicles.

Options for vehicle-mounted devices are similar to hand-held devices. These include various display sizes, color displays, various keyboard configurations, and choices in operating systems. Windows CE has become very common on vehicle-mounted devices.

If your workers are primarily working from a lift truck or other vehicle (tug, pallet truck, or even a stock cart), a vehicle-mounted device is likely your best option. If your workers need to occasionally step away from the vehicle to scan a bar code, you can use a wireless scanner with your vehicle-mounted device. There are even vehicle-mounted devices available that can be detached from the vehicle and temporarily used as a hand-held device.

Touch screens

Though I don't expect touch screens to do a lot for accuracy, they can certainly enhance productivity and are a relative topic in the context of this chapter. Touch screens have been available for quite some time as fixed devices in industrial applications and are becoming more widely available in hand-held and vehicle-mounted systems. The value of a touch screen system lies in their ability to configure a screen-based keypad that's relative to the specific task being performed. If you need to enter a quantity, a numeric keypad can be displayed, if you need to enter alpha data a full keyboard can be displayed, if you simply have a choice of a few options, only buttons for those options will appear.

Wearable systems

Wearable systems will likely have substantial growth in coming years. As the name would imply, a wearable system is a device or set of devices that are worn by the worker. While equipment manufacturers and a lot of computer geeks are still experimenting with wearable system designs, there are already a small offering of wearable systems commercially available. Most notable are Symbol's WS series device (nicknamed the Gladiator) and Vocollect's Talkman. Symbol's system has a complete portable computer with a screen and keypad that is worn on the wrist/forearm and uses a small bar code scanner worn on a finger like a ring. This same ring scanner device can also be used with other portable devices. Vocollect's Talkman system consists of a small ergonomic computer worn on a belt, and a wired headset to send and receive voice communications. Headmount displays also have potential applications, though I have some serious questions on the safety of the technology. A headmount display is a device that is positioned in front of one of the user's eyes and projects a viewable image of a computer screen. Though the technology is very interesting, I think some serious safety studies need to be done before you require workers to use these for extended periods of time.

With the exception of the wrist-worn computer device, most wearable systems use a small computer that can be worn on a belt or carried in a pocket. The peripheral devices (scanners, voice headsets, headmount displays) are then connected via wire to the computer. I should also note that there are some portable computer manufacturers that have tried to enter the "wearable" market by simply putting their hand-held devices into a fanny pack, connecting them to a ring scanner or a voice headset and calling them a wearable system. While these are technically "wearable systems" they are rather poor examples.

Wrist-worn device with ring scanner.

The primary benefit of wearable systems in inventory-related tasks should be obvious. It frees the worker's hands to do that thing…you know…WORK! I absolutely expect wearable devices to totally replace hand-held devices in material handling applications in upcoming years. Exactly what form they will take is the big question. Will they be a device on your wrist? Your belt? Your arm? Integrated into a headset, hat, or backpack, or hung from a workers neck like a necklace? Will they get so small that they can be integrated into the frames of a pair of glasses or woven into the fabric of clothing? What technologies will be used to communicate the data? Will it be bar code scanners? RFID? Voice recognition? A direct neural connection? My guess is that it will be all of the above (well, maybe not the direct neural connection) along with some things we haven't even heard of yet. I currently envision the integration of small wearable bar code scanners (such as Symbol's ring scanner) and voice technologies in the same wearable system to be the optimal solution for the next few years. Beyond that, I guess I'll just wait and see.

Personal wireless technologies are also making an entrance into wearable systems. Bluetooth is a wireless standard that is becoming very popular for personal wireless applications. Basically, a personal wireless system is the use of several devices within close proximity that communicate with each other. For a wearable system, this would mean that you could carry a small portable computer on your belt or in your pocket, and have a wireless headset or bar code scanner that communicates with the portable computer. The portable computer would then operate as a stand-alone system or use batch or RF to transmit data to and from the host system. While it's great to be able to get rid of all of the wires, there is a catch. Since the devices are now wireless, they will each need their own communications hardware and power source (a battery). This is going to increase the size and weight of each device and also require recharging each device. Due to this, I don't to expect this technology to replace all of the connecting wires on wearable systems in the near future.

"YEAH, THE BOSS JUST READ AN ARTICLE ON WEARABLE COMPUTERS AND FIGURED WE COULD SAVE SOME $$$ BY BUILDING ONE OURSELVES"

Voice systems

I've developed a real liking for voice technology in recent years. Though the technology is far from mature, it has advanced to the point where it is now a very viable alternative to computer screens, keypads, and even bar code scanners. The basic idea here is, "why not communicate with our information systems the same we communicate with each other?" What could be a simpler user interface?

Voice systems are actually composed of two technologies: **voice directed**, which converts computer data into audible commands, and **speech recognition**, which allows user voice input to be converted into data or commands. Though stationary voice systems have been used for years in applications such as quality inspection processes, portable systems used in inventory-related tasks are relatively new. A portable voice system consists of a wearable computer and a headset with headphones and a microphone. Tasks are converted to audible commands that are sent to the headphones while confirmation of completion of tasks and requests for additional information are communicated through voice commands to the computer.

The advantages of voice systems include hands-free and eyes-free operation. Applications for voice systems include order picking, shipping, receiving, put-away, and cycle counting. Though speech recognition technology has improved over the years, it still is not at the point where you can just talk to the computer and expect it to understand everything you are saying. If you are thinking, this sounds like a problem (since you are trying to implement systems that increase accuracy) you are only partially correct. As long as you work within the capabilities of the voice technology, you can be very accurate. To compensate for the problems related to speech recognition you need to limit the speech input to a fairly short list of keywords and phrases for commands and primarily numeric characters for voice data input. Alpha characters would have to be spoken phonetically (Alpha, Bravo, Charlie, ...Zulu) to maintain acceptable levels of accuracy. Fortunately, many warehouse and shop floor tasks can be performed very effectively within these limitations.

It's fairly easy to see how voice technology can increase productivity by directing workers through their tasks. You may, however, be wondering how this technology can actually increase the accuracy of these tasks. The answer lies in the use of "check characters." Unlike the check characters used in bar codes that are the mathematical result of the contents of the bar code, check characters in voice systems are more likely to just be preassigned values given to items or locations. The idea here is that the worker is sent to a specific item/location to pick or put away inventory. When the worker gets there, he reads the check character on the item/location back to the system. This verifies that he has indeed found the correct item/location. If you are wondering why the worker doesn't just read back the item or location, there are actually several reasons. First, it would probably result in reading alpha characters that would require your workers to memorize the phonetic alphabet. Second, you simply don't need to read back that much data (saving time), and third, you could still be at the wrong item/location and simply be repeating the information the system has given to you. Since the system has not given you the check characters, you have to actually read them from the item/location; this gives you the accuracy validation. Usually a two to three digit numeric check character is used.

Let's describe a picking task using a voice system.

Worker:	"ready"
Computer:	"go to aisle B R"
Worker:	"ready"
Computer:	"go to slot one seven three"
Worker:	"ready"
Computer:	"check character"
Worker	"seven five nine"
Computer:	"pick five"
Worker:	"Five"

This is just an example of a script that may be used during a voice-based picking task. I would again apply the concepts that we used in optimizing documents and programs to these voice prompts. Since, in this case, an aisle (two alphabetical characters) sounds distinctly different from a slot (three numeric characters), I would probably eliminate the "go to aisle" and "go to slot" commands. In addition, since the picker knows that after he has found the location he must read the check character, there is really no reason for the computer to prompt for this. The picker can simply say "ready" and immediately read the check character, or you may even omit the need to say "ready" and just read the check character. This would result in this script:

Worker:	**"ready"**
Computer:	**"B R"**
Worker:	**"ready"**
Computer:	**"one seven three"**
Worker:	**"seven five nine"**
Computer:	**"pick five"**
Worker:	**"five"**

Though eliminating a few words may seem like an insignificant change, it can add up to a significant time savings in a high-volume picking operation. Using the previous examples, an order picker averaging 500 picks per day would eliminate the need to say "ready" 500 times per day. Just say "ready" 20 times and I think you will appreciate this "minor" change. Now add to that the fact the picker can eliminate listening to "go to aisle," "go to slot," and "check character" 500 times per day. I think as this technology advances, science will develop that adds greater efficiency. For example, it may be determined that having the worker say "next" or "go" or some other command rather than "ready" is quicker and less stressful on the worker's voice. This brings ergonomics to a whole new level, doesn't it?

You will also need to design in commands and scripts for any exceptions that may occur. A command like "again" would prompt the computer to repeat the previous information, while a command like "short" would initiate a script for reporting an inventory shortage.

Speech recognition programs require that each user "train" the system to their speech patterns. This is done by repeating a series of commands into the microphone. Since we are using only numeric entry and limited commands, the system only needs to be trained for these sounds. This makes the training process much quicker and the resulting system much more accurate.

As I stated, I really like this technology and expect substantial growth in this area. I don't, however, see voice as a replacement for everything. I think using voice combined with other technologies (bar code, RFID, light systems) will provide the ultimate in accuracy and productivity. For a small-parts picking operation, this may be a wearable voice system to direct the activities combined with a small wearable scanner (to scan the item/location rather than reading back a check digit). For a receiving/putaway operation, this may include a vehicle-mounted computer combined with a wireless headset and a wireless bar code scanner. The worker would scan the incoming materials, initiating the receipt/putaway process. The voice system would then direct the worker to the putaway location where the worker would scan the location to verify. As RFID (discussed next) becomes more popular, I would expect to see it also enter this combination of technologies.

> *Voice systems provide a hands-free and eyes-free user interface.*

Radio frequency identification (RFID)

RFID encompasses a diverse range of devices that are capable of transmitting data to an RF receiver. Many of us already have RFID devices in our vehicles that allow us to zip through express tollbooth lanes at 55 mph while others wait to pay cash. Similar devices are being used to track ocean containers as they are loaded and unloaded. Veterinarians are implanting small RFID devices under the skin of pets to allow identification if the pet is lost and then later found. Hospitals are starting to use RFID bracelets to track patients. RFID tags are worn on the shoes of runners during marathons and triathlons to track racers through checkpoints. There are areas where you can use an RFID button hanging from your key chain to pay for gas and even fast food. And there are RFID circuits so thin that they can be integrated into a paper label (called smart labels). You may have seen a television commercial that airs occasionally depicting a person that appears to be shoplifting. The person is seen in a grocery store placing merchandise into his trench coat. As the person leaves the store, he passes through a scanning device that beeps. A security guard then approaches the person and reminds him that he has forgotten his receipt. This commercial is depicting RFID technology in action. By using smart labels on all products combined with the shopper carrying an RFID version of a credit card, this scenario is entirely possible.

There are several terms you should understand when considering RFID systems. Active tags (I am going to refer to all RFID devices as tags) contain their own power source (a battery), while passive tags are powered by the signal generated from the reader device. I'll admit that I don't quite understand how a radio signal generated from a reader, several feet away, can actually provide the power source to a tag without touching it. And, until I do understand it, I'm going to make a point of not standing between a reader and a tag unless I'm wearing lead-lined underwear and a tinfoil dew rag. Hey, you can't be too careful.

Since passive tags do not require an internal power source, their useful life is essentially as long as the life of the materials from which they are manufactured. Read/write tags are capable of having their data changed on the fly, while read-only tags contain fixed data.

The advantages of RFID over bar codes includes the ability to hold more data, the ability to change the data at various points in the process, the ability to read RFID tags without having direct line-of-sight (even reading through many materials), and the ability to use RFID tags in harsh environments where bar coded labels would have problems. On the minus side, RFID tags are significantly more expensive than bar codes, you can't selectively read a specific RFID tag from a distance, and certain materials (metals) may cause problems with reading RFID tags.

The potential applications of RFID technology are limited only by our imaginations, however, the practical applications will most likely be limited by the costs of the RFID tags. In many applications, the cost of a bar code is less than one cent. Though the cost of RFID tags is going down, it's going to be a long time (if ever) before bar codes and RFID tags will compete on a pure cost basis. Instead, RFID technology is being applied where bar codes don't work, or where productivity savings related to the application of RFID over bar codes exceed the cost of the RFID technology. If we take the grocery store example (from the "shoplifting" commercial), there are obvious labor savings if the checkout process can be automated. The only thing preventing this automation from being implemented is the cost of the RFID tags and the reading technology (I guess I should also mention the requirement to change the entire grocery and retail industry). This is a situation where the current costs of the RFID tags make this application unrealistic (you obviously can't have the cost of the RFID tag being greater than the value of the product it's being placed on).

More effective applications of RFID tags result when the number of tags required is limited, the cost of the tag is negligible in comparison to the value of the product it's being placed on, or when the RFID tags can be reused. Most current applications of RFID in inventory-related tasks incorporate the reusable capabilities of RFID tags into reusable pallets, totes, or containers. This minimizes the investment, and allows the cost of the tags to be spread over the lifetime of the pallet, tote, or container. Examples would include using RFID tags on totes within an automated conveyor system to initiate sortation, using RFID tags incorporated into pallets to track loads into and out of trailers, and using RFID tags incorporated into pallets or containers to track product movement on the shop floor.

One of the more interesting concepts that have come out of RFID technology is the real-time locator system (RTLS). One version of this concept implies that you could track your entire inventory within your facility automatically by placing RFID tags on each moveable unit of measure and incorporating strategically placed readers throughout all storage and staging areas. This would suggest that your workers could move product throughout the facility without ever executing a transaction. The RTLS would read all areas and determine what you have and where it is located. No matter what your employees do, they cannot lose your product. Sound too good to be true? This is another situation where theoretical possibilities do not easily translate into practical applications. Depending upon the nature of your product, product movement, and storage characteristics, a RTLS may or may not be in your future. These characteristics can dramatically change the cost and complexity of this application of RFID technology.

A more likely application of RFID in determining product locations would involve using RFID tags to identify locations and having an RFID reader on a lift truck or other automated storage device read the tags to determine the vehicle's location. For example, in a bulk floor storage area, you could embed RFID tags in the concrete floor designating each location. A reader on the lift truck could read the location tag whenever product is put away or picked to confirm the location. Application of bar code technology in this same application would usually involve hanging bar coded signs from the ceiling above each location and using long range hand-held laser scanners to read the location. This sometimes requires a little "trick shooting" by the lift truck operator to read the sign since the operator cage and lift truck mast tends to get in the way. Having an RFID location tag in the floor and another RFID tag on the pallet would allow the worker to complete the transaction by simply pushing a button on a vehicle-mounted terminal or even giving a voice command via a headset.

Some of the difficulties in using this technology are related to designing a system that ensures you are reading the tags that you intend to read and do not read the ones you do not intend to read. Since RFID does not require line-of-sight, it is also not restricted by it. Which means that you need to make sure you are not accidentally reading a nearby pallet, tote, container, or location. When you read a bar code, you must point the reader directly at the bar code being read. While this is a limitation of a bar code system, it is also an advantage since the worker absolutely knows which bar code is being read. With RFID, these issues must be resolved through the technical design of the system. In some cases this may result in the need to be very close to the RFID tag to get the read (to prevent reading nearby tags). This may result in a situation where the use of bar codes would make more sense since the user can be more selective in the scans.

Light-directed systems

Light-directed systems have been used for years in order picking operations to increase accuracy and productivity. Though there are many configurations of light systems being used, the most common involves having a small light module on each picking location. Each light module will include an LED display that displays the quantity to pick, and a button to confirm completion of the pick. There may also be additional buttons to deal with shortages or other problems.

Let's describe a picking task using a **pick-to-light** system.

Order picking route is started.

First pick location lights up.

Order picker locates lighted location.

Order picker reads quantity from LED display.

Order picker picks quantity.

Order picker presses [task complete] button on light module.

Next pick location lights up.

Sounds pretty simple, doesn't it? In the right environment, pick-to-light can prove to be the best combination of productivity and accuracy. So what is the right environment? Well first of all, pick-to-light modules would need to be installed in each picking location. This requires a significant amount of hardware, and the corresponding costs of this hardware make pick-to-light systems only cost effective where you have very high picks per SKU. You also need the picking area to be small enough to allow the picker to easily see the next lighted location from the previous one. And you generally need to limit your picking to one order picker per pick zone (though there are some technologies being implemented to get around this). A "standard" pick-to-light scenario would be an operation where fast-moving, small items are picked from carton flow rack into totes onto a conveyor system running parallel to the flow rack pick face. Each individual pick zone is generally rather small — consisting of 20 to 50 feet of pick face.

Because pick-to-light systems are generally paperless picking systems, the entire physical picking process is solely controlled by the lights. Having multiple order pickers working in the same zone would result in a picker potentially picking another picker's next task. One way around this would be to maintain a safety buffer between each picker. If one picker's next pick were beyond the current position of the picker ahead of him, the system would have to stop him and hold him until the other picker progresses beyond this pick. While this is possible, you probably don't want to invest this kind of money into technology that is going to

force one worker to stand there and wait for another worker. I've heard of another solution recently that uses RFID technology to communicate a picker's location relative to the picks. Though I'm not clear as to the exact specs of this combination of technologies, I still suspect there would be potential problems when one picker passes another near a pick. Yet another solution would combine voice directed or hand-held computer directed picking with pick-to-light. While I don't like the hand-held computer option (no surprise here) the voice option has potential. Obviously these technology combinations are getting rather expensive. The most common solution is to avoid the problem by limiting your process to one picker per zone.

Another common use of pick-to-light involves picking from horizontal carousels and using a "light tree" to identify the pick location and quantity. The light tree is a series of stacked LED displays mounted on a vertical device (more like a pole than a tree) that stands next to the carousel. The carousel will stop at the appropriate position, and the light tree will light up at the level corresponding to the pick. Since many carousel applications will consists of several pick bins per level, the light tree will identify the bin position and quantity via the LED display. Because the light tree is a separate device, there is still an opportunity for error if the picker picks from the wrong bin. This will result in a slightly lower level of accuracy with a light tree than you would get with a standard pick-to-light system that has a separate pick module for each location. On the plus side, since a single light tree can be used with hundreds or even thousands of pick locations, the cost per pick location is much lower.

Light systems are also frequently used in batch picking operations where multiple orders are picked at the same time. In this scenario, **put-to-light** systems are used to designate the correct order to place the picked item in. Often this involves a multilevel pick cart or a section of conveyor with a light for each order position. Cartons or totes are placed into each position of the pick cart or conveyor (and often require scanning a bar code to identify each order with a pick position). As each item is picked, the corresponding "put" location will light up, signaling the picker where to place the product. Operations that use pick-to-light will often also incorporate put-to-light in the same system (the carousel example previously discussed would generally be a batch picking system also using put-to-light).

Because of the simplicity of a light-directed system (from the workers standpoint), you should expect substantial gains in accuracy since the workers can now place most of their focus on quantities. The biggest potential accuracy problem associated with pick-to-light systems results when inventory is incorrectly stocked. Since pick-to-light is only validating location, there is no way for the worker to identify that the wrong parts are in the location. In a fast-paced operation you may have tens or hundreds of picking errors before you realize that the incorrect item is in the location. Because of this, it is highly recommended to use a comprehensive validation system (probably bar code) for putaway processes in a pick-to-light environment.

Pick-to-light is also the most productive technology used in order picking. For the most part, your choice to use light-directed systems will be dependant upon your storage equipment and the pick volume per SKU. If you are using horizontal carousels, you can assume you will also be using a light tree. When incorporating pick-to-light into static picking locations, you need to balance the cost of the system against the potential productivity and accuracy gains. As previously stated, this generally requires very fast moving items to justify the cost of pick-to-light. I should also note that pick-to-light is not an all-or-nothing application. You may set up a portion of your facility with pick-to-light for your faster moving inventory and use a more conventional (manual) system for slower moving inventory.

There are also some pick-to-light designs that have looked to achieve a compromise between cost and functionality by using only a single light module per section or aisle, rather than per each bin location. In these designs, the light module will usually be larger and display the item/location and quantity to pick. My general opinion on these is that they really don't offer you much, if anything, over a manual paper-based system. I think operations that have implemented this technology were focused more on finding a way to go paperless, than actually finding a way of improving operations.

Full automation

For those with very deep pockets, there is automated equipment available that takes the largest source of errors (people) out of the process. These include fully automated picking systems such as A-frames, robotic picking and putaway systems, automated storage and retrieval systems (ASRS), automated guided vehicles (AGV), and automated truck-loading systems. There is no doubt that a machine is capable of being more accurate than a human. Unfortunately the costs associated with these systems can only be justified in a small percentage of operations. Generally you need enough volume to support running these machines continuously over multiple shifts to gain a reasonable return on investment. It's also unlikely that you will completely eliminate people from the process. People are usually required to stock A-frame picking machines, people will often be the ones that put together the loads that are handled by automated systems, and people may be involved in counting piece quantities out of or into some of these systems.

Integration

When exploring the various technologies described previously, you will find that the costs of much of the equipment used in these systems has decreased substantially in recent years. That's the good news. The bad news is that most of these systems require integration (software and programming) that can cost substantially more than the equipment. It's the integration costs that often put these technologies out of the reach of many operations.

Systems integration has been a rather lucrative business in the past couple of decades. Plug-and-play is not a term that can be used with business software and industrial equipment. Businesses wanting to utilize the technologies available today must deal with the integration issues. Since most companies don't have the internal expertise to take on these specialized projects, they have no recourse but to outsource the integration to independent system integrators or software or hardware suppliers. The costs associated with these services can be extremely high. In my opinion there are several contributing factors to these high integration costs.

Integrator's expertise. Integration is a specialized field and requires specialized skills. Certainly there is a cost associated with this.

Integrator's lack of expertise. Some integrators aren't very good at their jobs. Unfortunately, the client will usually pay for this through endless billable hours required to get the system to actually work.

Integrator's profit expectations. As with many other specialists, integrators expect to make a lot of money; some of them are quite simply overpriced.

Client's lack of knowledge. Unrealistic expectations and misapplication of technology by the client will drive up implementation costs.

Client's lack of commitment. The more difficult the client makes the implementation, the greater the implementation costs.

Complexity of systems. Some integration projects are extremely complicated. Unless you have a very good understanding of systems, you should avoid making "that shouldn't be too hard" assumptions.

Fishing expeditions. Costs associated with time an integrator spends with "prospective" customers that claim they are serious about a project but are actually just conducting research (fishing). These costs must be made up by their paying customers through inflated fees. Though it can be a hard sell, some integrators are starting to limit the amount of free up front work they will conduct. This is a good thing since it can help to keep the costs down for their paying clients.

Finding a really good systems integrator or programmer is almost like winning the lottery. Since the clients don't have the expertise to implement the system themselves, they also lack the expertise to adequately evaluate prospective integrators. Even during and after the implementation, they are unlikely to know if they are being "taken" or not. It's a lot like dropping your car off at the repair shop. If you knew how to fix it, you probably would have fixed it yourself. Therefore when the repair bills start piling up, you are scratching your head trying to figure out if the costs are legitimate or not. After a series of very expensive repairs, you may decide that you should be looking for another mechanic, however you still probably don't have the skills to evaluate the next one.

This can be a very frustrating process and even the standard methods of asking for references may not be effective. Though a good reference is probably better than a bad reference, you have to realize that the person recommending an integrator is likely no more capable of evaluating the integrator's performance than you are. Integration projects are so diverse and infrequent within an organization that it's difficult to try to compare one integrator on one project with another integrator on another project. There are undoubtedly some very happy clients that got "ripped off" as well as some very unhappy clients that were provided excellent service.

The best piece of advice I can give on these projects is to get involved and get educated. A good integrator will appreciate and encourage educated and involved clients. A bad integrator will prefer ignorance and a hands-off approach. Prior to starting the project, try to educate yourself as much as is reasonable about the technologies available. Use your integrator to help educate you on the details of the technology as the project develops. Use your internal resources to reduce the

amount of work the external resources have to perform. Be involved in the detailed decisions of the project to ensure your requirements are being met.

An educated and involved client can reduce integration costs by setting realistic requirements, limiting and maintaining the scope of the project, and providing
the internal resources to support the external resources. Changing requirements
and project delays due to lack of internal support will drive up the costs of the
project. An integrator will "assume" a certain amount of incompetence by the
client and likely build this into the costs in the bid (don't look for a line that says
"client incompetence costs"). If you can convince the integrator of your compe-
tence, and then perform to this standard, you are more likely to get the integrator
to quote a more reasonable rate. You also want to be heavily involved to prevent
an incompetent integrator from providing an inferior product.

There is also no clear roadmap as to how an integration is conducted. Each
integrator tends to have their own preferences on the best methods. This is another case where a lack of expertise by the integrator may force them to use
technologies they are "comfortable" with rather than using the "best" technology
for your application. Your best bet is to talk to several integrators and ask them
how they would technically implement the system. You may find that you will get
different answers from different integrators. You should then ask each why they
are not using the methodology recommended by the others. This may give you
some idea as to their technical knowledge. Here are a sampling of options used to
integrate portable industrial computers with business software:

> Write a program for the portable device that reads and writes directly
> to the underlying files.
>
> Write a program for the portable device that communicates with
> middleware that performs the transactions.
>
> Modify the standard transaction program from your host system to work
> on the portable devices.
>
> Use a terminal emulation program that allows you to use your host
> system programs "as is" on the portable devices.
>
> Use a terminal emulation program and modify the host system programs
> to work on the portable devices.
>
> Use a terminal emulation program combined with a screen mapping util-
> ity that allows you to use your host system programs on the portable
> devices.

While the options will be limited, to some extent, by the platform of the host
system and the capabilities of the devices, there are always alternate means of
achieving the same objective. You should also consider issues related to system
security, the integrity of data communications, and the ability to continue to process transactions if communications are temporarily lost. Each method has its
own merits and problems. It's not so much that one method is inherently better
than another, but rather that one method is better for your specific application.

If you are having custom programming done, you are strongly encouraged to get the source code. Source code is the actual code written that is later compiled into a computer program. If you have the source code, you can later have another programmer modify it, or fix the mistakes made by an incompetent programmer. If you don't have the source code, you are at the mercy of the company that did the original programming. If you are no longer interested in doing business with them, you must either purchase the source code from them (not the best time to negotiate a price) or you must start from scratch. You also run the risk that the company may no longer exist when you need additional programming done.

I should also note that many of the technologies described in this chapter do not need to be implemented in an all-or-nothing strategy. Restricting the scope of the application can often greatly reduce the project costs. In many cases, implementing the technologies in selected processes and then expanding the implementation later (if needed) will have only a small impact on total costs. You may also find that you don't really need the technology in all processes. Focus on only implementing the technologies where you expect the greatest return on investment. Also, by applying these technologies to one process at a time, the knowledge you gain during the first application will help you in making smarter decisions for subsequent applications.

DIY integration

Want to do the integration yourself? You need to determine your own internal expertise and the technologies that can be implemented within this skill set. Certainly the keyboard wedge devices fit into the DIY category. In addition, there are products available to assist nonprogrammers with developing programs for portable industrial computers. These products go under the names of "code generators," "program generators," and "development tools." Though you don't need to write code to use these programs, you do need a certain level of technical aptitude. These development tools are usually windows-based programs that let you use a graphical interface to "assemble" applications for the portable devices. These tools can do a pretty good job of developing the prompts for the data collection device, and may be capable of reading and writing information to a separate compliant database. While these tools are not capable of developing highly complex applications, they are useful for simple applications or as the basis for a more complex application that will supplement the code generated by the development tool with some custom code.

Unfortunately, in today's complex integrated software systems a single transaction may need to read and write to a number of files with some complex validation throughout the process. In these cases it's often better to integrate the portable devices with programs from the integrated software system. This is more difficult than just writing to a file and is probably not a DIY project.

There is a lot of pressure on software and hardware suppliers to find solutions to these integration problems. In the case of portable industrial devices, where the software and integration costs can easily be three to five times the costs of the hardware, suppliers are realizing that the key to increased hardware sales lies in reducing integration costs. Though I don't expect to see true plug-and-play integration in the near future, I do expect to see advances in the development tools and the compatibility of technologies.

Software technologies

Though there are many software technologies that affect accuracy, there are a few optional software technologies that tend to have a more significant impact than others. We've already covered cycle counting and physical inventory counting programs, so I won't go into these again. I've mentioned locator systems throughout this book and will cover them in a little more detail here. I will also give brief descriptions of warehouse management systems and manufacturing execution systems. Though there are many reasons to use these systems, I will be focusing primarily on the accuracy-related implications.

Locator systems

Locator systems (also known as location systems and bin location systems) are inventory-tracking systems that allow you to assign physical locations to your stored inventory. Prior to locator systems, warehouses needed to store product in some logical manner in order to be able to find it (stored in item number sequence, by vendor, commodity, by product description, etc.) By using locator systems you can increase space utilization by slotting your product to a location whose physical characteristics best match that of the product. You can also increase productivity by locating fast moving product to closer, more accessible locations, and by making it easier to find items. Accuracy is improved by separating similar items and by narrowing down the area where a picker will look for specific product (thus reducing the chances of picking a wrong item). Locator systems also make it much easier to perform cycle counts, audits, and physical inventories.

Location functionality in software can range from a simple text field attached to an item that notes a single location, to systems that allow multiple locations per item and track inventory quantities by location. The latter (multiple locations with quantity tracking) is considered the norm for a locator system.

Though I rarely make general recommendations, I feel comfortable stating that most warehousing and manufacturing operations should be using a location system. Unless you are in a very small facility with a limited number of SKUs, you will find the benefits of using a locator system far outweigh any drawbacks. I am very surprised to find that some inventory management software packages still do not come with location functionality. Fortunately, most of them will offer it as an added module or as a program offered by a third party supplier.

The primary down side of using a locator system is that it adds one more piece of data that now needs to be managed. With a locator system, you now need to complete a transaction whenever you put away or move inventory. For those of us that have used locator systems for years, this is just standard operating procedure. However, for workers that have not had to do these transactions in the past, it can be grounds for mutiny. Which leads me to my first point. If you are not going to enforce the use of the locator system, don't waste your time trying to implement one.

There is no standard method for setting up the location identification scheme. To optimize accuracy and productivity, you should design your location scheme to fit your specific operation. Focus on designing a system that is simple and consistent. Do not add unnecessary data to the location, or design completely different location schemes for different areas of the facility unless it is absolutely necessary. An example of unnecessary data would be adding a location designation for the front and back pallet locations in double-deep pallet rack. In most applications this added designation is not providing any real value and only clutters and complicates the location system. Here are some standard descriptions that are used within a location scheme:

Zone
Designates a large storage area that has unique storage characteristics, is in a unique area of the facility, or designates a specific work area (such as pick zones where each worker is limited to a single pick zone). Zone is usually a single character and may be alpha or numeric.

Aisle
Designates a storage aisle. There are two variations on the aisle designation. In one variation, a pick face is the aisle designation. This results in the pick faces on either side of a physical aisle (the area where you walk or drive a lift truck) having different aisle designations. In the second variation, the aisle is "the aisle" and the pick faces on either side of the aisle are considered to be in the same aisle. Section designations will usually determine which side of the aisle you are referring to by designating one side of the aisle with "odd" section designations and the other side of the aisle with "even" section designations. Once again, there is no single "best" method; I generally prefer the first method for wide-aisle lift truck operations, and the second method for manual piece picking or very narrow aisle lift truck operations. Aisle is usually one or two characters and is usually

alpha. This helps to set it off from the remainder of the location, which is generally numeric.

Section

Designates a physical section of a specific storage medium. Usually designates the storage locations between uprights in pallet rack or static shelving. Section may also describe a single pallet width area of racking. Sections are almost always numeric and are generally two or three characters.

Shelf

Though it seems obvious, there are some variations of the shelf designation. In pallet racking, a physical shelf may be divided based upon pallet locations (usually two per shelf). In most cases, however, a shelf is a shelf. Shelves are normally numbered from the ground up. Shelf is usually two characters, but may be only one character if using alpha designations or numeric designations with less than ten shelves per unit.

Bin

A bin (also known as a slot) is a single item storage location. When multiple items are stored on a single shelf, a bin location is often used to designate the specific item storage location. Sometimes specific pallet locations within a section are designated as bins. If this sounds like the alternate shelf description, it is essentially the same thing. Sometimes each pallet position within an aisle is considered a bin. This eliminates the need for section and shelf designations. Bin is usually two characters but may be only one character if using alpha designations or numeric designations with less than ten bins per shelf. Bin may be three characters when eliminating section or shelf designations.

Lane

Lane is used in floor storage and usually designates a single pallet width location that is multiple pallets deep. Lane is generally two numeric characters.

There are also other terms that have similar meaning to those above. "Bay" is often used in place of "Section" or "Lane," "Row" is often used in place of "Aisle," "Level" is often used in place of "Shelf," and "Slot" is often used in place of "Bin" or "Lane."

Examples of location schemes.

Zone, Aisle, Section, Shelf, Bin

Zone, Aisle, Section, Bin

Zone, Aisle, Bin

Zone, Aisle, Lane

Maintaining consistency requires developing location schemes that can be used throughout the organization. In addition, consistency within storage areas is achieved by carefully planning the physical storage areas and matching location schemes to them in a manner that makes it easy to determine exactly where a location is by its ID. When I say exactly I mean that you should know how far a section is down an aisle and how high a shelf is from the ground before you arrive at the location. This means that section "34" should be in the same relative position in every aisle and shelve "4" should be at the same height in every section. If the maximum number of shelves you will have in any section is six (including the floor) then the top shelf should always be "6" regardless of whether you have three, four, five, or six shelves in that section.

You should also plan for potential expansion of physical storage. If it may be possible in the future to add one or two aisles prior to your current "first" aisle, you should designate your first aisle "aisle C" rather than "aisle A" to allow for this expansion. The same concept applies to sections, zones, shelves, and lane; if you could potentially add sections to the beginning of aisles, you should designate the sections accordingly.

Careful thought should also be put into setting up staging locations. Most commonly used in manufacturing operations, staging locations are generally areas of open floor used to temporarily store materials. You want to break up these staging areas into individual locations that are small enough to easily find the materials, yet not so small as to make all movements within staging areas require transactions. An example of a "too big" location would be if you decided to set a single location ("PLANT," "FLOOR," "WIP") to anything that is staged in any of your production areas. For most operations this is simply too broad of a designation and will result in having to search for materials. An example of a "too small" designation would be breaking up a small staging area (capable of holding 30 palletized loads) into individual pallet locations. Since most staging areas have loads stacked in front of other loads, you often have to move some loads to access the load you need. If this requires performing a transaction for each moved load, or having to keep track and put each moved load back into its original position, you are not following the "make accuracy easy" principle and will likely have problems maintaining this level of detail.

Staging locations are also used for receiving areas and shipping areas. It's generally good practice to receive into a receiving location and then transfer the inventory into a storage location during the putaway process. In most operations, a single receiving location is usually adequate, though there may be times when you would want to use multiple receiving locations. This is especially true when you have receiving processing conducted in several different physical areas of the facility. If conducting putaway transactions manually, you need to make it clear to the worker which receiving location was used. With a WMS, this will generally be handled automatically. Using staging locations for shipping areas requires you to transfer the inventory from the picking location to the staging location as orders are picked. For most manual systems, this will prove to be a lot of extra work and is generally not done. In these systems you will have the shipping transaction process relieve inventory directly from the picking location. If you are picking materials early and staging them for future shipments (I really don't recommend doing this) you can use a shipping staging location to help in cycle counting and related processes. If you are using a WMS, it will likely automatically transfer picked inventory to a shipping staging location as part of the picking process.

Logical locations are location designations that do not refer to a specific physical location. I had already discussed using a logical location within a cycle counting program to move variances to and from. In this case the logical location represents variances. Another reason for using a logical location would be if you had an item or group of items that were very difficult to maintain under your normal location policies. An example would be if you operated a fixed location system that was rather cumbersome at changing locations, and had a group of very large products that you couldn't designate fixed locations for without wasting a lot of space. You may chose to set up a logical location, assuming these items are so large and unique that they can easily be spotted with a quick look at the storage areas.

Sort order should also be a consideration during the setup of a location scheme. You should try to design a location scheme and apply locations in such a manner that a standard alphanumeric sort will result in a workable sequence for order picking, cycle counting, location auditing, etc. Though some warehouse management systems will allow you to define alternative sorts — which can be very useful — there is often a lot of work required in setting these up. And, most standard locator systems will not have this added functionality. These same considerations will also help in data selection for additional reporting and auditing purposes. For example, you may want to create a unique zone for all staging locations to allow you to easily select and report on them. The same would apply to logical locations.

When setting up a location scheme you should carefully consider the effects on accuracy and productivity of different schemes. Sometimes it may make sense to use different schemes within the same storage area. An example would be in a racked storage area where the floor level constitutes the picking locations and all higher racked locations are only used for reserve storage. You can simplify the picking location scheme by just listing zone, aisle, and slot, with the first floor level pallet position being "Slot 001," the second "Slot 002," etc. The locations above may have a zone, aisle, section, bin designation.

Warehouse management systems

A warehouse management system is an execution system that controls the movement and storage of inventory as well as related activities. Though there is no real standardization among WMSs there are several core functions that they should provide.

✔ They should have a flexible location system.

✔ They should utilize user-defined parameters to direct warehouse tasks and use live documents to execute these tasks.

✔ They should have built into them some level of integration with portable data collection devices.

This is my opinion of the minimum functionality a WMS should have to be called a WMS. Since there are no real standards, there are products out there that are called WMSs that do not meet my base criteria. There is also a whole lot of additional functionality being added to WMSs that is far beyond the scope of this book.

So how can a WMS increase accuracy? We've already covered the benefits of a location system. In addition, the functionality to direct tasks through live documents provides confirmation transactions, which are inherently more accurate than manual transactions. Since the WMS should be telling you where to pick from, putaway to, or replenish from/to, and in what specific quantities, all the worker needs to do is confirm that he has done what he was directed to do. Also, the live documents (not necessarily paper documents) provide an audit trail with data useful in identifying and resolving errors. For example, without a WMS a worker may put away a receipt and forget to enter the transaction. If this is in a random storage area, the receipt is essentially lost. With a WMS, the live document would state the putaway location the worker was directed to. Even if the worker doesn't complete the transaction, you should expect to find the receipt in the location specified on the putaway document. You may also have information on the worker that did not complete the transaction. These live documents may be called move tickets, move tags, tasks, or instructions. They may also be distinguished by task type such as, putaway tickets, replenishment tickets, or pick tickets. Audit reports that identify overdue open move documents can be used to quickly identify process problems.

I also mentioned that a WMS should have some level of built-in integration with portable data collection devices. Some WMS suppliers will mislead buyers by providing statements like "easily integrates with," "seamlessly interfaces with," "works with," and "supports." It's important to ask the supplier to clarify the meaning of these statements. In fact, any software system can be integrated with portable data collection devices; therefore, these statements can be used to describe any software. What you really want to know is, what has been done to the WMS software to make it easier to integrate with these devices. In some cases the WMS will be designed with all the programming you need to integrate with specific devices (often restricted to specific models). In other systems, there may be some general programming and tools in place that allows integration with many more devices, however some additional integration is needed based upon the specific devices used. And in still other systems, you may find that nothing has been done to the WMS software to simplify integration with portable data collection devices.

Though the WMS may reduce implementation costs associated with data collection devices you still need to integrate the WMS with your other systems. Your decision to implement a WMS will likely have more to do with productivity and other business requirements, than with accuracy. Functionality related to first-in-first-out processing, lot tracking, cross-docking, batch and wave picking, directed putaway and replenishment, special storage requirements, and integration with automated material handling equipment will often drive the decision to use a WMS.

As with the addition of any technology, you need to consider the potential negative impacts. Warehouse management systems are large, complex, data intensive applications. They tend to require a lot of initial setup, a lot of system resources to run, and a lot of ongoing data management to continue to run. A WMS is very data intensive and restrictive by design. You must be committed to working within the restrictions of the WMS. Failure to work within the WMS and maintain data integrity may result in disaster. Companies often "want to have" directed picking, replenishment, and putaway, but then proceed to allow workers to vary from the WMS directions and choose their own locations or change quantities. This is sooooo wrong. In doing so, you are reducing or eliminating the benefits that drove the decisions to implement a WMS. You should set up your WMS to direct tasks the way you want them done, and then enforce compliance to the WMS directions. Occasionally there may be situations where there is an easier alternative to a WMS directed task, however you are still better off working within the WMS than allowing exceptions.

A WMS will likely improve your inventory accuracy, but it is also extremely dependant upon accuracy. You will need to achieve a reasonable level of accuracy prior to implementing the WMS system and then maintain consistently high levels of accuracy to fully utilize the system.

Unlike a locator system, I do not believe that every company should have a full-blown WMS. If you have a small operation and only require a small portion of the functionality of a WMS, you may be better off modifying your standard inventory system to provide this functionality. There are also trimmed-down versions of WMSs becoming available. Though they don't offer the same functionality as the larger systems they may be effective in smaller operations. A simpler software package is also generally much easier to implement than a larger, more complex one. For large, high-volume facilities, a full-blown WMS is likely the route for you.

Manufacturing execution systems

Most standard manufacturing software systems are primarily planning systems and tend to have inadequate functionality when it comes to the detailed execution of manufacturing tasks. A manufacturing execution system basically does for the shop floor what a WMS does for the warehouse. It's an execution system that controls shop floor activities, including data collection and movement of materials.

Like a WMS, an MES should be expected to simplify and automate inventory-related transactions through the use of integrated technologies. Also like a WMS, this functionality may vary significantly from one system to another. The same questions should be asked related to integration capabilities.

Although warehouse operations can be diverse and complex, manufacturing operations are much more so. This results in MES's functionality being much more diverse and less standardized than WMS's. When looking to select an MES, you will likely limit your search to MESs that are designed for your specific industry.

An MES can provide accuracy gains through the simplification and automation of transactions and through greater control of activities and a more structured shop floor environment. As with a WMS you need to be committed to working within the MES and maintaining the necessary data.

General technology comments

Technology can make us faster. Technology can slow us down. Technology can make us more accurate. Technology can make us less accurate. Technology can make us smarter. Technology can make us stupid. Technology solves existing problems. Technology creates new problems. Technology can make your company more profitable. Technology can suck the profits out of your company.

All of these statements are true. I like to use "spell-checking" technology as an example. Certainly spell-checking has improved the accuracy of our documents and written communications. But has it made us better spellers? I've become so dependent upon spell checking that I don't dare communicate without it. When I occasionally have to write down comments on a whiteboard in a group brainstorming session, I realize that I no longer know how to spell. In addition, if you blindly allow spell-checking programs to "fix" all of your errors you will soon find out that spell-checking technology has its limitations. Occasionally it will replace a misspelled word with a wrong (but correctly spelled) word. A failure to understand the technology will give you less-than-optimal results.

If you now look at applying bar code scanning technologies to your processes, you will find similar issues. When workers manually enter transactions, they have a better understanding of the transaction process. When you automate the process and give them bar code scanners, they get really stupid (related to transaction knowledge). They tend to think "the bar code system knows what it is doing," therefore they scan and beep and scan and beep and scan and beep, totally oblivious to what is actually happening. If you don't put systems in place to prevent it, you will likely have duplicated transactions when a worker isn't sure if he processed a transaction and decides to scan it again. You will also find that if there is a problem with an automated transaction (a bad bar code, a wrong bar code scanned, a closed transaction document, a validation error) the worker may have no clue as to how to handle it. He may not even realize that there was a problem. Careful planning in system design and an ongoing employee training program are critical to optimally utilizing technologies.

Summary

Invest in technology if that technology makes your company better. Technology can be wonderful when applied effectively and a nightmare when misapplied. If these types of technology are new to you, don't feel the need to jump in headfirst. Start with something simple like using a keyboard wedge bar code scanner to automate document-based transactions. As you get more comfortable with this technology, you can start to look at other technologies that may benefit your operation. Always evaluate the real benefits, the potential problems, and the costs associated with the technologies. Every additional layer of technology that you add will need to be managed. Companies often overlook or underestimate the resources required to manage their technology systems. Systems like WMSs and MESs may require additional resources to manage the data required by and produced by these systems. "Exception handling" is a critical part of most automation systems, and can quickly become a resource hog.

When you are implementing these technologies, take the time to ensure the detailed system design takes full advantage of the technology. This includes being very picky about device choices, voice commands, screen prompts, and manual entry. Make sure you explore "what if" scenarios to ensure you have procedures in place to handle variations that are likely to occur during the course of completing these automated tasks.

And, as always, don't forget about training.

9

Specific Processes, Tips, & Misc.

This is my "everything else" chapter. There are a variety of topics here that relate to inventory accuracy. Some of them are topics that were referred to in previous chapters, while others are topics that may be useful but did not justify a separate chapter. Since some of these topics only relate to specific types of operations, it is not necessary to read everything outlined here.

How to count? 248
Receiving process tips 252
Putaway process tips 256
Order picking / shipping process tips 258
Returns processing 262
Negative inventory. 265
Non-stock inventory 268
Units-of-measure. 271
Unit packs, multi packs, inner packs, kits, and sets. 274
Lot and serial number tracking. 276
Multi-plant processing. 277
Substitutions 279
Outsourcing 280
Theft. 283
Manufacturing processes general observations 288
24/7 289
Point-of-use inventory and floor stock 292
Outside operations 293
Scrap reporting. 297
Work-in-process tracking 299
Backflushing and other issuing techniques 302
Transitions. 308

How to count?

Wipe that smirk off your face. There are actually specific techniques that can increase both accuracy and productivity when manually counting inventory. These include organizing materials so they can be counted in even layers, hand counting in multiples of twos or fives, counting large quantities in smaller batches, and counting from one container to another. Don't assume that common sense will prevail here. Yes, eventually many employees will likely develop good counting techniques through trial and error, but why risk it when you can teach them to count smarter?

☐ **Organizing materials so they can be counted in even layers.** This applies to any stackable product, whether it is in parts bins, in cartons, on pallets, hand-stacked on a shelf, or in other types of containers. Generally this product is initially stacked in even layers, but becomes disorganized during the picking process as workers pick product from more than one layer at a time. You are just asking for an error if you allow workers to count the product when each layer has a different quantity. Whenever counting stacked layered materials, workers should restack the materials, if necessary, so that they have no more than one odd layer. The product is then counted by multiplying the quantity per layer by the number of full layers and adding the quantity in the odd layer. This should be a required (not optional) part of the counting procedure for cycle counting, physical inventories, and order picking processes. This is one you'll have to enforce, since the natural tendency towards laziness will tempt workers to count the product "as is" regardless of the difficulty it adds to the counting task.

☐ **Counting materials from one container into another** is another method you may want to consider making a mandatory part of the counting procedure. When loose product (not stackable layered product) is in containers (cartons, gaylords, crates, cages, etc.), workers will often try to count the materials in the container by "eyeing it" and moving the materials around in the container. This is another situation where you are just asking for trouble. Unless there is a very small quantity of parts in the container, you are very likely to miscount this way. Removing the parts from one container and counting into another, or dumping the parts out and then counting them back into the container is the most accurate way to do it. And, in many cases, it does not require any significant additional effort. This is a little tougher to put in place as a mandatory procedure since there may be valid exceptions depending upon the types of materials you are counting. If you can clearly document the exceptions, I would recommend making the procedure mandatory; otherwise, make it clear that it is a strong recommendation.

❏ **Counting in multiples** can make counting easier and more accurate, but there is some training that is involved here. Most of us can count fairly effectively in multiples of twos (2, 4, 6, 8, ...) or fives (5, 10, 15, 20, ...), but counting by threes or fours is likely to create problems, and counting by ones is just plain wasteful. When hand-counting inventory where workers are physically picking up the parts (as in counting from one container to another) they should always count by twos unless the parts are so large that they can only pick up one at a time. This requires that the employee picks up exactly two pieces every time and counts two, four, six, and so on. Often, workers will try to count by picking up several parts (inconsistent quantities) at a time and counting each "grab" individually. For example, first grab "one, two, three, four," second grab "five, six, seven," third grab "eight, nine, ten, eleven, twelve," etc. This is another method that is more highly prone to error and is also usually less productive than consistently counting by twos. I also mentioned counting by fives which is done less frequently and primarily only when you are counting very small parts on a flat surface (discussed next).

❏ **Counting very small parts.** I would characterize very small parts as parts that are sized such that you could easily hold at least ten pieces in one hand. Though you could count very small parts from one container to another, it's much better to carefully dump them on a clean flat surface, such as a table top or the top of a stock cart, and use your fingers to slide them by twos or fives across the surface into another pile or into a small container held against the edge of the flat surface. If the parts are extremely small, you can use a small card (such as a business card) to separate and slide the parts from one pile to another.

❏ **Counting in batches.** When hand counting very large quantities, you should stop at logical points (every 50, 100 or 200 pieces) and create a physical separation of the parts. This can be done by using multiple containers or creating multiple piles on a flat surface. This can save a lot of time and aggravation should you lose count at some point in the process or decide to recount the entire quantity for other reasons. If you lose count you would only need to recount the quantity since the last separation, and, if you are recounting the entire quantity and find a variance, you can isolate the variance to a smaller group that can then be recounted once again just to be certain. Obviously, if you frequently hand count very large quantities you should consider using counting scales.

❏ **Touch as you count.** When counting large parts or layered and stacked parts, you will find that it's less likely you will lose count or miscount if you actually use your hands to keep your place as you count. For example, if you are counting the layers on a stacked pallet, you would put one hand on the second layer and count "2" then put your other hand two layers up and count "4" and so on. It's very easy to miscount if you are just using your eyes, even when counting rows or layers that are only eight or ten units deep or high.

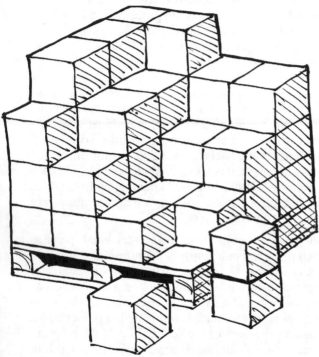

This is an example of a disorganized pallet of inventory that would be very common in a picking location. Your workers are much more likely to make an error if they try to count inventory in this condition.

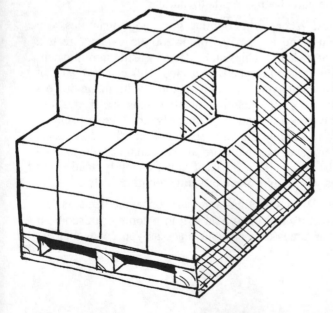

Here, the same pallet has been restacked so there is only one odd layer. The odds of getting a correct count of this pallet have just increased significantly.

Counting small parts this way is both slow and more prone to error.

This is a more accurate means of counting small parts. Slide the parts, two at a time, from one pile to the other.

Counting from one container to another (again in multiples of two) will be more accurate than trying to count the parts within the container. You can also dump the parts out onto a clean surface and then count them back into the container.

Accuracy is in the details, and though you may feel these counting tips are just "common sense," you should not assume that your employees would instinctively develop accurate counting techniques. Training employees at this level of detail can be a little uncomfortable, especially with your experienced employees, however you should not let that stand in the way of progress. As long as you communicate the training in a positive manner, your employees should accept it. If they claim they were already counting this way, fine, you are simply reinforcing what they think they already know.

Receiving process tips

The first part of any receiving process involves unloading of the delivery vehicle. While a delivery vehicle may be a delivery van, trailer, rail car, or even a ship or barge, there are still two very simple things that need to be done to assure accuracy here. First, verify the delivery address on the bill of lading. That's right; make sure the stuff is yours. You certainly hate to waste the time and effort involved in unloading and then setting up a return pickup for an incorrectly delivered load. Next, you need to verify that the count used on the bill of lading is verified. Usually this is just a listing of the number of pallets or number of cases. This is a very important step that often gets missed in the hustle and bustle of unloading the vehicle. That is the extent of the check required prior to letting the delivery driver leave (you should also look for any damage).

Once the materials are in your facility, there are primarily two steps in the receiving process. The first step involves checking the receipt against what the vendor claims was shipped (usually based upon a packing slip). The second step involves getting the information into your inventory system. I should note that these two steps do not necessarily need to be conducted in the pre-stated sequence. In fact there is a significant benefit to reversing the steps, which I will discuss later.

Probably the most difficult decision made in defining a receiving process is related to the level of checking that occurs in the check-in process. Do you just accept the vendor's packing slip as accurate? Do you just count pallets or cases? Do you open cases and containers and physically verify each item and quantity? There is a movement in some industries to eliminate the entire receipt check-in process. These "dock-to-stock" programs involve having incoming materials delivered directly to the point of use. The receipt transaction process is handled automatically via electronic communication from the supplier. The reasoning behind this is that receipt check-in is not a value-added process and should therefore be eliminated. In doing so, they not only eliminate the labor required to conduct the incoming check, but also reduce lead times and inventory by eliminating the delay caused by a formal check-in process. On the down side, your accuracy is now limited not only by the accuracy of your own processes, but also by the accuracy of your suppliers' shipping processes. If you are going to go this route, you need to make sure your supplier has processes in place that provide very high levels of accuracy. Even with that, I would still recommend conducting spot checks.

For most operations, you will be conducting some level of receipt check-in. Generally, standardized case quantities are accepted without opening and counting the contents. You will still count the cases, but there is little advantage to opening the cases to verify the contents. This is especially true when the cases are designed such that the correct number of pieces fits exactly into the case. With cases of non-standardized quantities, I generally recommend opening them up and counting the contents.

With cases containing large quantities of loose materials, such as cases of bolts or screws, conducting verification via a counting scale is a good idea (See technology chapter for counting scale procedures). One thing to consider when using a counting scale at receipt is the level of accuracy of the supplier's equipment and processes. It may be that the supplier has counting scales and processes that are tightly tuned to the specific materials they supply. This may result in a situation in which their quantities are more likely to be accurate than the quantities that would result from your own scale counting process. This may suggest that you would be better off not counting these materials, but I would suggest an alternative. At the piece level, their counting capabilities may be better than yours, however, they are still capable of making mistakes. I would suggest that you conduct a quick scale count at receipt, and, if your count is close to their count, I would suggest accepting their count. What this quick check does is ensure that you would be able to catch a "screw up" by the supplier, such as shipping 2,000 instead of 3,000. Now if your count comes up 2,989, and you know that your supplier's process has a higher level of accuracy at the piece level, it would make sense to accept the 3,000 count. I should emphasize that I only suggest this process if you have specific knowledge of the accuracy of your supplier's process. Otherwise, I would suggest conducting a more thorough scale count and using your own results.

As for materials that are received in bulk such as powders, granules, or liquids, or materials that are received in rolls, bails, or bundles, your check-in process will usually be more limited. If the quantity per container, roll, or bail is not consistent, you should at least verify the quantity on each unit (you should expect that there is a label from the supplier on the unit with the quantity). You may also periodically use a scale or other measurement method as a spot check. It's unlikely that you would do this on a regular basis unless you have a history of problems with the supplier. As with the small parts, it's likely that your supplier has greater capabilities of accurately determining quantities, though you should still look for the obvious errors.

When checking in receipts against the supplier's packing slip, you should have a clear procedure in place as to exactly how the packing slip is marked to confirm the check-in process. Since you will likely have multiple suppliers — and therefore multiple versions of packing slips — you will need to build in some flexibility here. But you can still maintain a reasonable level of consistency. Make sure your workers understand there may be several quantities listed on a packing slip (ordered quantity, shipped quantity, backordered quantity) and that they should only focus on shipped quantity. I recommend that the procedure require the worker to circle the shipped quantity to confirm that they verified the quantity. This will be much more obvious than a check mark, especially since there are often check marks already on the packing slip from the supplier's checking process. I also suggest supplying your receiving personnel with green pens and requiring that they only use these green pens to write on the packing slips. It's very common for incoming packing slips to have marks on them such as checks or circles as a result of the supplier's processes. It's extremely unusual to encounter a green pen mark (red, blue, and black are very common). By enforcing a "green pen rule" in receiving you will make it much easier to identify your internal marks versus external marks. By the way, shipping should use the "red pen rule" to avoid screwing up your customer's green pen process. Hey, just trying to start some standardization here.

You should also have a clear procedure for documenting the number of cartons, pallets, totes, rolls, bails, etc. associated with the line item and their quantities. This is usually done by variations of "5 ctns @ 50" which reads "five cartons at fifty each." Companies often have no procedure as to how to document this important information, resulting in each worker developing their own abbreviations, which will ultimately result in confusion. I strongly suggest you document the exact syntax for this information. I also suggest you consider the "make accuracy easy" approach and use nice short abbreviations, and please, don't make your workers draw that "@" thing. A simpler version of the previous example would be "5c/50" where "c" is the abbreviation for cartons or cases. Use "p" for pallets, "r" for rolls, "b" for bails, and you have a nice simple procedure here. Document it, and train the workers, and you will have a nice simple and consistent process.

It's usually fairly easy to be accurate at checking in receipts. Unlike a shipping process where you are picking and putting together the shipment, the receipt check-in is actually a checking process. You are simply verifying that the materials received match the materials claimed shipped by the supplier. For this reason, it doesn't really make sense to put in place a check of the check-in process. If you have a reasonable check-in process, your biggest source for errors in receiving will be the receipt transaction process — that is, the process of entering the receipt into your inventory system. Often times, purchase orders have multiple line items on them and the sequencing of the line items on the vendor packing slip rarely matches the sequencing of the line items on the computer screen. You also have confusion over materials identification (supplier item numbers and descriptions) on the packing slip not matching those in your system. All of this combined, makes it relatively easy to make mistakes in the receipt transaction process.

Herein lies the benefit to reversing the normal receipt sequence. By entering the transaction first, and then producing receipt documents that will be used for the check-in process, you are able to use the receipt check-in process to not only check the supplier's accuracy, but also the accuracy of the receipt transaction, with no additional labor. You can also include information on the receipt document that can make the check-in process easier, such as consistency of the information, cross-reference numbers, unit-of-measure and unit-of-measure conversions, and internal material description. Before doing this you need to make sure you can reverse or otherwise adjust a receipt should you encounter a discrepancy, and also determine any possible complications related to reversing or adjusting a receipt. A receipt document can be a piece of paper, a label, or a display on an RF terminal. The receipt document will also likely provide the putaway information for the materials.

This reversed receiving sequence also leads us to the use of advanced shipment notifications. To repeat the information on ASNs described in "Making Accuracy Easy" ASNs are used to automate receipt processing. ASNs will include PO numbers, SKU numbers, lot numbers, quantity, pallet or container number, and carton number. ASNs may be paper-based, however electronic notification (usually through EDI, however use of XML is growing) is preferred. Since an electronic ASN will transfer detailed shipment data to your inventory system, all the receiving personnel have to do is confirm the receipt at the ASN level and all transactions are automatically completed. This is usually done by scanning a bar coded compliance label associated with the entire shipment, or separate labels for each pallet, each crate, or each carton. Since transaction-related errors tend to account for the majority of receiving errors, the use of ASNs can significantly increase accuracy in receiving operations as well as increase productivity. The nature of ASNs lends them well to the "receive first and then check-in" process. Unfortunately ASNs require that your suppliers are willing and capable of applying compliance labels and sending ASNs. Smaller businesses or businesses that have an extensive supplier base often find it difficult to achieve this level of cooperation from their suppliers. Some supply chains, such as the automotive industry, have achieved some levels of standardization, however there is currently no widely accepted standard for ASNs and compliance labels. As the trend towards collaboration and information sharing grows, especially through the use of the Internet, more businesses will gain access to these technologies.

Pay attention to the physical layout of the receiving areas. Make sure staging lanes are clearly identified, and have methods in place that make it clear at what stage of processing the materials currently are. This may require either physically moving the materials as they are processed or using physical methods of identification (labels, paperwork, flags, special marks, etc.). Do not allow materials that have completed receipt processing to remain in the receiving area. Have clear processes in place to handle problem receipts. Process today's receipts today. For the most part, receipts should be processed and moved out of the receiving area within a few hours of when they hit the dock. This is a reasonable expectation in almost any receiving operation. There is no reason for receiving operations to "store" inventory. Allowing receiving departments to have days or weeks of backlogs sitting on the dock creates accuracy, productivity, and material planning problems. If your receiving department occasionally needs some extra help during peak periods, get it for them.

A well-designed receiving process including a check-in step can provide high levels of accuracy without adding significant labor or delays in getting the materials into stock. Unless you have extremely accurate suppliers or an alternate means of verifying a receipt, I do not recommend bypassing the receipt check-in process.

Putaway process tips

The most significant accuracy problems related to the putaway process occur in random storage areas where the worker decides where the materials will be stored. In a manual system this generally requires that the worker fill out a form stating the item number, the quantity, and the location where it was put away. Problems occur when the worker forgets to write down the transaction, incorrectly writes down the transaction, or incorrectly enters the transaction. The result is "lost" inventory.

If operating in a manual-transaction random-putaway environment, an aggressive location-audit program is often a necessity. You can also consider implementing a formal checking process for putaways by having each worker verify their own work or having someone else verify it. A checking process should include checking all transactions to see that they were entered correctly, as well as physically checking the locations to see that the transactions were written down correctly. While this seems like a lot of extra work — and it is — it still is much better than constantly having to conduct "walk-throughs" to look for lost inventory.

Because of the high error rate in this type of environment, it is often the first place to consider implementing the use of portable computers and bar code scanners. This is a task where the implementation of ADC technology will provide substantial increases in both accuracy and productivity. You will also find that using a WMS to direct the putaway tasks will also provide increases in accuracy. While the use of bar code scanners in a random storage area may not completely eliminate the need to conduct location audits, it will greatly reduce the frequency of these audits.

Putaway into fixed locations is less problematic than putaway into random areas, the reasons being, putaway into a fixed location is essentially a "directed" putaway regardless of whether you are using a WMS, and, the worker can expect to usually find more of the same item in the location. This is a built-in check, since finding something else in the location will point out that the worker is likely in the wrong location. And, even if the transaction is missed, you still know where the materials "should be."

Putaway tips:

✔ Have the worker write down or scan the item(s) that are going to be stocked as they are picked up for putaway. This will help in reducing the possibility of missing a transaction.

✔ Use putaway documents to aid in the putaway process. These may be a receipt document that also includes putaway information. Include a bar code on the putaway document that can be used to complete the transaction later at a fixed terminal with a bar code scanner (assuming portable computers and scanners are not being used).

✔ Strongly consider using portable computers and bar code scanners, especially if stocking in random storage areas.

✔ Enforce first-in-first-out when stocking small parts in parts bins. This forces the worker to "see and touch" the materials in the bin, which ensures that he will notice if they are not the same as the materials he is stocking.

✔ Apply license plates to palletized materials with item number and quantity, preferably on a large label that can be read from a distance. Make sure materials are stocked with license plates or other labels facing the aisle.

✔ Always place partial pallets or partial cases in front of or on top of full pallets or cases. This may occasionally violate first-in-first-out policy. Also consider marking partial pallets or partial cases (using special labels) to help identify them.

✔ If possible, consider scheduling putaway areas in random storage putaway environments. For example, all putaway this week is confined to aisles A, B, and C, next week all putaway will be confined to aisles D, E, and F, and so on. This way you can follow up by conducting location audits in the areas. You will also have a smaller area to conduct a "walk-through" should you suddenly need something that was recently lost.

Order picking / shipping process tips

I've certainly touched on order picking throughout this book. Because of its immediate effect on customers, accuracy in order picking tends to get a lot of attention (or at least it should get a lot of attention). Because of the amount of labor often dedicated to order picking and shipping, it also gets a lot of attention related to productivity. This all results in a great variety of methods used to pick orders, with each method having it's own accuracy characteristics. You also have a great variety of item profiles and order profiles that also impact accuracy. Putting all of this together to provide some simple tips on accuracy in order picking is not an easy task. Tips that I would apply in one operation will likely not apply to the next operation. I have, however, tried to assemble a list of considerations and tips.

Paper-based picking.
Use the suggestions from "making accuracy easy" to improve your order picking documents. I prefer the use of pick tags (see chapter 2) to pick slips. Pick tags provide a separate tag (piece of paper or label) for each line item on an order. This allows the order picker to more easily focus on the details of the specific line item, reduces the chances of forgetting to pick a line item, and makes order checking much easier. Pick tags are usually attached to the materials as they are picked. The use of removable labels is advised.

Paperless picking.
I'll admit that I prefer paper-based picking in most operations. I just don't like the hand-held computers and little LCD screens used to direct picking tasks in many paperless applications. I do think paperless is effective when using pick-to-light, voice-directed wearable systems, or vehicle-mounted computers. If these technologies fit your application, they can provide high levels of accuracy without negatively impacting productivity. Pick-to-light is the only technology that I feel offers productivity gains over a well-designed paper-based system. The others offer accuracy gains but may have productivity levels equal to or less than a well-designed paper-based system.

Locator systems.
Locator systems (described in technology chapter) can provide increases in both accuracy and productivity in order picking processes. Unless you are running an extremely small operation with a very limited number of SKUs you should strongly consider using a locator system.

Availability checking and allocations.
It is ridiculous to produce picking documents for materials that are not available (in stock). A picking document should print the quantity to ship. If there is inadequate inventory available it should automatically backorder the difference. This is base functionality that should be expected with any inventory system that has order processing capabilities. Unfortunately there are still some software packages in use that do not have the functionality to check availability and allocate

based upon availability. If you have anything that even closely resembles an order picking process you need a system that automatically determines availability. Get a new system or modify the old system, but do not settle for anything less.

Directed picking.

Usually associated with warehouse management systems, directed picking functionality is also included in many standard inventory systems (with more limited options). Though it may just be called an "allocation system," as long as it identifies a specific location to allocate against, it is essentially a directed picking system. Some systems may provide a manual pre-allocation program that allows you to designate the picking locations before you print the picking documents. While an automated allocation system is preferred, a manual pre-allocation system will ultimately produce the same result — just with a little more work. When using directed picking, do not allow workers the flexibility to decide to pick from a different location.

Transaction by exception.

If you have a picking system that checks availability and allocates against specific locations, you should be using transaction-by-exception methodology to complete the picking transaction. By using a simple confirmation transaction that essentially says, "yes this entire order was processed as expected" you eliminate the possibility of making detail level transaction errors. There is no reason to have to go into the details of orders and tell the system the picked quantities and the pick locations if the system already knows. I'll again mention the importance of having procedures in place that make it clear that the information on the picking documents (locations, quantities) is not to be changed.

Same day processing.

Do not release orders to the warehouse that are not scheduled to ship that day. Pick and ship all orders that are released on the same day they are released. Order picking can be a very fast, streamlined process. There is little value in picking orders in advance and staging them. There are, however, numerous problems that can result from staging orders days before they are going to ship. Mixed shipments, inventory taken out of one staged order to satisfy another order, additional releases needing to be added to the existing shipments, all add to the possibility for errors. In addition, semi-processed staged orders can make cycle counting extremely difficult. You will find that in many operations, a same day shipping policy can be more of a benefit than a burden. The effort required to meet same day shipping requirements, though substantial, are often less than the efforts required to manage backlogs and staged orders at various levels of processing.

Order checking.

I have yet to encounter an order picking operation that should not be conducting some type of order checking. Develop a method of order checking that best fits your operation. Even some very simplistic checks such as counting total number of pallets prior to loading a truck, weight verification while manifesting parcel shipments, or verifying the number of pick tags in each order can greatly reduce certain types of errors. For shippers that regularly pick larger quantities of small parts (greater than 25 pieces), you should consider periodically conducting 100 percent inspections with full recounts of picked quantities. This is important in not only catching counting errors, but also in preventing the "throw in a few extra" technique some pickers will develop "just in case they miscounted" to prevent a short shipment (customers are unlikely to report a few extra pieces as an error). While this technique may reduce customer complaints, it can be very harmful to your inventory balances. If you're unsure as to the level of checking appropriate for your operation, conduct a 100 percent inspection over a short period of time, and then analyze the results. If the vast majority of errors caught, could have been caught with a less comprehensive inspection process, you can probably go that route. In either case, you now have a baseline that can be used in the decision-making process.

Training.
Certainly accuracy training should be part of any process; however its importance should be emphasized even more in order picking activities. Order pickers may be conducting hundreds or thousands of transactions per day, and errors that occur are much more likely to directly affect a customer than errors in other processes. Workers should understand the importance of "focus" in the order picking process and be trained on the most common types of errors that occur in your specific operation.

Batch picking and wave picking.
Batch picking, also known as multi-order picking, is a great way to increase productivity in piece-picking operations. It also increases the chances of mixing orders. Using put-to-light technology, or generating pick tags that include a designation of the tote position will help in avoiding mixed orders. Wave picking involves multiple workers picking the different parts of the same orders at the same time. This then requires a consolidation process that combines the materials into individual orders. Because of the increased chances of mixed orders or missing items in these processes, I very strongly recommend a formal order checking process be put in place.

Limit order picking to order picking.
Basically what I'm trying to say here is that since order pickers are processing large amounts of transactions and require a high level of focus to maintain high levels of accuracy, you should try to limit their activities during the order picking process. If they are also packing the order, custom packaging the items, kitting, doing light assembly, or conducting cycle counts as part of the order picking process, they will not have the same level of focus on accurately picking the orders as they would if they were only picking orders.

Pick-to-trailer.
In pallet-load or similar unit-load picking operations there are productivity gains that can be achieved by picking directly into a trailer, rail car, or container, rather than picking, staging, and then later loading the shipment. The primary down side is that it eliminates the possibility of a formal order check after the shipment

is picked. Pick-to-trailer is another very good application for portable terminals and bar codes. Having bar codes on the unit-loads and on the loading dock will ensure the correct product is picked and that it is loaded into the correct trailer. RFID is also applicable in these environments by having RFID tags embedded in the pallets or containers and readers located by the loading dock doors.

Task interleaving

Task interleaving is used to reduce travel time by mixing picking and putaway tasks. If using a WMS to control task interleaving through portable terminals in a full pallet or unit-load environment, you will find that you can achieve these productivity increases without sacrificing accuracy. I do not recommend manual task interleaving.

Fixing errors.

This really applies to all processes but has a little more significance in order picking and shipping processes. When an error is identified or perceived (sometimes an error isn't an error), additional errors are often made trying to correct the initial error. This is much more common that most would suspect. Any time something "out of the ordinary" occurs, your potential for making an error dramatically increases. You should have procedures in place for handling errors. Sometimes these can be rather extreme but nonetheless necessary. For example, in a full-truckload shipping operation, if there were any reason to believe that there was an error in a shipment during or after the loading of the truck, I would require the entire truck to be unloaded and rechecked. This was a firm rule even when the person doing the loading "was positive" as to what was already on the truck.

Waiting for more.

This is a common problem in manufacturing operations. You have a shipment going out, the truck is at the dock, and you are still waiting for part of the shipment to come off of the line or machine. **Do not load that truck!** Even though the driver and the person loading the truck won't like it, you are risking errors if you load part of the shipment and then add more as it comes off the line. Wait until the entire shipment is together and complete, check it, then load it. This is a very similar situation to that described in "fixing errors" in that it is out of the ordinary (though in many places it is the norm) and it is very easy to screw things up.

Staging areas.

As in receiving operations, it's very important to have clearly identified staging lanes and ways of identifying the status of materials in those areas. There should be clear delineation between one order and another, as well as clear identification as to if an order is finished, has been checked, and is ready to load. Loading paperwork should always state the number of pallets, and the person loading the shipment should verify this. Accuracy in order picking and order checking does no good if a shipment is mixed during loading or a pallet is left off of the truck.

Returns processing

Problems with returns processing are usually the result of a lack of formalized processes, a lack of system support, and a lack of dedicated resources. Unless you are in a very large fulfillment operation, you have likely paid little attention to your returns processing. A lot of this has to do with the perception of returns. Returns are not perceived as a critical business process, they are not perceived as a process that contributes to profitability, they are perceived as a "necessary evil" of doing business. With these perceptions, it's not surprising that businesses do not formalize their returns process, businesses do not invest in equipment and technology to support their returns process, and business software developers tend to deal with returns processing as an afterthought.

The returns process starts with notification of need for a return. It's imperative that the reason for the return is assessed and properly communicated to anyone needing that information. Items involved in returns related picking or shipping errors must be counted as soon as notification of the problem is made. It's important that those taking the calls for returns have some training in asking the proper questions to get a reasonable assessment of the cause of the return. A claim of "you shipped the wrong part" does not necessarily mean a picking error. It could be an order entry error or a catalog/cross reference error, or even a quality problem. A claim of "the part doesn't fit" should not be assumed to be a quality error. It may be a picking error where a similar part was picked. If you don't properly assess the cause for the return, you are not getting the proper information that may be needed to correct current inventory and prevent future problems. Sometimes you will find that by doing some quick investigation in-house (counting inventory, verifying paperwork) you may determine that the reported problem was not a problem at all, and was actually just some confusion by the customer. If you have a process in place that handles these situations quickly enough, you can catch these and explain your "theory" to the customer. I use the term "theory" because ultimately the customer is "right." Even if you are absolutely certain the customer received the correct materials, if you fail to convince the customer of that, it is still an error.

Let me give you an example of how some quick investigating can change you from a villain to a hero. A regular customer calls and claims he received the wrong item. He had ordered part "A" but had received part "B." He's furious because part "A" is needed for a repair of a critical piece of equipment. You quickly count both items and determine that both counts are correct. You now look at the customer's recent order history and see that he had two orders that week, one containing part "A" and the other containing part "B." It is now obvious that he actually needed both parts, and that he is confusing one order with another. By calling the customer back and explaining your "theory," you are actually resolving two problems for him, since eventually he would realize that he needs the part "B" that he was about to return. Now I'm not going to tell you that you will be getting these "hero" opportunities every day, but they do come up. Obviously if you have no confidence in your inventory accuracy, this situation is not possible.

Now back to returns processing. In previous chapters, I've talked about the importance of using live documents to move, receive, consume, or ship inventory. These live documents help to direct activities, automate transactions, prevent duplication of transactions, and provide tracking of missed transactions. The most common method for dealing with returns within business software is to simply use the standard sales order process, replacing the quantity to ship with a negative quantity (return quantity). The sales order now becomes a return authorization, and the resulting invoice now becomes a credit, simply by using a negative quantity. While this is fairly reasonable logic, there are some inherent problems. A return does not necessarily follow the reverse flow of a shipment, and the updating of on-hand quantities and allocations at the same points you would in a sales order process is not necessarily the best methodology for returns.

A negative allocation is not the same as an inbound quantity. Negative allocations will actually create positive availability in some inventory systems. This is a big no no. If your system does this, try to find a way to turn this off. Even if your system has more advanced functionality that allows the return to show as an inbound quantity, you may not want it to. This depends on the likelihood that the return will actually be put into stock. Ideally you would want the results of the assessment conducted during the return notification process to be able to control whether or not the return will be treated as an inbound quantity.

Next we need to deal with the determination of the need to adjust on-hand balances and the timing of the transaction. In the standard return system, the acceptance of the return or issuance of the credit (invoice with negative quantity) will also adjust the on-hand balance. Often systems will have an "adjust on-hand Y/N" option that is designated during the creation of the return authorization. The problem here is that you may not know for certain whether or not the materials will go into stock, and the timing of the issuance of credit may not coincide with the timing of the materials actually being placed in stock. In some operations, as a response to customer demand, credit is being issued as soon as the return hits the dock. Later the materials are evaluated for disposition; rework or repack may be required before the materials are put into stock. Meanwhile the materials have already been added to your inventory system via the credit. In other operations, the return is checked in, the materials processed, and then the paperwork is forwarded to "the office" for completion. Should a cycle count occur during these timing disconnects you will likely end up with an errant adjustment. You also do not have a direct connection to ensure that materials put back into stock are "added in" while those discarded or otherwise routed elsewhere are not "added in."

What is needed, is to maintain a connection between the credit and the inventory adjustment, but remove the need to have both activities occur at the same time. Yes accountants, this probably means a returns-related WIP (work-in-process) account. This would allow the credit to be issued at whatever point best meets your business objectives and allow the inventory adjustment to independently occur at the point that the inventory is actually placed into stocked or determined not to be placed in stock. It would also maintain the "live document" functionality for both activities.

Another option would be to create a logical location that is not included in availability calculations (this is not standard functionality in most inventory systems), have the credit adjust to this location, and have the final stocking of the materials move from this location. While this does not guarantee that the adjustment designation of the credit will coincide with the final designation of the materials, it at least provides a means to isolate the placing of the materials in stock from the credit adjustment. Careful monitoring of the logical location would be necessary to identify and correct disparities.

One problem that is not resolved through either of these options occurs when processing a return for a picking/shipping error where the wrong item was shipped. For correct costs, pricing, and historical usage updates, you need to issue the credit for the item that was ordered, yet to correct the inventory balance, you need to adjust inventory on the item actually shipped (this assumes that you already adjusted inventory on this item previously through an inventory count initiated by the reporting of the error). There is no easy resolution to this, and it will likely need to be handled through some manual adjustments. Since you are focusing on accuracy throughout your organization, you should have very few of these, right?

If you have frequent returns, you should also make an effort to get a return authorization with a bar code in the hands of the customer. In many cases this is provided as a shipping label. With technologies available today, you can email a printable image to the customer that can be used for this purpose. They simply print the label on plain paper in a laser or inkjet printer, trim the excess, and tape it to the return. This simplifies your customer's process, but also provides a bar code that you can use to automate your processing. A scan of the bar code at the dock can initiate the credit, while a subsequent scan when the material is placed in stock can execute the inventory adjustment.

Certainly the level of effort and technologies applied towards returns will have a direct relationship to the frequency of returns. Though a manufacturer that may only incur one or two returns a month will likely not be investing in automated data collection technology just for returns, and will certainly not have dedicated return staff, they should still have a formalized process and they should still train their employees on the procedures.

Negative inventory.

"That's impossible!"

"How can we have negative inventory?"

"How can you have less than nothing?"

"Is it like a black hole, sucking inventory into it before the inventory even exists?"

"Is negative inventory like anti-matter? If it comes in contact with positive inventory, will it create a fracture in the time-space continuum?"

Yes trekkies, I've heard them all.

People can get rather excited over negative inventory because the concept seems so ridiculous. Surprisingly, negative inventory is a very common occurrence and may even be a "normal" part of some processes. Though negative inventory balances certainly reflect some type of problem, it should not be assumed that you must manually adjust inventory up to "fix it." In many cases, negative inventory is simply a timing issue. For example, if materials are coming right out of manufacturing and into an outbound shipment, the shipment transaction may be completed before the production-reporting transaction if the production run is still in process. This will result in a temporary negative balance until the production quantity is reported. While it would be nice to have had the production quantity reported prior to the materials being moved to shipping, there is no real harm being done here. When the production is finally reported (hopefully later that same day) the quantities will all be fine.

Transaction timing is certainly not the only cause for negative inventory balances. Any transaction that affects on-hand balances can create a negative inventory balance if the transaction is incorrectly executed. It's important to be able to make a distinction between negative balances caused by timing issues and those caused by transaction errors. It's also important to make a distinction between location-level negative balances and item-level negative balances.

A location-level negative balance occurs when an incorrect location is used in a transaction or when an incorrect quantity is transferred in a location transfer transaction. For example, if I had 100 pieces of an item stored in location "X" and picked 50 pieces for a shipping order but mistakenly issued the material from location "Y"; the end result would be 100 still showing in location "X" and -50 showing in location "Y." Though I now have a negative balance in location "Y," my item-level inventory balance of 50 pieces (the sum of location level inventories) is actually correct. A similar situation occurs when you transfer inventory from one location to another and enter an incorrect "from location" or enter a quantity greater than was actually moved. For example, if I had 100 pieces of an item stored in location "X" and moved the entire 100 pieces to location "Z," but mistakenly entered a quantity of 1,000, the end result would be 1,000 showing in location "Z" and -900 showing in location "X." Once again, my item level inventory balance of 100 is still correct. Though these location-level balances will create problems in the warehouse, they should not be causing problems with planning systems.

Item-level negative balances, on the other hand, may be affecting planning system. These can occur from a variety of transactional mistakes. Over-reporting scrap quantities, cycle count adjustment errors, over-reporting production when using backflushing, overissuing materials to production, duplicate transactions, and overissuing inventory to shipping orders are just some examples of errors that can create item-level negative balances.

The reason it's so important to make the distinction as to the type of negative balance (timing, location-level, or item-level) is to ensure that your subsequent actions to "correct" the negative balance don't result in more serious inventory problems. If you were to adjust up a negative balance caused by a timing issue, you would create an inventory problem since, once the other transaction goes through, you will now be overstating your inventory by the amount of the adjustment. The same is true if you were to adjust up a negative location-level balance. Where your item-level balance was previously accurate, your adjustment would now result in overstatement of your item-level inventory.

Item-level negative balances not related to timing issues should also be carefully investigated before taking any actions. Usually you will want to identify the transaction that caused the negative balance and use the same transaction program to enter an offsetting transaction. This is especially true in manufacturing environments since the incorrectly executed transaction may have also created errors with other items (such as with backflushing transactions).

Despite the seemingly complex aspects of negative inventory balances, they are actually very easy to manage. They are easy to identify since all you need is a report that shows any items with a quantity on hand less than zero. In addition, it is usually very easy to track down the source of the error since the errant transaction is usually the transaction that brought the inventory balance below zero (if not, it very likely occurred within a very short timeframe prior to the negative balance being created).

In addition to understanding the sources of negative inventory balances, it's also very important to understand their effects on planning and execution systems. In most planning systems, a negative item-level balance is treated the same as positive demand. Basically your system will tell you to make or buy more to offset the negative balance. Obviously this is a problem when a large negative balance occurs but can also create serious problems with small negative balances under certain conditions. For example, if you have an item that is set up as an "order as needed" item, meaning that you do not want to order or stock any unless you have actual demand (orders), an errant adjustment that drives the balance to -5 will result in a recommended buy of 5 pieces. Since "order as needed" is often associated with very slow moving or obsolete items, you may have just added to an obsolescence problem. In a manufacturing environment using MRP, a negative balance of a single end-item, will result in demand cascading throughout the bill of material structure, potentially resulting in unnecessary orders for hundreds of lower-level items. This is what occurs if your system handles negative balances as would normally be expected. Some programs, either purposely or due to poor programming practices, may not execute properly if they encounter a negative balance. They may ignore the records with negative balances or simply "blow up" because they weren't designed to incorporate negative balances into their calculations.

Though there are valid reasons for not wanting a program to execute if it encounters a negative balance, there are also potential problems with this logic. You may actually need to take action, but because the calculations were suspended due to a negative balance, you did not get the information needed to initiate an action. Due to the complexities of demand-planning systems, especially MRP/DRP systems, there is no "best" way to handle negative balances within the programming. Execution systems such as warehouse management systems and manufacturing execution systems can also have problems with negative balances. While you may not be willing to modify your systems to handle negative balances in a specific way, you should at least understand what your systems are doing when they encounter negative balances.

Ultimately, avoidance of negative balances in the first place is the best solution. However, since perfection is pretty tough to achieve, you should have a backup plan. Since most planning systems still operate in batch mode (run nightly or on weekends) you can eliminate conflicts by resolving all negative balances prior to running these programs. With execution systems that are more likely to run real-time, you don't have this same luxury. Fortunately, the impact on execution systems is generally less dramatic than on planning systems.

I'd once more like to emphasize the importance of thinking through your actions when trying to "fix" negative balances. A "run the report and adjust them all up" mentality will most certainly cause problems. Remember, you should not make adjustments to timing-related negative balances, you should only correct location-level problems with a location transfer program, and you should try to correct other negative balances by entering an offsetting transaction in the same program that created the problem.

Non-stock inventory

Non-stock inventory, also known as non-inventory or special order inventory, is inventory that is not tracked as inventory within your perpetual inventory system. This means it does not have an internal SKU number or an item master record. I need to distinguish non-stock from "order as needed" inventory that does have an SKU number and item master record, but is only ordered when specific demand is present.

Though non-stock inventory can include other materials (such as office supplies or maintenance supplies), I am going to focus on non-stock inventory that is purchased for resale, as samples, prototypes, or to be used in a special manufacturing run. Though non-stock is not tracked the same way your normal inventory is tracked, it is still inventory, and therefore must be accurately processed. There are also situations where the accuracy of your regular inventory can be negatively impacted by non-stock inventory.

The nature of non-stock is that it is not tracked through your normal inventory systems. There are no internal SKU numbers, item master records, on-hand balances, locations, allocations, demand, forecasts, bills of materials, or item-based transaction histories. The reason for this is it's not worth the effort to go through the entire item setup process for an item that will only be handled once. Also, in the past, when database size was much more of an issue than it is today, you didn't want to fill up your databases with records for non-stock items.

Unfortunately, the fact that you are not setting up the item in your inventory system results in you being unable to process, track, and manage the item the way you can an inventory item. Because of this, I really dislike non-stock inventory. All of my finely tuned processes and systems are useless when a non-inventory item hits the receiving dock. Non-stock inventory tends to disrupt every process that it touches. Often, manual processes have to be put in place to track the non-stock inventory; these often include special staging areas, forms, and ID tags. And these manual processes are always problematic.

So what is the solution? Well, some software systems have developed added functionality to track the non-stock items, such as linking the purchase order line directly to a sales order line. While this helps — and is far superior to other systems that do not maintain any added functionality — it is still not near as good as the inventory tracking systems you already own. The real solution is not related to creating systems to track non-stock, but rather in creating systems that allow you to eliminate non-stock. The non-stock problem is caused by the difficulty in setting up inventory records and the added system resource requirements to maintain these records. I think the system resource issue has been resolved through the evolution of computer hardware. So now the only issue is, "what needs to be done to allow us to get this non-stock inventory into our regular inventory system with minimal effort?" This is hardly an insurmountable problem. All you need to do is to create a program that will automatically create the inventory records with mostly default data during the normal order entry process. Don't like all those added records cluttering up your database? All you have to do is purge or archive them periodically — no big deal. I'm not suggesting that everyone goes out and modifies their software to do this. This is more of a message to software developers to add this functionality to their systems. In doing so, they negate all of the issues related to non-stock inventory processing.

Now back to reality. Your system probably doesn't have the functionality I am proposing and your non-stock volume probably does not support modifying your system. You still need ways to process and track your non-stock inventory. Non-stock inventory is ordered for a specific purpose. That purpose is known when the order is placed and should, therefore, be included somewhere in your purchasing system. Find a place in the system where you can put this information, preferably in an extended description field or a notes field associated with the purchase order line. If the non-stock inventory is purchased for resale, include the sales order number (sales order should be entered before the purchase order is created) on the purchase order line. Systems that automate this will usually have "related order" fields on both the purchase order line and the sales order line. This gives the direct two-way tracking you are looking for. Automated systems for production orders will likely use this same technique.

Design your receiving documents to print this information. This will clearly identify the materials as non-stock as soon as they are received and also provide the receiving personnel with the information they need to properly route the materials. In a good automated system the associated sales order will automatically release, allowing you to immediately ship the materials. In a manual system, a daily report showing all non-stock receipts and their associated information can be used to release the sales orders or production orders.

Do not allow non-stock inventory to be stored with stock inventory unless there are no other reasonable options. The chances of losing it, having it mistakenly consumed as an inventory item, or confusing cycle counters, are much greater if your non-stock items are not segregated. Generally, special storage areas should be set up specifically for non-stock inventory. If you cannot segregate some non-stock materials (as is sometimes common with very large bulk materials that can only be stored in specific areas used for inventory items), I recommend using really big obnoxious labels, markings, flags, or signs to clearly designate the non-stock materials.

Your next challenge is to put processes in place to prevent shipping or consuming non-stock inventory as stock inventory or vice versa. This is how non-stock can contribute to screwing up your stock inventory. The reasons for these problems may be the result of simple errors, or efforts by customer service or planning personnel to circumvent allocation systems and other control systems. For example, you have an allocation system that locks up inventory based upon user-defined rules. The entire quantity of a specific item is locked up for a future customer order (based upon company policy), meanwhile a customer service person gets a request for the item by one of his "special" customers. Knowing the system will prevent him from shipping the item to his customer, but also knowing that the items are just sitting there in the warehouse, the customer service person decides to put his customer's interests above another customer's interests (and company policy) and enters the item on an order as a non-stock item. In doing so, no availability checking is performed; therefore the order hits the warehouse floor showing the quantity in the "quantity to ship" position. If the warehouse does not recognize the "deception" they will ship the item. Eventually, the other customer's order will be released (you know, the one that was supposed to get the item), but when the picker goes to pick it, there's nothing there.

Now you have pissed off a customer that was kind enough to give you advanced notification of demand, wasted the warehouse personnel's time since they probably spent some time looking for the inventory, and have increased the "our inventory is a mess" attitude within your organization. There is only one way to deal with this clear violation of company policy. You either have policies or you don't. Allowing these types of activities makes it clear that you do not have policies.

You can avoid these situations with clear policies, procedures, and employee training (no big surprise here). You should also look at your systems and documents and identify data elements that make it easy to tell the difference between inventory and non-inventory. If you use a locator system, you will find that non-stock inventory will not have a location pulled into the programs and picking documents. This is a simple and obvious way of identifying non-stock picks. Make sure you educate your warehouse personnel on this "check." Now it is possible that a clever customer service person will figure this out and find a way to look up and manually enter the location. Fortunately there are not too many clever customer service people out there (is it obvious that I come from a warehousing background?).

Similar problems can occur in manufacturing processes when non-stock materials are used. For the most part, I recommend that you set up inventory records for anything used in manufacturing. Non-stock within manufacturing processes can get really messy. It's extremely rare that a material used in a manufacturing process will only be a onetime purchase. And, even if it is, you are still better off taking the time to set it up in the inventory system. Sometimes non-stock materials are substituted for inventory items during production processes. It may be that the non-stock materials were special ordered for another purpose but were not used, or they were test materials from a different vendor. I have no problem with these substitutions as long as they are reflected on the materials list so they don't screw up inventory. Substitutions are discussed in more detail later in this chapter.

Ultimately, resolving the non-stock issues leads us to eliminating non-stock and replacing it with special order "inventoried" items. Until the functionality to do this becomes "standard," most companies will need to rely on good old-fashioned manual processes. They can be effective, it just takes more work.

Units-of-measure.

The unit-of-measure (U/M), describes how the quantity of an item is tracked in your inventory system. The most common unit-of-measure is "eaches," which simply means that each individual item is considered one unit. An item that uses "cases" as the unit-of-measure would be tracked by the number of cases rather than by the actual piece quantity. Other examples of units of measure would include pallets, pounds, ounces, linear feet, square feet, cubic feet, thousands, hundreds, pairs, gallons, and dozens.

A unit-of-measure conversion is needed whenever you work with multiple units of measure for the same item. For example, if you purchased an item in cases (meaning that your purchase order stated a number of cases rather than a number of pieces) and then stocked the item in eaches, you would require a conversion to allow your system to calculate how many eaches are represented by a quantity of cases. This way, when you received the cases, your system would automatically convert the case-quantity into an each-quantity.

The unit-of-measure you use to track your inventory within your facility is called the "stocking unit-of-measure." Your stocking unit-of-measure will usually be the smallest unit-of-measure that you will ever need to handle. For example, you do not want to set up cases as the unit-of-measure if your customers can order quantities that are not equal multiples of the case quantity. The need for multiple units of measure (along with associated conversions) arise when the stocking unit-of-measure that best meets your needs is not the best unit-of-measure for other parts of the supply chain (customers and suppliers).

Whenever using units-of-measure other than "eaches," and especially when using multiple units of measure, you need to carefully consider the training requirements and the system setup requirements. Choosing the right stocking unit-of-measure can do a lot for simplifying internal transactions, but can also create confusion and inventory problems if the workforce doesn't understand them. This starts with the receiving department, when using stocking units of measure that differ from purchasing units of measure. The people handling the receipt transactions will need to understand that the unit-of-measure and quantity on the supplier's packing slip and on the purchase order will differ from the unit-of-measure they will be using to put the materials away. Usually you will enter the receipt transaction using the purchasing unit-of-measure and let the system calculate the stocking unit-of-measure. This is another reason why using a receipt document can be so important. You can have the receipt document print out the results of this conversion, clearly showing the quantity and unit-of-measure that will be used to put the materials away.

In manufacturing environments you may encounter situations where you can actually have portions of units-of-measures in stock. For example, if you were stocking a raw material by pounds or gallons, it is very likely that the "quantities per" on your bills of material would actually be fractions of the stocking unit-of-measure. This is a situation where you do not want to use the "smallest unit of measure" rule. The smallest unit of measure actually used in manufacturing may actually be thousandths of a pound or gallon. Changing the stocking unit-of-measure to "thousandths of pounds" would result in a material handler having to enter a quantity of 2,000,000 to move a load containing 2,000 pounds of materials. In this case you are better off using pounds as the stocking unit-of-measure. You may even want to consider using "thousands of pounds" as the unit-of measure if the quantities you handle are generally very large. In this case, the material handler would move the 2,000 pounds as a quantity of 2.

This does bring us back to the "portion of a unit-of-measure" issue since sometimes you will have quantities that are not exact units-of-measure. If you were moving a container of 1,538 pounds of materials that were stocked using "thousands of pounds" as the unit-of-measure, you would need to enter your transaction as 1.538 units. This is the point where you will realize that many of your workers do not understand decimals. I was caught a bit off guard several years ago by this exact issue. Fortunately we were using "thousands of eaches" as the unit-of-measure and the workers were able to understand "put a dot where the comma would go." Had we been using "hundreds of eaches" they would have been lost because they just didn't understand decimals. We would have needed to conduct some basic math training (which isn't a bad idea anyway) to get them back to the level of knowledge that I'm sure they had when they were ten years old.

There can also be confusion created when inventory screens are formatted to only show whole units-of-measure. For example, that 1.538 units of materials would show as 2 units on inventory screens. This is actually very common, and is not a problem as long as those using the screens understand that they are looking at rounded numbers. For those that need to know exact quantities, you either need options within the program to show these or may need to create reports that print exact quantities.

There are also other problems related to unit-of-measure conversions that can come up in more unexpected areas. For example, I ran into a situation where several incidences of product damage resulted in the quality and engineering departments getting together and making a decision to reduce the pieces per carton for a certain product line. They informed the machine operators and floor supervisors of this change, who in turn started putting fifty fewer pieces in each carton. They knew that the customers ordered in eaches (actually thousands of eaches) and they even made sure that they changed the piece quantity printed on the case labels. What they failed to do was realize the stocking unit-of-measure was cases not eaches. Therefore they should have also changed the bills of materials and the unit-of-measure conversion for the selling unit-of-measure. This operation was also using backflushing to issue raw materials. The result was, every time production was reported (in cases) the system backflushed more raw materials than were actually used because the bills of materials were now wrong. In addition, the customers were all getting short shipped because the system was using the wrong unit-of-measure conversion to convert the order quantity (in thousands of eaches) to cases.

Math skills were not the issue here since quality and engineering folks certainly understand simple mathematics. The problem was a lack of awareness of the entire process and the ramifications of making this type of change. Now some may look at this problem and think this would have been avoided had they just used eaches as the unit-of-measure and not used backflushing to issue raw materials. I strongly disagree. Their choices to use cases as the stocking unit-of-measure and backflushing as the method for issuing raw materials were definitely the best choices for that environment. In fact, I was extremely impressed in the way they had their systems set up. Had they used eaches as the stocking unit-of-measure, the material handlers would have had to pull out their calculators every time they moved a pallet, since the case quantities ranged from 500 to 3,000 depending upon the specific product family. Also since they were using bulk point-of-use materials in manufacturing, backflushing was a much easier and more accurate method of issuing materials. The only thing they neglected to do was train their people properly.

As an additional note, you will also find that warehouse management systems may also allow multiple stocking units-of-measure. Multiple stocking units-of-measure allow you to move materials within your facility using different units of measure. More simply put, I can put away, pick, or move the same item as either a quantity of pallets, a quantity of cases, or a quantity of eaches. Once again, you need to balance the benefits of using this functionality with the potential confusion and errors that can be created through this added level of complexity. And, of course, train your workforce!

Unit packs, multi packs, inner packs, kits, and sets.

Inner packs, also called unit packs and multi packs, are smaller containers within a container used to separate smaller quantities of an item. Inner packs are usually smaller chipboard boxes or poly bags used within a case to break down the larger case quantity into smaller, easier to handle and count quantities. Kits and sets are items that are made up of multiple parts. A kit is usually made of different parts, while a set is usually made up of a quantity of a single part. The definitions of these terms are not standardized. In some operations, multi packs and unit packs follow the same definition as sets. It really doesn't matter which terms and definitions you use as long as your employees (and possibly your customers) understand your definition.

Inner packs.
Inner packs cause frequent inventory problems when workers mistake an inner pack containing multiple units for a single unit. Due to the nature of inner packs, errors associated with mistaking an inner pack for a unit are often significant. For example, if you have small plumbing fittings that are packed 25 units each into a small chipboard box, and an order picker mistakes each inner pack as a single unit, he would be shipping 25 units for each unit ordered. If a customer ordered 10 units, it would result in an inventory shortage of 240 units from a single picking error. Errors related to inner packs are more common when the same packaging used to package multiple units is also used to package single units of other items. They are also more common when your inventory is made up of inner packed materials as well as kits and sets.

Tips for eliminating inner pack errors:

✔ Remove units from inner pack packaging when receiving or putting away the inventory. The person receiving or putting away inner-packed materials should be able to identify them since he knows the full quantity he is handling. Removing the packaging and dumping the loose parts into a bin or bulk case will eliminate any chance for confusion by order pickers. Unfortunately, it will also make it more difficult to count the materials when cycle counting or if order picking quantities are larger than the inner pack quantity. If you usually handle relatively small quantities of the item, I would recommend this solution; otherwise I would try other solutions.

✔ Clearly mark the inner packs at receipt. Sticking a special label (choosing a unique color is suggested) on each inner pack will help to identify them. It is best to use a label with a unique color (something that stands out) and either preprint them with "inner pack," "multi pack," "unit pack," or print the actually quantity per pack on them.

✔ Clearly mark the picking locations. Since inner packs are more of a problem with small parts picking, and since most small parts picking operations use fixed picking locations with parts bins, you can mark the front of the bin to identify that the contents are in inner packs. The same concept as above, using a special label, will work. You may also choose to purchase unique colored plastic parts bins for your inner pack items.

✔ Group all inner pack items into a single area. This is a good option if you have a small number of inner pack items. Just store them all in a single area (a single section of static shelving) and find a way to mark that section in a manner that gets the attention of the order pickers. Painting it a unique color, using colored tape or labels, or hanging a big sign will help.

✔ Identify the items as unit packs on the picking documents. This will be more effective if you use conditional formatting such as only printing a message if it is an inner pack item and then printing it in a large bold font (use color if you have this functionality). Changing the formatting of the quantity data element on the pick document can also be useful to make the pick stand out.

Kits and sets.
Errors associated with kits and sets are usually just the opposite of the errors that occur with inner packs. An order picker opens up a bag containing a set and treats each piece as a unit. An order picker opens up a corrugated carton thinking it is a case and pulls out a part when the case was actually a kit. An order picker picks one box of a kit made up of several boxes. In addition to picking errors, kits and sets are also more likely to have receiving errors when the individual pieces are confused with single units.

The tips described previously for eliminating inner pack errors related to using special labels on the items, marking the locations, grouping the items into a single area, or identifying the items on the picking documents will also apply to eliminating errors with kits and sets. In addition you can try things like using special tape (again a unique color is helpful) to seal the outside packaging of kits and sets. For large kits that consist of multiple boxes, you should consider assembling the multiple boxes into a single unit by taping or strapping the boxes together or banding them onto a pallet. Clearly mark them so that someone does not separate them. If they cannot be assembled into a single unit, large labels that identify each separate item as being part of a kit are helpful.

Lot and serial number tracking.

Lot numbers are unique numbers assigned to discrete batches (usually individual production runs) of items. Serial numbers are unique numbers assigned to discrete units of an item. Tracking lots or serial numbers is usually done based upon a need to meet regulatory or warranty requirements. If you don't absolutely have to track lots and serial numbers, don't track them. Lot numbers and serial numbers are just one more data element that needs to be managed. Tracking them complicates every task that involves inventory transactions. The largest impact occurs when conducting order picking tasks or cycle counts and physical inventories.

Lot tracking.
Here are some recommendations related to tracking lots.

✔ If practical, do not mix lots within a location. This will make both cycle counting and order picking much easier. If you do mix lots, follow first-in-first-out practices and even consider creating a physical separation between each lot.

✔ Use directed tasks that specify the lot number. This will be much easier if you follow the previous tip and avoid mixing lots or use FIFO when mixing lots.

✔ Pick by lot number, not item number. If using directed tasks that specify the lot number in an environment where lots are not mixed in locations, there is little value in having the order pickers look at the item number. The task should send them to a location to pick a lot.

✔ Strongly consider using bar codes and portable computers with bar code scanners during all material handling tasks. The need to track lots makes it much easier to justify implementing automated data capture technologies.

Serial number tracking.
Since serial numbers are unique to each unit, it is unlikely that you will be able to avoid mixing serial numbers or be able to mix them in a manner that would lend itself to directed tasks specifying the serial numbers. You don't want to make your employees go to a location and then have to sort through the units looking for a specific serial number. Instead, use bar codes and scanners to capture the serial number data as the inventory is processed. If the cost of a portable computer system is not justifiable, you can at least implement a wired scanner at a fixed checking or shipping station to capture the serial numbers.

In many environments, the serial numbers are not tracked through internal processes (receipt, movement between facilities or storage locations). They are only documented when the unit is shipped. If you do need to track serial numbers internally by storage location, you should use license plates on all unitized loads (pallets, cases, totes, etc.) to track the movement. The license plate will have a single number (usually bar coded) that is the key to all serial numbers contained in the unitized load. This will allow you to use the single license plate number to complete transactions for all units in a single transaction.

Multi-plant processing.

Multi-plant processing is very common and may or may not create some unique accuracy issues. In older less-functional systems, each plant is treated as a separate entity (often on separate inventory and accounting systems) and the same sales order and purchase order processes that are used with customers and outside suppliers are used with the other plants. Under these systems, the accuracy issues are no different than they would be with your customer and vendor shipments. However, as you get into true multi-plant systems that provide much better planning information, you also have additional data that needs to be maintained. Distribution requirements planning (DRP) is the name given to inventory systems that are able to plan and manage inventory across multiple plants by setting up relationships between the plants and calculating demand through these relationships. A DRP relationship is basically data that says, "This item is supplied from plant "A" to plant "B."

While I don't intend to get into the complete inner workings of DRP, I do want to address "inbound quantities," "outbound quantities," and "in-transit quantities." Inbound and outbound quantities are very similar to quantities used to identify incoming materials from purchase orders or allocations for sales orders. In fact, the documents used to transfer materials from one plant to another (called transfer orders) are usually specialized versions of purchase orders and shipping orders that have a built-in relationship. It is this relationship between inbound, outbound, and in-transit quantities and their related transfer orders that make it very important to maintain the accuracy of this data.

Essentially, DRP outbound quantities plus in-transit quantities should equal inbound quantities. All of these quantities should also be "current," in that they represent quantities that are actually being transferred or are going to be transferred. Any discrepancy between the quantity shipped from one plant and the quantity received at the other plant will result in a problem. For example, let's start with a simple situation where plant "A" requires 500 units of an item from plant "B." A transfer order is placed, creating an inbound quantity of 500 on plant "A" and an outbound quantity of 500 on plant "B." After plant "B" ships the 500 units, the system will show an inbound quantity of 500 on plant "A" , and in-transit quantity of 500 units, and an outbound quantity of 0 on plant "B." Now let's say that plant "A" receives the materials, but counts only 450 units and enters the receiving transaction accordingly. This will result in an on-hand quantity of 450 units in plant "A" and inbound quantity of 50 units on plant "A," and in-transit quantity of 50 units and an outbound of 0 on plant "B." Under this situation there needs to be a process in place to communicate the discrepancy and "figure it out," because doing nothing will create serious planning problems

Let's go through the possible ramifications of not figuring this out:

✔ If this was a plant "B" shipping error, eventually plant "B" will count the item during a cycle count and adjust its inventory up by 50 pieces. Now plant "B'" on-hand balance is correct, but the overall inventory (plant "A" plus plant "B" plus in transit) is overstated by 50 units, and the planning system still thinks that 50 units are on their way to plant "A."

✔ If this was a plant "A" receiving error, eventually plant "A" will count the item during a cycle count and adjust their inventory up by 50 pieces. Now plant "A'" on-hand balance is correct, but the overall inventory (plant "A" plus plant "B" plus in transit) is overstated by 50 units, and the planning system still thinks that 50 units are on their way to plant "A."

✔ If 50 units were "lost" by the carrier, the planning systems still think that 50 units are on their way to plant "A," and the accounting system still has the 50 units in-transit on the books. Or, if you deduct the 50 units from the in-transit quantity via a manual adjustment, you still show 50 inbound units on plant "A."

Basically, you need to be sure that every item shipped in a DRP environment, is received by the other plant in the exact quantity as was shipped. While this sounds simple, there are a lot of very out-of-whack DRP quantities out there that are creating serious problems for these highly functional planning systems.

Maintaining this data requires monitoring open transfer orders, inbound, outbound, and in-transit quantities. This can be done through a variety of exception reports including:

❏ Received quantity different than shipped quantity.

❏ Received quantity different than ordered quantity.

❏ Shipped quantity different than ordered quantity.

❏ In-transit quantity more than a certain number of days old.

❏ Past due transfer orders.

❏ Items where inbound does not equal outbound plus in-transit quantities.

I'm not suggesting that you create all of these reports since some of them are actually redundant. You should, however, develop some key exception reports to monitor DRP data based upon your activity. It's much easier to stay on top of these quantities than to try to clean them up after a long period of inattention.

The DRP relationship setup is also extremely important. Depending upon how your system works, an incorrectly set up DRP record may prevent the transaction from occurring, or may result in really messed up inbound, outbound, and in-transit quantities. Consider setting up exception reports for DRP relationships to spot errant records. You also have to be very careful in changing DRP relationships when you currently have open transfer orders for the specified items, as this may also result in out-of-sync quantities.

Substitutions

Substitutions are often a source of inventory problems. What really annoys me about inventory problems related to substitutions is that they are almost always easily avoidable. This includes substitutions in both manufacturing and distribution environments. All that is required is a simple policy and an environment that makes it clear that policies are the "only way."

Here is the policy:

> "Substitutions are to be implemented at the document level by planning or customer service personnel only. Under no circumstances are warehouse workers or plant workers to substitute materials listed on a production order materials list or shipping order with other materials."

You can simplify the policy even further if you are only dealing with either manufacturing or distribution substitutions.

I have yet to see an inventory system that does not allow a planner to change the materials list associated with a production order or prevent a customer service person from entering the substitute item on the order. These are the "only ways" substitutions should be handled. Not through notes on the production order or shipping order. Not through a phone call to the shop floor or warehouse. And, definitely not at the discretion of warehouse or shop floor personnel.

"Use this instead and have Bob make the adjustment" just doesn't cut it. For the most part, the realization that a substitution is necessary is known before paperwork ever hits the shop floor or warehouse. All that is required is the person responsible for planning the production run or entering the shipping order changes the document in the system to reflect what is actually going to happen. Even if the need for a substitution is realized after the paperwork has hit the warehouse or shop floor, you can usually still make the changes in the system and then generate new paperwork. Certainly some training is needed, especially for planning personnel that may need to make changes to materials lists, however, the minimal level of effort needed to maintain this policy is far outweighed by the benefits of not screwing up your inventory every time a substitution occurs.

This "right way" of doing substitutions not only helps your inventory accuracy, but is also very important should you ever need to know exactly which item was shipped or which materials were used in the manufacturing process. The only potential down side is that your usage history will reflect the substituted materials rather than the normal materials. This may be a problem if you use this history to forecast future demand. If this is a critical problem, I suggest you transfer the substituted inventory balance to the original inventory item prior to the substitution, and then just treat the substituted materials as though they were the original materials. There can be some problems with this, but it is still better than trying to clean everything up after the substitution has occurred.

Outsourcing

There's little doubt that current trends towards outsourcing specific business functions will continue to grow. Outsourcing brings up some unique accuracy issues. These include risks associated with double entry of data, integration and communication problems, and the transfer of control responsibilities to "outsiders."

Though virtually any business function can be outsourced, I'm primarily focusing on the outsourcing of warehousing or manufacturing functions. Whenever your inventory is going to be stored or processed offsite, you need to be very concerned about accuracy. As I've previously mentioned, most companies have inadequate levels of inventory accuracy. Third party warehouses and contract manufacturers are not excluded from this generalization. When outsourcing, it's very important to evaluate the processes and systems the service provider has in place. The fact that they may use bar code scanners, have a cycle counting program in place, or conduct monthly physical counts really doesn't tell you anything. In fact — based on the way most companies perform cycle counts and physical inventories — I would rather they didn't count my inventory. Instead, you need to know how they process and control transactions, how they train their personnel, and how they handle variances. I feel it's very important to go to their site and see firsthand how they operate. Look at the paperwork used in the warehouse and shop floor, observe the organization of their storage and staging areas, evaluate their technologies, question their employees to evaluate their knowledge of procedures. Try to conduct an "impromptu" location audit. Sure, this is going to make them nervous; it's also going to make it clear that you are serious about accuracy.

There are some distinct differences between outsourcing warehousing versus outsourcing manufacturing processes. Inventory accuracy is a much larger "order winner" for a third party warehouse than it is for a contract manufacturer. Not surprisingly, you can expect much higher levels of accuracy with warehouse services suppliers than those providing manufacturing services. To throw in another generalization, if you have an "average" operation, you will likely increase your overall accuracy by outsourcing warehousing/distribution functions, while you very well may decrease your accuracy by outsourcing manufacturing functions. It's very important to educate the people that make decisions related to outsourcing manufacturing on the importance of accuracy. Certainly manufacturing capabilities, price, lead times, capacity, and quality, will likely fall higher on the list of priorities, but you should make sure accuracy is a consideration.

In most outsourcing processes you will have related data maintained on two separate systems (your inventory system and that of your service provider). This brings up the issue of keeping data in sync between separate systems. The choice to do this manually versus automatically will generally depend upon the number of transactions and your access to technology. While having systems share data is getting easier, it is still a complex and often expensive undertaking.

Manual processing

✔ **Set a formal process for sharing information**. This should include specific times, formats, and methods of communication. You should work together to determine the best formats. Preferably you will be able to download transactions directly from one system into a text file, spreadsheet, or database file and send them as email attachments.

✔ **Set a formal process for validating data.** This is usually achieved in the form of a periodic comparison of on-hand balances between the two systems (monthly or weekly). This can get tricky since you need to closely synchronize the timing of the data. This comes down to making sure that all transactions are completed on both systems, and reports or data are then extracted from both systems at the same time. The reports or data are then compared, and hopefully they match. Any data than doesn't match needs to be investigated. Never assume one source is more accurate than the other. You may even need a way to share transaction history information from each system to track down the error.

Both manual and automated systems

✔ **Monitor the transactions.** It is especially important to monitor miscellaneous transactions such as scrap, cycle counting, and physical inventory transactions. You should review these transactions the same way you would if you were conducting this in-house.

✔ **Question the transactions.** Any questionable transactions that are identified through the monitoring process need to be questioned. Once again this is primarily geared towards miscellaneous adjustments. I have frequently contacted outside service providers and said "you cannot possibly have had that much scrap, I need you to verify or explain further," "you must have these, I am absolutely certain they were shipped to you and there is no way you could have used them," "you cannot possibly have these, you should have used everything we shipped in the last production run of item #Z," or "you must have miscounted 10 cases of item #A as item #B." Be prepared to be forceful in these situations since you can expect to get responses like "my system shows ..." or "we just did a physical last week so I'm sure our numbers are correct." If the transaction is wrong, it is wrong ... period! Taking the easy road and accepting it will leave you with incorrect planning data that will certainly come back to bite you later.

Tracking inventory located at outside suppliers or service providers is generally done by setting up the supplier location as a separate facility in a inventory system that supports multi-plants, or setting up a logical location for the supplier within your facility. Choosing one method over the other will generally relate to your system's functionality, the need to segregate inventory for availability calculations, and the need to use DRP-type planning to move materials between facilities. Either method can be accurate. I generally prefer just setting up a logical location unless you need the added functionality of a separate facility setup.

Ultimately, maintaining accuracy when outsourcing comes down to the capabilities of your service provider and your efforts to manage the process. Taking an active role in managing the process goes beyond just monitoring transactions; in some cases you may be able to help your service provider become more accurate. This is especially true when outsourcing to small contract manufacturers that often have little expertise in inventory management, but also applies in using your experience with your product to assist third party warehouses set up their processes. Sending them a good book on inventory accuracy couldn't hurt either...hint, hint.

Also see "Outside operations processing" later in this chapter.

Theft.

Theft, pilferage, shrinkage — many names for the same problem. Theft is likely the ugliest of inventory accuracy problems. Unlike accuracy problems caused by incompetence — which tend to be reluctantly accepted — management and business owners very often take a discovery of missing inventory due to theft personally. Having worked mostly with industrial goods, my experience with theft is significantly less than had I worked extensively with consumer goods. This isn't to say that I haven't bumped into it from time to time. For most businesses, it's unrealistic to put in place measures that would absolutely prevent theft. If someone wants to steal from you bad enough, they will probably find a way. What you can do is put in place measures that will make it more difficult to steal from you. This will likely prevent the "casual thieves" from supplementing their income with your inventory and reduce your exposure to the more serious thieves.

Let my try to create "thief categories" for a workforce.

- ❐ **Workers that don't steal**. Yes, these are the workers that absolutely will not steal regardless of need or opportunity. They have strong personal convictions that stealing is wrong and will not allow themselves to even be tempted.

- ❐ **Workers that only steal certain things**. These are the ones that can justify in their minds that taking office supplies or similar items is not really stealing. They would never consider actually taking "inventory," and would never admit that they have ever stolen anything. They tend to think of these things as "benefits" of their job. Since they started working for your company, they have ran thousands of copies of personal materials on your copy machines, have drawers full of company pens, markers, paperclips, and staples, maybe have a couple of tape dispensers and a handful of razor knives. They may have even helped themselves to company coffee, trash bags, toilet paper, and maintenance supplies. Recyclable scrap materials often fit into this category of "not really stealing."

- ❐ **Workers that only steal under certain circumstances.** These are the workers that will steal if an "opportunity" presents itself. They are not going to develop an elaborate plan to steal something, however, if you have no controls in place, they will take advantage of the opportunity to take something. They may also be workers that will "justify" their stealing based upon perceived mistreatment by the company or by unethical activities conducted by the company.

- ❐ **Workers that will steal anything anytime.** These folks don't care about the value of what they are stealing or any security measures you have in place. They will steal stuff they cannot even use or sell. They steal as a compulsion rather than a need. It's very difficult to prevent these people from stealing, but you will likely eventually catch them.

❑ **Internal professional thieves.** These are employees that will steal large amounts of inventory. They may be working with other employees and will carefully plan out their activities. The inventory they are stealing will likely leave your facility through your loading docks. They may even be selling to one of your customers or suppliers.

❑ **External professional thieves.** OK, these are not part of your workforce. These are people that will break into your facility to steal inventory.

So how do they do it?

The put it in their pockets.

They take materials out in a lunch box, briefcase, or backpack.

They just walk out with it in a box.

They slip it out an unsecured exit door and pick it up later.

They throw it in the trash and pick it up later.

They throw it in the trash or recycling container and make a deal with the guy that picks it up.

They make a deal with a truck driver, and load it on a truck from your loading dock.

They make a deal with a truck driver and sign for more than they actually unloaded.

They make a deal with a supplier and receive more than was actually received.

They make a deal with a customer and ship more than was supposed to be shipped.

They use your computer system to have inventory shipped out and then delete the records.

OK, so there are many types of thieves and many ways to steal. Now what do you do about it?

✔ **Control access.** This includes not allowing employees free roam of your facility. If it's not their work area, they shouldn't be there. It also includes control of exits and docks. Do not allow use of emergency exits for anything but emergencies. Install audible alarms on any exits that are not used as part of normal operations. Have employees enter and leave the building from specified entrances. Strictly enforce these policies.

✔ **Consider installing cameras.** This is especially important in loading dock areas. Employees are less "freaked out" about cameras than they were years ago. Just make it clear as to the purposes of the cameras and then stick with that purpose. I have no problem with using cameras to monitor productivity as long as you inform the workers of that, but if you tell the employees you are only using the cameras as a security issue and then use them for other purposes you are building an atmosphere of distrust.

✔ **Don't allow lunch boxes, coolers, briefcases, backpacks, purses, jackets, etc. into warehouse and manufacturing areas**. This is a pretty easy one. Just provide lockers and have a firm policy of no personal belongings in the work areas.

✔ **Don't allow employees to park or drive their vehicles near the building.** Especially near warehouse and plant exits, dock areas, or trash removal areas.

✔ **Security guards?** This really depends upon the types of materials you are handling and the risk of theft. Some operations will actually conduct physical "pat downs" of employees as they enter and leave the facility.

✔ **Undercover detectives?** I know this is a very popular recommendation by loss prevention specialists, but I have some real problems with it. Employees are well aware that they are being watched by managers and supervisors, and that they may even be monitored via video cameras. But finding out that a "coworker" was specifically brought in to spy on them can create some real problems with management/employee relationships. Remember the comment I previously made about employees that feel entitled to steal due to mistreatment by management; you may actually be creating thieves by treating employees with a lack of respect. If not, you will likely at least create a morale problem that will result in reduced productivity, a lack of pride in their work, a lack of respect for management, and increased turnover. I would suggest only using this as a last resort when you have a significant theft problem. Probably more applicable to the "internal professional thief" scenario than the others.

Those were the most well-known methods for curtailing theft. Here are some more factors to consider:

✔ Remember the "materials cannot be stored, moved, shipped, consumed, or produced without proper documents" policy we discussed in chapter three? **Use it!**

✔ **Know what's going on.** Walk around the storage areas and dock areas and look for "suspicious" activities. Watch for employees that are not doing what you would expect them to be doing. Look for materials that are not where they belong, or are being moved or staged without the proper documentation. There's nothing wrong with asking, "What are you doing?" or "What is this material doing here?" These are questions that should be asked anyway just to maintain operational control. If an employee is going to steal materials by loading them on a truck, he still needs to get them to the truck. While you may not just happen to run into a theft in progress, the fact that you are frequently checking will be a significant deterrent.

✔ **Be very cautious when allowing an employee access to both the docks and the storage areas**. While this may not be practical, you should at least consider it. This is especially true when handling materials that are more highly prone to theft.

✔ **Maintain high levels of inventory accuracy.** If you have accurate processes and thoroughly investigate inventory discrepancies, you will have a much better chance of knowing if someone is stealing from you. If employees are aware that process problems regularly cause significant inventory errors that are accepted as "normal," they are more likely to steal because it is unlikely that you will notice the theft. They may even feel they are doing you a favor by putting that "overage" in their lunch box.

✔ **Avoid, or tightly control, situations where employees would legitimately leave the building with company property.** This may include work-at-home programs, giving away old equipment or unneeded inventory, or selling "seconds" to employees. When it is normal for employees to leave the building with inventory, you have greatly increased your chances of getting ripped off. Often times in their pursuit of being "employee friendly," organizations are hesitant to say no to employees. An employee sees something being scrapped that they could use at home, such as damaged inventory, obsolete computer hardware, or unneeded hardware that comes with purchased materials, and asks if they can have it. Yes, I agree that it's a shame to throw away something that could be used by someone, but consider the potential for theft that you are opening up. If you are going to allow these activities, you need to have a bulletproof formal process for it. Including having a person of responsibility sign off on the materials to ensure that they actually are unusable or obsolete.

✔ **Run an ethical business.** If the employees know that management lies, cheats, and steals, are they more likely to follow suit? Those at the top levels of organizations are often the ones that most unashamedly rationalize their unethical practices into "acceptable" practices. The "corporate accounting scandals of 2002" are in full swing as I am writing this book, and I don't believe anyone that has been involved in business management can honestly say they were surprised. Do you use "creative accounting" methods to reduce tax exposure or mislead shareholders? Do you reward managers for obtaining confidential information and trade secrets from competitors? Do you violate confidentiality agreements with customers or suppliers if you think it can increase your bottom line? Do you look for ways to get around software licenses? Do you save a few bucks by making copies of copyright-protected training materials and internal-use forms? Do you do these things and still have the nerve to be "appalled" when one of your employees steals from you?

There is no doubt that you have people in your workforce that are willing to steal. However, just because someone is willing, does not mean that they will steal from you. Put in place control policies, eliminate opportunities for theft, pay attention to what's going on throughout your operations, and provide a fair and ethical work environment that promotes honesty. Though no industry is immune from theft, there are certainly varying levels of risk. For those in higher risk environments, it is advisable to get professional help from a loss prevention specialist.

I've primarily covered theft as it occurs within the four walls of your facilities. Theft during transportation is also a potential issue. Once again the accuracy of internal processes will play a key role in identifying this type of theft. If you have high levels of confidence in your picking and loading processes, you are much more likely to "know" if a shortage is related to theft or not. For truckload and container shipments you should also have clear policies in place related to applying and removing seals. Allowing the pickup/delivery drivers to apply or remove seals is a ridiculously common practice. If you are concerned about the security of your loads, you need to make sure they are sealed and unsealed by your staff. You also need to make sure the person unsealing the load verifies the seal identification.

Manufacturing processes general observations

Is it possible to use the terms "manufacturing" and "inventory accuracy" together without cringing? There is no doubt that inventory accuracy in manufacturing operations is usually far worse than in warehousing/distribution operations. While a portion of this can be attributed to a difference in priorities, there are also some significant factors related to manufacturing processes that contribute to this industry-based disparity. Basically, converting something into something else is far more complicated and more highly prone to error than just moving something around. Dealing with variable scrap and yields, bulk materials, substitutions, prototyping, custom products, setup scrap, outsourced operations, and rework, all contribute to the challenges faced by manufacturers in maintaining accuracy. Though I can't possibly cover every manufacturing topic, I will cover some of them in this chapter. And, of course, the concepts discussed in the first three chapters can be applied to any process.

I do need to address the issue of attitude in manufacturing operations towards accuracy since it can be a tremendous hurdle to overcome. Resistance to change is present in any operation, but seems to be significantly greater in manufacturing operations. This is especially true (though not exclusively so) in manufacturing operations that have been in existence for a long time. "Set in their ways" would be a considerable understatement in describing attitudes in many of these operations. They have probably gone through many a failed attempt in the past to improve accuracy and operations in general, and have resigned themselves to the thought that "this is how it will always be" and " why should I make an effort to change if it ultimately isn't going to work anyway." Significant efforts need to be made to convince the manufacturing folks that the changes you are suggesting will actually help them. And once the decision-makers have agreed to the changes, strict enforcement must be applied. You will have to "force" some people to change their ways.

And you better be damn certain that the initial changes you are planning on implementing will work. You will likely have some people expecting the changes to fail and possibly others that will actually try to make the changes fail. You absolutely cannot afford a single bad decision in the early stages of an accuracy initiative in these types of operations.

That being said, there is no reason that you cannot expect to achieve high levels of accuracy in manufacturing operations. Though you may not achieve the same levels of accuracy possible in pure distribution operations, you can likely achieve levels that are far above that which you are currently experiencing.

24/7

I'm not going to kid you. Maintaining inventory accuracy in an operation that never stops is tough. When we discuss 24/7 we are most likely talking about manufacturing operations. For Monday-Friday workers (materials managers, production planners, inventory analysts, cycle count administrators) that are often responsible for managing the inventory in these operations, the "Monday morning damage assessment" becomes part of their weekly routine. If you've never had to manage an operation where the majority of activities occur when you are not there, you have likely not experienced the difficulties and frustrations that go along with these environments.

The biggest issues with nonstop, multi-shift operations are that there are no clean end-of-days or end-of-weeks where you can easily run cycle counts or review exception reports. There is also more likely to be a lack of ownership of processes due to the multiple shifts, communication across all shifts can be very challenging, and the lack of management presence on nights and weekends contributes to the usual problematic activities (you know — horseplay, shenanigans, tomfoolery and the like).

Now for the good news . . . OK, there may not be much real good news here. 24/7 is tough, and it takes a lot of work to maintain accuracy in these environments. Well-designed processes and a well-trained workforce are even more critical in these operations. For the most part, the accuracy improvement methods you would apply to a single shift operation also apply to a multi-shift one. The emphasis on training is very important here since the level of supervision and availability of expertise found on the day shift is rarely the same as that found on night and weekend shifts.

Accountability is critical in 24/7. Multi-shift operations are plagued by the "it's the other shift" syndrome. It's extremely beneficial to have measurements in place that allow you to isolate specific shifts and individual worker's performance measures. This includes performance related to productivity, quality, accuracy, safety, and housekeeping.

Communication is another real challenge in 24/7 environments where you may have combinations of fixed and rotating shifts. This was actually one of the most difficult challenges that I faced when I moved from a simple split shift operation to managing a workforce in a 24/7 environment. The operation had some real inventory problems and I was implementing process changes almost daily (I know this is not the way I recommend implementing process changes, but this was a very special set of circumstances). Coming from an environment where I could readily assemble entire departments to educate them on changes, to an environment where I never had more than 25 percent of the workforce in the building at the same time (I actually had one employee that I would not see for months at a time) forced me to quickly find new communications methods. Email accounts, physical mailboxes, a bulletin board with daily updates, and even a web site can all prove to be very useful in making sure everyone is informed. Stay away from voice mail; written communications are much better and I just plain hate voice mail. Set a formalized format for the communications and make sure everyone is aware of their responsibilities towards checking and updating any communications.

Cycle counting in 24/7

The end-of-the-day or first-thing-in-the-morning time slots that are usually used for cycle counting in other environments rarely apply in a 24/7 operation. Since suggesting, "operations need to be shut down so I can cycle count" will probably get you fired, you're going to need some other options. Cycle counting in a 24/7 environment requires imagination and flexibility. It's all about looking for "count opportunities." Free yourself from the constraints of conventional cycle count methodology and find ways to isolate and count inventory without stopping production.

Here are some tips on cycle counting in a 24/7 environment:

✔ **Isolate storage areas for counting.** Though your manufacturing operations may be running nonstop, you can usually find or create short periods of time when storage areas can be isolated and counted. If you are issuing as you pick inventory for production, all you need to do is make sure everything picked has been issued. If you are using backflushing or issuing materials as they are consumed, you need to create logical locations or physical locations that represent manufacturing areas (machine-specific locations are common). You then must use a location transfer program to transfer quantities from storage areas to production areas as they are moved. Now, as long as you can hold off on any activities in a specific storage area for a short period of time, you can conduct your counts. I recommend using the "variance location" scenario I detailed in chapter four. Granted, any items that have quantities in the production areas will not have a complete "item-level" count completed. You will, however, be validating all stored quantities, which is often the majority of your inventory. We will take care of the production quantities another way.

✔ **Count items that are not currently running.** This is a pretty obvious one, but it's surprising how many companies fail to take advantage of it. In many manufacturing environments, only a small portion of the total SKU base is running at any given point of time. It's usually fairly simple to cycle through all or most of your inventory by counting items when they are not currently active. As discussed in the cycle counting chapter, counting materials immediately after a production run can be a very effective count approach.

✔ **Count during shift changes.** Again, this is unique to the operation, but if there are short periods of time at shift changeovers where production is not actually occurring (even just 5 or 10 minutes), you can take this opportunity to count inventory at the machines or assembly stations. It is imperative that transactions are completed each shift for the materials used and produced during that shift. For example, if the machine operator stops production five minutes before the end of the shift to enter transactions and forward paperwork, you can start counting as soon as they stop producing. Then just compare your counts to the system after they have entered their transactions. Yes, I know, you are only going to get a few counts at a time this way, but remember you are only doing this for items that are currently running. In most operations, this is not that much.

✔ **Count during machine setup/changeover or during preventative maintenance.** This is the same principle as the shift changeover scenario outlined above. Time your counts to coincide with times when production is not running. This can be between production runs, during preventative maintenance, or even when a machine breaks down. Just try not to seem so excited about the fact that a machine has broken down. Again, it's important to make sure all transactions have been processed.

✔ **Count during production?** This is certainly not my preferred method, but it is possible if you are really on top of your game. If you can figure out what has been run but not yet reported, and how much is currently at the machines, you have enough information to compare and adjust inventory.

It is not unreasonable to use all of these techniques in an operation in order to count all materials. Since the execution of the count process must be completed in a very short period of time in some of these situations, it is unlikely that you will use formal cycle count programs (select counts, freeze inventory balances, count, enter counts, recounts, investigate, approve) to achieve this. Quick inventory reports, screen prints, or handwritten forms, combined with manual adjustments, are more likely to be the method of choice for these types of counts.

Exception reports and process audits are also very important in 24/7 environments. Figure out the common types of errors that occur in your operation and try to find ways to identify them quickly.

One of the benefits to 24/7 is that the use of equipment and technology over multiple shifts results in a much more favorable return on investment on accuracy-related technologies. I highly recommend that those in 24/7 environments exploit this advantage.

Point-of-use inventory and floor stock

Floor stock is inventory that is consumed in production but is not tracked in the perpetual inventory system. Floor stock is different from non-stock inventory since it does actually have an SKU number and item master record. But rather than tracking quantities in the inventory system, the materials are expensed as they are received. These are usually lower cost items such as hardware or consumables such as adhesives, oils, etc. The primary reason for designating inventory as floor stock is you don't want to have to execute inventory transactions every time you use it. If you have an inventory system that is capable of backflushing inventory (discussed later), I see no reason to designate inventory as floor stock since you can automate the inventory transactions.

Point-of-use inventory may or may not also be floor stock. Point-of-use inventory is basically stored at the place where it is used (makes sense). The reason for storing inventory at the point-of-use is you don't need the additional handling of discretely picking quantities and moving them to the production areas each time they are needed. It is also useful for bulk materials that can't be easily picked in specific quantities. Though the machine operator or assembler could discretely issue point-of-use inventory as it is used, the preferred method is to use backflushing. Point-of-use inventory may also have additional reserve storage areas. When reserve storage areas are used, a method for replenishing the point-of-use inventory as it is depleted is necessary.

Counting point-of-use inventory is achieved through the methods described previously in "cycle counting in a 24/7 environment." Basically you need to find points in the production process when you can isolate the inventory, make sure all transactions have been processed, conduct your counts, and make your adjustments.

Outside operations

"Outside operation" is a term used to describe a specific step in the manufacturing process that is outsourced, and the associated transactions used to process and track it. There are two significant problems with outside operations. First, most people don't understand how the inventory system tracks and processes outside operations. Second, the process for transacting outside operations is cumbersome and difficult in most software systems.

Resolving problems related to outside operations is primarily an educational issue (though systems can be used to simplify the processing). Those involved with planning or processing outside operations need to understand both the physical process and the transactional systems used. An outside operation exists when an outside supplier is used to transform materials that are not owned by the outside supplier. The outside operation may be the entire manufacturing process or any part of the manufacturing process. You may have several outside operations as well as several internal operations used within a manufacturing process.

The basic flow involves sending materials to the outside supplier to undergo some type of processing. The materials are returned after the processing, and are either received into stock (if the manufacturing process is completed) or forwarded to the next operation (internal or external).

The problems don't really lay with the physical flow — which is relatively straightforward — but rather with the complex transactions that are needed to track the activities. In standardized accounting/MRP systems, transactions related to transformation of materials are achieved through the production order process, and transactions related to purchasing of materials and services are achieved through the purchase order process. In the case of an outside operation, you are doing both. The most common way to achieve this is to associate a purchase order line with a step in the manufacturing routing. A routing is a mechanism used to describe and track the various steps (operations) in the manufacturing process. Each operation will represent a separate transformation activity, such as extruding, cutting, drilling, welding, heat-treating, painting, etc. If heat-treating is outsourced, that step in the routing is considered an outside operation and will have a purchase order associated with it. It's important to note that the purchase order is not used to purchase and receive an item, but rather to purchase and receive a service. When an outside operation purchase order is received, though you are receiving a quantity, that quantity is representing a service, not an item. The receipt provides the information that allows you to pay the supplier, and also adds the cost of the service to the production order (via WIP account, discussed later) to allow proper accounting of costs. This cost information associated with the routing, is also used during the cost-rollup process to estimate product cost.

In order to properly advance the production order, you will also have to post production associated with the outside operation against the production order. If this is the only operation or last operation in the manufacturing process, on-hand inventory will be updated at this point. If additional operations need to be completed, on-hand will not be affected; the production order will simply be advanced to the next operation.

This can be extremely confusing to the folks on the receiving dock. They need to first identify that the receipt is an outside operation. They then need to process the receipt through the receiving program, and also process the production order through the production-reporting program. Often times this requires them to "figure out" the production order number either through paper documents or computer inquiry programs. They also need to know which specific operation they are reporting against. Once they report against the production order, they need to know what to do with the materials. If the operation was the last step in the process, the materials are now "inventory" and can be put into storage. If it was not the final operation, the materials are part of WIP and need to be forwarded to the next manufacturing operation (internal or external). Add the fact that they may also need to report scrap associated with the outside operation, and may also need to determine if this is the entire receipt associated with the outside operation or a partial shipment, and you can see the opportunities for confusion and error.

If all of this isn't confusing enough, you'll find that many software packages do a very poor job of simplifying and error proofing the transaction process. In some systems, the complexity of correctly executing these types of transactions is simply beyond the skill level of many receiving personnel. In fact, the complexity is also often beyond the skill level of the planning personnel responsible for planning and managing these processes. What is really needed here is automation of the transaction process along with system validation to ensure the various transactions are completed in the correct sequence and quantities. While some software packages have automated various parts of the process, I have yet to see one that has achieved a level of automation and validation that significantly reduces the opportunities for error.

Here are some suggestions for improving outside operations transaction programs:

✔ Receiving an outside operation should not require a multistep process. The entry of the receipt should automatically report production against the production order. With the exception of scrap and received quantity, all information related to reporting production is known by the system. There is no reason to have to enter this info manually through additional steps.

✔ The only additional information required at receipt would be related to production scrap. A simplified popup window can provide entry of this information.

✔ System should not allow processing against an operation if the previous operation has not yet been reported against.

✔ System should not allow reporting a total quantity (good and scrap) against an operation that is greater than the total quantity reported against the previous operation.

✔ System should provide warning if the total quantity (good and scrap) reported against an operation is less than the total quantity reported against the previous operation.

✔ System should automatically update on-hand if the final operation is reported against, and should produce a receipt document similar to those produced for a normal purchase order receipt.

✔ System should not produce a receipt document if the operation being reported against is not the final operation. Instead it should produce a routing that clearly identifies the current and next operation.

✔ System should similarly allow the reversal of receipts with proper validations.

✔ System should provide referential integrity between the production order and all associated purchase orders. It should prevent the cancellation of any document if other documents remain open. It should also prevent differences in quantities between the production order and all associated purchase orders.

These do not fall into the category of "simple modifications." As with some of the other suggestions in this book, this one is pointed more towards the software companies. If you have a large operation with frequent outside operation transactions, you may want to consider these modifications. It may even be that there are already packages available that do all of this. I have just not run into them.

For those unable to fix their system, there are steps that can be done to help in preventing errors in the outside operation process.

✔ Find a way to easily identify outside operations at receipt. This will vary from system to system but may include separate purchase order numbering systems, a popup window in the receipt program, employee education as to specific vendors and materials that are outside operations, or systematically preventing processing of an outside operation receipt in the standard receiving program.

✔ Have the outside operation receipt produce a bar-coded document that can then be used with a programmable keyboard-wedge scanner to automate the processing of the production order.

✔ Use a locator system and a receiving staging location. This way, if someone tries to put away in-process materials as though they were the finished item, you would end up with a negative balance in the receiving location (see, negative balances can be helpful).

✔ Use exception reporting to identify variances between sequential operations.

✔ Use exception reporting to identify variances between outside operation purchase orders and their associated production orders.

In addition you need to train your people on the outside operation process. And, you need at least one person that has an exceptional understanding of the entire process. This person needs to be consulted when anything unusual comes up related to outside operations. Some examples of when serious problems can occur would include:

❏ Someone trying to change the vendor for an outside operation after the production order has been initiated.

❏ Someone trying to delete an outside operation production order or related purchase orders.

❏ Someone trying to outsource an operation after the production order has been initiated.

❏ Someone trying to reverse a receipt against an outside operation.

It's very important that all system setup that is associated with outside operations is correct before initiating the production order. Any changes that occur after the production order has been created are very likely to cause problems.

Scrap reporting.

Production scrap.

Production scrap falls into two categories — scrap associated with the manufactured item, and scrap associated with individual components or raw materials. If you are assembling cameras and break a lens during the assembly process, the broken lens would be considered component scrap provided you could remove it and replace it with a good lens. If the entire camera were determined to be bad, that would be manufactured-item scrap. Knowing the difference is important, since you will report it in different ways. While this sounds simple, it is not always so. Let's say that we are machining a casting, and then adding bushings, bearings, and grease fittings. It may be obvious that a bad casting, bushing, bearing, or grease fitting would be component scrap, and a defective completed item would be manufactured item scrap, but what happens when you have machined the casting and added the bushings (but not the bearings and grease fittings) before you noticed the casting was defective? Depending upon the way that you issue materials and report production, this can be a real problem. More on that later.

Reporting scrap associated with the manufactured item is usually a fairly straightforward process. When you report production against an operation, you will usually have the option to enter a "good quantity" and a "scrap quantity." Though the basic transaction is simple, there are frequent problems with this type of scrap reporting. The most common problem is inaccurately counting scrap or failing to report scrap. Since scrap covers such a wide range of materials in manufacturing processes, there is no single solution for this. What you should try to do is make it as easy as possible to determine the scrap quantity. Machine counters, scales, or containers designed to hold a specific quantity of scrap, are techniques that can be used to assist in tracking scrap. Another problem sometimes encountered is related to confusion over units-of-measure when reporting scrap. If your stocking unit-of-measure is cases, it is likely you will report production in this unit-of-measure. While employees may understand this for reporting "good" quantities, they sometimes become confused when reporting scrap, and instead report the piece quantity. This can be a very serious problem if you are backflushing components since you will end up significantly over issuing materials.

Reporting scrap associated with components or raw materials can be tricky. If you are backflushing components, you will generally need to go into the detail screen of the backflushing program and enter scrap quantities on specific components. This can be problematic, and I will generally try to avoid this type of scrap reporting unless you have frequent scrap and relatively simple bills of materials. An option in a backflushing environment is to just keep component scrap separate and use manual scrap transactions to account for it. If you are issuing materials as they are consumed, all you really need to do is make sure that you issue the full quantity used (good and scrap). If you are pre-issuing as items are picked from storage areas, you will need a process to request more materials (since exact quantities are generally picked in a pre-issue process) and have them issued to the specific production order. Since it is possible to use several issuing methods within a single production order, you may need to have several scrap reporting procedures in place.

The way you process scrap will have a lot to do with your manufacturing processes, reporting systems, and the frequency of scrap. If scrap is a rare occurrence, you may want to have a limited number of trained individuals that are authorized to approve and report scrap. Where scrap is a normal part of the manufacturing process, you will want to try make the scrap reporting as simple as possible. In addition, you will need to train the workers and make sure they are held accountable for accurately reporting scrap.

Damage.

Scrap associated with damage incurred during material handling and transportation processes can also be a challenge. Often called shrinkage, this type of scrap often goes unreported due to a lack of procedures or a fear of retribution. Here are some tips on minimizing inventory problems related to damage.

✔ Design material handling processes to minimize risk of product damage.

✔ Train material handling equipment operators on safe use of equipment.

✔ Hold material handling equipment operators accountable for following procedures related to operating material handling equipment.

✔ Have a formal process in place for reporting damage.

✔ Hold employees responsible for reporting damage.

✔ Don't discipline workers when they report damage they have caused. Instead, discipline them when they are observed not following procedures.

The last tip is very important. If your lift truck operators are driving in an unsafe manner, you should be stopping them and disciplining them when this behavior is observed. You should not wait until they damage inventory or cause injury before disciplining them.

Work-in-process tracking

Work-in-process (WIP), also known as work-in-progress, presents some very unique challenges. Outside of maybe one or two people in the accounting department, it is unlikely that there are others in the organization that actually understand what WIP is and how it is tracked. In most manufacturing systems, WIP is simply an inventory account. It is not an inventory tracking system. It is the summarized value of in-process materials.

I need to clarify a little further what is considered "in-process materials." In-process materials are materials that no longer exist as specific SKUs. Subassemblies or partially processed materials that can be tracked by an SKU number do not fall under this category and are not considered as WIP, provided they have not yet been issued to a production order. WIP classification is actually the result of your bill-of-material structure. Let me again use the example of a casting that gets machined, and then has bushings, bearings, and grease fittings added to it. If your bill-of-material structure is set up such that the casting, bearings, bushings, and grease fittings, are on a single-level bill, and your manufacturing process performs the machining and the assembly steps all under the same production order, these materials will be part of WIP from the time they are issued to the production order until the time the finished item is produced. However, if your bill-of-material structure is setup so that the casting is on a bill that only has the machining process, and there is an SKU set up for the "machined casting" that is on another bill along with the bushings, bearings, and grease fittings that is used to assemble the finished item, the machined casting is now a "stockable" item and is therefore not part of WIP (that is, it is not part of WIP from the time it is reported as being produced, until the time it is issued to the assembly production order).

This is probably the biggest misconception among shop-floor personnel (management and general workforce) about WIP. They tend to think it is based solely on the physical state of the materials, when, in fact, it is based upon the structure of the bills-of-materials and the transactional status of the materials. The transactional status of the materials is a result of the issuing process. If I pick materials and issue them to production orders as I deliver them to the production area, they are now part of WIP. However, if I deliver those same materials to the production area, but they will be issued as consumed or backflushed, they are not part of WIP until they are issued.

As you can see, before you attempt to "count" or "track" WIP, you need to understand what it is in your environment. You also need to understand that you cannot count or track WIP the way you do your other inventory. From a system standpoint, WIP does not exist as discrete units of inventory, therefore you cannot run a cycle count or standard inventory report on it.

WIP basically works like this: The value of materials issued to a production order, the value of labor reported against a production order, and the value of overhead applied to a production order (usually tied to labor or machine hours reported) are all added to the WIP account. The value of the finished materials (good and scrap) reported against a production order are deducted from the WIP account. Hence, what's left in the WIP account should be the dollar value of in-process materials.

Unfortunately, there are a lot of reasons for the WIP account being out-of-whack. Costing methods, scrap, inconsistent production rates, specific operator pay rate, labor reporting errors, and inventory reporting errors will all create WIP problems. Because of all of these contributing factors, ownership of WIP accuracy cannot be easily placed in any single department. This often results in no ownership of the WIP process. Since an "out-of-whack" WIP account does not directly impact planning or execution systems, its accuracy is often not given priority by those that work in these areas.

Though I mentioned that problems with a WIP account may not directly impact operations, they can help to point out related inventory problems. While a WIP problem is not necessarily an inventory problem, any inventory error associated with production reporting will result in a WIP problem.

In most operations, the production order is the key to WIP tracking. By monitoring variances at the production order level, you can identify problems and take appropriate actions. This will allow you to maintain a relatively accurate WIP account and identify potential inventory problems related to the manufacturing process. Most systems will have a "variance-by-production-order" report available. If your system doesn't have this, you should look into having one created. Though most systems will have the data necessary to create this report, it is not necessarily a simple report to create. A production order variance report lists the WIP inputs and outputs associated with a specific production order and calculates the difference, which is essentially the WIP associated with that production order. If your production runs are relatively short, you will likely only review this report for production orders that are completed. This allows you to identify potential errors and write off any WIP variances associated with each production order. In doing this as a formal process, you will ensure that your WIP account is not accumulating variances from past production orders. Though this doesn't ensure that WIP is correct, it does at least ensure that any problems with WIP are related to current production orders.

My basic recommendation related to actually counting WIP is to do everything possible to avoid it. If you monitor production order variance reports, write off variances, and improve processes to reduce WIP variances, your WIP account should be relatively accurate (absolute WIP accuracy is impossible in most manufacturing operations). If you haven't been writing off variances as production orders have been completed, you can run a production order variance report against all current active production orders. The sum of the variances is essentially the total value of WIP associated with these open orders. The difference between this amount and the amount in your WIP account is basically the value of WIP variances from previous production runs and should therefore be written off.

If you do want to try to physically validate your current production against the WIP count you need to find a way to calculate piece quantities associated with each production order. This can be done by subtracting the quantity produced (good and bad) at an operation from the quantity produced (good only) at the previous operation. This will work for all but the first operation. Depending on how you handle production runs, you may be able to calculate the first operation as requested quantity minus produced quantity of all active orders at that operation. While this gets you some quantity info, you can't easily translate these quantities into dollars since the value of these in-process materials is not usually tracked. Often times, companies will develop "estimations of value" that are used to help in validating WIP. These will vary by industry, but are essentially little "shortcuts" or "cheat sheets" used to estimate WIP value for comparison to the WIP account. These are often used on month-end or year-end to validate the WIP account. Though this doesn't sound like the best approach to accuracy, it can be a reasonable compromise.

I have described the most common WIP environment (production order-based system). Make sure you first consult with your accounting department before you try to reconcile WIP. You may find that your organization uses different methods to track WIP. You may also find variations such as generically issuing materials directly to the WIP account without tying transactions to specific production orders. These variations will require different validation strategies.

Backflushing and other issuing techniques

I've referred to backflushing at many points throughout this book, and I want to make it clear that I am not suggesting that every manufacturer should be using backflushing. I do, however, feel many manufacturers that could benefit by backflushing have dismissed it as an option due to a lack of understanding of backflushing. I also feel that many companies already using backflushing can improve their accuracy by having a better understanding of the process.

Backflushing is a somewhat misleading term used to describe a method used in manufacturing operations to issue materials to production orders at the point that production of a specific operation is completed. To make things clearer, for a portion of this chapter, I will refer to backflushing as "postproduction issuing." I will also use the term "preproduction issuing" to describe the method(s) for issuing material most people are familiar with. It's important to discuss the similarities in the programs used to execute postproduction issuing and preproduction issuing to demonstrate that the two methods are essentially small variations of a single process.

Preproduction issuing.
When you create a production order, you will usually enter some very basic information such as item number, requested quantity, and requested date (in most MRP systems this information is automatically entered when you convert a planned order). This information (known as the production order header) is then used to create the materials list (also called parts list or pick list) and the routing for this specific production order. The materials list is created by multiplying the quantity required from the order header by the quantity per of each component on the bill of materials, which results in a detailed materials list showing each component, the quantity per, and the total quantity required to produce the requested quantity of the finished item.

When it comes time to start production, there are several methods used to accumulate the materials required for production. One method is to simply use the materials list and pick all of the materials, transporting them to the production area. You then use a program designed to issue the components to a specific production order. This program will generally require you to enter the production order number to bring up the materials list. You can then accept the entire materials list as a single transaction and the program will issue the quantity on each detail line to the production order, reducing on-hand balances by that quantity. If the materials list did not specify the locations the materials were to be picked from (directed picking) you would have to enter that detail information before completing the transaction. The program will probably also have an option to increase or decrease the entire materials list at the header level by changing the quantity required of the finished item; all detail lines will then recalculate based on this quantity. You would also have options to change quantities on individual detail lines or only issue individual detail lines.

While this is the most common method for accumulating the required materials and issuing them there are quite a few variations. You may have some materials that are stocked at the machine; these are referred to as point-of-use materials. You may have the person that picked the materials also go ahead and issue the point-of-use materials even though they haven't actually picked them or you may have the operator issue these during production. You may also have situations where the amount of materials required to complete the entire production order is too large to stage at the machine all at once and smaller quantities are picked and issued as production requires. In this type of issuing you may use the previously described program, selecting individual lines and specifying quantity picked on each trip, or you may use a separate program where you enter the component item number, the quantity, and the production order number to directly issue individual transactions to the specific production order. This type of transaction program and process will likely be highly prone to errors unless used with an automatic data collection system and bar coding.

Postproduction issuing.
In postproduction issuing (backflushing) you are not issuing the materials until production is posted (reported) against the operation. The materials may be accumulated through whatever means are most efficient for your operation. Once the operation is completed the operator will use a program to post the production against the operation. The operator will generally enter the production order number, operation, quantity good, scrap quantity, and labor and machine information. The production-reporting program will then bring up the issuing program (essentially the same program as in the preproduction issuing) using the sum of the good and scrap quantity to recalculate the materials required. You generally then issue all of the materials as one transaction just as you would have in the preproduction issue. You would also have options to change individual item quantities and add individual scrap quantities to detail lines. Another option commonly used in postproduction issuing is to have the issuing program work in the background without the operator ever seeing it (blind backflushing).

Now you can see that the difference between preproduction issuing and postproduction issuing is essentially just the timing of the transactions and a little transaction automation. So where is it advantageous to use backflushing?

- ❏ In operations where scrap is common in the finished item and you continue to produce until you have a good quantity equal to the ordered quantity, you will find postproduction issuing will simplify the issuing process since you won't know how many you will run until you have completed production.

- ❏ When you use point-of-use materials, postproduction issuing simplifies the issuing process and makes it easier to perform counts on the point-of-use materials. If you were to preproduction issue these materials you would need to rectify the system counts with any orders that had quantities issued but not yet consumed. However, if you postproduction issue you should have a system-to-actual-count match after each production posting.

❏ In very long production runs (days or weeks), where preproduction posting takes the materials out of the on-hand inventory balance days or weeks before they are being used and puts the dollar value into a WIP account. Anyone that has tried to rectify WIP accounts will tell you that the less you have in the WIP account, and the quicker things come out of the WIP account, the better off you are. It's far easier to track inventory than WIP. You also may have situations where you don't have enough of the raw materials for the entire production run, however more will be arriving during the run (JIT/Kanban); preproduction posting would force inventory of the raw materials negative. It's important to note I am assuming that if you are doing long production runs you are periodically (each shift or each day) posting quantities produced rather than waiting until the entire run is complete.

❏ When you are using bulk materials such as bar stock, roll stock, sheet goods, and dry goods or liquids in bulk containers, where the exact quantity cannot be picked. For example if you need 1,000 linear feet of material that comes in bulk rolls of 300 linear feet, preproduction issuing of 1,000 even though the material handler delivered 1,200 causes a confusing inventory situation, and issuing the entire 1,200 would require you to reverse issue 200 when you return the remainder.

For a simplified example of an operation where postproduction issuing would make sense I'll create a fictitious company that makes prepackaged food products for vending machines. This company, called *The Taste Like Cardboard Snack Company*, has set up a production work cell for their sandwich assembly that makes several combinations of sandwiches on white or wheat bread, with ham, turkey, or beef, American or Swiss cheese, and mustard or mayonnaise. This results in about one hundred separate finished combinations, and they will generally run about thirty production orders per shift.   The final step in the assembly is to run the sandwich through an automated heat-seal packaging machine which, despite their best efforts, manages to trash about one percent of the sandwiches run through it. Since they are a make-to-order manufacturer with no tolerances allowed the company must produce the exact number of good sandwiches as ordered.

Since they are dealing with very few components (only nine) to make up all of these combinations it would make sense to treat these components as point-of-use materials, especially since they are stored in bulk form. Trying to pick and segregate exact quantities of mustard, mayonnaise, meat, cheese, and bread for each production order would be inefficient (and probably messy). Due to the scrap problem you really don't know how many sandwiches you will need to make to get the correct quantity, so preproduction issuing would force you to go back and enter additional transactions for the scrap materials. While it may be possible to use digital scales for the meat and cheese, flow meters for the mayonnaise and mustard, and a counter for the bread to try to automatically capture exact quantities used per production order, it just isn't a cost-effective option, and having the production operators manually track actual usage will likely prove to be an accuracy nightmare. The best option here is to use blind postproduction posting (blind backflushing). All the operator needs to do is enter the good quantity and the scrap quantity and let the system calculate the rest.

A real-world example of postproduction posting I recently encountered was for a manufacturer of paperboard based packaging materials. One of the families of products produced were round lids that consisted of a custom printed insert, rim base material, rim label material, and adhesive. The inserts were stocked on pallets of anywhere from 20,000 to 200,000 depending on size. The rim base material and rim label material were on bulk rolls, and the adhesive came in bulk containers. The forming of the lids was a single operation on a single machine. This forming operation was highly prone to scrap and the company was a make-to-order operation that required a specific good quantity be produced. Production runs could go from several hours to several days and would be grouped so that multiple orders using the same rim base material and rim label material were run consecutively.

All of the raw materials were stored in random location storage in the warehouse. Material handlers would deliver rim base material, rim label material, adhesive, and inserts as needed to keep the machine running. Material handlers would enter location transfer transactions to move the materials from the storage locations to a specific machine location set up for the lid forming machine. When the production operator finished an order, or when the shift ended, the operator would post quantity good and quantity scrapped; the backflush program would then calculate material requirements and issue them from the machine location.

By using machine locations for the backflushing we essentially isolated the storage locations from the production reporting system and were able to maintain cycle counting in the storage areas. By the way, did I mention that this was a 24/7 operation? This also gave the benefit of very quickly catching production reporting errors just by monitoring the inventory at the machine locations.

Tips on implementing postproduction issuing (backflushing)

✔ Backflushing is performed by operation; in the bill of material you will have to link the component to the specific operation and set the backflushing flag. You may also have to set backflushing flags on the specific operation in the routing, the program used for production posting, and at the machine/cost center level. The details of each system may vary, so read the documentation for your specific software.

✔ You may also find backflush flags on the item master. If so, this is likely used only as a default in setting up bills of material. Changing this to backflush will probably not change any existing bills previously created.

✔ Changing an item on a bill of material to backflush will likely not change the item on the materials lists on any existing production orders previously created. You will probably have to change these manually or delete and recreate the orders.

✔ Backflushing is generally not a global setting, which means you can choose specific bills of materials to backflush and even specific items within a bill of material. For example, you could backflush only point-of-use items and perform preproduction issuing on other items within the same production order.

✔ Bills of material often have options for entering scrap percentages. Note that this scrap information is usually only used for materials planning purposes and will probably not have any effect on the backflush quantities, however you should test to see how your system handles this.

✔ I highly recommend setting up machine locations and backflushing from these locations rather than backflushing from specific storage locations (this is often set up at the machine/cost center level, however, it may be set up on the item master, bill of material, or routing). Items stored in specific locations should be transferred to the machine location when picked for production.

✔ You may need to set up some alternative picking documents. Creating a report that consolidates all materials required at a specific operation for all production orders expected to be run during that shift gives you the efficiency of batch picking. Point-of-use items can be treated similar to the way you would replenish forward picking locations in a distribution operation.

✔ If you are using lot tracking of components, you may not be able to perform blind backflushing, you will probably need to enter lot information in the detail of the issuing program.

✔ Need I mention that accurate bills of material and routings are critical.

✔ Thoroughly test your system. Verify the effects on inventory accounts, on hand balances, allocations, and locations.

Backflushing is simply a method for issuing materials that — like any other method — works well when applied correctly and works poorly when applied incorrectly. People that fear backflushing usually don't understand it. Operations not using point-of-use materials, bulk materials, or those where production scrap does not force an increase in run quantities will find little benefit to backflushing. Contract manufacturers and engineer-to-order manufacturers may find system setup too extensive, or bill of material accuracy inadequate, to support backflushing. Operations that have or can easily put in place automated data collection systems to accurately issue exact quantities to production orders will also have no need to consider backflushing.

I like backflushing because it automates the materials issuing process (a process frequently plagued by errors). If you know the exact quantity of each raw material or component required to make one unit of the end item, why not automate the issuing process? Backflushing ensures that if "it should have taken these parts to make this other part" then "these parts" are actually issued to that production order.

Transitions.

The topic of "transitions" is very broad, covering everything from software implementations, to plant relocations, to new product line introductions, to new storage configurations. Though these are infrequent occurrences, their potential for creating disastrous inventory problems is fairly high. These problems are generally the result of a lack of planning, a lack of knowledge of the systems and related processes, and a lack of training of the workforce affected by the transition. Yes, these are all management-decision-related problems.

The problems start when those managers responsible for the planning of the transition oversimplify the implications of the transition. This is followed by an inadequate plan that is characterized by bad process decisions and an underestimation of resource requirements. Next comes a chaotic implementation, which usually spurs some additional bad process decisions when it becomes obvious that the original plan was inadequate. Soon the chaotic implementation progresses into the chaotic aftermath. In the chaotic aftermath stage, more hastily made bad decisions are implemented to try to quickly dig your way out of the hole created by the previous bad decisions. Eventually, through a lot of unnecessary work, most of the problems created by the transition are fixed. Now the managers wipe their foreheads, pat themselves on the backs for a job well done, and proceed to screw up the next transition, having learned nothing from their previous mistakes.

I don't mean to be unduly abusive to managers, but these problems fall squarely onto their shoulders. When it comes to inventory-related problems created by these transitions, the lack of systems knowledge of managers tends to be the biggest contributing factor. With today's highly complex integrated information systems, it becomes increasingly important that those people planning the transition are very knowledgeable in the systems and processes that control or are affected by the transition, or include people in the decision-making process that have the detailed technical knowledge. While I agree that a sign of a good manager is one that can make decisions even with limited information, I also think that many times managers are making these decisions without making an effort to get adequate information.

After the lack of systems knowledge, a lack of understanding of related processes becomes a critical problem. On top of that, add an underestimating of the types of errors that may occur during the transition, a lack of resources during the transition, and a lack of training of those involved, and the outcome is likely going to be problematic. While each transition is different, there are some general tips that can help in being successful.

✔ **Have a plan. No, I mean a REAL plan!** A transition is a process, and should therefore have a plan detailing the tasks associated with it. All of the considerations you would apply to any new process or process change should be applied to a transition plan. In fact, it's even more important in a transition since there is rarely time to react to a process problem.

✔ **Be very careful of "batch-type" data changes.** There is no doubt that the use of batch-type data changes (where a computer program is used to change, import, or create large amounts of data) can save a lot of labor as well as prevent a lot of mistakes that would occur should these changes be made manually. However, there is also a lot of risk when conducting these types of activities. If you don't thoroughly understand the way the manual program would have affected the data, your batch program may not update all of the files or fields correctly, resulting in serious system problems. Whenever practical, you should conduct test runs of the batch data changes to ensure the changes worked and that critical programs work correctly with the changed data.

✔ **Have data validation occurring during and immediately after the transition.** Data validation may be physical counts, audits, or exception reports. This should be a documented part of the transition process. Don't wait until the dust settles to start checking your data.

✔ **Contingency plans?** This really depends upon the type of transition. I generally prefer to put all efforts into making sure the primary plan works rather than spending time on backup plans. You should at least have a pretty good idea of the types of problems that may occur during the transition. Base your contingency plans on the likelihood and potential severity of these potential problems.

✔ **Big bang versus phased approach.** Think through this very carefully. There is no one best method for all transitions. As a general statement, big bang tends to be more of a risk since there is inadequate time to address unforeseen problems. Phased approach will usually require additional efforts since the transition will occur over a longer period of time and may require "work-arounds" to be performed during this extended time period. Basically you're balancing the risk of big bang against the work-arounds and ongoing disruptions caused by a phased approach.

✔ **Preparation.** Do whatever you can prior to the transition to make the transition easier. If you go back and read the preparation portion of the physical inventory chapter, you should get an idea as to the preparation process that should accompany any transition or project. Any tasks that can be conducted prior to the transition implementation should be considered.

✔ **Train your workforce.** This involves training personnel on the tasks they will perform as part of the transition as well as training them on changes that will occur as a result of the transition. I am going to keep hounding you on the training issues because they are absolutely critical to operational success. Most transitions are hectic and stressful; making sure those involved are well trained on their responsibilities will significantly reduce the stress and the chaos.

The best single piece of advice I can give on transitions is "think." Think hard about the objectives of the transition. Think hard about the potential problems that can arise as a result of the transition process. Think hard about processes that can be put in place to reduce, eliminate, or compensate for potential problems.

Glossary

1D bar code—a bar code that uses a series of bars and spaces to represent data. 1D barcodes (also called linear bar codes) are read scanning across the width of the bars (one dimension).

2D bar code—a bar code that uses small geometric shapes to represent data. 2D codes stack the shapes or use a matrix to allow more information to be stored in the same space as a 1D bar code. Whereas a 1D bar code only requires the scanner to read a single narrow band across the bar code, a 2D bar code requires the scanner to read the code both horizontally and vertically (two dimensions).

24/7—refers to operations that run non-stop 24 hours per day, 7 days per week.

ABC classification—stratification of inventory using a specific activity-based driver. Examples of ABC classifications would include ABC by velocity, ABC by units sold, ABC by dollars sold, and ABC by average inventory investment. ABC classifications may be used to determine cycle count frequencies, tolerance levels, and to break down accuracy measurements.

Absolute variance—a numeric representation of a variance that ignores whether the variance is positive or negative. A summarized variance number or amount where positive and negative variances are not allowed to offset each other.

Accuracy—correctness of data to reality. Inventory accuracy is the consistency to which the data in your inventory system is in agreement with the actual inventory in your supply chain.

Accuracy audit—a periodic verification of the accuracy of inventory by using a sampling of inventory data and physical counts to determine correctness. Accuracy audits can be used as a replacement for the annual physical inventory for financial accounting purposes.

ActiveX control—a small computer program that can be plugged into compliant applications to provide added functionality. ActiveX controls are often used to add bar code printing functionality to applications.

ADC—automated data capture. Systems of hardware and software used to automatically pass data used to process transactions in warehouses and manufacturing operations. Data capture systems may consist of fixed terminals, portable terminals and computers, radio frequency (RF) computers, and various types of bar code scanners and RFID readers.

A-frame—a type of automated picking system. A-frames are large machines that dispense items onto a conveyor that runs down the center of the machine.

AGV—automated guided vehicle. Vehicles that can be programmed to automatically drive to designated points and perform preprogrammed functions

Aisle—the physical passageway used for the travel of material handling equipment and pedestrians. Also, the location designation of the set of locations on either side of the physical aisle.

Allocations—refers to actual demand created by sales orders or production orders against a specific item. The terminology and the actual processing that controls allocations will vary from one software system to another. Basically a standard allocation is an aggregate quantity of demand against a specific item in a specific facility, standard allocations may be referred to as normal allocations, soft allocations, soft commitments, regular allocations. Standard allocations do not specify that specific units will go to specific orders. A firm allocation is an allocation against specific units within a facility such as an allocation against a specific location, lot, or serial number. Firm allocations are also referred to as specific allocations, frozen allocations, hard allocations, hard commitments, holds, reserved inventory. Standard allocations simply show that there is actual demand while firm allocations reserve or hold the inventory for the specific order designated.

Annual physical inventory—a yearly count of all inventory. *See also* Physical inventory.

APICS—American Production and Inventory Control Society. www.apics.org

ASN—advanced shipment notification. Advanced shipment notifications are used to notify a customer of a shipment. ASNs will often include PO numbers, SKU numbers, lot numbers, quantity, pallet or container number, and carton number. ASNs may be paper based, however electronic notification is preferred. Advanced shipment notification systems are usually combined with bar coded compliance labeling that allows the customer to receive the shipment into inventory through the use of bar code scanners and automated data collection systems.

ASQ—American Society for Quality. www.asq.org

ASRS—automated storage and retrieval systems. A system of rows of rack, each row has a dedicated retrieval unit that moves vertically and horizontally along the rack picking and putting away loads. Versions include unit-load ASRS and mini-load ASRS.

Audit—a verification of the accuracy of data.

Automatic mode—describes the manner by which people process information and apply actions when their attention is divided while performing repetitive tasks.

Autodiscrimination—the functionality of a bar code reader to recognize the bar code symbology being scanned thus allowing a reader to read several different symbologies consecutively

Backflush—method for issuing (reducing on-hand quantities) materials to a production order. In backflushing the material is issued automatically when production is posted against an operation. The backflushing program will use the quantity completed to calculate through the bill of material the quantities of the components used and reduce on-hand balances by this amount. *See also* Transaction by exception.

Backorder—an order that is past its required date for an item that has inadequate inventory to fill the order.

Batch computer—portable computers that are designed to periodically download data to a host system through a wired connection.

Batch picking—order picking method where orders are grouped into small batches. An order picker will pick all orders within the batch in one pass. Batch picking is usually associated with pickers with multi-tiered picking carts moving up and down aisles picking batches of usually 4 to 12 orders, however batch picking is also very common when working with automated material handling equipment such as carousels.

Bar code—a series of bars and spaces that are encoded to represent characters. Bar codes are designed to be machine-readable.

Bar code font—a font that is used to create bar codes. Additional programs are often needed to convert the bar code data into the proper format prior to applying the bar code font.

Bar code printer—a printer capable of converting characters into a bar code. A bar code printer can provide faster printing by allowing the computer to send special codes to the printer designating the data to be converted into a bar code. The printer then generates the bar code rather than requiring the computer software to generate an image of a bar code and send the image to the printer.

Bar code reader—any device that can convert a bar code image into data. Common bar code readers consist of pistol-type scanners, wand scanners, and fixed position scanners.

Bar code verifier—a device used to check the quality of a printed bar code.

Bar code symbology—a "bar code version" consisting of a set of specifications that determine how the bars and spaces are produced and later converted to numbers, letters, and characters. Bar code symbologies are broken into two primary groups: one-dimensional bar codes, and two-dimensional bar codes.

Batch-level transactions—transactions that are executed in large numbers through the use of a batch program. Batch-level transactions are usually confirmation-type transactions where the system is automatically completing a large group of transactions based on the assumption that all tasks were completed based upon the computer's recommendations. Batch-level transactions are only possible with directed tasks.

Benchmark—a measurement that is used for comparison purposes.

Benchmarking—the act of comparing measurement to a benchmark. External benchmarking seeks to compare internal measurement to measurement from an external source. Internal benchmarking seeks to compare internal measurements to historic internal measurements.

Bin—a physical storage container such as a small corrugated or plastic parts bin. Also used interchangeably with the term slot to designate a single storage location.

Blind counts—describes method used in cycle counting and physical inventories where your counters are provided with item number and location, but no quantity information.

BOM—bill of materials. Lists materials (components or ingredients) required to produce an item. Multilevel BOMs also show subassemblies and their components. Other information such as scrap factors may also be included in the BOM for use in materials planning and costing.

Brainstorming—method used to generate ideas on causes and possible solutions to process problems. A brainstorming session usually involves a group of people getting together and listing ideas. Analysis and commentary on ideas is held off until after the brainstorming session has concluded.

Built-in check—a check that intrinsically exists as part of a process.

Business objectives—the strategic goals of the organization.

Capacity—the capabilities of a process, machine, location, or facility.

Carousel—type of automated material handling equipment generally used for high volume small parts order picking operations. Horizontal carousels are a version of the same equipment used by dry cleaners to store and retrieve clothing; they have racks hanging from them that can be configured to accommodate various size storage bins. Vertical Carousels consist of a serious of horizontal trays on a vertical carousel. Vertical carousels are frequently used in laboratories and specialty manufacturing operations.

Carton—a corrugated box.

Case—a container (usually a corrugated box) that contains multiple units of an item.

CCD—charged coupled device. Used to describe a type of barcode scanner that acts like a small digital camera that takes a digital image of the barcode as opposed to the standard barcode scanner that uses a laser.

Check—any type of verification of a process or data.

Check character—characters added to a bar code to verify a correct read of the bar code. Check characters are usually the result of a mathematical calculation based upon the data in the bar code. Not all bar codes contain check characters.

Check-weighing—a method that uses scales as a check to verify the accuracy of orders or containers.

Clonable—functionality to copy programming from one device to another.

Code 128—a linear (1D) bar code symbology commonly used in warehouse and inventory tracking applications.

Commodity—a logical grouping of inventory based upon user-defined characteristics. Different industries will define commodity classifications differently. For example, in one industry they may have a classification of "building materials" that encompasses anything that would be used to describe all construction materials while another industry may have separate commodity classifications for "framing lumber," "decking materials," "fasteners," and "concrete products."

Compliance labels—standardized label formats used by trading partners usually containing bar codes. Compliance labels are used as shipping labels, container/pallet labels, carton labels, piece labels. Many bar code labeling software products now have the more common compliance label standards set up as templates.

Components—inventory used in the manufacturing process. Though some would categorize components as lower level manufactured discrete items, I consider anything used in the manufacturing process a component. I use the term synonymously with the term "raw materials." I also consider a subassembly a component.

Compounding a sample—method used with counting scales to use a smaller sample and then use the scale to build a larger quantity that is then resampled to represent the final sample.

Conditional formatting—formatting of data on reports or computer programs that changes based upon specific criteria. Examples of conditional formatting would include printing and displaying negative quantities in red, only printing the unit of measure if it is not "eaches," or printing an item number in reverse text if there are special handling instructions associated with the item. Conditional formatting is used to help focus attention on data elements when the importance of the data element may be different from one record to the next.

Configuration processing—software functionality that allows a product to be defined by selecting various pre-defined options rather than having every possible combination of options pre-defined as specific SKUs. Placing an order for a computer and specifying hard drive, processor, memory, graphics card, sound card, etc. would be an example of configuration processing.

Confirmation transactions—transactions that are completed by a simple confirmation step rather than by entering details of the transaction. Confirmation transactions are only possible when the computer already "knows" the details of the task. *See also* Transaction by exception.

Container—can be anything designed to hold (contain) materials for storage or transport including cartons, totes, drums, bags, etc.

Containerization—using standardized containers for the storage and transport of materials within a facility or supply chain. Materials are ordered in multiples of the container quantity. The benefits of containerization include reduced product damage, reduced waste (by using reusable containers), less handling, and greater levels of inventory accuracy by simplifying counting process.

Continuous improvement—a quality philosophy that assumes further improvements are always possible and that processes should be continuously reevaluated and improvements implemented.

Contract warehouse—a business that handles shipping, receiving, and storage of products on a contract basis. Contract warehouses will generally require a client to commit to a specific period of time (generally in years) for the services. Contracts may or may not require clients to purchase or subsidize storage and material handling equipment. Fees for contract warehouses may be transaction and storage based, fixed, cost plus, or any combination. *See also* Public warehouse and 3PL.

Control group—a small sample of items that are repeatedly counted over a period of time to identify process problems.

Control policy—a documented policy that describes process controls.

Coproduct—the term coproduct is used to describe multiple items that are produced simultaneously during a production run. Coproducts are often used to increase yields in cutting operations such as die cutting or sawing when it is found that scrap can be reduced by combining multiple-sized products in a single production run. Coproducts are also used to reduce the frequency of machine setups required in these same types of operations. Coproducts, also known as byproducts, are also common in process manufacturing such as in chemical plants. Although the concept of coproducts is fairly simple, the programming logic required to provide for planning and processing of coproducts is very complicated.

Counting scale—a scale that converts weight information into piece count information and vice versa.

COGS—cost of goods sold. Accounting term used to describe the total value (cost) of products sold during a specific time period. Since inventory is an asset, it is not expensed when it is purchased or produced, it goes into an asset account (the inventory account). When product is sold, the value of the product (the cost, not the sell price) is moved from the asset account to an expense account called "cost of goods sold" or COGS. COGS appears on the profit and loss statement and is also used for calculating inventory turns.

Cost of errors—the costs associated with errors. Costs of errors include both tangible and intangible costs. Tangible costs would include costs such as transportation costs incurred by expediting materials or by correcting shipping errors, cost of production delays and interruptions related to inventory errors, labor costs associated with searching for lost product, clerical costs of correcting errors, and even costs associated with a cycle count program. Intangible costs include cost of customer dissatisfaction and costs associated with employee frustration.

Count frequency—the number of times per year you plan on counting an item. Count frequency is used to calculate cycle count period. *See also* Cycle count period.

Count sheet—a document used in cycle counting and physical inventories to facilitate the counting of inventory. A count sheet will contain multiple items and locations to be counted and can be a simple report or a live document produced by cycle counting programs.

Count tag—a document used in physical inventories to facilitate the counting of inventory. A separate count tag is created for each item/location combination and a unique ID number is assigned to each count tag to facilitate data entry and verification of counts.

Cross-docking—in its purest form cross-docking is the action of unloading materials from an incoming trailer or rail car and immediately loading these materials in outbound trailers or rail cars thus eliminating the need for warehousing (storage). In reality pure cross-docking is rare outside of transportation hubs and hub-and-spoke type distribution networks. Many "cross-docking" operations require large staging areas where inbound materials are sorted, consolidated, and stored until the outbound shipment is complete and ready to ship. This staging may take hours, days, or even weeks in which case the "staging area" is essentially a "warehouse".

Cross-training—training workers in tasks outside of their normal job responsibilities.

Cube utilization—term used in warehouse management systems. Cube logic is often incorporated but seldom used in WMS systems because of its tendency to treat your product as liquid (fitting a round peg in a square hole).

Custom form—any form designed for a specific task in a specific environment.

Cycle count—any process that verifies the correctness of inventory quantity data by counting portions of the inventory on an ongoing basis. In other words, any process that uses regularly scheduled counts but does not count the entire facility's inventory in a single event.

Cycle count number—number assigned to a group of cycle counts used to facilitate tracking and updating of transactions associated with the group.

Cycle count period— a time period used in cycle counting programs to calculate the next count date based upon the previous count date. Count period is generally stated in the number of days between counts. An understanding of whether your system uses calendar days or work days is necessary to properly convert count frequency to count period. *See also* Count frequency.

Cycle time—the time that transpires from the time a task (or series of tasks) is initiated to the time a task is completed. For example, from the time a shipping order is printed to the time it is loaded on the truck and the system is updated.

Data elements—individual pieces of data in a database, on a report, or on a computer screen. Individual fields in a database file such as the item number or quantity from an inventory record are examples of data elements.

Data element identifier—text used to describe a data element. For example, the text that reads "PHONE NUMBER" that appears on a report used to identify the data element that contains the customer's phone number.

Data formatting—the specific way data elements are displayed or printed on a report or computer screen. Data formatting not only includes the font and style (bold, italics, etc.) of the text but also the inclusion of spaces or special characters to make the data element more readable.

Data identifier— a character or set of characters added to a bar code to identify the type of data included in the bar code.

DataMatrix—a two-dimensional (2D) bar code symbology.

Data selection—term that describes the "filtering" of data to only display certain records on reports or computer screens. Setting a count program to only release counts for a specific aisle is an example of data selection.

Data sequencing—refers to the sorting of data on reports and computer screens. Sorting a count sheet by location is an example of data sequencing.

Decoded scanner—scanner that has built-in logic to convert the bar code into ASCII characters and then pass the ASCII characters to the connected device.

Decoder—interface device that allows you to connect one or more undecoded scanners or other devices (such as scales and credit card readers) to a computer or terminal. Decoders are often called wedges because they frequently use a keyboard wedge interface to connect and communicate with a computer or terminal. The decoder will convert the scanner output into ASCII characters and then pass this data to your computer.

Demand—The need for a specific item in a specific quantity.

Depth of field—describes the working distance of a particular scanner from the bar code. This cannot be listed as a single range since the depth of field is also dependant upon the density (size) of the bar code and the reflectivity of the media on which the bar code is printed.

Directed tasks—tasks that can be completed based upon detailed information provided by the computer system. An order picking task where the computer details the specific item, location, and quantity to pick is an example of a directed task. If the computer could not specify the location and quantity forcing the worker to choose locations or change quantities, it would not be a directed task. Directed tasks set up the opportunity for confirmation transactions.

Direct thermal—printing method used to produce bar code labels. Direct thermal uses a heated print head to darken areas on special thermal activated label stock.

Discrepancy—*See* Variance

Discrete manufacturing—manufacturing of distinct items (items you can easily count, touch, see) such as a pencil, a light bulb, a telephone, a bicycle, a fuel pump, etc. Discrete as opposed to process manufacturing. *See also* Process manufacturing.

Dock-to-stock—receiving method whereby materials are delivered directly to the point of use (storage or manufacturing) skipping the normal receipt check in process.

Document—a physical piece of paper produced by a computer system used to execute a task, or the electronic representation of a set of data used to execute a task.

Document-level transactions—confirmation transactions where multiple detail-level transactions are executed by confirming the completion of a set of tasks at the document level. For example, using the confirmation of a shipping order to automatically complete transactions for all items shipped on the order. Document-level transactions are only possible with directed tasks.

Double-deep rack—pallet rack designed to allow storage of pallets two-deep. Requires use of a double-deep reach truck to place and extract loads.

DRP—distribution requirements planning. Software used to plan inventory requirements in a multiple plant/warehouse environment. DRP may be used for both distribution and manufacturing. In manufacturing DRP will work directly with MRP. DRP may also be defined as distribution resource planning, which also includes determining labor, equipment, and warehouse space requirements.

Drive-in rack—racking system designed to allow a lift truck to drive into the bay creating very high-density storage for non-stackable loads. Useful for operations with limited SKUs and high quantities of pallets per SKU. FIFO is difficult to maintain in drive-in racking systems.

Eaches—term used to describe a unit of measure where each individual piece is tracked as a quantity of one in the computer system.

EDI—electronic data interchange. A method for exchanging data between systems based on a set of standardized specifications.

Environmental factor—any characteristic of the operating environment. Environmental factors include anything from storage methods and product packaging to facility temperature and lighting.

ERP—enterprise resource planning. Software systems designed to manage most or all aspects of a manufacturing or distribution enterprise (an expanded version of MRP systems). ERP systems are usually broken down into modules such as financials, sales, purchasing, inventory management, manufacturing, MRP, DRP. The modules are designed to work seamlessly with the rest of the system and should provide a consistent user interface between them. These systems usually have extensive set up options that allow you some flexibility in customizing their functionality to your specific business needs.

Event-triggered counting method—any method used to determine when to count an item that is based upon a specific event occurring. Examples of events that could trigger a count would include inventory level dropping below reorder point, the completion of a production run, or on-hand inventory reaching zero.

Exception handling—the process of managing atypical events that occur during a process. Exception handling is critical in automated processes.

Exception report—a report that uses data selection based on a very specific set of circumstances to identify process exceptions. Reports that identify items with negative on-hand quantities or locations with more than one item stored in them would be examples of exception reports.

Facility—a physical building or property used to store or transform inventory.

Faking the count—the activity of changing a count quantity in a cycle count program to make it match the expected quantity.

FIFO—first-in first-out. Describes the method of rotating inventory to use oldest product first. Actually an accounting term used to describe an inventory costing method. *See also* LIFO

Finished goods—inventory that is in a salable or shipable form based upon its location within the supply chain. An item considered a finished good in a supplying plant might be considered a component or raw material in a receiving plant.

Fixed location storage—storage method where an item is always stored in the same physical location.

Fixed-position scanner—stationary bar code reader that requires the bar code to be placed in front of the reader to scan.

Floor stock—inventory that is consumed in production but is not tracked in the perpetual inventory system. Floor stock is different from non-stock inventory since it does actually have an SKU number and item master record, but rather than tracking quantities in the inventory system, the materials are expensed as they are received

Floor-to-system count— describes a method of counting inventory where you document inventory balances found in storage and staging areas and then compare this data with the system information

Flow rack—racking system that incorporates sections of conveyor to allow the cartons or pallets to flow to the face of the rack. Stocking is performed from the rear of the rack.

Focus-related errors—errors caused by a lack of attention to the task at hand. Focus-related errors are common in repetitive tasks where divided attention allows the worker to incorrectly execute the task.

Forced count—counting an item based upon an expected error. When there is reason to suspect inventory of an item may be incorrect, the item is manually added to the next cycle count.

Forecast—a forecast is an estimation of future demand. Most forecasts use historical demand to calculate future demand. Adjustments for seasonality and trend are often necessary.

Fork lift—*See* Lift truck.

Form—anything that requires a worker to write on it. A document may also be a form. Data entry programs are also sometimes referred to as forms.

Freezing inventory balances—in most cycle counting programs the term "freezing" refers to copying the current on-hand inventory balance into the cycle count file. This may also be referred to as taking a snapshot of the inventory balance. It rarely means that the inventory is actually frozen in a way that prevents transactions from occurring.

Gaylord—a large corrugated container usually sized to match the length and width dimensions of a pallet. Gaylord is actually a trade name that has become synonymous with this specific type of container.

Good count bad count—accuracy measurement method that compares the number of good counts to the number of total counts. Tolerances are often used to allow counts that are close but not perfect to still be categorized as good counts.

GUI—graphical user interface. Computer interface normally associated with operating systems like Windows and Macintosh where a mouse can be used to navigate the screen. A graphical user interface will allow the use of graphics such as icons and buttons to execute actions and also uses drag-and-drop to perform actions.

Hand-held scanner—a bar code reader that that is manually pointed at a bar code to read it. Most common are the wired pistol-shaped devices used in retail stores. Hand-held scanners can also be wireless.

Hand-held computer—any portable computer that can be operated while holding it in one hand.

Headmount display—a wearable device that is positioned in front of one of the user's eyes and projects a viewable image of a computer screen.

High-density storage—describes a variety of storage methods where unit loads such as full pallets, crates, rolls, or bales are stored more than one unit deep and/or high. Stacked bulk floor storage, drive-in/drive-thru racking, pushback rack, flow rack, and to a lesser extent, double-deep rack, are examples of high-density storage methods.

Host system—the primary computer system. The computer system on which the primary database resides.

Housekeeping—the orderliness and cleanliness of work areas and storage areas.

Human-machine interface—any point where data is communicated from a worker to a computer or from a computer to a worker. Data entry programs, inquire programs, reports, documents, LED displays, and voice commands are all examples of human-machine interfaces.

IF THEN ELSE—describes the most common logic used by software to make decisions. IF THEN ELSE is used to describe a situation and then describe what the program should do if the situation is true and what it should do if the situation is false. For example, for your computer to tell you when you have email, the software is programmed such that IF there is new mail in your mailbox, THEN execute the sound file that has the "you've got mail" message, ELSE do nothing.

IIE—Institute of Industrial Engineers. www.iienet.org.

Incentive—any type of reward given when a specific goal is achieved.

Inner pack—a smaller container within a container used to separate smaller quantities of an item. Inner packs are usually smaller chipboard boxes or poly bags used within a case to break down the larger case quantity into smaller, easier to handle and count quantities. Also known as unit packs.

Integration—process of making separate software and hardware systems and devices communicate with each other.

In-transit inventory—usually refers to inventory in a multi-plant environment that has been shipped from one plant to another. When it is shipped, the inventory is reduced in the shipping plant and added to the in-transit inventory. When received, the inventory is reduced from the in-transit inventory and added to the inventory at the receiving plant.

Inventory adjustment—any transaction that increases or decreases on-hand balances.

Inventory characteristic—any distinguishing trait that describes the types of inventory you are handling. The physical size, the form, and the method of unitizing are examples of inventory characteristics. More specific examples of characteristics would be rolls of steel, liquids in drums, or cases of small parts on pallets.

Inventory system—the software used to plan and track inventory balances and activities.

Issue—to reduce on-hand inventory and assign it to a specific document or process. Such as issuing raw materials to a production order or issuing finished goods to a shipping order.

Item—any unique material or product stored or handled, or any unique configuration of a material or product stored or handled. Item is used synonymously with SKU.

Item master—a collection of data that describes a specific item. Item master is also used to describe the database file that contains this data.

Item number—the identification number assigned to an item. Also called the part number, SKU number, or SKU.

Item numbering scheme—the format or template used for assigning item numbers.

Item history file—a database file that contains detail records for each inventory transaction that has occurred.

JIT—just-in-time Term usually thought of as describing inventory arriving or being produced just in time for the shipment or next process. Actually JIT is a process for optimizing manufacturing processes by eliminating all process waste, including wasted steps, wasted material, excess inventory, etc.

Kanban—used as part of a just-in-time production operation where components and sub-assemblies are produced based upon notification of demand from a subsequent operation. Historically, kanban has been a physical notification such as a card (kanban cards) or even an empty hopper or tote sent up the line to the previous operation.

Keyboard wedge interface—an interface that allows you to connect a bar code scanner or other device between your keyboard and the computer or terminal. Any data scanned will be sent as ASCII characters and immediately appear on the computer screen just as though it were typed on the keyboard.

Key data element—pieces of information that are critical to the completion of a task.

Kit—items that are made up of multiple separate parts (not assembled).

Lane—a row of stored or stage materials. Also used to designate the location associated with a physical lane.

Laser scanner—bar code scanner that uses a laser to read the bar code.

Last count date—date maintained in the inventory database that records the last date that the item/location combination was on an approved count sheet. Last count date is used in combination with cycle count period to calculate the next count date.

Lead-time—amount of time required for an item to be available for use from the time it is ordered. Lead time should include purchase order processing time, vendor processing time, in-transit time, receiving, inspection, and any prepack times.

Lead-time demand—forecasted demand during the lead time period. For example, if your forecasted demand is 3 units per day and your lead time is 12 days your lead time demand would be 36 units.

License plate—a document, tag, or label used to identify a unitized load.

LIFO—last-in first-out. In warehousing, LIFO describes the method for using the newest inventory first (I've never seen an operation that uses this). In accounting it's a term used to describe an inventory costing method. *See also* FIFO

Lift truck—vehicles used to lift, move, stack, rack, or otherwise manipulate loads. Material handling people use a lot of terms to describe lift trucks, some terms describe specific types of vehicles, others are slang terms or trade names that people often mistakenly use to describe trucks. Terms include industrial truck, forklift, reach truck, motorized pallet trucks, turret trucks, counterbalanced forklift, walkie, rider, walkie rider, walkie stacker, straddle lift, side loader, order pickers, high lift, cherry picker, Jeep, Towmotor, Yale, Crown, Hyster, Raymond, Clark, Drexel.

Light-directed—systems that use visible lights or displays to direct activities. *See also* Pick-go-light, Put-to-light.

Line item—a single detail record.

Live document—a document that can be tracked within a computer system by a status designation.

Load—in manufacturing, describes the amount of production scheduled against a plant or machine. In warehousing, describes the materials being handled by a piece of equipment. In transportation, describes the materials being transported.

Location—the place where the inventory is physically stored or staged. Also used to describe the identification number assigned to the specific storage slot.

Locator System—locator systems are inventory-tracking systems that allow you to assign specific physical locations to your inventory to facilitate greater tracking and the ability to store product randomly. Location functionality in software can range from a simple text field attached to an item that notes a single location, to systems that allow multiple locations per item and track inventory quantities by location. Warehouse management systems (WMS) take locator systems to the next level by adding functionality to direct the movement between locations.

Logical location—location set up within a locator system that does not exist as a specific physical location.

Lost inventory—inventory that probably still physically exists somewhere within the facility or supply chain, but cannot be found.

Lot number—number assigned to a discrete batch of an item. Lot numbers are usually assigned to each separate production run of an item.

Lot tracking—the process of tracking inventory by lot number through manufacturing and distribution processes.

LTL—less-than-truckload. Transportation term that describes shipments that are less than a trailer load in size. LTL also is used to describe the carriers that handle these loads.

Machine counter—any device that counts output of a machine. Machine counters may count cycles, pieces, length, volume, weight, etc.

Macro—a simple computer program that scripts a series of actions. Macros can usually be created without writing any programming code. The simplest way to create a macro is to record a series of keystrokes that can then be reused later.

Manufacturing order—*See* Production order

Materials list—a listing of material required for a production order. The manufacturing planning system will use the bill of material to calculate the material requirements for a manufacturing order resulting in the materials list. Materials lists can also be created or edited manually.

MES—manufacturing execution system. Software systems designed to integrate with enterprise systems to enhance the shop floor control functionality that is usually inadequate in ERP systems. MES provides for shop floor scheduling, production and labor reporting, integration with computerized manufacturing systems such as automatic data collection and computerized machinery.

Memory-related errors—type of focus-related error where your memory accesses incorrect detail information during the execution of a task.

MHMS—Material Handling Management Society. www.mhia.org/mhms

Middleware—software designed to integrate separate software and/or hardware systems. Middleware provides the communication between the separate systems.

Minimum standard—a statement of the lowest acceptable level of performance.

Modification—a change to software that requires changing or adding to the source code.

Move ticket—a document used to move inventory within a facility. Warehouse management systems use move tickets to direct and track material movements. In a paperless environment the electronic version of a move ticket is often called a task or a trip.

MRP—manufacturing resources planning. Process for determining material, labor and machine requirements in a manufacturing environment. MRPII (manufacturing resources planning) is the consolidation of material requirements planning (MRP), capacity requirements planning (CRP), and master production scheduling (MPS). MRP was originally designed for materials planning only. When labor and machine (resources) planning were incorporated it became known as MRPII. Today the definition of MRPII is generally associated with MRP systems.

MRO—maintenance, repair, and operating inventory. Term used to describe inventory used to maintain equipment as well as miscellaneous supplies such as office and cleaning supplies.

Multi-plant—environments where multiple facilities are managed. DRP is often used to plan inventory in multi-plant environments. *See also* DRP

Negative inventory—situation where the system tracking of inventory results in an on-hand balance that is less than zero.

Net variance—a summarized variance number or amount where positive and negative variances are allowed to offset each other.

Next count date—date used in cycle counting programs that is calculated by adding the cycle count period (in days) to the last count date.

Non-stock inventory—inventory that is not tracked within your perpetual inventory system. Non-stock inventory will not have an item-master record or internal SKU number.

Obsolescence—the process by which inventory becomes obsolete.

Obsolete—the condition of being no longer of use due to passage of time. Usually associated with old, outdated designs.

Omni-directional scanner—bar code scanner that can scan in several directions negating the need to orientate the scanner with the bar code.

Open order—a live document (usually a shipping order, purchase order or production order) that has been initiated but has not been completed or closed in the computer system. An active order that still has tasks associated with it that are not yet completed.

Operation—in manufacturing an operation is a step in the manufacturing process. In more general terms, an operation is the combination of a physical facility and the processes that occur within that facility.

Opportunity counts—counts that are timed to take advantage of a specific set of circumstances.

Order picking—the process of selecting and assembling inventory for shipments or for use in production processes.

Order selector—lift truck designed specifically for manual handling of less than pallet load quantities in racking. Man-up design has fixed forks attached to a platform that elevates the load and the operator to facilitate manual loading and unloading from racking.

Outside operation—a step in the manufacturing process that is performed by an outside supplier.

Outsourcing—the act of transferring responsibilities for a process to an outside supplier.

Overhead—indirect costs associated with facilities and management that are applied to the costs of manufactured goods through the manufacturing reporting process.

Pallet rack—storage racking specifically designed to store palletized loads.

Paperless system—any system that replaces the paper-based interface with other forms of communication such as using computer screens, lights, or speech technology.

Pareto principle—states that a small number of causes are responsible for a great number of effects. Also known as the 80/20 rule.

Part number—*See* Item number.

Parts list—*See* Materials list.

Past due—a status at which the tasks associated with an order are not yet completed by the required date on the order. Usually refers to purchase orders, production orders, or shipping orders.

PDF—portable document format. A standardized computer file format that is used for documents that can be printed or displayed on a computer screen. A PDF file retains all graphics, fonts, and formats of the original document and incorporates compression to reduce the overall size of the file.

PDF417—a two-dimensional (2D) bar code symbology.

Perpetual inventory system—an inventory system that uses transactions to adjust on-hand balances to coincide with physical activities that are occurring.

Physical inventory—the process of counting all inventory in a warehouse or plant in a single event. Also called a wall-to-wall inventory.

Pick-and-pass—*See* Zone picking.

Picking accuracy—accuracy measurement associated with the order picking process.

Pick slip—the document used to pick shipping or production orders. Also known as a pick list.

Pick tag—a version of a pick slip in which each line item is printed as a separate document (usually a smaller paper document or label)

Pick-to-clear—method often used in warehouse management systems that directs picking to the locations with the smallest quantities on hand.

Pick-to-carton—pick-to-carton logic uses item dimensions/weights to select the shipping carton prior to the order picking process. Items are then picked directly into the shipping carton.

Pick-to-light—pick-to light systems consist of lights and LED displays for each pick location. The system uses software to light the next pick and display the quantity to pick.

Pick-to-trailer—order-picking method where the order picker transports the materials directly from the pick location to the trailer without any interim checking or staging steps.

Planned order—term used within MRP and DRP systems for system generated planned order quantities. Planned orders only exist within the computer system and serve multiple functions. One function is to notify the materials/planner or buyer to produce or order materials, which is done by converting a planned order into an purchase order, production order, or transfer order. Another function is used by the MRP or DRP system to show demand that is used by subsequent MRP and DRP programs to generate additional planned orders.

PO—*See* Purchase order.

Point-of-use inventory—material used in production processes that is physically stored where it is consumed.

Portable computer—any computer that can be used while being transported. Portable computers can be hand-held devices, wearable systems, or vehicle-mounted systems.

Postponement—a manufacturing /distribution strategy where specific operations associated with a product are delayed until just prior to shipping. Storing product in a generic state and then applying custom labels or packaging before shipping is an example of postponement.

Procedure—a listing of the rules and instructions associated with a task.

Process-correction cycle—describes a condition that exists when processes are changed without considering the impact of the changes on other business objectives. The result is that each correction creates additional problems that require additional corrections.

Process manufacturing—type of manufacturing where a product is produced or transformed through mixing, chemical reactions, etc. Examples of process manufacturing would be refining crude oil into gasoline, extracting copper from ore, combining materials to make paint. Process as opposed to Discrete manufacturing. *See also* Discrete manufacturing.

Production order—the document used to process a production run of an item. Also known as a job, work order, or manufacturing order, a production order is usually made up of a production order header, a materials list, and a routing.

Production run—the physical act of performing all tasks associated with a production order or a group of production orders that require similar setup and processing.

Programmable—describes the functionality of some bar code decoders and scanners. Programming functionality may include the ability to take different actions for different bar codes based upon data identifiers, format the data from the barcode, and script the keyboard wedge input — and do all of this without actually writing any "code."

Program generator—software programs that generally provide graphical user interfaces and tools that allow a user to create a program without having to write actual computer code. Currently these programs are more frequently referred to as "development tools" and are usually designed to write code for specific applications such as data collection programs for portable computers. While a user does not need to be a programmer to use this software, the user does need to have a higher level of technical skills than that of most standard software users.

Public warehouse—a business that provides short or long-term storage to a variety of businesses usually on a month-to-month basis. A public warehouse will generally use their own equipment and staff however agreements may be made where the client either buys or subsidizes equipment. Public warehouse fees are usually a combination of storage fees (per pallet or actual square footage) and transaction fees (inbound and outbound). Public warehouses are most often used to supplement space requirements of a private warehouse. *See also* Contract warehouse and 3PL.

Purchase order—document used to approve, track, and process purchased items.

Push-back rack—racking system that incorporates a carriage or other sliding device to allow you to feed multiple pallets into the same location "pushing back" the previous pallet..

Putaway—the process of physically placing inventory into storage.

Putaway accuracy—the measurement of the accuracy of the putaway process.

Put-to-light—method that uses lights to direct the placement of materials. Most often used in batch picking to designate the tote to place picked item into.

Quantity per—the numeric representation of the quantity of a specific item required to make one unit of another item. Quantity per exists on the bill of material and on the materials list associated with a production order.

Queue—computer term referring to data that is awaiting further processing. Also describes inventory that is staged awaiting further processing.

Queue time—the amount of time inventory is staged prior to processing.

Query program—computer program that allows the extracting of data from a database. Query programs will usually have the ability to pull data from multiple files (tables), perform calculations, apply selection criteria (filtering) to the data, sequence (sort) the data, and summarize data for reporting or output to a file or other program.

Quiet zone—clear area on either side of a 1D bar code required for an accurate read of the code. Quiet zones for 2D bar codes must exist on all four sides.

Random location storage—storage method where a product may be stored in any location. Random storage has higher space utilization and generally lower accuracy than fixed location storage.

Raw materials—inventory used in the manufacturing process. Though some would categorize raw materials as very base materials in bulk form such as carloads of ore or unitized loads of paper, plastic, or steel, I generally consider anything used in the manufacturing process as a raw material. I use the term synonymously with the term "components".

Reach truck—a narrow aisle (8'-10') truck designed specifically for racked pallet storage. It consists of outriggers in front and telescoping forks that use a hydraulic scissors type mechanism that allow you to pick up the load and retract it over the outriggers reducing the overall truck and load length allowing you to turn in a narrower aisle. Double-deep versions use an extended reach mechanism that allows you to store pallets two deep in specially designed double-deep rack. Also known as stand up reach, straddle reach, and double-deep reach.

Receipts—the materials or transactions associated with the receiving process.

Receiving—the process of placing materials into inventory. Also describes the department in which receiving activities take place.

Reconciling variances—the process of evaluating and correcting inventory variances.

Recounts—additional counts that are conducted after an initial count has resulted in a variance or when checking the accuracy of initial counts.

Reorder point—the inventory level set to trigger an order of a specific item. Reorder point is generally calculated as the expected usage (demand) during the lead time plus safety stock.

Replenishment—within a warehouse, replenishment is the process of moving inventory from secondary storage areas into fixed storage locations. Within a supply chain or a multi-plant environment, replenishment is the process of moving inventory between facilities to meet demand.

Replenishment accuracy—measure of the accuracy of the internal location replenishment process.

Reverse logistics—fancy term for returns. Reverse logistics covers activities related to returned product, returned pallets and containers, and returned materials for disposal or recycling.

Reverse sampling—the process of using a known case quantity as the sample for a counting scale rather than manually counting a sample. Materials can then be removed from the case to count out the required quantity.

RF computer—refers to the portable data collection devices that use radio frequency to transmit data to the host system.

RFID—radio frequency identification. Refers to the technology that uses devices attached to objects that transmit data to an RFID receiver. These devices can be large pieces of hardware the size of a small book like those attached to ocean containers or very small devices inserted into a label on a package. RFID has advantages over bar codes such as the ability to hold more data, the ability to change the stored data as processing occurs, does not require line-of-sight to transfer data and is very effective in harsh environments where bar code labels won't work.

RFID tag—small RFID devices attached to objects.

Root cause—the ultimate source of an effect.

Root cause analysis—the process of evaluating, assigning, and measuring root causes.

Routing—a list of operations used in manufacturing in conjunction with the bill of materials. While the BOM contains the material requirements, the routing will contain the specific steps required to produce the finished items. Each step in the routing is called an operation, each operation generally consists of machine and labor requirements.

RTLS—real time locator system. A real time locator system uses RFID technology to transmit the physical location of RFID tagged objects. System requires some type of RFID tag to be attached to each object that needs to be tracked and RF transmitters/receivers located throughout the facility to determine the location and send information to computerized tracking system.

Ruggedized—describes devices designed for industrial environments.

Safety stock—quantity of inventory used in inventory management systems to allow for deviations in demand or supply.

Sales order—document used to approve, track, and process outbound customer shipments.

Scrap—inventory that must be discarded or recycled as a result of a manufacturing process or damage that occurs during storage or material handling.

Screen mapping—the functionality to change the arrangement of data fields on a computer screen. Screen mapping is frequently used in combination with terminal emulation software to "remap" data fields from a standard mainframe program to be used on the smaller screen of a portable handheld device. Also known as screen scraping.

Scorecard—*See* weighted scorecard.

Sequence of events—the order in which the specific steps in a task are performed.

Serial number–a unique number assigned to each discrete unit of an item.

Serial number tracking—the process of tracking serial numbers through manufacturing and distribution processes.

Set—item that is made up of multiple units of a single part.

Shipping—the process of removing materials from stock and transporting them to a customer or other facility.

Shipping accuracy—the measure of the accuracy of the shipping process.

Shipping order—document used to approve, track, and process outbound shipments.

Shrinkage—term used to describe the undocumented loss of inventory.

SKU—stock-keeping unit. Referring to a specific item in a specific unit of measure Also refers to the identification number assigned to each SKU. Used interchangeably with the terms item and item number.

Slot—a single storage location.

Slotting—describes the activities associated with optimizing product placement in locations in a warehouse.

Smart label—a label that has an RFID tag integrated into it.

Smart stand—device that allows a hand-held bar code scanner to be used as a fixed-position scanner.

Speech-based technology—also known as voice technology, is really composed of two technologies — voice directed, which converts computer data into audible commands, and speech recognition, which allows user voice input to be converted into data. Portable voice systems consist of a headset with a microphone and a wearable computer.

Staged inventory—inventory that is in a temporary storage area awaiting further processing.

Staging location—a physical location used to temporarily store queued inventory that is awaiting further processing.

Start character—a character placed in a bar code to designate the beginning of the bar code.

Standard—a specific level of performance. Also a standardized set of specifications.

Static shelving—fixed shelving units.

Stocking type—a classification used by planning and execution systems to identify the primary stocking characteristic of the inventory. Examples of stocking types would include classifications that distinguish manufactured inventory, purchased inventory, direct ship inventory, or non-stock inventory.

Stocking unit of measure—the unit of measure used to track inventory within a facility. Stocking unit of measure is usually, but not always, the smallest unit of measure handled.

Stop character—a character placed in a bar code to designate the end of the bar code.

Subassembly—an item that has gone through an assembly process, but is also used in the assembly of other items. A subassembly is also a component.

Substitution—the replacement of an ordered item on a shipping order or a required item on a production order with another item.

System-to-floor count—describes a method of counting inventory where you take the system quantity information and then go to the storage areas to verify the accuracy of the system information.

Tag count—counting method that use individual tags for each item/location in place of a count sheet. Tags are often attached to the inventory or locations prior to the count.

Tare weight—the weight of the container that holds the materials you are weighing.

Task interleaving—term used in describing functionality of warehouse management systems to mix tasks to reduce travel time. Sending a forklift driver to put away a pallet on his way to his next pick is an example of task interleaving.

Terminal emulation—software used on desktop and portable computers that allows the computer to act like a terminal connected to a mainframe system. If you have a networked desktop PC and are accessing mainframe programs you are using terminal emulation. Terminal emulation is also a common method used to connect portable computers (as in warehouse bar code data collection systems) to mainframe software. *See also* Screen mapping

Test count—a count used to test the counting process.

Thermal transfer—common method for printing bar code labels. Thermal transfer uses a heated print head to transfer an image from a ribbon to the label.

3PL—third party logistics. Describes businesses that provide one or many of a variety of logistics-related services. Types of services would include public warehousing, contract warehousing, transportation management, distribution management, freight consolidation.

Three-way match—an accounting practice that compares a vendor invoice against a receipt and a purchase order.

Tolerance—an allowable variation. Tolerances are sometimes used in accuracy measures and in decision-making processes.

TQM—total quality management. A management strategy that focuses on continuous improvement.

Transaction by exception—any method that automates the completion of transactions that are executed consistently with system instructions. Only the exceptions require the manual entry of transaction details.

Transaction history file—the database file that contains a detail record for each transaction that has changed the on-hand balance of an item.

Transfer—the movement of inventory between storage locations within a facility or between facilities. Also describes that transaction associated with the transfer activity.

Transfer order—document used to move inventory between facilities in a multi-plant environment. Inventory moved between locations within a facility will usually use a move ticket rather than a transfer order.

Unapproved check—a process check that is initiated by a worker, but is not approved as an official check.

Undecoded scanner—a bar code scanner that requires a separate device or software to convert the scanned image into ASCII characters.

Unit load—any configuration of materials that allows it to be moved by material handling equipment as a single unit. While smaller manually handled configurations could be considered unit loads, the term generally defines larger configurations that would be moved by a lift truck such as pallet loads, crates, bales, etc. Short for unitized load.

Unit of measure—the unit of measure describes how the quantity of an item is tracked in your inventory system. The most common unit of measure is "eaches," which simply means that each individual item is considered one unit. An item that uses "cases" as the unit of measure would be tracked by the number of cases rather than by the actual piece quantity. Other examples of units of measure would include pallets, pounds, ounces, linear feet, square feet, cubic feet, gallons, thousands, hundreds, pairs, dozens. *See also* Unit-of-measure conversion.

Unit-of-measure conversion—a conversion ratio used whenever multiple units-of-measure are used with the same item. For example, if you purchased an item in cases (meaning that your purchase order stated a number of cases rather than a number of pieces) and then stocked the item in eaches, you would require a conversion to allow your system to calculate how many eaches are represented by a quantity of cases. This way, when you received the cases, your system would automatically convert the case quantity into an each quantity.

Unit pack—*See* Inner pack.

User interface—*See* Human-machine interface.

Variance—a situation where the physical quantity does not match the system quantity. Also describes the numeric representation of the discrepancy.

Vehicle-mounted computer—a portable computer designed to be mounted to a vehicle such as a forklift.

Verification count—counting method where the counters are provided the system quantity of the item being counted.

VMI—vendor managed inventory. Phrase used to describe the process of a supplier managing the inventory levels and purchases of the materials he supplies. This process can be very low tech such as an office supplies supplier or maintenance supplies supplier coming into your facility once per week to visually check stock levels and place a re-supply order or high tech such as an electronic component supplier having remote access to your inventory management and MRP system and producing and automatically shipping to meet your production schedule. Vendor managed inventory reduces internal costs associated with planning and procuring materials and enables the vendor to better manage his inventory through higher visibility to the supply chain. Vendor managed inventory may be owned by the vendor or the customer.

Voice directed—*See* Speech-based technology

Wall-to-wall inventory—*See* Physical inventory.

Wand scanner—pen-type device used to read bar codes.

Wave picking—a variation on zone picking where rather than orders moving from one zone to the next for picking, all zones are picked at the same time and the items are later sorted and consolidated into individual orders. Wave picking is the quickest method for picking multi-item orders, however, the sorting and consolidation process can be tricky. *See also* Batch picking, Zone picking

Weighted scorecard—a measurement compilation method that takes several separate measurements and weights them to come up with a single numeric representation of the measurements.

Wearable computer—a small portable computer that can be carried on a worker. Examples of wearable computers are computers that are worn in a fanny pack, clipped to a belt, or worn on the wrist.

Wearable system—a system that includes a wearable computer combined with one or more other devices such as a bar code scanner or voice headset.

WERC—Warehouse Education and Research Council. www.werc.org

WIP—work-in-process. Generally describes inventory that is currently being processed in an operation or inventory that has been processed through one operation and is awaiting another operation. Is actually a financial account that contains the dollar value of all inventory, labor, and overhead that has been issued to production but has not yet produced a finished product.

Wireless device—any device that can communicate with other devices without being physically attached to them. Most wireless devices communicate through radio frequency.

WMS—warehouse management system. Computer software designed specifically for managing the movement and storage of materials throughout the warehouse.

Work order—*See* Production order.

XML—extensible markup language. A method for exchanging data between systems based on a set of standardized specifications. XML was designed for communicating over the internet and is more flexible than EDI.

Zone—location designation that represents a storage area.

Zone picking—order picking method where a warehouse is divided into several pick zones, order pickers are assigned to a specific zone and only pick the items in that zone, orders are moved from one zone to the next (usually on conveyor systems) as they are picked (also known as "pick-and-pass"). *See also* Batch picking, Wave picking

Index

Symbols

1D bar code 207
24/7 289–291
2D bar code 207–208
2D scanners 214
80/20 rule. *See* Pareto Principle

A

A-frames 234
ABC classifications 84–89, 160
   ABC by average inventory invest-
     ment 84, 180
   ABC by dollars sold/consumed 84
   ABC by units sold/consumed 84
   ABC by velocity 84
   calculating 86, 87
   what's wrong with 92
Absolute dollar variance 155, 161
Absolute piece variance 155, 161
Accountability 69–75. *See also*
   Responsibility
Accuracy
   importance of 64–65
   perception of 79
   proving 183
Accuracy audit. *See* Audits: accuracy

Accuracy measurement. *See* Measure-
   ment
Active RFID tags 228
ActiveX control 211
ADC. *See* Automated data capture
Advanced Shipment Notifications
   45, 255
AGV. *See* Automated guided vehicles
Aisle 239
Allocations 80, 97, 103, 258, 263
Annual physical inventory. *See*
   Physical inventories
APICS 27
ASN. *See* Advanced Shipment
   Notifications
ASQ 27
ASRS. *See* Automated storage and
   retrieval systems
Audits
   accuracy 134, 160, 180–183
   data 190–192
   locations 118, 185
Autodiscrimination 215
Automated data capture 43
Automated guided vehicles 234
Automated storage and retrieval
   systems 234
Automatic mode 5

Automation 43, 233
Availability checking 258

B

Backflushing 43, 302–307
Backorders 170
Bad ideas 27
Bar code
    1D symbologies 207
    2D symbologies 207–208
    and physical inventories 147, 207–217
    bar code fonts 211
    on cycle count sheet 131
    on pick tags 38
    printing 209–212
    scanners 212–216
        programmable 41–42, 216–217
    verifiers 210
Bar code printer 210
Batch computers 218
Batch data changes 309
Batch picking 233, 244, 260
Batch-level transactions 44
Benchmarking 163–164, 172–178
Big bang 309
Bills of material 190, 191, 305
Bin 240
Blind counts 106–108, 147
    and physical inventories 141
    example of count sheet 122
    recounts 110
Bluetooth 224
BOM. See Bills of material
Brainstorming 27
Bulk materials 253, 304
Business objectives 26, 64

C

Calculators 197–198
Capacity 61
    locations 190

Carousel 232
Carton 12
CCD scanner 213–214
Check characters 208, 226
Check digits. See Check characters
Check-weighing 204–205
Checks
    as basis for performance measures 72, 166–169
    as control methods 77
    built-in checks 77
    cost of 170
    putting formal checks in place 59–61
    receiving 252–255
    shipping 259
    unapproved 78
    verifying 78
Clonable 216
Code 128 207
Commodity 98
Compliance labels 207
Compliance to procedures. See Accountability
Computer error, 18
Computer programs 40–45
    modifying 33, 40. See also Integration
    setup options 40
Conditional formatting 33, 37, 124
Confirmation transactions. See Transaction by exception
Containers 12
    standardized 12
Continuous improvement. 26, 28
Contract manufacturers 280
Control group 105–106
Control methods 75–80
Control policy 67, 75
Cordless scanners 212
Cost of accuracy measurement 172
Cost of checking. 170
Costs of errors 27

Count frequencies 84–89
Count opportunities 290
Count sheets 90, 142
Count tags 90, 144–147
Counting
    how to 248–251
    mechanically 116, 199–204
Counting scale 199–204, 253
Cross-docking 244
Cross-training 56–57
Custom forms 39
Custom reports 192
Cycle count period 88
Cycle Counting
    and accuracy measurement
        152, 160–162
    as replacement for annual physical
        inventory 134
    blind counts 106–108
    combining count logic 100–102
    count options 95–102
    count sheet examples 122
    definition of 81
    in 24/7 operations 290–291
    making adjustments 103
    purpose of 82
    recounting variances 110
    setting up and running 102–121
    standard cycle count program 84–
        94
        approving counts 91
        entering counts 90
        recounts 90
        running 89
        setting count frequencies 84
        variance report 90
        what's wrong with 92–94
Cycle time 25, 61

D

Damage 298
Data auditing 190–192

Data elements 31–40
    data element identifiers 32, 38
    formatting 33
    grouping 32
    key data elements 31, 35
    secondary data elements 31
Data identifier 209, 217
Data Matrix bar code 207–208
Data selection 33
Data sequencing 33
Decoded scanner 214
Decoders 215–216
Demand 97
Depth of field 213, 214
Difficult to count items 93
Direct thermal printing 209–210
Directed transactions 44, 243, 259
Discipline 48, 70, 74
Distribution requirements planning
    97, 277–278
Dock-to-stock 252
Document-level transactions 44
Documents
    designing/modifying 30–40
    examples
        count tags 145, 146
        count verification labels 143
        cycle counting 122
        location audit 186
        picking 34
    training materials 50
DRP. *See* Distribution requirements
    planning

E

EDI 45
Empty location report 187
Entering counts 90
Enterprise resource planning
    29, 34, 41
Environmental factors 9–19
    housekeeping 11

inventory characteristics 12
item identification 13
item packaging 12
lighting 9
noise 10
storage methods 15
temperature 10
transaction profiles 18
weather 10
Equipment
and physical inventories 140
ERP. *See* Enterprise resource planning
Errors
communicating 74
cost of 27
error type profiles 19–20
individual's relationship to 20
picking 262
problems when fixing 261
task relationship to 19
types
computer 18
focus-related 2–3, 7
knowledge-related 2
memory-related 6
Event-triggered counting methods
95, 96–97
Exception reports 187–190. *See also*
Reports: exception
Expediting 170

F

Faking the count 120, 121, 160
First-in-first-out 244, 257, 276
Fixed-position scanner 213
Floor stock 292
Floor-to-system 182
Flow chart 50
Focus-related errors. *See* Errors:
types: focus-related
Forced counts 99, 159
Forms 39, 50

Freezing inventory balances 89, 103
Frontline Solutions Expo 196

G

Gaylord 12
Gender 21
Good count bad count. 152–154, 161
Graphical user interface 30
Green pen rule 254
GUI. *See* Graphical user interface

H

Hand counting 248–251
Hand-held computers 218–222
Hand-held scanners 212
Headmount display 223
High-density storage 17
Housekeeping. 11, 139
Human-machine interface 29

I

IF THEN ELSE 101
Implementations 308
In-transit quantity 277–278
Inbound quantity 277–278
Incentives 57, 73
Inner packs. *See* Unit packs
Integrated scanners 221
Integration 234–238, 243
Inventory adjustments
cycle counting 103
physical inventories 149
understanding the effects of 117–120
Inventory characteristics 12
Inventory system
understanding 103–104, 192
Item
identification 13–15
numbering schemes 13–15
Item history file. *See* Transaction
history file

Item master 190, 191, 268, 306
Item register. *See* Transaction history
    file

J

JIT. *See* Just-in-time
Just-in-time 13

K

Keyboard wedge interface 215, 216–
    217
Kits 275

L

Labels 39
    bar code label software 211
    compliance 207
    used in physical inventories 143
Lane 240
Laser scanners 213–214
Last count date 88, 121, 149
License plates 257
Light tree 232
Light-directed systems 231–233
Line spacing 31, 35
Linear bar code. *See* 1D bar code
Linux operating system 222
Locations
    auditing 118, 185, 256
    capacity 190
    counting by 98
    fixed 15
    identification 18
        numbering schemes 239–242
    logical. *See* Logical location
    machine 290, 306
    random 15, 256
    slotting 16
    staging 18, 105, 189, 241
Locator system 3, 61, 238–242, 258
Logical location 264, 281, 290
Logical variance location 118, 121

Lost inventory 93, 117–
    120, 170, 182, 185
Lot tracking 244, 276

M

Machine counters 206
Machine locations 290, 306
Macros 41, 217
Management's responsibility 65–69
Manufacturing 288
Manufacturing accuracy 168–169
Manufacturing execution systems 245
Material requirements planning 97
Materials list 302
MaxiCode 207–208
Measurement 151
    benchmarking 163, 172–178
    general accuracy 152–162
        absolute dollar variance 155
        absolute piece variance 155
        good count bad count 152–154
        net dollar variance. 154
        net piece variance 154
        root cause 158
        transactional variance calculations
        158
    impact of inaccuracy 169–172
    individual performance 71–73
    specific-process accuracy 165–169
Memory-related errors. *See* Errors:
    types: memory-related
MES. *See* Manufacturing execution
    systems
MHMS 27
Middleware 236
Minimum standard. *See* Measurement:
    individual performance
Modifications. *See* Computer pro-
    grams: modifying
Move tag 44, 189, 243
Multi pack. *See* Unit packs
Multi-item location report 187

Multi-plant 190, 277–278. *See also* Distribution requirements planning

N

Negative allocation 263
Negative inventory 190, 265–267
Net dollar variance. 154, 161
Net piece variance. 154, 161
New location report 187
Next count date 88
Non-English speaking employees 56
Non-stock inventory 268–270

O

Obsolete inventory 170
Omni-directional scanner 213
Open manufacturing orders 188
Open shipping orders 187
Opportunity counts 99
Order as needed 268
Order checking 259. *See also* Checks: putting formal checks in place
Order picking process 258–261
Outbound quantity 277–278
Outside operations 293–296
Outsourcing 280–282

P

Packaging 12
    inner packs 12
Pallet rack 17
Palm operating system 222
Paperless 30, 220, 225, 231
    picking 258
Pareto Principle 85
Part numbering scheme. *See* Item: identification: numbering schemes
Partial pallets or cases 257
Parts list. *See* Materials list
Passive RFID tags 228

Past due receipts 189
PDA. *See* Personal digital assistant
PDF. *See* Portable document format
PDF417 207–208
People
    dedicated accuracy personnel 120
    relationship to errors 20
Periodic physical inventories. *See* Physical inventories
Personal digital assistant 222
Personal wireless 224
Physical inventories 99, 133–150
    avoiding 135, 150, 183
    conducting 135–149
        execution 148–149
        methodology 140–148
        preparation 137–140
    objectives of 140–141
    problems with 133, 135–137
    reasons for 133
Pick tags 38, 258
Pick-to-light 231–233
Pick-to-trailer 260
Picking accuracy 166–167
Piece weight 201
Pilferage. *See* Theft
Planned order 97
Point-of-use inventory 292, 303
Portable bar code printer 210
Portable computers 218–224
    and cycle counting 99
    and physical inventories 147
    and putaway 257
    and WMS 243–244
Portable document format 51
Postproduction issuing 303–307
Preproduction issuing 302–303
Presentation programs 51
Printing bar codes 209–212
Procedures 46–62
    documenting 46–49
    formatting 49–52
Process evaluation 26–29

accuracy measurement 165–169
alternatives 27
and cycle counting 82–83
brainstorming 27
monitoring for compliance to
    procedures 76
objectives 26
reevaluating 28
Process-correction cycle 19
Production run 96
Production scrap 297
Program generators 237
Programmable scanners and decoders
    216–217
Put-to-light 233
Putaway accuracy 168
Putaway documents 256
Putaway process 256–257

Q

Quality initiative 64
Quality strategies. *See* Total quality
    management
Quantity per 191, 302
Query program 192
Quiet zone 208

R

Radio frequency identification 228–
    230, 230, 232, 261
Real-time inventory system 206
Receipt 96
    early 189
    past due 189
Receiving accuracy 167
Receiving process 252–255
Reconciling variances 110–117
Recounts 90, 110, 148
    sample recount document 125
Reorder point 96
Replenishment accuracy 168
Reports

exception 77
Resources 69
Responsibility
    everyone 69–75
    management 65–69
Returns process 262–264
Reverse sampling 204
RF computers 218, 224
RFID. *See* Radio frequency identifica-
    tion
Ring scanner 223, 224
Root cause measurement 158
Root causes 117
Routing 190
Ruggedized 222

S

Safety 136
Safety stock 64, 93, 170
Same day processing 259
Sampling 182–183
Scales 198–206
    check-weighing 204–205
    counting 199–204
        sample size 201–204
Scorecard. *See* Weighted scorecard
Scrap 297–298, 303, 306
Screen mapping 236
Screen scraping. *See* Screen mapping
Section 239
Security. *See* Theft
Selection criteria. *See* Data selection
Sequencing. *See* Data sequencing
Serial number tracking 276
Sets 275
Shelf 240
Shipping accuracy 165–166
Shipping process 258–261
Shrinkage 298. *See also* Theft
SKU. *See* Item
Slotting 16
Smart label 228

Smart stand 213
Software implementations 308
Source code 236
Speech recognition 225
Speech-based technology 223, 225–228
Staging areas 18, 255, 261
Standardized containers 12
Standards
    performance 71–73
        enforcement of 73
Static shelving 17
Stocking type 191
Stocking unit-of-measure 271
Storage methods 15
Subassemblies 299
Substitutions 279
Symbol's WS series wearable computer 223
System-to-floor 182

T

Tag count. *See* Count tags
Tare 199
Task authorization 76
Task interleaving 99, 261
Technology 19, 192, 195–246
Terminal emulation 236
Test counts 138
Testing
    on procedures 57–59
    pre-employment 22
    sample test 58
Theft 283–287
Thermal transfer printing 209–210
Tolerances
    and check-weighing 205
    and cycle count reconciliation 110
    and recounts 110
    with accuracy measurement 152–154
Total quality management 26, 28

Touch screen 223
TQM. *See* Total quality management
Training 28, 46, 52–57, 260, 309
    assisted 56
    classroom 54
    cross-training 56
    cycle counters 109
    new employee 56
    on-the-job 55
    physical inventories 139
    self-paced 56
    training materials 49–52
Transaction by exception 43–45, 259
    and cycle counting 94
Transaction control
    with cycle counting 89, 104–105
    with physical inventories 148
Transaction history file 111–112
Transactional variance calculations 158
Transactions
    profiles 18
    type codes 112
Transfer
    between facilities 119. *See also* Multi-plant
    between storage locations 105
Transitions 308–309

U

Unapproved checks 78
Undecoded scanner 214
Unit load 117
Unit of measure
    2, 37, 112, 116, 191, 254, 271–273
Unit packs 12, 274
User interface 29–45

V

Variance report 90, 126, 128

Variance-by-production-order report 300
Variances
  and recounts 110
  measuring. *See* Measurement
  reconciling 110–117, 148
    questions to ask 113–117
Vehicle-mounted computers 222
Verification counts 106–108
Vocollect 223
Voice directed 225
Voice systems. *See* Speech-based
    technology

W

Wall-to-wall physical inventory. *See*
    Physical inventories
Wand scanner 212
Warehouse Management System
    44, 189, 243–244
Wave picking 244, 260
Wearable computer systems 223–
    224, 225
Website design programs 51–54
Weight verification 204–205
Weighted scorecard 160, 161
WERC 27
Windows CE 222
WIP. *See* Work-in-process
WIP variance report. *See* Variance-by-
    production-order report
WMS. *See* Warehouse Management
    System
Word-processing and page layout
    programs 51
Work-in-process 299–301, 304
Wrist-worn computer 223

X

XML 45

Z

Zero on hand. 95
Zone 38, 239

A special thanks to Dave May at CustomCartoonArt.com
for turning my scribblings into some really great cartoons.

Accuracybook.com

Accuracybook.com is the companion website to *Inventory Accuracy: People, Processes, and Technology*. Here, you will find updates, corrections, and additional information related to inventory accuracy.

Rather than printing references to other sources of related information in the book, I am able to keep the information current by maintaining it online. The site also allows me to provide updates on technology, notifications of errors, clarification of concepts and terminology, and any additional information I feel is relevant.

Accuracybook.com provides:

✔ Updated glossary.

✔ Links to sites related to products described in the book.

✔ Links to other sites of interest.

✔ Additional products (when available).

✔ Technology updates.

✔ General information updates.

✔ Clarifications and corrections.

✔ Contact information.

Order additional copies online.
Quantity discounts available.

http://www.accuracybook.com   **Code: TG4385**

From the author:

I have been working with inventory in one form or another for almost twenty years. In 2000 I started Inventory Operations Consulting LLC, a small consulting company providing services related to inventory management, material handling, and warehouse operations. In that same year I started Inventoryops.com, a website that provides information related to "inventory operations" (a term I use to describe the planning aspects of inventory management combined with the physical aspects of storage, material handling, and transportation).

I started writing articles for my website as sort of a "hobby" to fill my time between consulting work (there was a lot of in-between time when I started the company). The positive responses I have received from readers of my articles published on the website and in several magazines have encouraged me to continue writing. In addition, my involvement in recent years with online forums and with groups such as APICS and WERC have reinforced my belief that people involved in the day-to-day execution of manufacturing and distribution are far more interested in finding **real** information about improving operations than they are about reading more "next new thing" hype.

I strongly believe that most businesses can achieve significant improvements in operations by simply evaluating and improving the way they execute the detail-level tasks that run the business. I try to write on subject matter that follows this belief. My focus is on helping readers develop an understanding of the subject matter rather than just an understanding of terminology related to the subject. I combine my knowledge of systems, software, and equipment, with years of hands-on experience in warehouses and manufacturing operations to provide insights on how people, processes, and technology can all work together to achieve operational excellence.

I sincerely hope you have enjoyed reading my first book. More to come.

David J. Piasecki